AF552755

INDIA
PERSPECTIVES ON POLITICS, ECONOMY & LABOUR 1918-2007

Vol. 1 : The Age of Gandhi, 1918-1957

By the same other:

- Monetary Policy in a Developing Economy: A study of the Policies of the Reserve Bank of India and their Effect on the Operations of the Banking System, Calcutta, 1965.
- Management of Public Debt in India, New Delhi, 1965
- Unionism in a Developing Economy: A study of the Interactions betweer Trade Unionism and Government Policy in India, 1950-1965, Bombay, 1967
- Issues in Indian Labour Policy: (Edited), New Delhi, 1969
- Employment Relationship in the Building Industry, with S.M. Pandey, New Delhi, 1972.
- Incomes Policy and Industrial Relations (Edited), New Delhi, 1974.
- Industrialism and Employment Systems in India, Delhi, 1992.
- India monograph on Labour Laws and Industrial Relations in the International Encyclopaedia of Laws, Netherlands, 2002.

INDIA:
PERSPECTIVES ON POLITICS, ECONOMY & LABOUR 1918-2007

Vol. 1 : The Age of Gandhi, 1918-1957

C.K. JOHRI

INDIA: Perspectives on Politics, Economy & Labour 1918-2007
Vol. 1 : The Age of Gandhi, 1918-1957
C.K. Johri

First Published, 2011

ISBN 978-93-5002-151-4

Published by
AAKAR BOOKS
28 E Pocket IV, Mayur Vihar Phase I, Delhi 110 091
Phone : 011 2279 5505 Telefax : 011 2279 5641
aakarbooks@gmail.com; www.aakarbooks.com

Printed at
Mudrak, 30 A, Patpargang, Delhi 110 091

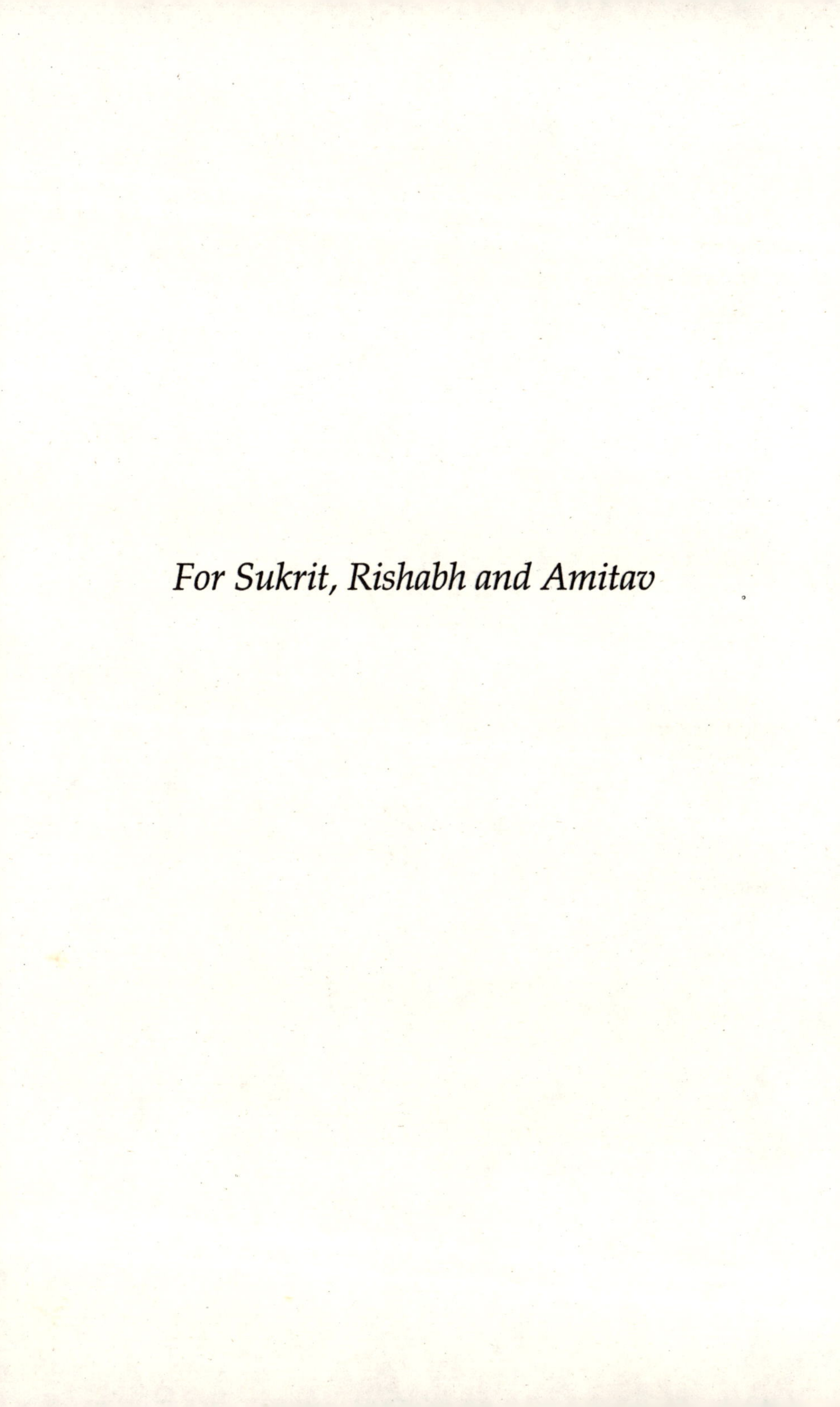

For Sukrit, Rishabh and Amitav

CONTENTS

Preface

The distinctive nature of India's struggle for freedom from bondage formed the essential context to usher in political democracy in a backward country. Six decades later, based on a written Constitution, the government is still struggling and trying to cope with manifold problems of illiteracy, high birth rates, malnourished children and several other dimensions of poverty and backwardness.

The book shows how India managed the change from a colonial economy of a subject people, first, into a self-governing country under a Constitution with an electoral system resting on the decisively important principle of universal franchise of free citizens. Second, under the state's direct planning, led by Nehru, the economy began to advance and acquired considerable strength by industrialization, though mostly through import substitution. Largely due to Cold War competition between the two superpowers, India received foreign aid and technology infusion in a wide range of industrial and other economic spheres. But it remained dependent on food imports to feed its growing population for several decades after independence and this emerged as a major shortcoming of Indian planning. Gradually over the last four decades, India has become self-reliant in food. However, this means maintaining large food reserves, so that when the monsoon fails, the government would still be able to feed the people and prevent avoidable hunger, distress and food-related unrest. This has been a major gain.

Following the collapse of the planning model, the government charted a new kind of economic growth towards liberalization, market dependence and globalization. This was led by the new information technology and software development industry. It is an altogether new economy where India enjoyed a head start and still retains a competitive advantage. It is obvious, though, that the Indian IT industry will have to make an extra effort to stay ahead in a competitive world. On the other hand, liberalization and globalization have progressed erratically.

Contemporary India has several weaknesses. Democracy has undoubtedly struck deeper roots, but a stable government at the Centre which enjoys majority support is a thing of the past. Coalition governments are inherently unstable, while uneven quality of governance is a common experience, as are complaints on corruption, criminality and shoddy administrative practices. India is among the most corrupt countries in the world. Alongside, is the country's low ranking on the indices of quality of life. High illiteracy, poor education, malnourished children, persisting high levels of infant mortality and poor health care are among the glaring shortcomings of the Indian politico-economic system. People have become more assertive and restless and it may be that they are less governable.

India's conflict systems have come out of the repressed mode and show little tendency to wane and weaken. Most of these are embedded in society and based on religion, caste membership, and ethnicity of tribal and language and sub-national identities. They have raised new demands for special political rights and status. Together, these make for a powerful centrifugal force. Even though it may be possible to control their dissents politically, or suppress the more militant tendencies, there is no denying that they weaken India and produce a train of disaffection among the people with occasional disruption of normal life. Though the nation state is secure and strong, the idea of Indian nationhood is not. In contemporary India, it is hazardous to suggest that nationalism is still a great binding force and retains the cohesive, uniting quality of the people of India as a common nation.

Politics has to deal with a variety of contradictions which are built into the social system and are a product of India's long history. Electoral politics also produces several kinds of conflicts, then seeks to resolve them, and in the process, lays fresh grounds for new tensions around unresolved issues. Whether it is in the course of electoral contests; choosing the particular mix of economic policies; the right mix of statism and market orientation; or protective policies and globalization; or profit motive and public welfare, contradictions unavoidably develop and divide society.

Politics is unavoidable in any action plan; so are the conflicts in the methods of coping by the government to resolve divisive issues. The political system mainly provides for representation and a voice to every conceivable interest or class of political concerns. It leads a life of its own. So every conflicting issue acquires a political colour. At the level of the state, it involves all its branches, viz. legislative, executive and judiciary. Unrelenting pressure is created for actions which are routed through the democratic and administrative channels where delays occur, the issues themselves become distorted or merge with other politically divisive subjects and press on the agenda of the government for initiative and purposive response even though it may not be possible to do so.

Politically-conscious people have pushed the government system in conflicting directions, to grapple simultaneously with mutually opposite goals, thereby forcing it to play roles of alternately repressing people and redeeming promises. These matters are described as they occurred in the last six decades and were dealt with by the government. Subject-wise, the themes are classified as political and constitutional developments; economic development or retardation, and effect on inflation and the parallel economy; and industrial relations and labour policy. It also includes brief accounts of progress or non-progress in these areas. The combination of the three broad themes is the unique feature of the book. As far as the author is aware, this book is the first endeavour to present the complex nature of developments over nine decades in a connected, unbroken sequence.

This book follows the method of history, but it was not my aim to produce a work of history. Up to 15 August, 1947, the broad-ranging narrative rests on a nationalist perspective and follows accounts of political events and the personalities connected to them, as presented by historians, biographers and political analysts. It is a very large body of written works and I had to decide on picking and choosing the salient events and episodes which were obviously of significance. My responsibility lay in piecing them together in a single narrative, reflecting the change of contradictory forces at work and the uncertainty of outcomes.

At the first stage was Mahatma Gandhi's unique leadership style which made it possible to create a large aggregation of nationalist forces and lead the entire movement to face and overcome a very powerful adversary in the British Empire. He used idioms of righteousness, converting political struggle into a moral purpose. He employed the technique of Satyagraha for self-purification as well as a non-offensive weapon for nationalist advancement, unity and discipline in action, along with an unswerving commitment to non-violence in speech and action. These were the most extraordinary aspects of the first period covered in the book, viz. January 1918 to January 30, 1948 when the Mahatma was assassinated. I have called it the Age of Gandhi.

The constitutionally arranged transfer of power in 1947 was what the Gandhian movement had aimed at and on accomplishing it, though at a heavy cost, Gandhi's political mission ended. What followed was the unexpected, un-Gandhian Nehru era. On Nehru's death, following a short interregnum in which Shastri led India, another phase, which shaped politics powerfully, followed in two stages, and has been referred to as the era of Indira Gandhi. It was prominently as un-Nehruvian in form, content and style of leadership as Nehru's was un-Gandhian.

Reflecting over the past and perceiving the future in an objective light, one thing that may strike an observer is the extraordinary scale of disconnect which the political class in India has made with Gandhi and his norms and values. On moral and ethical dimensions, contemporary political India and the India Gandhi bequeathed at independence, appear as two contrasting poles of Indian society.

The book is divided into nine chapters and covers a period of nine decades, 1918 to 2007, both years inclusive. The style combines objective narrative, description, analysis and evaluation. The book is about a developing India, struggling against many odds and obvious dangers, as one stage after another came and passed. Trade unions, industrial relations and labour policy form an important part of the book. Industrial relations are quieter now and demonstrate that trade unions are able to adapt to market conditions, though the market-based economy does not serve them the way the state-run controlled economy did. Ideas of liberalization, free trade and globalization do not appear to fit with the collective interests of the working class. Labour has done what it could to obstruct the policy of privatization and slow down liberalization. In the process, it has forced the government to do some rethink on the matter. As a result, the reform agenda is on the back foot and put into slow motion. This may not be in India's long-term interests, but for organized labour, there must be some limit to the reforms which rest on privatization and free trade.

The three themes, viz. politics, the economy and labour are the subject matter of Chapters two to eight. The ninth Chapter has the limited aim of projecting the immediate future as it is observed to emerge from the present. Deeper forces are at work and discussed under the nine subject headings. The population growth and its demographic distribution, climate change and the finiteness of natural resources in relation to the claims made for development, are discussed briefly and separately. The Constitution is accorded the highest priority. Unemployment and poverty are placed as aspects of backwardness and uneven progress on different parameters. The related subjects – over-population, insufficiency of economic progress and increasing disparity among states – are viewed as resulting in part from social inertia or resistance of traditional society to modernization and change. People have gone through tumultuous events, but have craved for continuity and social connectedness even though the result is a dull pace of progress. India unfailingly presents the two sides of its complex, conflicting nature. These are rapid progress at one end and, sloth or very slow motion at the other.

The work is the result of five years of readings and research in the libraries at Delhi as a solo undertaking. Most of the work was done at the India International Centre Library. I have also worked at the IIPA library, The Zakir Husain Library at the JMI, the Indian Council of Historical Research Library and the CITU library. I have received much help and cooperation from librarians and library staff. I may refer to the kindness and consideration shown by Dr. H.K. Kaul and Sushma Zutshi of the IIC Library and Dr. H.J. Abidi of the Zakir Husain Library as decencies in work life which smoothened the path and facilitated progress. I gratefully acknowledge their help and the qualities which make libraries so special for researchers. My friend over five decades, D.K. Agrawal, Senior Advocate, Delhi High Court and a CPI(M) activist not only lent me books from his private collection, but also sponsored me to use the CITU library.

I write in longhand and depend on someone who patiently reads my handwriting and produce a word processed printout to be corrected by me and returned for further word processing. I have received consistent support in this respect from Pratap Singh, who has worked for me on a part-time basis in a most friendly spirit. I acknowledge the support he has lent me over nearly two years. The manuscript was carefully edited by Jehanara Wasi and Sherna Wadia. I acknowledge their joint contribution to making the final product as free from various deficiencies as possible.

As for the final product I cannot apportion praise or blame on anyone and hold myself fully responsible for what is included and what is left out. Preeti, my wife, found it hard to accept my absence from home and in activities where togetherness was desired, and complained about it. I can only acknowledge it in appreciation and hope she will regard her part as an essential contribution to the preparation of this work. This book is meant for the new generation of readers, I dedicate this book to my grandsons, Sukrit, Rishabh Nalin and Amitav Krishna.

C.K. Johri

Chapter 1

INTRODUCTION

I. The Themes of the Book

This book covers a period of nine decades, 1918–2007, describing, interpreting and evaluating developments in India with respect to its politics, economics and labour. Political developments have received close attention since politics pervades all organized activity. Indeed, since Independence, the pervasiveness of politics and recognition that power is a factor which influences every branch of organized behaviour in society has steadily grown. Power games are not only played as an end in themselves, but also quite often to advance collective interests, to promote or undo existing policies or, in the hands of the government, to strengthen the institutions of the state.

India's economy in the last 90 years has functioned in close concert with politics. It is, accordingly, treated as a political economy functioning under the shadow of political ideologies, international power relationships and the profoundly deep, enervating social context of India's backwardness and inertia. Before independence, it was asserted by the colonialists and nationalists alike, that economic exploitation and military power were the two compelling reasons for perpetuating India's status as a subject colony and stalling constitutional advance.

Indian nationalism did not end with the complete break from Great Britain. For the nationalists, independence was the primary condition for India's economic development. Once freed from colonial tutelage, the country would develop naturally to provide greater material prosperity to its people. However, both politics and economics are enveloped in the multi-dimensional contradictions embedded in Indian society and in the very nature of things, these are centred in conflicts of various kinds. Economic advancement through the agencies of the state was the obvious answer and it could not possibly be otherwise.

Agrarian and labour relations form the core themes of conflict-centred formulations and the conduct of policies which have produced wide-ranging political outcomes. Industrial labour policies are unique since they have shown unbroken continuity and an organic growth over the entire period through successive governments and have received precedence over the agrarian. This is primarily due to the preponderance of the urban-industrial system in the making of economic policies since Independence. Earlier too, industrial development was accorded predominance by the nationalists though, in the 1930s, it was moderated by concern for the well-being of peasants. Agrarian questions do find a place in this book but these belong to a world apart and cannot be satisfactorily dealt with in a study which has an altogether different focus; their connection with the freedom movement was of a somewhat general nature, never very deep. In the building of the nation state agrarian issues and attempts at their resolutions played a secondary part. In the demarcation of the boundaries for the conduct of the study covering a long period, extensive exclusions had to be decided. Accordingly, considerable social unrest and upheaval originating in the many contradictions of India have been excluded.

In all three dimensions—politics, economic development and industrial relations—India's political system has avoided sharp breaks. This is the most powerful legacy of the Gandhi-led nationalist revolt against British imperialism. The doctrine of *satyagraha* and insistence on non-violence produced several sweeping agitations and mass movements, but not once were they aimed at seizure of power or furtherance of any act which might produce violence at the hands of agitators.[1] It was a pacifist conflict, conducted as resistance to evil. However, the purpose was not to inflict defeat or suffer and admit defeat in turn, but to overcome the wicked nature of imperialism and open the gates to an ultimate reconciliation. The imperial hegemon was confronted with the collective moral voices of Indians led by Gandhi as the counter-hegemon. The extraordinary style of conducting the nationalist revolt was productive of continuity with change, a transition from the old to the new. This could be smooth or rough but it completely eschewed any suggestion of a revolutionary transformation of the character of the state. The basic premise of continuity with change has informed the conduct of political affairs, economic policies and troublesome industrial relations during the entire nine decades. Much change has undoubtedly occurred over the long run.

It is also observed that the relationship between the state, as the primary change agent, and the people, who are urged to move faster and accept basic changes in their lifestyles, is full of contradictions. There was change as well as resistance to change, and the interaction process has severely impacted politics. Economic policies were used to facilitate the adaptation of economic actors and politicians to hard realities, while left ideology and its slogans were used as an aid. Yet the social forces, not reconciled to the forced pace of the state, reasserted their resilience and used their latent capacity to electorally fight back and reverse the unacceptable parts of earlier decisions. These are described and explained here.

The profound contradiction between British colonialism and the interests of the entire people of India could never be reconciled. It first produced the violent uprising of 1857 and later took the form of the Congress-led nationalist revolt which grew into a powerful challenge. Moreover, though the nationalist leaders and followers were predominantly

Hindus, the movement was broadly democratic and secular. It was not based on religion, caste membership, ethnic affiliations or any ties of birth or origin. The nationalist platform stood for civil liberties, universal franchise, elected assemblies, freedom of expression and a unified doctrine of Indian nationhood. These were great strengths and were passed on to free India as a total package. The fact that, at the end of six decades since Independence, the Indian state continues to adhere to these values and is engaged in expanding freedom by enfranchising the common masses is in no small measure due to this noble legacy.[2]

It is equally important to acknowledge and weave into the analysis the many contradictions of Indian society. Over many centuries, the people of India have developed considerable diversity of cultures. Most of these are among the Hindus but also in the clashing norms, values, beliefs and presuppositions of the six or seven other religions professed by non-Hindus. Among them, Islam and its contentions were used by Muslim leaders for a separate, compact political identity and, fostered by the colonial administration, it led to Partition. The Christians either stayed aloof from the nationalist movement or identified with the alien rule. Their respective political legacies were also transferred to free India and, despite the passage of time, they remain politically alive, seeking various ways to protect their distinct identities and advance collective communal interests. Together with several other more or less manifest contradictions, these make up the contemporary political map of India.

The position taken in this study is that the entire Indian people are still in the process of developing into a common nationhood. However, there is also a simultaneous striving among different ethnic groups and states or regional societies to assert their sub-national identities, engage in sub-national politics and yet promote their collective concerns as members of the nation state within the four corners of the Indian Constitution. In extreme cases, some of them have exceeded permissible limits and opted for the harsh consequences of violent means to achieve impermissible ends. The primary duty of the state is to defend the unity of India unequivocally. This is accepted as the unassailable foundation of India as a nation state.

Unlike the political history of the British period which may be read and interpreted in at least five different ways, which Bipan Chandra has accordingly classified and characterized, there is less controversy regarding the Indian economy during the colonial period. British writers pointed to the obvious prosperity which a stable government made possible and the broadly beneficial effects of the development of railways and post and telegraph as well as the growth in foreign trade. On the other hand, the nationalist critique pointed at rural distress, poverty and recurring famines in the nineteenth century. The land revenue policy, the drain of India's export surplus to Britain and growth in public expenditure (mainly on the army) Britain's military expeditions and the civil service were cited as the causes which perpetrated India's poverty. The employment of so many Europeans at British salaries was a burden on India's economy because their lavish lifestyles and remittances conferred no economic benefit on India. To these causes may be added the burden of interest on public debt which had to be tax financed. Other arguments followed in this train.

It is undeniable that India gained substantially by British investments which grew steadily between 1852 and 1912, inclusive of reinvestment of retained profits. This period comprises the expansionary phase of British investment leading to industrialization and infrastructural development. However, this phase ended by 1914.[3] There is no comparison between this period and the one which commenced with the conclusion of the First World War and continued up to 1947, in fact for several more years. Growth and decline are non-comparable terms. The nationalist critique relied on such facts which showed British rule in a poor light, highlighting its discriminatory and exploitative nature. The rise of the Indian bourgeoisie produced racial antagonism as well as contests between the two interests. In the age of Gandhi, more reasoned arguments were advanced but they were heard as often as they fell off unresponsive ears.

In this study, the first period is certainly accepted as an important dimension of India's political economy but, even more, as the context for the second period. The latter period is more closely examined to bring out the conflicting interests of Britain and India, the long-term effects of the Great War on the former and the manner British investments in India came under pressure, the primacy accorded to the exchange rate and the monetary policy and the critique that was directed at it. The Depression (1929–33) and the Second World War, of which the Great Bengal Famine was the harshest blight, were the two terrible traumas which the Indian people had to suffer. To these was added the trauma of Partition. These produced deeper distress than was realized by the governments then and their long-term consequences had to be borne by the government of free India for at least one decade. Thereafter, on different premises, the government started on a journey of planned economic development with controls. The links with India's colonial past weakened steadily and were replaced by a new relationship based on altogether different terms. This is a period of 50 years, from 1957 to 2007.

Labour has an important though disjunctive place in India's political and economic development. The formation of a modern industrial force began as a concomitant of the growth of the factory system and the railways. However, excepting the tea plantation where conditions of serfdom prevailed, elsewhere labour was legally free to engage in employment contracts. Yet, it was not sufficiently free to exercise any choice in the matter. The organization of industry necessitated the creation of a substratum connecting employers with the labour market and the villages where unemployed young workers looked for opportunities to move out and find work. This substratum is described as jobbers and their main function was to recruit and control labour. This included maintaining the stability of the workforce, discipline and loyalty. Apparently this institution was found to be so efficient by mill owners that they let them discharge the duties of first line supervisors. It may also be due to this novel institution that labour learnt the habits of servile obedience, to protest but rarely and to turn to their jobbers for relief or redress for individual or group complaints.

The objective fact that workers had no real choice rests on the operation of the push factors in the village economy. These, in turn, were related to the destruction of village crafts and cottage industries as the long-term causes while the frequent occurrence of famines was the immediate cause. Mill hands mostly found themselves in defenceless conditions of work without choice. High turnover of labour was common but, since the jobbers found substitutes, the mills generally didn't have to cope with a shortage of hands. Moreover, no one had heard of trade unions or voluntary organizations to build a spirit of solidarity among fellow workers; so several decades passed before anything resembling associations of labour began to emerge.

The village nexus and labour turnover, together with the extreme dearth of institutionalized training and skill development, largely contributed to the retarded growth of a settled, organized and skilled labour force in India. This stage usually precedes the emergence of an early, rudimentary form of unionization. In its absence, the second stage didn't arrive till the closing years of the First World War. However, labour and politics were far removed from each other. The nationalists remained engaged in various protest activities but, except for an occasional glance at factory hands, they ignored them. This was so till the period 1917–20 when, in a great tumult, the Bombay textile mill workers sought out any leaders who might help them. Furthermore, while the concerned provincial government, not unsympathetic to their plight, looked on, the politicians laid the foundations of the trade union movement in India.

As labour learnt to organize, it became increasingly evident that political parties' agendas would not be separated from trade union goals. This may appear an unnecessary distinction because trade unions, as a collective, acquired the traits of a labour movement by at least formulating a line of political action aimed at government policies and legislation. The government too, in its own interests, found it necessary to develop a labour perspective or policies which would minimize excessive use of power in the conduct of industrial disputes. In India, these were not matters which could be settled by looking for common grounds between the two camps, partly because they gave rise to sharply divided positions based on ideology. The secular constitutionalist position on industrial relations is entirely separate from the Marxist and both are far removed from the Hindu democratic nationalist. Politics based on ideology has become a great divider in the entire society and it is no less so in the ranks of labour.

As Indian democracy progressed, so did political divisions on the many issues which confronted society. Industrial relations is one such subject on which the stated positions of politically-led rival trade union centres are far apart and the few common grounds that are discovered occasionally, are speedily lost. These have weakened the labour movement. It has done considerable harm in recent years to the formulation of a more meaningful labour policy by the government which could subserve the broad thrust of market-oriented economic policies. Labour and government are in a stalemate which cannot be broken because neither the government, nor the employers or the unions have the strength to do so.

There are indications that, at the company or plant level industrial relations, political leaders and their failed styles face rejection. Workers want solutions to their collective problems and settlements at the end of open conflicts. Strikes may not be called, not because these are no longer the theatres in which lessons of class struggle are learnt, but because strikes are painful and often produce deprivation and hunger, besides indebtedness for many. In several cases, the pronounced disinterest in ideology has produced a shared willingness among workers to offload the leaders and elect union office bearers from the ranks. These are the grass-root-level manifestations of independent unionism. However, as yet such unions have not acquired an all-India presence and it is quite possible that they would not be able to do so in the near future. Their urges, aspirations and drive are local, and if management styles could become more compatible with the independently run unions, there may not appear even the need for wider organizational links.

In the last ten to fifteen years, a new complexity has emerged in the organized employment system. This is the English-educated workforce in the modern, technologically upgraded organizations and multinational companies. By their education, upbringing, work habits and lifestyles, they are rooted in the middle class though the same labour laws apply to them as the majority of the working class, and they, too, may have to engage in conducting industrial relations, even call strikes. However, English is a great divider in Indian society and a partitioned workforce may be in the making. It is difficult to visualize the patterns of industrial relations which will take shape once this subclass of workers has learnt to organize itself.

Among the many diversities and contradictions which feature in India, the rural-urban divide has become more turbulent, apparently in step with the gathering pace of the market-led economy. Rural-urban disparities touch every aspect of human life—the economic rather more prominently, but also the non-economic. Rural societies are still dominated by the traditional, pre-modern and pre-industrial attitudes and these affect market-centred relationships as well. The rural youth may have received several years of schooling but neither the village schools nor the education they impart are at all comparable to the older, better-equipped schools in cities and towns, and the students who emerge from them. It is a lifelong disadvantage which may bring in its train the entire baggage of disparities in economic prospects, standard of living and expectations in life.

Demographic pressure is also felt most acutely in rural areas, though its grave consequences may still meet with disdain or dismissal. The average land holdings are becoming smaller and in several states and regions the average farmer cannot cultivate his land as an economic holding any longer. The condition of farming in the un-irrigated, rain-fed areas may be altogether precarious. Yet, the rural economy complements the urban-industrial economy and still produces most of the agricultural raw materials for industry. However, in more ways than one, rural India is becoming economically dependent on the urban and is in need of government-funded schemes to provide the means for supporting life, upgrading the technologies in use, preserving agriculture as an economic activity, weakening the inevitable grip of moneylenders, averting farmers' suicides and combating poverty. The economic relationship between agriculture and industry is now completely reversed. Instead of the government mobilizing agricultural surpluses to finance industrialization, as it attempted to do in the first fifteen years of planned development, it is the latter which must now release its surplus to keep the former in a workable condition.

Political India has not only adapted to the political economy of this dramatic reversal of roles but, so far, it has managed it skilfully. However, a new wholly bewildering dimension was added to the ongoing rural-urban conflict-prone relationship. It is the villagers' organized resistance to government acquiring agricultural lands at below market prices for industrial development. Pushed to its logical end, the portentous development implies and may result in a major reversal in the government's attitudes towards industrialization. It may one day have to abandon this policy plank and let the companies, singly or in groups, acquire land, develop it at their cost and set up industries thereafter.

On the face of it, it is a hard decision and unlikely to find political acceptance. However, the only way the special economic zones (SEZ) system of industrialization can be kept going is by acquiring farmlands at low cost. Either the government will do it as at present and succeed by raising the level of compensation to farmers, or market forces would have to be released on farmlands with greater vigour to obtain large parcels of lands currently cultivated in tiny holdings. These possibilities are too speculative and are left undiscussed.

II. Scope and Method of the Study

The scope of this book is defined by those aspects of political development, economy, industrial relations and labour policy which are either intertwined or are of separate interest due to their far reaching importance. Each of these may be broadly described. Politics is all encompassing and the only sensible way to deal with this subject is to limit it by applying the rule of exclusions. This rule is reasonably exercisable by maintaining the focus on macro-political issues and the developments connected to them. The importance of Delhi in India, London in the British Empire, Washington and Moscow as the movers and shakers of Cold War world politics, and the people or leaders who have been at the helm at these capitals is accepted as given. In this study, all these capitals and several others grow or decline in importance as they relate to and impact India with energy and drive, or they withdraw from engagement.

However, a considerable amount of politics has been observed at lower levels in India especially since independence and it can be legitimately asked whether it is at all analytically defensible to exclude, for instance, state-level political developments altogether. Some of these developments have wider reach, or they have impacted India's survival as a nation state, so they must be accorded prime importance. All of India's Northeast falls in this category, as do political developments in Punjab, Tamil Nadu,

Jammu & Kashmir (J&K) and West Bengal. What has been aimed at in the limited confines of this book is to pick up the salient features, present the comparable perspectives of the central government relative to those of the dissident, militant or combatant political parties or movements and point at the positive or hopeful directions of change. The purpose of describing the incendiary nature of these subjects is to clarify the tangled web of issues and the length to which it may be possible to push them politically, while retaining an all-India national perspective and objectivity, but no more. In a national viewpoint, there is room for dispassion, greater understanding and considerable scope for political accommodation, as also, logically tenable and mutually negotiated compromises. What are excluded are the win-and-lose political games.

The Macro Perspective

The macro perspective is also the dominant mode for analysis of economic problems. The Indian economy and its developments are deeply connected with politics, the beliefs of its rulers and the nature of governance of the country. Hence the subject is political economy and considerable attention must always be focused on the key clusters of economic policies, the manner these are implemented and the results expected and achieved. During the later colonial era in the inter-war period, the belief system continued to favour laissez-faire, as was the case before the war. However, political compulsions had already produced the contending claims resting on 'discriminating protection' on the one hand and the equally, if not more contentious, pursuit of 'imperial preference' on the other. What the monetary policy achieved under those circumstances is a subject of absorbing interest, but a discussion in a summary form is all that is possible. What then followed was the economics of war, inflation, severe shortages and supply bottlenecks, rationing and the Bengal famine. These make for grim reading. The colonial government's handling of these problems showed an extraordinary lack of preparation at the administrative level, made worse by the political vacuum created by nationalist opposition. It became a task of economic management in the midst of a deep adversarial relationship. The economy was in dire straits when the imperial realm decided to fold up. Britain chose to withdraw from India, partition the country and grant full independence to the two dominion states.

Thereafter, a new chapter opened in economic management and formulation of nation-specific economic policies. Viewed from the standpoint of the people of India, in respect of their poverty, suffering, hunger and deprivations, it is difficult in retrospect to be sure when they suffered more, in the decade preceding the outbreak of the Second World War, or in the following decade. In this book, they remain at the centre of concern though, in the strict sense, the core subject of economics is the problem of scarcity and the consequent questions of choice and allocation of resources. Successive governments of free India have endeavoured and faced basic economic choices in a long-term political perspective. These are to raise the level of the economy, upgrade the complexity of its structure and augment the range of goods and services available for both investment and consumption. However, given the enormity of problems which the two World Wars and a Great Depression created, followed by the enormous pile up of tasks connected with the partition of the country, the goals had to be realistically set.

Much later, India began to have five year plans, but only the second, third and the fourth were designed as planning models. Subsequently, in the face of compelling circumstances, the strength of a pragmatic hand steadily gained in force and conviction over those of the planning dogmas and economic illusions which went into the making of earlier Five Year Plans. A major shift in the political direction of economic policies was made in 1991–3, actually in the face of exceedingly heavy odds, and the entire corpus of economic policies was retooled to bear greater accord with market forces. For many, it was regrettable that the system of controls was dismantled. However, gradually, the market has brought in new faces and faster growth as well but, unavoidably, more risks too, as the economy has moved closer to the worldwide swings of market forces.

Labour as a Category

Unlike politics and the Indian economy, developments in labour bore the characteristic features of the industries in which the workforce was employed.[4] In the nineteenth century, the most important industries were cotton textiles, jute textiles and coal mining. By the end of the First World War, two more employment segments were added—the railways and the iron and steel industry. Most of the workers were immigrants and they brought their specific sociocultural traits with them. These were vastly different from each other, and the mere fact that several linguistic, religious and geographic region-based differences were mingled in a common industry did not mean that in response to shared experiences they would think and act alike, or develop bonds of brotherhood. However, the Bombay textile workers stood up first to face the freshly mounted attacks on their living standards by demonstrating a capacity for united action, which the authorities had never expected. Other industrial centres took their time and followed their internal dynamics. The heterogeneous trait of the labour movement has stayed with it in the last nine decades; it will be profiled and evaluated in this book.

Labour's second unusual aspect has been that, though led by the political class, the working class acted mostly in defence of its own interests. This behavioural characteristic prevented its absorption into the larger political movements, including the earlier nationalist agitation for Swaraj. The autonomy of trade unions has been largely due to the asymmetric dependence of workers, primarily on their employers for their livelihood and security (hence their attitudes towards class relations) and secondarily on the cadre of outside union leaders who mitigate their day-to-day problems and provide guidance and leadership on critically important issues. It is the workers' collective survival instinct which has kept them away from political parties and has led them to downplay their doctrines and ideologies.

A political macro perspective emerged, however, with the development of an all-India labour policy and a philosophy of government action towards industrial relations. The laissez-faire philosophy of the colonial government had to be given up during the Second World War and, since then, the government has stayed with labour as an involved and interested party in moulding and managing industrial relations. The labour policy evolved in response to the demands of organized labour and the parties allied to their cause, so that the government remains active as an involved third party. The overriding theme of the government's legislative programme is to promote labour welfare within a politically managed paternalistic relationship. In return, labour is expected to conduct its disputes with management in a responsible manner and avail of the dispute settlement machinery created for the purpose. The irony of this vastly unequal political relationship is that, in return for the promise of preserving industrial peace, the government is asked to refrain from any legislative proposal which, on enactment, might hurt workers' interests in any way. It has worked because the labour policy has derived its strength on a practiced consensus, which requires agreement not just of private employers and the trade union centres but also the state governments. However, consensus precludes systemic change in the direction of policy. All parties are agreed to continue with the existing arrangements, because there is no possibility of developing another consensus on making any significant alteration in them, or in the direction of policy. This is a structure of non-progress and it is preserved as a mutually convenient and politically tolerable subsystem of Indian polity.

Regulating industrial relations involved the government

in an ongoing, conflict-centred power relationship. No other conflict relations have led to government involvement on a comparable scale and continuity. Among them, the most complex, pressing but intrinsically difficult to assuage is the thorny issue of land reforms, or the connected problems of agrarian relations in different parts of the country. This subject lies outside the scope of this book but is intimately linked to the distribution of power in the country, the social bases of parties, the development of highly militant forms of struggle for securing rights on land led by revolutionary Marxist parties, called Maoist and Naxalite, and the threat they pose to the security of the state. Actually, these aspects were never absent and Congress-led movements did get involved with agrarian tangles at varying levels of intensity and commitment. Consequently, as a sub-theme of political developments, they have been described or explained beginning with the assumption of power in 1937 and, later, following independence. Currently, it is acknowledged as a political threat; the same is noted in the book but left at that.

Dimensions of Conflict Management

There are two other related problems which dominate the country's economic development as well as its political systems and the already difficult tasks of conflict management. One is the size of India's population and the differential rates of growth by religions, linguistic distributions, castes and tribal identities. The politics of identity is inherently prone to conflicts. Demographic distribution tends to aggravate them, while leading elements of religious, language and caste groups seek to enter and dominate party structures and turn them into political instruments for capturing power or influencing the course of government policies. For the future of India's broad-based secular democracy, this is a most perverse development. Yet, all pointers show that identity politics will dominate India's immediate future.

The other problem is that of environment, climate change,

deforestation, silting of rivers and dams, floods, droughts and other natural disasters connected with rising temperatures of the seas. Population growth will inevitably magnify climatic adversity over people's lives, including agriculture and livelihood patterns. India has been very slow in waking up to the seriousness of the damage already done to the ecology and, much more, to the dangers that are in the making. The electorate shows minimal awareness, even as people raise loud cries in despair for help and redress when natural or climate-change-induced disasters occur in India. In the last three decades, these seem to have become more common or the visitations of nature-inflicted calamities more frequent. The politics of action for remedial measures, which involves heavy financial and administrative commitments, is not in sight. A few activists are in the lead and the government follows with as much speed or tardiness as it finds expedient. This is because the larger part of the political system is busy elsewhere and it will continue to dodge and dither over what is not of immediate consequence.

The British Legacy

It is a basic premise of this study that all the three political developments—nationalist, economic and labour—were by-products of British imperial rule over India. Tara Chand's first two volumes of the *History of the Freedom Movement in India* explain in considerable detail the wide sweep and deeply penetrating impact of British rule.[5] The educated middle class played the critically important role in building a new consciousness on the relationship of the people of India with their rulers. The yearning for freedom, which leading elements in the relatively small middle class in major cities acquired, was based only partially on their discovery of the glory and defeats of India in the past but, more positively, on the acceptance of British liberal values. Modern India was created under British auspices and it continues. The Indian nation state was reborn as an independent country as a successor state with all the elements of continuity that defined the British administrative system, which were taken over intact by the nationalists now in governance.

India has changed considerably since then but it is remarkable how little the state system has changed. It is the same with the people. Their circumstances have altered beyond recognition and they enthusiastically participate in politics but without breaking with bonds of religion, caste and tradition. Over the last six decades, in the deepest consciousness of the Indian people, a new awakening has taken shape—that they are a distinctive people and their country is unlike any other. As a country and as its citizens, more people probably accept it as a settled fact that they have a distinct identity.

The study rests on the affirmation that over-arching nationalism is a political reality and forms the principal bastion of India's unity. At the same time, all the contradictions of Indian society, the utter diversity, the unceasing craving for plurality, for recognition of every conceivable indicator or criterion of identity and the bewildering scale of political chaos these threaten to produce, are also admitted and are provided for in the descriptive and evaluative parts of the book. Social contradictions and political conflicts are an inseparable part of the functioning of the Indian nation state. At the macro level, India is still struggling to superimpose the notion of a pan-Indian identity over other identities.

What has been achieved is much less and that is a broad acceptance of the idea of India as a nation in the making. This discrepancy is probably the result of the clamour of other identities for acknowledgement and affirmation. The idea of a nation in the making is basically a product of the Indian people's greatest and foremost encounter with the far more developed and far better organized British civilization as an administrative, military-cum-economic power. This has expanded in recent decades into a wider and more enriching interaction with the entire Western civilization, including their politics, cultures and economic systems. These have simultaneously been a learning as well as a daunting experience. As a people, Indians are far behind Western societies and much as they may learn from them, what can be brought home to India is comparatively less. Only in science and technology is the vital second step of transference of knowledge achievable and progress continues to be made in this regard. However, it is a predetermined pattern overall: the West leads and India follows. The interactions have also awakened them to their many weaknesses, the hollowness of their pretensions and the considerable cultural and educational distance the people in parts as well as the whole must travel to catch up with the more advanced people.

Threat Perceptions

Writing on economic and labour developments has been relatively easier since the broad features have already been described and explained by established authors and there are fewer controversies. The close connection of Britain's economy to the political drive to retain India as a possession forms a significant part of Tara Chand's works as does the connection between the rise of Indian nationalism and the state of the economy in India. This dimension was carried over to the formulation of economic policies and planning exercises for future development during the post-Independence period. Six decades later, the articulation in the nationalist idiom of Indian business and wider economic interests is nearly as common as it ever was earlier. It is Swadeshi once again, the slogan first used by Tilak to counter British power over India. The difference is that currently India has the membership of GATT as well as reciprocal responsibilities towards its trading partners, while at the turn of the twentieth century, Swadeshi was a novel slogan and politically related only to Britain. Nonetheless, in the post-Independence period, the conduct of economic policies has never been free from criticisms from the nationalist perspective along with other controversial angles.

On occasion, the economy deteriorated to such an extent that it seemed to endanger the stability of the government. Indeed, it is arguable that the mismanagement of the economy in 1974–5 preceded sharp swings in politics and governance. Much political debate is currently focused on prioritizing the most significant and pressing issues among the many which have cropped up over a period of six decades. The perceived hopes of and threats to India's sovereignty and the integrity of the nation state, entailed by the liberalization and globalization processes and the consequent weakening of the state as a power system, are the latest concerns.

There was a strong patriotic appeal in the objectives of economic planning, expressed as self-reliance in food, diminished dependence on imports, the need to promote import substitution and so on, though some of them were indefensible on purely economic grounds. Appeal to nationalism was implied in the need to conserve foreign exchange, to cut down oil imports, to reduce dependence on foreign aid, et cetera. Most of the emotive appeal of planning was in the garb of nationalism as projected by the government and political leaders at the helm. The underlying theme was that this was the only solid way the gains of the freedom movement, for India, as a secure, free though developing country, could be retained and strengthened in the future. Now, in the face of globalization and the anticipated growth of foreign capital and its interests in the Indian economy, perhaps the threats which were receding may reappear and even cloud the political horizons of contemporary India. The controversy is between economic logic and economic nationalism. The left, the Marxist parties, have emerged as the strongest champions of the latter which is also shared by the BJP and its allies. Presently, the former appears to be winning against heavy political odds, though it is a case of the stronger side still having to build up its scores in the face of several setbacks and politically directed pauses.

A major handicap is the demographic pressure and the

heavy strain it imposes on the fiscal system. Moreover, demographic growth is starkly embedded in the backwardness of large parts of India with an overload of religious, casteist and tradition based loyalties which reflect in the attitudes towards work, progress-related issues and economic development in general. Most of the backward states show relatively greater deficits in education, health standards, mortality rates, gender inequality and, not surprisingly, in investors and entrepreneurs also. In several states, the real problem is the all-round pervasive backwardness of society which impedes progress in any direction. However, there are few differences of opinions on the great need for concerted state-led actions in these respects. The government is expected to take on the leading role and persevere in providing practically all inputs to give a strong thrust towards the realization of the connected socioeconomic goals. The fear is that in the event the central government, as the most powerful arm of the state, is weakened by the ongoing thrust of liberalization and globalization, it may not prove equal to the tasks.

New Labour Perspective

Labour's induction into politics may be traced to the Government of India Act, 1919, which conferred a formal status of interest, meriting recognition. Following this, was the inevitable process of choosing someone to represent labour's interests. The selection of the leading representatives of the All India Trade Union Congress (AITUC) to represent Indian labour's views at International Labour Organization (ILO) conferences was also political in nature. Thereafter, the colonial government only took action affecting labour after engaging in political consultations with the more trusted labour leaders. This habit was passed on to independent India without a hitch. The second stage arrived with the Marxist ideology and the emergence of communist cadres during the latter half of the 1920s. The sole exception to this was the trade unionism under Gandhi's guidance and leadership at

Ahmedabad, which has preserved its distinctive Gandhian character to this day.

Since Independence, the political element in trade unions gained in strength and, alongside this, grew the government's anxiety to steer workers' political consciousness towards its predetermined path of socioeconomic development. Accordingly, the day-to-day conduct of industrial relations is closely tied to the dispute settlement machinery. Over several years of schooling in practical politics, organized trade union centres learnt to use their powers to demonstrate by collective action, which government policies they approve of, and which they reject and demand their roll back. They have successfully thwarted government actions to accelerate privatization of public sector undertakings (PSUs) and induction of liberal policies. However, for all practical purposes, labour's protests have been effective mainly in the public sector on which there is a larger political agreement among political parties and the bureaucracy.

By comparison, in the steadily expanding private sector, labour's stance has been the opposite. Militancy is on the wane and trade unions appear to be more understanding and less obstructive, as managements seek to prepare themselves to face tougher competition. This is a dichotomous development, more the result of the reluctance of average workers to engage in fruitless strikes and instead seek more constructive ways to protect their jobs and earnings, as the firms themselves struggle to survive. This is not the result of any rehearsed policy planks by the union centres or of any specific policy initiative by the government. It is the result of markets at work which doused the aggressive brand of trade unionism and reaffirmed the principle of mutuality of interests.

III. The Immediate Context of the Age of Gandhi

Political Developments

The decade preceding the era of the pan-Indian national movement for Swaraj, which began under Gandhi in 1918, may be treated as the immediate context. Political India was already in ferment in the first decade of the twentieth century. In Bengal, the agitation against its partition remained unabated and there was considerable underground revolutionary activity.[6] In the Bombay presidency, Bal Gangadhar Tilak was the acknowledged political leader who pursued the Swadeshi programme together with the boycott of anything British and the demand for Swaraj. In 1907, the Indian National Congress suffered a major split between the moderates and the extremists resulting in the latter leaving the organization. Coincidentally, the government singled out the leading extremists for various punishments and deported several. In 1908, Tilak, in a sedition case, was sentenced to six years in jail at Mandalay in Burma. The transportation of a popular, respected leader of Tilak's stature caused deep resentment. The Bombay working class demonstrated their revulsion by going on a general strike.[7] The government had already decided on the policy of repression as a powerful arm of imperial governance against seditious writings and public utterances and acts of revolutionary violence, without bothering about the distinction between the two. The garrison state must be strong to rule a subjugated people, and it must be feared.

However, the other arm of imperial policy was to encourage the loyal elements and sustain the moderates' position with concrete reform measures. The Minto-Morley reforms of 1909 were produced by a complex mix of these attitudes. The moderates, though placated, were not satisfied with the meagre contents of the reforms and demanded much more, but continued to look up to Britain for India's political progress. The government had already rendered the extremist movement leaderless and bereft of guidance. The few reform steps taken to increase Indian representation in the governing bodies left practically everyone dissatisfied. From the perspective of alien rulers, the one thing the 'natives' respected most was governance on the basis of an autocratic but just rule. However, the demands made by the small class of educated urban politicians, democratic and secular in outlook, also had to be met. Broadly viewed, it was a mix of a policy of favours and persuasion for the loyal elements and coercion for the disloyal.

The benevolent among the rulers thought that while autocracy must be the permanent feature of an effective administration, it was equally important to prepare the Indians in institutions of self-governance. This was to be a long-drawn process, because those who aspired for self-rule must prepare themselves, not just in education but also in moral character and administrative principles of integrity and objectivity. The moderates generally bought this line of reasoning.[8] Yet, they looked up to the British with greater optimism and hoped that, in the many branches of administration and the army, Indians could be allowed greater participation, and there were no satisfactory reasons why progress could not be faster.

In Tilak's absence, there was little activity towards Swaraj, till Annie Besant took the stage. From a theosophical viewpoint, she picked up the plea for India to make faster progress towards the same principles of governance as were practised in Britain. She led a movement in which many dissatisfied thinkers and intellectuals found a source of spiritual renewal, a platform for constructive social reform and a more integrated understanding of the traditions and faiths of their ancestors. In 1914, she decided to launch a movement for Home Rule on the pattern of the Irish Home Rule League and started two papers, *New India* and *Commonweal*.

In 1914, Tilak was released and he picked up the threads of nationalism. On different platforms, Annie Besant and Tilak regrouped an entirely new body of young men with shining idealism, eager for action. Annie Besant was a loyalist and pleaded with the British government to move India rapidly towards dominion status. In 1916, the two leaders joined to make a common front but with the clear understanding that, while Tilak would confine his agitation in the Marathi and Kannada-speaking parts, Annie Besant would have the rest of India. In fact, she had already established a wide network of educational institutions, public libraries and units of the Home Rule League. The joining of the two streams of the nationalist movements happened at the same venue, Lucknow, where the extremists were readmitted to the Congress. The programme of Home Rule towards Swaraj was adopted by the Congress in that year.

In 1917, Anne Besant was served the order of internment and it caused a virtual uproar. For the first time, though baffled at the scale of protests on the detention of an Irish lady, the government saw the pervasive spirit of pan-Indian nationalism. Three months later, she was released and, in view of her great popularity, elected the president of the Congress. Her eloquence in support of free India was her greatest asset as were her fearlessness and total commitment to the cause. In 1916–17, the country found two idols, Tilak and Annie Besant.[9]

At the Lucknow meet Tilak had taken no chances and had brought 300 delegates with him. He was given a rousing reception on arrival and, at the Congress, he received an unprecedented ovation. From this stage onwards, the leadership of the Congress was vested in the Swaraj camp. The moderates continued to hitch themselves to the progressive British position, which sought cooperation from India towards further advance. This appeared to have been held out by the King at his Durbar in 1911, and the latest affirmation was Montague's statement in 1917. There were setbacks too, principally by the Secretary of State for India: Crewe's statement in 1912, that the British government had no intention of introducing home rule in India. He later reaffirmed this. Clearly there was a discrepancy between the two positions in Britain.

As the issue of political advance for Indians grew in importance, the British opted to become participants in India's politics. Two strands of political involvement are discernible. One was the inclination to grant legitimacy to the loyal oppositionists, of whom G.K. Gokhale was perhaps the most eloquent and acceptable spokesman. Gandhi accepted him as a political guru though both he and Tilak stood apart from his politics of accommodation with Britain. The moderates were most concerned at the rise of revolutionary activities and agreed that these had to be curbed. However, they also asked for a policy of concession and conciliation to politically disarm them. The government did think of a few concessions but these were altogether tardy and ineffective.

Instead, the rulers sought the loyal support of the princely order and asked for mutual cooperation in the face of a common danger. The princes began to be viewed as an important element in the future development of India's constitutional progress.[10] An idea was mooted, but deferred at that stage, to set up an advisory council of ruling chiefs and territorial magnates.[11] Earlier in 1911, a major political move towards conciliation was taken at the King's Durbar. The partition of Bengal was annulled and the capital was shifted from Calcutta to Delhi. A theory was advanced that there should be greater provincial decentralization while retaining the power to interfere in cases of misgovernance and matters of imperial concern. This gave rise to more hope of increased self-governance, which was then speedily laid to rest by the Secretary of State, Crewe. Thereafter, the influence of the moderates waned, while revolutionary activities increased. For all practical purposes, Crewe demolished the expectations that were roused by the King's pronouncements in 1911.

> Minto thought the Congress demand for 'self-rule' to be an impossibility. He firmly believed that the character of the Indian government must remain autocratic, but it could be tempered by giving Indians a larger representation on the legislative councils and more share in the administration of their country. He even thought of the admission of an Indian to the Executive Council, from which the Indians were barred by tradition.

Politically, there were a number of interests needing representation. Among them, the Muslim interest grew steadily in importance and eventually succeeded in a large measure.[12] The Muslim delegation was able to secure the concession of a separate electorate from Minto and recognition of their political identity as a nation in India. In course of time, the Muslim opinion would grow into a formidable counterpoise to nationalism. This was Minto's most significant achievement in preserving British rule in India. The other weaker counterpoise, was to move toward reforms while suppressing anarchical crimes. This initiative was addressed to the predominantly Hindu Congress. A political game plan thus evolved to defeat the anarchists, isolate the extremists, weaken the nationalist thrust towards Home Rule and strengthen the base of peace and order to preserve British rule over India.

The silent but powerful Muslim interest took a distinctly more critical view of British actions following the annulment of the partition of Bengal. The beginning of the First World War introduced a new element—the pan-Islamic sentiment of Indian Muslims. The few Muslim powers, including Persia and Turkey, were 'sinking lower into depths of submission or calamity'.[13] As far as India mattered, the position taken was that the advancement towards self-government should be compatible with the political interests of Muslims, not based solely on their share of population. It must be politically proportionate, or much greater than their numerical importance. The development of the idea that Muslims were a distinct nation had progressed over the preceding three or four decades. Several scholars, poets and public leaders had devoted their lives to the mission of reviving the spirit of loyalty to Islam and Islamic countries, of pan-Islamism as a true blend of religion and politics.

> The Muslim elite in India had always been conscious of their pan-Islamic identity, that is, their belonging to a wider world of Islam which extended far beyond India. In one sense, pan-Islamism, as an ideology or a sentiment, can be said to have

> been as old as Islam itself, for the brotherhood of all Muslims had been an essential part of the teaching of the Prophet.[14]

Syed Ahmed Khan was the foremost spokesman of this ideology but there were several others who are referred to by scholars.

Opposition to the Congress and support to British rule was the practical dimension of Syed Ahmed Khan's politics. The long-term interest of Muslims was to remain loyal to the British and promote their collective interests by forging closer ties with the rulers. This attitude received considerable encouragement at the hands of Anglo-Indian officials. Tara Chand summed up the British policy underlying the concession on separate electorates: 'The minority community was favoured and the majority spurned because it was necessary to thwart the purpose of the national movement.'[15] However, this policy was later reviewed and partly reversed and the King's Durbar was used for the purpose.

However, the Muslim reaction was adverse and an adversarial attitude towards British rule developed as the Balkan war unfolded and showed the unending misfortunes of fellow Muslims abroad. Meanwhile, the Muslim League underwent a change of leadership. Jinnah and Mohamed Ali were the new leaders and they steered it closer to the Congress. 'But the collaboration which now began was more of the nature of an alliance of two organized and self-conscious bodies representing two distinct communities with their special problems and ideologies, for mutual aid against a common foe, than of fusion.'[16] Muslim leaders received practically no hearing on their concerns over Turkey. Turkey had joined forces with Germany and was now Britain's enemy. In India, British interests coincided with the Congress which strongly supported British war efforts, though a large number of Muslim soldiers took part in the war.

India's war contribution received considerable appreciation in England and the moderate leaders of Congress viewed it positively, as well. In fact, Tilak too supported India's participation in the war. The extremists seemed to be steering towards the moderates. It is these objective forces which moved the Muslim League closer to the nationalists. Mohamed Ali set the goal of working 'shoulder to shoulder with the sister communities of India for securing the recognition of all the legitimate claims of India as a whole, while safeguarding at the same time, all the legitimate interests of the Muslim community.'[17] The spirit of common purpose produced a conclave at Lucknow in 1916 where the two groups of leaders worked hard over complex issues. The Congress conceded the principle of separate electorates, while it sowed the seeds of Muslim separateness. However, much bargaining preceded agreement as, for example, the compromise on the proportion of Muslim seats in UP and Bengal.[18] This pact was followed by more concerted action and it informed the Hindu–Muslim politics in the next decade but, later, it gradually and irreversibly withered away.

Independent of the Swarajists and campaigners for home rule, the nationalist pressure on alien rule was built up by the underground revolutionary groups. The expectation that the annulment of the partition of Bengal would end the cult of the bomb was belied. Instead, there was an upsurge of revolutionary activities in Punjab headed by the Ghadar Party, with failed attempts at inciting Indian soldiers to rebel and mutiny.[19] The Bengali revolutionaries and Ghadar activists thought that it would be possible to stage an uprising in India with German aid of money, weapons and logistics support. However, despite considerable planning and active German support, nothing much happened. The British government countered German moves, unmasked the conspiracies and nullified the revolutionaries' elaborate plans.[20]

Nevertheless, the spectre of revolutionary activities produced an entire body of repressive legal measures to suppress any form of dissent. Censorship was enforced at local levels and as a result, 'over 1,000 individual titles were banned between 1914 and 1918. Securities were demanded from 289 newspapers and 389 presses: securities were actually forfeited in the case of 11 papers and 33 presses. About 300 editors and publishers were actually warned.'[21] Yet, curbing political violence needed more than normal legal repression, it would have to rest on emergency powers. These were recommended by the controversial report prepared by a committee headed by the Scottish judge, S.A.T. Rowlatt, in 1918. Though considered necessary for the preservation of British rule over India, they ran totally contrary to the reforms proposed in 1917 by the liberal Secretary of State for India, E.S. Montague. The fact that a deep political impasse had occurred was hardly understood and never faced.

Subject to the overarching principle of the permanency of British rule, the imperial government took a major forward step towards greater self-governance by Indians. As Tara Chand put it, His Majesty's Government was of the policy 'of the increasing association of Indians in every branch of the administration and the gradual development of self-governing institutions with a view to the progressive realization of responsible government in India as an integral part of the British Empire'. However, progress can be achieved only in successive stages and the British government would decide the timing and measure of each advance. They would be guided by the cooperation received from the responsible Indians who would have to work the reforms and demonstrate by deeds what could be achieved and what might be aimed at in future.

This was accompanied by two announcements: one, to remove the bar on admission of Indians to the commissioned ranks and the other, that the Secretary of State for India would visit India and provide ample opportunities for discussion on proposals which would later be presented to Parliament. This fell far short of self-governance. Swaraj was not in sight, but the nationalists would get a fair opportunity to meet Montague and Chelmsford together and impress upon them their views on the proposed reforms. Meanwhile, the order of internment on Annie Besant and her political colleagues was withdrawn. More people on whom restrictions were placed would be freed and the government hoped there would be tranquillity in the country.

The War and the Economy

The First World War, 1914–18, made a deep impact on the Indian economy. It impacted manpower more directly since the combat involved a large-scale mobilization of both fighting and support personnel. 'By the end of December 1919 nearly 1½ million Indians had been recruited into combatant and non-combatant services, nearly 1,400,000 British and Indians had actually been sent overseas. So had 184,350 animals!'[22] India made substantial contribution to war finance, estimated around £146 million. The share of defence expenditure in total public expenditure rose from 25 per cent in 1913–14 to 33 per cent in 1917–18 and stayed at this level till 1921–2. To meet the military expenditure, taxes were increased and large war loans raised. In real terms, the economy did not grow at all, though its structure underwent significant changes.[23]

The changes in the economic structure can be deduced in a general way from the data on exports. Between 1900–10 and 1920–1 the percentage share of manufactured jute goods rose from 8.1 to 22.1, while indigo almost disappeared.[24] Due to severe curtailment in trade, there were extreme shortages of essentials, such as kerosene, while prices were steadily rising. The price level rose twice as high between 1914 and 1918 and continued to rise thereafter.

> The situation was aggravated by profiteering and speculation, despite government attempts to control prices. It was compounded by the monsoon failure in 1918–19. An official survey of Indian affairs accepted that during the war, prices of food grains had risen by 93 per cent, of imported goods by 190 per cent and by just over 60 per cent in the case of Indian-made goods.[25]

At the level of the masses, there was distress and also some disturbances taking the shape of grain riots, petty looting, et cetera. By 1917–18 the supply management was failing and the little that was officially done was utterly inadequate in view of the high prices of salt, cloth and oil.

On the other hand, industry profited and paid out handsome dividends. Yet, the manufacturing sector could not take advantage of wartime scarcities to expand the industrial base by import substitution. The Indian economy was still largely dependent on British manufacturers for technology, machinery and spares. The wartime dislocations did not create new opportunities, because all other trade sources, especially Germany, were shut off, and the dominant view in India was to wait for war to end before planning for new expansions.

The long-term economic forces at work produced a most adverse effect on the indigo plantations. Germany's advance in chemical dyes hastened the end of the indigo business. Indigo profits rested on the severely exploitative terms which the planters had imposed on the ryots. These were first criticized, then assailed and eventually whittled down. Gandhi made his contribution towards this end. Indigo was no longer the crop the ryot was forced to grow, nor was it profitable in the changed conditions. The entire indigo business steadily drifted towards eclipse.

By comparison, the tea planters continued to expand, the labour force grew from 609,000 in 1913 to 704,000 in 1918 in North India. However, by 1917, physical problems such as shortage of railway rolling stock and tea chests impacted tea export and it had to be restricted. Employment in the jute industry grew from 218,000 in 1914 to 234,000 in the course of the war.[26] The cotton textile industry earned high profits and, in Bombay, it was lavish with dividends.

Impact on Factory Labour

Labour conditions were never satisfactory in any industry and turned grim as prices rose following the outbreak of the war. Yet, labour failed to respond. In both Bombay and Calcutta industrial labour originated in rural areas in very poor conditions often bordering on destitution. Industry sought an abundant supply of labour to operate multiple shifts and nearly always managed to secure it. The declining rural economy rendered entire segments of rural population poor and helpless.[27] However, the development of railways opened up the village societies to the possibilities of migration. Industry too, developed elaborate institutional arrangements to ensure adequacy of labour supply even in seasons when factory hands returned to their villages. In years of prosperity, the mills were keen to conserve their supply of labour and be assured of replacements when the inevitably high turnover rates produced instability. Labour contractors, known by various names, were the intermediaries who performed this function and became indispensable.[28]

In the plantations, workers were mostly indentured and not only worked, but also lived, on the lands belonging to the masters in near serf-like conditions. There never were any labour organizations in village societies; they came to the cities as strangers and the only organizational element they knew was the mill and, in direct relationship to it, the labour intermediary. On their own they could not have, and did not, organize themselves. This was a task for high-minded social activists and social reformers. 'The characteristic features of this period of the Indian labour movement were the complete absence of radicalism, non-realization of the significance of labour problems, lack of class consciousness and hence of class conflicts and the inevitable communal colour of the social welfare movement.'[29] There were instances of unrest, protests, even strikes as spontaneous outbursts of agitating workers, but there were no unions. The guiding principle of social reformers was sympathy and moral uplift, not justice. Despite many years of exposure to industry, the working class still lacked education and the culture which would translate the wider meaning of wild-cat strikes to the importance of unity in organization and cohesion and solidarity for furtherance of their collective interests.

Among the mill hands of Bombay, the first signs of an emerging collective were observed during 1917–20. Though still predominantly rural from the Ratnagiri area, not far from Bombay, and first-generation mill workers, by this time a collective consciousness about their shared working conditions and the adversarial nature of employment relationship had obviously taken early root. The underlying factor was probably common ethnic bonding and a loose sense of fraternity resting on mutuality of trust and neighbourly helpfulness rather than class solidarity.

> World War I was a period of great tension in Bombay. The work force became increasingly restless as the cost of living rose rapidly. Strikes became even more frequent and threatened to take on city-wide proportions. The mill owners boasted that by their quick action in granting a cost-of-living allowance they were able to forestall a general strike in the middle of 1917, but in January 1919 an industry-wide strike involving 150,000 workers broke out and paralyzed the mills.[30]

India in 1917–18

To sum up, the situation in India in 1917–18 was far from reassuring. There was economic distress, labour was in a most disturbed mood and Muslim political opinion had veered away from ideas of loyalty to the crown, mostly in response to pan-Islamic concerns. The most loyal at this juncture were the entire body of nationalists, now broadly in the same camp as Tilak and Annie Besant. They sought from the government a plan of action toward self-rule or Swaraj within the British Commonwealth. For them, it was not a hallucination, nor a goal that was utterly unrealizable in the concrete circumstances of India, of which two were self-evident. First, there weren't enough trained Indians of a calibre and character to man the civil and judicial services and, with the best intentions of the world, it would still take many more years to accomplish this task. This, the moderates readily granted, while the Swarajists were keener on the goal being announced without any ambiguity and with transparent clarity, as well as the immediate steps to be taken to enable the country to move speedily toward goal realization. The Swarajist position produced a huge gap between them and the rulers and an agitation was mounted.

The second, and the older, was the Muslim question which the Lucknow Pact had apparently resolved, though the patchwork of compromises already had seeds of disillusionment built into it. Not many were convinced that it would last, because Muslim politics was led by other stronger motivating factors which flowed from their pan-Islamic sentiments as much as from their collective consciousness as a distinct people though, at this juncture, it was congruent to the nationalists' position.[31] The Muslim League had achieved one objective. Having entered into an alliance with the Congress, it secured for the Muslims the formal cognizance of their political identity. This was a major gain which received still greater weightage under the Montford reforms. However, the government's attitude toward the Muslim agitators had stiffened and leaders like Mohmed Ali and Shoukat Ali were detained.

The official attitude towards the Swarajists was not to countenance any idea of a radical change in the scheme of things. Lord Chelmsford, reassuring the King on this subject, wrote:

> In the domain of the Government of India we shall lay it down emphatically that there can be no transfer of power at the present time and that no transfer of power is in contemplation in the near future. Any such change must await the establishment of responsible government in the provinces and the results of such government. On the other hand, the composition of the Legislative Council is clearly defective on its representative side and we shall recommend changes to insure the more adequate representation of the varied interests and classes of India.[32]

The British were also most determined in ensuring for themselves a secure position in the legislative bodies. The nationalist position must be balanced by the voices of political counterweights who would no doubt see their interests better protected under the assured authority of a secure British rule. In the midst of so much politics, the economy showed worsening conditions. The people at large did not understand the reform proposals; they were in distress and 'looked anxiously for government measures to enable them to buy salt, oil and cloth at prices within their means'.[33]

IV. The Plan of the Book: Chapter Outlines

The book follows the method of dealing with time as comprising long periods and short periods. Each sub-period is preceded by earlier developments which determine the context. Analytically, it is the context which determined the conditions in society and the state of politics—mainly the attitude of the government in the face of concrete problems. In the short-run, a series of actions, counteractions and reactions took place which in turn generated a chain of consequences. The latter in turn define the context for the next short period and politics generally.

Connecting with the initial context, the first long period describes and interprets the extraordinary change that occurred over the earlier dominant and strategic perspective of imperial Britain: from the right to possess the Indian empire by the sword, economic accommodation, to half-attempts at self-rule, if necessary, to its becoming a liability and a burden towards the end. The sword was needed to safeguard an asset; it became worthless in relation to a growing liability or a burdensome political asset.

The empire may be viewed both as a given fact or a static element, with Indian nationalism as the principal dynamic entity which metamorphosed the broadly given relationship between the ruler and the ruled into one of concession and coercion. Among the British subjects, opposite forces were at work, to unite and to divide, also to demand more from the rulers but settle for less. Bipan Chandra has characterized it as a sequence of struggle-truce-struggle.[33] This formulation is undoubtedly more dramatic than can be justified by the actual course of important events.

The formalized sequence probably more accurately interprets Gandhi's long-term political strategy. The period, January 1918 to Partition and the independence of India is called 'The Age of Gandhi'. Gandhi was the most dynamic political factor in this period. The first long-period is 1918–31 (both years inclusive), a period of 14 years. It is subdivided into two short-terms of five years each, 1918–22, 1923–7 and one of four years, 1928–31. The second long-term, 1932–45, similarly comprises two sub-periods of five years each 1932–6, 1937–41 and one of four years, 1942–5. Each sub-period separately describes key developments in national politics, the economy and labour and an attempt is made to establish the interconnections. British rule ended in August 1947 formally, but the British phase continued beyond January 1950 when India's new Constitution came into effect. This forms the sub-theme of the four-year sub-period, 1946–9, which to all effects and purposes, marked the end of the great age of British rule over India, as well as the 'Age of Gandhi'. The former was a long historical era, while the latter gained in historical importance by the extraordinary coincidence of the decline of Great Britain as an economic power.

The same method is retained for the next great age which commenced on 15 August 1947 and continues. The nation state representing Indian nationalism acquired a formal structure with constitutional democracy as its principal mode of political expression and governance. Political India struggled to retain as much of former forms of governance, rules and procedure as it could, even as it strove hard to build new institutions, work the constitutional machinery and learn to cope with the ever new challenges to its paramountcy from the communal, class-based and sub-national political manifestations. This is an unending process and is bound to the working of the nation state. The following four long-term periods of 12 years each, beginning with 1946–57, again subdivided into three sub-periods of four years each, complete one stage of development. These are 1958–69, 1970–81 and 1982–93.

The final long-term happens to be of 14 years duration, divided into two sub-periods of five years and one of four years. This period is characterized by the most important, defining changes in the political economy of the country and the deep-seated political changes which gave rise concurrently to a minimum of four sets of contradictions and conflicts. These have demanded considerable responses and, if possible, resolutions from the government. They are based on the specific identities of India's religions, the caste sub-structure of Hindu society, language and regional loyalties, mostly of the Hindu faith, and class-centred confrontations, which again happen to be waged principally by Hindus. Thus viewed and placed in the perspective of India's immediate past, the contemporary political scene presents itself as an extraordinary spectacle of the state having to manage or suppress the revolt of its people.

The first chapter is the Introduction, followed by seven chapters in two volumes of chronicles, description and analysis. By transposing transitional phases and interregnums they bring out the accounts of separate as well as interrelated developments in the political, economic and labour spheres. In the ninth chapter, some of the deeper, underlying problems of India's development are discussed. These include demography, backwardness, poverty, hunger and neglected childhoods, as well as the environmental aspects and the overall unevenness of material and social progress made by the people in the hugely diverse climatic and economic circumstances of the country. The demographic dimension can be observed in all the principal departments of national progress.

In independent India, there have occurred two noticeable eras, one led by Nehru and the other by his daughter, Indira Gandhi. The Nehru era, of parliamentary democracy, decency in public life, probity, loyalty to ideals, service to the country and search for popular mandates at every election, began in

1951, after the death of Sardar Patel and continued till the end of 1964, roughly seven months after his death. In the first three and a half years, he was not on sure ground and had to defer to others, principally Sardar Patel. The termination of the Nehru era could not have been delayed much longer but its pace was speeded up by the adverse regional power balance in which India was placed and had to counter its foes across the borders mostly in isolation. Beginning in 1963, neither in economic policies nor in the broad reach of foreign policy were Nehru's doctrines or strategic policies of any relevance. These had to be shed.

The second era, of Indira Gandhi, also commenced three and a half years after she was prime minister and followed the bitter but inevitable power struggle within the Congress leadership, which led to the split in the party into two almost equal halves. It was marked at first by long stretches of struggle for political hegemony and later by the catastrophic breakdown of democracy for a period of less than two years during, 1975–7 when the Emergency was in force and fundamental rights suspended. Indira Gandhi very nearly succeeded in undoing what her father had painstakingly built. The second phase of Indira Gandhi's rule began with another split in the Congress but followed a much quieter tone in public life. There was great turbulence in Assam and the beginning of an armed revolt in the Punjab, led by the dissident Khalistanis on behalf of the Sikh community. It was communal rebellion for a separate Sikh state and had to be crushed. This sub-period of the 'Indira-Gandhi Era' was expeditiously ended, after her tragic assassination when her son, Rajiv Gandhi, became prime minister.

For political reasons, Rajiv Gandhi recreated the two forms of formidable compulsions of Indian society and political economy—religion in politics and liberalism in economic policies. Both have gained in strength since then, and it may be an extraordinary coincidence that, in contemporary India, politics appears inseparable from religion, as much as other sub-aggregates, like caste and language, while the political economy unsteadily moves on the chequered path toward increased liberalization and globalization. Clearly nationalism as a secular, democratic, liberal and humanistic ideal is in retreat.

ENDNOTES

1. The subject has received varied treatment, but there is no difference of opinion that Gandhi's aim was the attainment of Swaraj by peaceful and legitimate means. The Quit India movement was the most un-Gandhian because it had both non-violent and violent features since Gandhi was peremptorily arrested along with the entire Congress leadership and the movement was conducted by lower level leaders. However, Gandhi did say, 'There is no room left in the proposal for withdrawal or negotiation. There is no question of one more chance. After all it is an open rebellion.' He called it an unarmed revolt. 'We shall do or die. We shall either free India or die in the attempt.' The government's response was of unabated fury. See R.C. Majumdar, *History of the Freedom Movement in India,* Vol. III, Calcutta, Firma K.L. Mukhopadhyay, 1963, pp. 639–78 and Bipan Chandra, *India's Struggle for Independence, 1857-1947,* New Delhi, Viking, Penguin Books (India) Ltd., 1988, Ch. 35, esp. pp. 457–70.
2. Ibid., Bipan Chandra, 'Introduction', esp. pp. 2230.
3. See Tara Chand, *History of the Freedom Movement in India,* Vol. III, Government of India, Publications Division, Ministry of Information and Broadcasting, Ch. 2, Economic Stagnation: Agriculture' and Ch. 3, 'Economic Stagnation: Industry and Trade', also Vol. II, Ch 7, 'Economic Background of Indian Nationalism'. A brief political account of the Indian economy is provided by Judith Brown, *Modern India: The Origins of an Asian Democracy,* Delhi, Oxford University Press, 1984, pp. 101–29. A short statement on economic stagnation is presented by Russell Lidman and Robert I. Domrese 'India' in W. Arthur Lewis, (Ed), *Tropical Development 1980-1913, Studies in Economic Progress,* London, George Allen and Unwin Ltd., 1970. According to a British viewpoint, 'It can truthfully be said that the activities of the Indian National Congress delayed economic development. During the 1930s, there was a substantial withdrawal of British capital from India, and

the Congress Party's general tendency towards socialism—at least in public statements—made some Indian capitalists unwilling to expand the level of their investments.' Michael Edwards, *British India 1772-1947. A Survey of the Nature and Effects of Alien Rule*, London. Sidgwick and Jackson, 1967, p. 225. He also says that to charge that the British rule was for exploiting India, 'it would be more truthful to say that exploitation was far too limited.' p. 127. Clearly he observed very little and understood much less.

4. Bipan Chandra finds a closer connection between the Swadeshi upsurge of 1903-08 and the rise of the professional agitator together with the power of organization in the conduct of industrial strikes. However, the evidence is sketchy. See his magnum opus (loc. cit.), Ch. 17, esp. pp. 213–15.
5. In the Preface to Vol. I, Tara Chand says:

   > The achievement of freedom by India is a unique phenomenon. It is the transformation of a civilization into a nationality. It is the fulfilment of nationality through the establishment of national sovereignty. It is throughout the course of its advance a movement directed as much against the violence of the other as much against the unreason of the self. In essence, it is an ethical struggle both in relation to the foreigner as well as members of its own body. And where similar struggles have been accompanied with bloodshed, the movement in India, though intense and accompanied with much suffering, was non-violent. (p. xii).

   It is a four-volume study with a common title.
6. An excellent review is given in Majumdar's work (loc. cit.), Vol. II, Book III, Ch. VI, also by Ram Gopal, *How India Struggled for Freedom (A Political History)*, Bombay, The Book Centre Pvt. Ltd., 1967, Ch. VI, 'Seeds of Terrorism', and Ch. X, 'Sedition, Bombs and Reforms of 1909'.
7. Ram Gopal in his biography of Tilak, *Lokmanya Tilak. A Biography*, Bombay, Asia Publishing House, 1956, Reprinted 1965, gives detailed accounts of his two arrests, first in 1897 for sedition and the second in 1908 on the same charge. See Ch. XXIV, 'Not Loyal to the Queen' and Ch. XLIII, 'Most Dangerous Rebel', Ch. XLIV, 'The Historic 21-Hour Speech', Ch. XLV, 'License or Liberty and Ch. XLVI 'Six Years' Transportation, A Light Sentence'. Also by Theodore Shay, PhD, *The Legacy of Lokmanya. The Political Philosophy of Bal*

Gangadhar Tilak, Geoffrey Cumberlege, Oxford University Press, 1956, esp. Ch. V, 'The Battle with the Bureaucracy'. An account of the preceding phase of Tilak's political actions is given in Ch. IV, 'The Programme of the Nationalists'.

8. Gokhale, a loyalist, in support of the British position said in 1909, that Britain had done very well in India and, 'there was no alternative to British rule and could be none for a long time.' As for the future:

   > They would proceed in two directions: first towards an obliteration of distinctions, on the grounds of race, between individual Indians and individual Englishmen, and second by way of advance towards the form of government enjoyed in other parts of the Empire. The latter was an ideal for which the Indian people had to qualify themselves, for the whole question turned on character and capacity, and they must realize that their main difficulty lay with themselves.

   On another occasion, he said,

   > We have to recognize that British rule, in spite of its inevitable drawbacks as a foreign rule, has been on the whole a great instrument of progress for our people. Its continuance means the continuance of that peace and order which it alone can maintain in our country, and with which our best interests, among them, those of our growing nationality are bound up.

   The quotations are from a book written by a British civil servant after his retirement in 1920, Sir Verney Lovett, *A History of the Indian Nationalist Movement*, London, Frank Cass and Co. Ltd., First Edition, February 1920, New impression of Third Edition, 1968, pp. 80–3'.

9. In the accounts of the Home Rule League, Tilak and Annie Besant are seen working together. However, the last 20 years of Tilak's life were mostly devoted to politics, For Annie Besant, her educational activities and politics were conducted together, and mainly from her headquarters at Madras. Some of her supporters, such as the trading castes in Sind and Gujarat had no link with the Congress, also presumably with active politics. See Judith Brown (loc. cit.), p. 192.

   On the issue of accepting or rejecting the Montford reforms, 'Annie Besant herself indulged in a lot of vacillation on this question as well as on the question of passive resistance. At times she would disavow passive resistance and at other times, under pressure from her younger followers, would advocate it.' Bipan Chandra (loc. cit.), p. 169.

10. Lovett refers to the unusual step the Viceroy took of communicating directly with the ruling chiefs, 'on the subject of the active unrest prevalent in various parts of India and invited an exchange of opinions' with a view to mutual cooperation against a common danger'. Lovett (loc. Cit.), pp. 83–5.
11. Ibid., pp. 12–14. The idea of a Council of Princes would not be pursued because neither the leading princely houses were in its favour nor was it possible to clarify its precise functions. pp. 156–9.
12. A review and appraisal of Lord Minto's term as the Viceroy brings out his leading role in the formulation of ideas which produced the reforms of 1909. Syed Razi Wasti, *Lord Minto and the Indian Nationalist Movement 1905 to 1910*, Oxford, Clarendon Press, 1964.
13. Lovett, (loc. cit.), pp. 90–2, 104–5.
14. Bimal Prasad, *The Foundations of Muslim Nationalism*, New Delhi, Manohar Publishers and Distributors, 1999, p. 170. For an entirely different interpretation see Tara Chand, Vol. III, (loc. cit.) Chapter 5, 'Muslim Thought and Politics', and Chapter 9, 'The Muslim Problem'. Mushirul Hasan provides yet another perspective on the mixed and diverse reactions of Muslims to nationalist forces. See, *Nationalism and Communal Politics in India*, New Delhi, Manohar, 1994, Chs. 2 and 3.
15. Ibid., Tara Chand, p. 408.
16. Ibid., p. 413.
17. Quoted by Mushirul Hasan, (loc. cit.), p. 83.
18. Ibid., see Chapter 4, 'Congress-League Rapprochment. The Lucknow Pact'. The British historical perspective is presented by Judith Brown, (loc. cit.), Ch. IV, 'War and the Search for a New Order.' According to her, referring to the Lucknow Pact: 'Such unexpected cooperation was a repercussion of Turkey's alliance with Germany, which worried British administration in India as early as November 1914.' The Lucknow Pact 'was emphatically not an agreement between Congress and the whole Muslim community, any more than the foundation of the League had signified the emergence of a unified Muslim community with a single political voice'. p. 193. This is not a

useful formulation and it misses out completely on the political significance of the pact.

19. In a detailed study, it is reported that the Ghadar movement was to be carried forward by the Sikhs returning from Canada and California in the USA. About 8,000 returned emigrants were expected to spearhead the movement. But the police was on alert and found it unnecessary to maintain vigilance in the case of about 5,000 of them. 'Precautionary measures were taken in the case of about 1,500. A small number of more (sic) committed but without a centralizing leadership, made attempts to win over their fellowmen from the peasantry for the cause of rebellion.' Most of them failed to find an audience. See Harish K. Puri, *Ghadar Movement, Ideology, Organization and Strategy*, Amritsar, Guru Nanak Dev University Press, 1983, pp. 81–8, entitled, 'Rebellion 1915: Bang and Whimper'; quote on p. 85. For a very different interpretation see Bipan Chandra, (loc. cit.), esp. pp. 153–8.
20. R.C. Majumdar, (loc. cit.), Vol. II gives a summary of revolutionary activities on pp. 398-489. Most of what he writes is based on official accounts and the details narrated by the Seditions Committee (Report, p. 436).
21. Judith Brown, (loc. cit.), p. 195.
22. Ibid., p. 188.
23. B.R. Tomlinson, *The Economy of Modern India 1860-1970*, The New Cambridge History of India, Cambridge University Press, 1993, Table 1.2, p. 5. The GNP estimates show growth from the index number 83 (at 1938–9 prices) in 1900 to 100 in 1913 and it stayed at 100 in 1920. Another estimate shows a decline from 100 to 94 and yet another from 100 to 96 over this period.
24. Ibid., Table 2.1, p. 52.
25. Judith Brown, (loc. cit.), pp. 188–9. In another study she gives a sharper description of hardships caused by price disparities. In Bihar and Orissa, the price of rice fell suddenly between mid-1916 and 1918. 'Other food grains dropped in price in the period 1915–18', and as one official put it, 'Everything the cultivator had to sell, rice, oil seeds or gur, had either fallen or at least not risen in price, while everything he had to buy, cloths, salt, kerosene, had become extremely expensive.'

Gandhi's Rise to Power, Indian Politics 1915-1922, Cambridge, At the University Press, 1972, p. 66.

26. See Raymond K. Renford, *The Non-Official British in India to 1920*, Delhi, Oxford University Press, 1987. Ch. VIII, 'The War and its Impact'. It is a mine of information on businesses controlled by the British. The indigo planters who at first profited from the war eventually lost out. However, the jute industry was 'in a very satisfactory condition indeed.' p. 358.
27. V.B. Karnik quotes Annie Besant's work, *How India Wrought for Freedom*, to show how India was reduced to poverty, her industries dislocated and the way it made a severe drain on the country. *Indian Trade Unions. A Survey*, Bombay, Manaktalas, first Published, December 1960, pp. 17–18.
28. The credit for discovering the important role of jobbers is to the Royal Commission on Labour, 1931. They acted in multiple roles, even as supervisors or sub-employers. Most scholars who have worked on the subject have missed out their role in obstructing the development of unions. Morris D. Morris has developed the theme more fully in, *The Emergence of an Industrial Labour Force in India*, Bombay, Oxford University Press, 1965, Chapter VIII 'Administration of the Work force'.
29. S.D. Punekar, 'Trade Union Movement in India' entitled as Chapter XXVIII in V.B. Singh, (Ed.), *Industrial Labour in India*, Bombay, Asia Publishing House, Second Edition, 1963, p. 444. The origins of the trade union movement are placed in 1918–24.
30. Morris D. Morris, (loc. cit.), p. 179.
31. *Secret Papers From British Royal Archives*, Chief Ed. P.N. Chopra, Delhi, Konark Publishers Pvt. Ltd., 1998, p. 190 (Letter dated 4 April 1917).
32. Lovett, (loc. cit.), p. 172.
33. Bipan Chandra, (loc. cit.), Ch. 38, 'The Long-Term Strategy of the National Movement'.

Chapter 2

NATIONALISM GATHERS FORCE, 1918-31

I. 1918–22

Repression and Reforms, Satyagraha and Pan-Islamic Politics

Two astonishingly contradictory attitudes towards the demand for Home Rule in India emerged in the imperial system. One, published in July 1918, was politically best expressed by Montague and largely reflected in the tone and contents of the report on the proposed reforms. The other was the powerful voices of the British bureaucracy, the military and non-official Europeans who were anxious to reinforce British power in India with more coercive laws and use of military might—as much as would be needed to defeat and crush the nationalist revolt. While the former proposed the abolition of racial bars and raising the proportion of Indians in the civil service to 33 per cent, the latter could not think of the continuation of the empire if the British element in the military and civil service was diluted.

Reflecting the trench mentality of local governments and the fear of revolutionary activities in Bengal and Punjab principally, the government appointed a sedition committee headed by Justice Rowlatt. It had two British and two Indian members. The Report was published in July 1918, shortly after the Reforms Report, and was hailed with showers of abuse by the extremist press. The moderates generally reserved comment.[1] The legislative proposals were soon incorporated in two Rowlatt Bills which would be needed when, six months after the end of the war, the Defence of India Act would lapse. The Bills met with stout opposition from all the Indian members of the Imperial Legislative Council. The punitive and preventive measures which formed part of the two Bills denied an accused person any chance of fair defence or right of appeal. It was a travesty of justice under law. The committee had investigated revolutionary movements in different parts of India. However, it ignored the fact that these were already on the wane and acts of terrorism had practically disappeared in Bengal. They entertained the worst fears and sought to arm the government with extraordinarily stringent powers. Ignoring the opposition, the government proceeded to enact the Bills but political conditions changed at such a pace that these were never put into effect. Instead, the government put to work the direct force of guns as used by soldiers on combat duty.

The Rowlatt Bills did bring about a major change in politics. They galvanized Gandhi into experimenting with *satyagraha* against the Bills. This was the first time Gandhi's satyagraha, as a soul force in politics, was put into practice in India and it immediately put Gandhi in the limelight. Earlier, he had used the tactics of passive resistance at Champaran in north Bihar against the indigo planters. However, as the government saw that he was working for a just cause, they permitted him to proceed with his inquiry. He subsequently succeeded partially in securing some relief for the peasants. The Viceroy had interceded in the dispute because, 'it is not denied that Gandhi's inquiry was inspired by substantial grievances'.[2] He had also tried his methods in the dispute on land revenue at Kheda in Gujarat with considerable success.

Wherever Gandhi worked, he won supporters and colleagues who remained politically loyal to him. They achieved distinguished status in the Congress and later in independent India. Rajendra Prasad joined him at

Champaran and Sardar Vallabhbhai Patel at the Kheda agitation. However, in both places Gandhi's role was that of a mediator though, at Kheda, he used his methods politically to connect the educated elite Indian classes with the poor farmers while retaining the title of a public worker. Brown sums up the importance of the Champaran and Kheda movements:

> Kaira hammered home the lesson of Champaran that satyagraha could be used in virtually any situation of conflict, by literate and illiterate. It was a weapon for all seasons, and in Gandhi's hands, directed by his personal ideology, it gave him the edge over conventional politicians with their techniques of petitions, public speeches and debates, which were more suited to the educated.[3]

In 1919, Gandhi plunged into national politics on the question of the Rowlatt Bills and announced satyagraha to counter the government and undo a national wrong. He called for a *hartal* (a general strike) on 6 April. He had already organized a satyagraha *sabha* and a pledge that, while the members would civilly disobey all the laws that were subversive of liberty and justice, 'in this struggle ... [they would] faithfully follow truth and refrain from violence to life, person and property'.[4] For Gandhi, there was no politics outside religion and he announced that on the day of the hartal, people should observe a fast and offer prayers to purify the self. In Delhi, the hartal was observed on 30 March. The day ended in police and army action against the crowd in which heavy firing was resorted to and several people were killed. Hartals were observed on 6 April in Bombay and elsewhere but were generally peaceful.

In the established political circles, there was considerable opposition to satyagraha. The Home Rule League virtually split on the issue because Annie Besant was strongly opposed to satyagraha and civil disobedience. Despite their opposition, Gandhi took the next step to offer civil disobedience against specific laws. The government then decided to arrest anyone found defying laws. There was unrest in Punjab and it appeared to Gandhi that he could promote satyagraha there and appeal to people to take part in it without engaging in violence. However, the government arrested him in Delhi and sent him back to Bombay under police escort, where he was set free. At the news of his arrest, there was more unrest. Shops closed in Bombay, and there was stone throwing and forced interference with the city transport. Elsewhere too, there were instances of mob violence. In Bombay, a cavalry unit was summoned to control the crowd. However, Punjab saw the worst disturbances which led the government to impose martial law and thereafter it crossed all limits of civilized governance.

In 1918, Punjab was in the throes of unrest. The Lt Governor, Sir Michael O'Dwyer, was excessively harsh. He recruited men for the army by coercing the landowners (the *lambardars*) to furnish them or risk forfeiture of their land rights. Likewise, he raised funds for the war. The Governor had developed a particularly loathsome attitude towards the educated classes, on whom he heaped insults. 'He interned hundreds of local men with little or no cause. He gagged the vernacular press and prevented nationalist papers published outside Punjab from entering the province.'[5] Towards the close of 1918, unrest became palpable and the Lt Governor felt the need for extraordinary powers to suppress it. In February 1919, the Punjab government requested the Viceroy to permit use of martial law under a regulation of 1804 and secured it, though it is doubtful if the Rowlatt satyagraha had anything to do with it.

The call for hartal on 6 April did reach Punjab and it passed off peacefully. However, the government, already armed with the martial law, decided to take pre-emptive action on 10 April when the District Magistrate (DM) of Amritsar arrested two senior leaders of the province and removed them to an undisclosed destination. This infuriated the mob which sought information about the leaders. Upon the DM refusing to meet them, they threw brickbats. At this, the police opened fire killing at least two people and injuring several others. Thereafter, the mob engaged in more lawlessness. A bank was set on fire, public buildings were attacked and worse, five Englishmen were killed in revenge. The government then made a public announcement that martial law was in force so, in Amritsar, the people did know about it on 13 April, the fateful day, but not the larger masses, and certainly not the many villagers who came to the holy city on Baisakhi day for fun and pilgrimage.

However, official reprisals had already commenced.

> Troops were called out, and they opened fire indiscriminately unmindful of the deaths and injuries they were causing. Armoured cars and aeroplanes were used to disperse the mob. On the night of the 11th General Dyer, who commanded the district under General Beynon, took command of the troops in the city. On the 12th there was a round-up of people suspected of provoking trouble, many being taken into custody. All public gatherings and meetings were banned.[6]

Still, a public meeting was called at the Jallianwala Bagh at 4.30 p.m. on 13 April to be addressed by political leaders. A picket was posted there but it merely watched as people assembled for the meeting. A large crowd estimated at 10,000 or 20,000 gathered there and included women and children. General Dyer decided to teach them a lesson. He took his troops into the Bagh, ordered them to kneel and open fire directly into the crowd. 'He had to stop after firing 1,600 rounds as, he ruefully admitted later, his ammunition had run out and to this merciful lack of planning thousands of Indians owed their lives.'[7]

The government counted the dead at 379 and about 1,200 wounded, which show a close fit to the 1,650 rounds that were actually fired. However, Madan Mohan Malviya believed that at least 1,000 had died, mainly because curfew was imposed and no one was allowed to enter the place to attend to those still alive. Later, the Seva Samiti counted 500 bodies, which figure the government was prepared to accept.

Yet, the purpose was to strike terror in the whole of Punjab and more gruesome acts followed. Horrible, vengeful orders were issued: Dyer ordered that every person passing through the lane where Miss Sherwood, a missionary teacher, was attacked would have to crawl on his belly. Flogging and whipping became common. Earlier in Lahore, on 10 and 12 April, processions were fired upon. In Kasur, the crowd went wild and attacked a train in which some Europeans were travelling. They opened fire at the crowd and, in turn, received a fusillade of stones whereupon two Europeans were killed. The police arrived and opened fire. Revenge was in the air. At Gujranwala, people were ordered to alight from their carriages and salute British officers, failing which they might be whipped, fined or punished in other ways.

This continued while Gandhi was denied entry into Punjab.[8] He criticized violence and incendiary behaviour by the crowds. In July, he suspended the Rowlatt Bill satyagraha and token civil disobedience. In December, Gandhi asked the Congress to condemn the mob violence but the resolution was rejected and later a modified resolution was passed. There was a huge gap between what Gandhi wanted people to do while protesting and what they actually ended up doing in the surge of anger. The government or the bureaucracy in India imagined that only by an active display of the iron fist and state violence would their supremacy be maintained. There could be no other reason for recalling the atrocious regulations of 1804 and putting them into effect.[9]

The reforms were announced in December 1919 with a royal proclamation. Major political changes were made in the manner India would be governed and a window opened to the moderates to move from criticism to collaboration. The Congress was divided and a large body of opinion favoured rejection because, in totality, the new Act fell far short of what appeared to have been promised by Montague in 1917, and was later formally declared in the Montford Report. This was nowhere near Swaraj; nor was there any hint that the next step would soon follow. A review was promised at the end of ten years. The 1919 Act could in no way be viewed as a necessary step that led to the dominion status.

Under the 1919 Act, the legislatures at the Centre and the provinces would have a majority of elected members. However, the franchise was rather small, and it varied from province to province. Only 3 per cent of the adult population in the whole of British India had the right to vote in the Assembly. At the Centre, there were two houses—the Council of State and the Legislative Assembly. The introduction of the second chamber was a new feature in India. The Assembly comprised two parts—the nominated and the elected. The former group had 26 official and 15 non-official members. The elected members were composed of seven distinctive constituencies: the non-Muslims with 52 seats, Muslims 30, Sikhs two, Europeans nine, landholders seven, and Indian commerce four. Thus, there were 41 nominated and 104 elected members. The nominated official members represented the government, while the non-official ones represented those constituencies which did not return elected members, labour being one of them. The basic philosophy of the Act was to recognize a wide range of general, communal and interest-based constituencies. The representation given to the Europeans reflected their prominence in Indian industry, trade and commerce and the political weight they already had in the country.

The Council of State comprised 60 members, of whom 33 were elected and 27 nominated. The franchise for this body was more restricted. The Government of India and 10 provinces, including Burma, would be represented in the Council but, in doing so, five interests would also be elected or nominated. In the elected part of the constituencies the non-Muslims were 16, Muslims 11, Sikhs one, non-communal interests two and European commerce three. Among the nominated, 17 were official and 10 non-official. All bills had to be passed in both houses. The finance bill could be discussed in the Council but not for vote on grants, which privilege was vested in the Assembly. The Council was designed to act as a bulwark against progressive legislature passed by the Assembly in its capacity as a revising chamber. The total electorate for the Council was only 17,000 for the whole of British India at one point and was divided into several interest constituencies.

Moreover, the government used the Council to pass laws which the Assembly did not adopt. The Governor-General also had the power of certification which he unfailingly used when the Assembly did not follow his proposals. The Act introduced a system of diarchy in the provinces, retaining several subjects as reserved for the Governor to be administered by the councillors and the transferred subjects by the elected ministers. The Governor distributed the portfolios to the councillors and the ministers. He summoned the legislative council, could extend its life by one year or dissolve it before the expiry of its term.

A major change was made in the Act in dividing the subjects between the Centre and the provinces in accordance with two lists. There was a provision for the devolution rules which enabled the Governor-General to transfer any subject from the Centre to the provinces if it was predominantly of local interest. On the other hand, the Government of India was also given concurrent powers to legislate on the provincial list, subject to previous sanction of the Governor-General. The 1919 Act created a system of governance in which the Governor-General and the governors were responsive to the legislatures without being responsible to them.[10]

The 1919 Act did not concede the principle that India was fit for full responsible government, nor did it shed the doctrine that even with the association of Indians running the administration, the central pillar of British rule would still be the autocracy of the aliens and their responsibility only to their Parliament and King. This doctrine informed British administration in India in the past and led to many excesses, including the massacre at Amritsar. However, it was a unifying principle in which a selected few Indians at various levels could be inducted, subject to the binding commitment of loyalty to the Crown. The new Constitution was, nonetheless, more than a discrete step towards associating Indians in governance. It imposed domestic political constraints on the structure, style and procedure of governing India. Contradictions were built into the system and implied in the more difficult political role prescribed for the governors. They would have to cope with elected ministers and the voice of the electorate. These were positive features and there was hope that further progress could be made in the next ten years. However, Congress leaders were divided. The moderates extended the hand of cooperation and Gandhi too thought that the reforms should be worked. However, for political reasons he soon abandoned this attitude and went over to non-cooperation.

The most astute and politically the wisest position, was taken by Tilak and defined by him as responsive cooperation. In fact, he announced a new political front, named the Congress Democratic Party and issued a manifesto in April 1920. However, Tilak recognized Gandhi's growing influence. Though he did not accept the politics of satyagraha, he would not break with Gandhi on this issue. He also supported Hindu–Muslim unity on the Khilafat agitation but wanted the Muslims to demonstrate a sincere bent on non-cooperation with the government. It appears that for all intents and purposes, Tilak granted the leading role in the joint Khilafat and Non-Cooperation movements to Gandhi. Tilak was not inclined towards a leadership tussle though he had serious reservations on both satyagraha and Non-Cooperation. So he preferred to withdraw and play a supportive role to Gandhi.[11] On 1 August 1920, Tilak suddenly died. Annie Besant, who did not agree with Gandhi on non-cooperation steadily lost popular support in the Congress and devoted her energies to other causes dear to her.

Gandhi made an extraordinary political turn about between the end of 1919 and the beginning of 1920 as he saw an immense strategic advantage in joining hands with the

Muslim leaders on the Khilafat agitation. He pleaded strongly for the release of Mohamed Ali and Shaukat Ali, whose friendship he valued and saw in their sincere devotion to pan-Islamism a fruitful basis to forge unity in action towards speedier progress in the realization of Swaraj. His efforts, though logically inconsistent and confusing, did produce an unusual result. On June 1–2, 1920 the Khilafat Committee decided to start the combined Non-Cooperation Movement from 1 August 1920 and Gandhi returned the three medals awarded to him for meritorious services. Meanwhile, following the declaration of amnesty by the King the Ali brothers were released and they played a leading role in the Non-Cooperation movement.[12]

The Khilafat movement was fundamentally pan-Islamic and reflected in the overriding brotherhood of Muslims as a religious people regardless of their race or nationality. In India, Maulana Mohamed Ali and his elder brother Maulana Shaukat Ali, were foremost in championing Turkey's cause and were most anxious that following its defeat it would not only lose all its occupied territories but also the sacred cities of Islam to the Christian powers. This fear ignited strong feelings among the Muslims and they were urged increasingly by the ulema and clergy to denounce the British openly. The Government of India made public the very unequal terms imposed on Turkey by the Allies on 14 May 1920. The Ottoman Empire vanished.

The Muslims were keen on expressing political opposition to British power in India and found in Gandhi a most valuable ally. They accepted his leadership, also to condition themselves to stay within the disciplinary bounds of truth and non-violence. In September 1920 at the Calcutta session, Gandhi asked for approval and support for the progressive, non-violent, non-cooperation movement 'until the Khilafat wrongs were righted and Swaraj established'. This was combined with protest at the manner the government had light-mindedly exonerated the wrongdoers in Amritsar and elsewhere in Punjab and the deep disquiet it had caused among the people of India. The only effectual means to redress the two wrongs was the establishment of Swaraj.[13] The Muslim clergy declared a fatwa (religious commandment) to the Muslim people to engage in non-cooperation. According to Mushirul Hasan,

> It is no doubt true that the introduction of the Muslim divines was fraught with dangers because it heightened the religious aspects and weakened the anti-colonial dimension of the Khilafat movement. However, their adherence was vital to the success of the movement, a fact that influenced both the Western-educated Muslims and Gandhi to cultivate the ulema and to ignore the repeated warnings about the obvious dangers of their involvement in politics.[14]

The presence of the ulema and their active participation meant that as far as they were concerned, it was the Hindu leadership of the Congress that supported the Muslim cause, but it did not mean that they were either subordinating their communal interests to the higher interests of Indian nationalism or willing to give up their separate identity. The reason for this priority to Islamic brotherhood over Indian identity was due to their status as a prominent minority, recognized as a political interest by the rulers, but it also reflected a search for an alternative centre.[15] This was the Khalifa who was also the Sultan of Turkey. The Khilafat movement was for the restoration of their centre. The Indian Muslims derived vicarious pride in identifying themselves with the achievements of the Turks, ignoring or condoning the oppressive tyrannical rule Turkey had imposed on an entire Arabic population in several countries. That facts and valid reasons were ignored by Gandhi and his many supporters, as much as by leaders like the Ali brothers, may be beyond reason, or incapable of intellectual understanding. However, such was the momentum of the unique unity forged by Gandhi with the Khilafat leaders that the sheer absurdity of their demands were left to be exposed only by the most powerful developments later, which transformed

Turkey from a theocratic sultanate into a secular state. The new Turkey abolished the institution of Khalifa.

The unity between the Hindus and the Muslims was a contingent reality which rested on an uncertain measure of trust between the two communities. The issue of non-violence formed the very core of Gandhi's politics, while the Muslim leaders accepted it as a political necessity and not necessarily in conformity with the Islamic tenets. However, collective action produced an uncommon unity between three streams of political consciousness. These were the Hindu religious nationalism as espoused earlier by Tilak and now donned by Gandhi, the Muslim religious nationalism which was largely pan-Islamic and also partly Indian nationalism while the third, the smallest component comprised modern secular nationalism but it had such men of promise as Jawaharlal Nehru and of stature as C.R. Das.

Gradually the unity weakened and Muslim leaders complained of lack of support from the Congress rank and file for their movement. On the other hand, the Muslim masses did not recognize the same necessity for Swaraj as the Hindus did. They did not come to public meetings as did the Hindus and there was a question whether the Muslims even thought of India as their home. In 1921, the combined movement suffered a major blow when the overplayed Khilafat sentiment led to rebellion of the Moplah community in Malabar. They engaged in horrible acts of retribution, massacre, forced conversions and violation of Hindu women as necessary steps for the setting up of an Islamic state or Khilafat. Every Hindu was seen as a potential enemy—partly for the reason that the Hindus were landlords and the Moplah were the exploited peasant tenants—and the only option the Hindu had was conversion to Islam or death. Ultimately, 1,000–1,500 were converted and 500–600 people killed. By the time the Moplah rebellion was crushed, about 2,337 were killed and 1,652 wounded and more than 45,000 were either captured or surrendered. The figures show the huge human tide that had risen to set up an Islamic state in Malabar.[16]

Apparently Gandhi was getting disenchanted with the Non-Cooperation movement as news of disorder trickled in, and also because the Muslim leaders felt that the option of violent protest could not be permanently foreclosed, especially if non-violent means failed to deliver results. In November 1921, the Prince of Wales arrived in India and the Congress decided to boycott the visit. However, in Bombay the mob went out of control. There occurred violent scenes and the police used force to restore normalcy. In February 1922, a most tragic sequence of events resulted in the killing of 26 policemen and a young son of one of the policemen by the violent mob. For Gandhi, this was the last straw that broke his resolve to continue with the movement. He decided to discontinue it, though in different parts of the country it continued and showed few signs of weakening. For Gandhi, the time was not yet ripe to extend it into a civil disobedience movement. Instead, the movement was suspended, virtually given up, and it produced considerable anguish and bewilderment in the rank and file. Even the leaders reacted angrily. Congressmen were asked to stop courting arrest and instead devote themselves to constructive activities. The Muslims felt abandoned, let down and betrayed. Some Muslim leaders openly attacked Gandhi. The suspension of an active movement was tantamount to admission of defeat and the Muslim leaders deeply resented this. Apparently, Gandhi remained unrepentant and failed to realize the far-reaching consequences of this decision.[17]

A major consequence of Gandhi's abrupt, unilateral decision was that his popularity plummeted. The public mood changed and Gandhi became the object of sharp comments for his various failings. The Viceroy, taking advantages of the sudden drop in political activities in the country, and reckoning that Gandhi's public standing was at its nadir, arrested him in March 1922 and tried him on the charge of sedition.

> When he was brought into the courtroom clad only in a loin cloth, everyone stood up to do him honour. He pleaded guilty

> and made a verbal statement explaining why, from a staunch loyalist and cooperator he had become an uncompromising disaffectionist and non-cooperator. He accepted full responsibility for the outrages at Madras, Bombay and Chauri Chaura saying, 'I knew I was playing with fire. I ran the risk and if I was set free I would still do the same', and invited the full penalty of the law.[18]

He was awarded a sentence of six years of jail, the same sentence that was pronounced on Tilak in 1908 on the same charge of sedition. Gandhi's courage, truthfulness and defiance portrayed him as a true *satyagrahi* in the court and won back the love of his people, he had only recently lost. Gandhi in prison produced the effect of his portraits being reproduced and displayed in the homes and shops of his numerous admirers.

It is difficult to find an unequivocal opinion on the important questions of whether it was prudent of Gandhi to join hands with the Khilafatists in launching a combined movement and promising the totally impractical goal of 'Swaraj in one year'; and second, whether the non-cooperation movement could be viewed as a success though it had evidently failed this time.[19] To the first question, the one plausible answer is that having announced the decision to work the reforms, as Tilak had wanted to, the 1919 Act had already yielded four annas in a rupee and perhaps they could wrest more in the next round of deeper reforms. Several Congress leaders, including C.R. Das, had concurred; Gandhi should not have abandoned it. Instead, he was attracted by the prospect of Hindu–Muslim unity in action with himself as the top and undisputed leader to put his political ideas into practice. However, the opportunity lost was also a substantial one, in the sense that the possibility of 'responsive cooperation' which opened in 1920 was closed.

Gandhi took the political decision to follow the wholly new path of confrontation and exposed the people of India to a non-violent struggle and sacrifice; one on which people, risked loss of life and limbs, their careers and comforts. It was the arduous path of sacrifice, courage and fearless defiance of the might of the imperial power with truth, non-violence and supreme self-confidence that the cause was just and the method right. Perhaps, if not then but at some later date, the British would have to face and concede the unassailable fact that their rule was exploitative and unjust, that it solely rested on their might and they could not stay in India. If Gandhi erred at all, it was on the timing of the movement. It is not that the satyagraha against the Rowlatt Acts, and then against the Amritsar massacre and severe repression in the Punjab and elsewhere should not have necessarily been followed by even more concerted demonstration of active public rejection of foreign rule. This was needed to demonstrate the defiant will of the people which could not be ignored.

Elections to the legislative councils were held in 1920 and electoral politics made steady progress as a distinct political stream in India. As was the purpose of the 1919 Act, the newly created electorate learnt to regroup around their well-defined constituencies and start bargaining on ministerial posts and other appointments in respect of which the ministers could issue orders or had influence. Under the new dispensation swifter progress was made while the Muslim interests were safeguarded better in provinces like Punjab where they were more backward. If an underlying motive of separate electorates electing their respective representatives to the councils and the Assembly was to wean the Muslim from the general constituency in which the Hindus were predominant, it was effectively served under the system of diarchy. In Punjab, the dynamic leader Fazl-i-Hussain was able to introduce reservation in admission to the Medical College and the Government College at Lahore distributing seats among the Muslims, Hindus and Sikhs in the ratio of 40:20:20. This was far above the seats Muslim students had been able to secure on merit earlier.

> A similar quota was also fixed for recruitment to medical and educational services. However, no attempt was made to

> introduce such a quota to recruitment to the police force which was dominated by Muslims. The same objective of helping Muslims to improve their position lay behind the Municipal Amendment Act of 1923, which redistributed seats where communal electorates already existed and redrew electoral boundaries where joint electorates were still in operation.[20]

By comparison, in Bengal the less organized and generally poor Muslim population took longer to derive similar benefits. However, everywhere the Hindus and the Muslims began to view themselves not just as separate people but also with non-convergent, even conflicting interests. The Hindu Sabha in Punjab won new adherents and expressed disenchantment with the working of reforms. By comparison, the Muslim block in the legislatures worked for the reforms. In Bengal, the Lucknow Pact was questioned because Muslim seats were fixed at 40 per cent, while the 1919 Act had raised it to 45 per cent though they were in a slight majority of 52 per cent. The Moplah uprising in Malabar and their atrocities on the Hindus was relived politically and it convinced several Hindu leaders that the future of Hindu–Muslim unity was bleak, although this also implied that attainment of Swaraj in the near future was less likely without it.

> At the same time a feeling grew that the primary loyalty of Muslims was to their community and not to India, and that such loyalty was so strong that in the event of a clash between India and a Muslim power, Muslims in India would side with the latter. Indeed, some even felt that the Muslims in India might combine with their coreligionists abroad in a bid to re-establish Muslim rule over the country.[21]

Annie Besant argued that the fear was entirely well grounded, because in independent India the Muslims would follow those who spoke in the name of the Prophet and become 'an immediate peril to India's freedom'.[22] Muslim pan-Islamism as a political creed worked as a counterweight to Indian nationalism.

On the positive side, the liberals had successfully contested the election to the Central Legislature where they worked for the success of the reforms and achieved some creditable results. Several undesirable laws were repealed. 'The liberals were instrumental in placing some useful acts on the statute book, e.g. the Press Law Repeal and Amendment Act, 1922, the Special Law Repeal Act, 1922, the Indian Criminal Law Amendment Repealing Act, 1922 and the Criminal Law Amendment Act, 1923...'[23] The work of liberals was aided by the Non-Cooperation Movement in the sense that while they had to demonstrate that they were not less nationalist while cooperating with the government; the latter too wished that the liberals should achieve some success during their first tenure. The political climate was conducive to fruitful cooperation. Yet, the Viceroy had to legislate by certification two unpopular bills, one of which related to books and periodicals which might cause disaffection in the populace against the rulers and the other doubled the salt tax. It may be mentioned that European interest was opposed to abolition of racial discrimination in criminal trials in 1922, but the Viceroy sided with the liberals.

Within the Congress there was already a strong body of opinion that favoured entry but the leaders who thought along these lines were swept into the Gandhian surge and they took part in the Non-Cooperation Movement. On its suspension and Gandhi's imprisonment, the cooperators revived and regrouped around C.R. Das and Motilal Nehru. In December 1922, C.R. Das presided over the Congress session and strongly pleaded for entry into the councils but failed. He resigned from the presidentship and organized the Swaraj Party along with Motilal Nehru to contest the elections in 1923. They added a new chapter in national politics.

Meanwhile, Reading worked on the imperial government to do something tangible to allay the misgivings of Muslims in India on the fate of Turkey. The telegram he sent to London was duly published and demonstrated beyond doubt that he was a man of goodwill who understood Muslim sentiments and was keen to restore the position of the Caliph.

This weakened the Khilafat movement further and nearly succeeded in causing a breach between the non-cooperators and the Khilafatists. Later in 1923, the Treaty of Lausanne greatly improved the terms for Turkey. In the meantime, the Turkish nationalists abolished the Sultanate, and in October 1923, Turkey became a republic. The post of the Caliph was also abolished. This ended the political vision of the Caliph as the centre of Muslim allegiance in India and knocked off the premises on which the Khilafat movement had rested. 'When the Khilafat movement died down the Muslims came out of Gandhi's shadow but they were bewildered. They had been so wholly occupied with the fate of the Sultan of Turkey that there was now a void in their political life.'[24]

Thus in 1922, two chapters of agitation politics and the sole episode of Hindu–Muslim unity came to an end. The Khilafat movement had reinforced ideas of Muslim nationalism separate from Indian nationalism, or that they were Muslims first and Indians next. They had joined hands with Gandhi only to get the Christian British rule out of India. Now they would have to reverse their stand and work on the rulers' side to protect their interests.

Gandhi's motives for suspending the Non-Cooperation Movement was certainly the one that was the immediate cause, that is, violence at a remote village in UP. The decision was also influenced by two additional considerations. One, as the movement merged in several places with the incipient revolt of the peasantry against the landholding classes, it took on the character of a class struggle.[25] This happened because the central control which was never very effective lost its grip on local factors and the leadership passed on to the leaders of the Kisan Sabha or variants of peasants' organizations. Gandhi never wanted the peasants to stop paying land taxes or rents and start an agitation against landlordism or the government's land revenue settlements. Moreover, any violent agitation, regardless of the genuineness of the underlying causes, would cease to be legitimate and invite government repression. Gandhi's assessment took into account the possibility of overreaction by the violent state. Bipan Chandra says:

> The government would have had an excuse to remove him and other activists from the scene and use force to cow down the people. Mass civil disobedience would be defeated even before it was given a fair trial. By taking the onus of withdrawal on himself and on the working committee, Gandhiji was protecting the movement from likely repression and the people from demoralization.[26]

Gandhi could not allow unauthorized movements to proceed alongside the strictly guided individual satyagrahi-centred Non-Cooperation Movement, though the movement undoubtedly gathered force because it sucked in wider streams of society which had thus far remained politically aloof. This was a built-in contradiction in the call to people to move forward to claim Swaraj but with only one effective control, the voluntarily pledge taken by the satyagrahis which could never be binding on the masses.

Brown also analyses the tension that was building up between Gandhi and the Ali brothers in 1921. The latter were apprehensive that, in case Gandhi was able to meet the Viceroy, there could be some compromise that would be detrimental to the Muslim cause. The two did meet and unexpectedly Gandhi agreed to an apology by Ali for a speech which the Viceroy had interpreted as incitement to violence.[27] Gandhi had secured an assurance from the Viceroy that, should an apology be rendered, they would not be prosecuted. The Ali brothers were not votaries of non-violence but had agreed to practice it as a condition precedent to accepting his leadership. Perhaps the strained relations between them marked the weakening of the spirit of unity and solidarity between the Khilafat and the non-cooperation movements. Several Muslim leaders openly expressed serious reservations on accepting Swaraj as a political goal for the Muslims because it would amount to admitting the legitimacy of a Hindu majority government. In the absence of a pact between the Hindus and Muslims through their political organizations, the realization of Swaraj would be detrimental to their interests as the largest and strong minority in the country. Hasrat Mohani thought that the goal of complete independence should be accepted in place of Swaraj and Congress should alter its creed. He did not succeed but still sowed seeds of doubt and distrust. To the ulemas, the creed of non-violence was repugnant as also the continuing leadership of Khilafat by a non-Muslim.

The Post-War Economy, Famines and Unstable Conditions

The five years before the war were of relative prosperity in British India. The monsoon had not failed and agriculturists had recovered from the famines and drought-inflicted calamities of the preceding decade. The recovery from the 1907–8 famine was aided by expansion in the railway network and better preparation by the government to cope with it. The notable long-term trends that emerged were increase in commercialization of agriculture, expansion of the area under irrigation and penetration of transport and communications into the economic system, which favoured the farmers who had the marketable surplus that could be sold at higher prices, bringing in profits. This process was accelerated at the end of the war.

However, 1918–19 was a very bad year. The monsoon had failed and famine conditions prevailed. The war had severely dislocated international trade and there was acute scarcity of essential commodities. The government's relief measures received support from restrictions on exports and, 'it was extremely fortunate that the necessity for the exportation of large quantities of food stuffs to the allies began to diminish owing to the advent of armistice conditions just at the close of the 1918 monsoon'. The government imposed controls and a system was instituted for provinces with surplus food stocks to share them with the rest of the country. In 1918–19, the surplus rice crop in Burma was transferred to India and, in addition, 20,000 tonnes of wheat was imported from Australia. 'The imports of grain, pulses and flour into India in 1919 reached a height as never before.'[28] The monsoon was normal in 1919 but not in 1920 and 1921. The yield of wheat declined and its price soared. The data produced in Gadgil's book shows that the area under cultivation of food grains increased from 177.844 million acres in 1918–19 to 186.890 million acres in 1920–1 and there was some substitution of the former for cash crops, especially sugarcane and cotton. Farmers did put in some effort to increase food production but yields fell due to low precipitation.[29] Famine conditions developed again in 1921 and the government had to provide relief to about 4.5 lakh people. Food grains had to be imported on an increased scale. It was suggested that 'wheat yields began to decline in north India around 1880–1900 and that the trend continued till 1948'.[30]

Charlesworth investigated a more manageable question pertaining to the average land under cultivation per capita and found that since new land was being brought under the plough it increased between 1901 and 1921. 'And in no part of Bombay was there serious famine between 1901 and 1921.' A difficult question follows: 'Was new land brought under the plough at times of hardship as part of an urgent quest to find more land for food or in times of buoyancy as the product of profit maximizing expansionism?' The answer is that in years of good monsoon and harvest, a short-term increase in land use took place and in poor years, it declined. There was also the problem of grazing land and it seems to have declined in favour of cultivation. So fodder crops had to be grown, perhaps for the first time in this period. Clearly such land, though under the plough, did not produce either food grains or other cash crops.[31] Broad trends point to buoyancy in the area under acreage and, hence, in agricultural performance.[32]

In other parts of India, less than buoyant even disquieting accounts were reported. In Gujarat, average fields showed declining or fluctuating trends. Choksi reports that the average yield of rice and wheat declined from 1145.2 lbs per acre and 510 lbs per acre respectively during 1910–15, to 893.0

and 462.1 lbs per acre respectively during 1920–5. Yields show some recovery during 1930–1 to 1934–5. He attributes fluctuations to seasonal variations and the downward tendency to deteriorating standards of tillage. As the population multiplied, the pressure on land grew progressively. Furthermore, as there was little or no improvement in the cultivation techniques, the tendency of diminishing returns asserted itself.[33] He also says that the area under cotton and tobacco expanded at the cost of rice and *jowar* and traces this trend to 1921. Choksi affirms the pressure on lands producing cattle fodder and grazing grounds which declined from 3.3 acres of cultivated land in 1891 to 2.2 in 1925.[34]

For Tamil Nadu, Baker writes,

> In the tough conditions after 1920, the desire to cultivate more and more commercial crops dictated that resources of labour, manure, and managerial attention should be concentrated on these crops. It was not just that there was a simple transfer of acreage from grains to commercial crops, rather there was a tendency to concentrate resources on the production of 'good' crops on 'good' land to the extent that the production of 'poor' crops was neglected and thus overall acreage declined. For it was not only the acreage under grain which declined but probably also the yields.[35]

In Tamil Nadu, tastes and preferences shifted in favour of rice and the excess demand for rice, well over its production levels, resulted in a steady increase in imports. Overall, the steady rise in population coupled with increase in acreage under cash crops and constant or declining yields resulted in increased import dependence in food grains.[36] Baker adds, 'The weakening in the position of lower ranks of rural society was revealed in the sharp decline in the production of their staple foods. The poor must have had much less to eat.'[37]

The behaviour of affluent farmers is consistent with the profit maximization hypothesis. Through the agencies of traders who engaged in export and import of agricultural produce these farmers secured structural connections with foreign markets and derived some share in profits when international prices rose, though the larger part of profit was undoubtedly pocketed by the traders. A major import item was bullion which may be viewed either as a commodity meant for ceremonial display or security and a liquid asset in adverse times. Tomlinson views bullion imports as a form of capital, in the sense that it was the most acceptable asset for obtaining credit.

> The established view that peasant profits were simply hoarded as bullion, and so were lost to the credit networks, is probably mistaken, for holdings of precious metals were regarded as an indication of credit rating for loans from moneylenders and bankers for agricultural capital. Some proportion of India's imports of treasure ought to be regarded as imports of capital for they certainly acted as the basis for credit expansion within the indigenous money market.[38]

This system of credit probably supplied 90 per cent of the total credit in the country.

Subsistence farmers too needed credit and generally faced grossly unfair terms. They pledged what they had, ornaments and, more often, the standing crop at a negotiated or dictated price which was usually well below what the produce would fetch in the market. They would soon enter the lifelong trap of indebtedness from which there could never be an escape. The rates of interest were high and on sums borrowed for unproductive purposes still higher. In Gujarat, 'the rate of interest charged by the moneylender varied from 9.5 to 18 per cent and the tenant cultivator borrowed sometimes at a rate higher than 20 per cent. While good agriculturists got advances at rates as low as 6 per cent the backward class of farmers had to pay 30 per cent or more.' The best placed borrowers could get loans at a low rate of interest of 3 per cent. Elsewhere, moneylending to poor farmers was on security of farm produce, at about half the current rates.[39] Evidently, rural India at the end of the First World War could be placed into well defined economic segments—mainly, the few who profited from the globalized market economy and the many who settled down to the permanence of a subsistence economy. The latter held uneconomic sizes of farm lands. In Gujarat, around 60 per cent had five acres or less while the economic holding should have been 20 acres. The government realized that to reach the goal of economic farming, a large number of cultivators should give up farming and become landless labourers. The alternative was to create opportunities for earning supplementary incomes.[40] The nature of uneconomic farming, high indebtedness and absence of choice for subsistent farmers have stayed with India and, at the end of eight decades of varied developments, are as stark as they were in the early 1920s.

At the end of the war, wages rose and along with them the cost of cultivation also increased. Cotton cultivation became more profitable while other crops suffered. Expansion in cotton cultivation appears to be the proximate cause of the steady climb in wages. Labour was in short supply. There had been a high incidence of death due to influenza, plague and cholera. Charlesworth finds that in Ahmednagar and Bijapur districts, 'any population growth was accurring at rates much below the norm. In Ahmednagar, hard hit by influenza the population actually fell substantially from 838000 to 732000 between 1901 and 1921, against the Presidency, wide trends of 4.1 per cent rise. In Bijapur there was no acceleration. These are subregional factors and are correlated with other indices.'[41] In Gujarat, mortality rates due to the aforesaid epidemics were very high. 'The toll in life was heavy, Ahmedabad district paid the heaviest in life. All others were affected in varied proportion.'[42] The other reason for shortage of labour was migration—from the villages to towns and from the latter to bigger cities. Profits in cotton trade raised the bargaining capacity of poor labourers. Wages rose faster than the price indices of food grains and real wages improved. The steady increase in employment in the manufacturing industries in Gujarat raised rural wages. It is doubtful if an all-India inference can be deduced from Gujarat's experience.

The rural economy of India, in fact, continued to suffer from the twin paradoxical characteristics of under-investment and under-consumption. Tomlinson puts the responsibility for producing such outcomes on the colonial institutional structures. Privileged groups were created and favouritism was rife. These favoured people used their power to manipulate land and the sale of output. However, economic returns were low though moneylending and income generated by it did account for about 10 per cent of total agricultural income. This is not a low figure of net returns. Rent may have been a major attraction, but buying land to earn rent generated a mere 3–4 per cent of the purchase price. Trade produced higher profits, 'but this remained a risky and uncertain business in the difficult conditions of inter-war years. Thus farm profits were often used to spread and avoid the risks that resulted from practising under-capitalized agriculture at times of ecological adversity and unstable market conditions.' One more reason why agriculture remained under-capitalized is that the surplus produced in working the land was used partly for reinforcing the social power of favoured people and the state agencies which were the ultimate arbiter of how scarce resources would be used and surplus appropriated.[43]

For Punjab, Mridula Mukherjee writes that though commercialization reached a very wide section of peasantry and the profits earned from it were by and large retained in the agricultural sector, yet the level of cultivation remained low owing to,

> the investment of capital accumulated by some sections of rural society in land purchase and land mortgage rather than in improvement of agricultural techniques, the use of mechanized implements, fertilizers, etc. and the intensification of semi-feudal, semi-colonial relations, i.e. an increasing concentration of landholding accompanied not by growth of large-scale farming with wage labour but by rapid increases in areas under tenancy (cultivated primarily on a sharecropping basis), as well as by an actual shift from rent-in-cash to rent-in-kind.[44]

The basic fact about Indian agriculture is that by and large yields were low due to low capital intensity and the combined share of land taxes including land revenue, interest or usury claimed by moneylenders and other credit providers such as traders who exported the crop or engaged in domestic trade. Profit from trade was high, leaving a very small return for the cultivator. He received the residual after meeting all other claims. An average farmer still wanted to save in order to buy or lease more land to raise the operational holdings and overcome his deficit status, or invest in a pair of bullocks, et cetera. Quite apart from the poverty syndrome of deficit farming, the thriftiness of farmers, even if savings were invested in bullion or ornaments, would be suggestive of systemic under-consumption as a general condition and, together, the two formed an unbroken vicious circle producing poverty and economic stagnation. Under-consumption was also consistent with the reported rise in real wages in Gujarat and the Punjab between 1915 and 1925. Money wages rose in a lagged response to rise in crop prices and cut into profit margins.

Before the war, there were only two large-scale industries in India—manufacture of jute in the Calcutta region and cotton textiles mostly in Bombay but also in Ahmedabad. The Tata steel plant was commissioned in Jamshedpur in 1912 and it was struggling to overcome initial difficulties. The importance of industrial development for the Indian economy was primarily in two respects. The backward linkage was obvious in respect of the cash crops of jute and raw cotton which were partly exported and partly consumed by the mills. In the domestic economy, both industries led to expansion in trade, transport and banking. However, of greater importance were the international linkages created and sustained by the two industries. The fact that foreign markets were created in manufactured and raw jute, as well as in cotton yarn and raw cotton is an important indicator of the low level of economic development that took place in India.

India was heavily dependent on Britain for the supply of capital goods and the business connections which formed the essential linkage in foreign trade. Though there were hardly any barriers on foreign investment and opening of trade channels, India was an integral part of the extended British economy. At the end of the war, India's connections with the rest of the world underwent changes and, with the passage of each decade, British connections weakened. Correspondingly, within the domestic economy, the presence of Indian owned and financed industrial development and trade steadily grew.

At the end of the war, the jute, cotton textile and iron and steel industries emerged more prosperous and with ample liquidity to finance renewal of capital stock as well as expansion. On the negative side, the famine of 1918–19 and the influenza epidemic destroyed much of the unsatisfied demand due to war conditions and the immediate outlook for industrial goods. Nonetheless, 'there was a boom through the years 1919–20 to 1921–2, which was reflected in, among other things, the number of joint stock companies registered and the capital involved in these companies'. The latter was at about twice the level of 1913–14.[45] The value of machinery and mill work excluding agricultural machinery rose steadily from the stagnant level of Rs. 46.879 million in 1918–19 to Rs. 84.55 million in 1919–20, Rs. 202.322 million 1920–1 and Rs. 315.205 million in 1921–2, and then tapered off and could not reach this level again. On a comparable basis, the index number of textile machinery rose from 100 in 1904–5 to 103.67 in 1913–14 and in 1920–1 it stood at 370.10 in 1920–1. Thereafter, the index number declined and stayed below the peak year.[46]

Data show that despite setbacks, because of exogenous factors, boom conditions prevailed and industry took advantage of its resources to expand its base. Industries other than jute and cotton textiles also expanded though these two were still more important than all others. However, Bagchi says: 'A major part of the increase in investment during the years from 1919–20 to 1923–24 must have been frittered away in increases in the prices of capital goods, leaving the real average levels of investment only slightly higher than in 1913–14.'[47] Overall, the weight of cotton textiles increased while the jute industry diminished. Alongside, Bombay's importance relative to Calcutta's rose steadily.

Trade and industry established Bombay's pre-eminence. According to Chandavarkar, 'In 1914, Bombay received over 87 per cent of the total value of Indian capital investment while Indian capital accounted for nearly half the total value of private industrial investment centred in the city. In the late nineteenth and twentieth centuries, Bombay remained the bastion of Indian capital.'[48] He gives a detailed account of the emergence of Indian capital in a subordinate status to European merchants, yet drawing on the considerable industrial and commercial background of Gujarat, where the local merchants established a foothold as early capitalists. Gujarat's capital played a vital role in the development of commerce and industry in Bombay. However, most of the early industrialists were only marginally important in Gujarat society. Yet, they found entirely new opportunities in Bombay and prospered. Chandavarkar includes in this class the Ismaili sects of the Khojas and Bohras as well as the Parsis. The China trade enabled risk takers in India to accumulate capital and there was considerable tension, based on trade rivalries, between the Khojas and the Parsis. This factor was present in the Prince of Wales riots in November 1921.[49]

The initial constraints which limited the options for the subordinate Indian capital could never have permitted a logical progression from trading to industry. However, pushed into the export trade, Indian businessmen discovered an outlet in spinning and weaving while finding it difficult to raise the needed capital, since it could only be mobilized in small pools. Nonetheless, once the industry was established and found its place in the impoverished Indian markets it began to attract capital. Yet, the mortality rates of mills were high. Between 1855 and 1925, 97 mills were erected in Bombay, but only five survived till 1925. Though production expanded, sometimes in spurts of growth, the demand for cloth did not rise as much; in fact, it often fell. Cost of production was high in the smaller mills and several crashed or went into liquidation. 'In 1911 the 25 mills which shut down were all spinning mills.'[50] The mills were characterized by short-term attractions of high profits and took individualistic decisions. There was no understanding of total industrial capacity relative to demand and there was much idle capacity in the industry as a whole, even while new units were installed. In 1922, depressed conditions set in and the future looked bleak. In Bombay, the mills were slow in replacing their capital stock and it was further stretched to produce more cloth during the post-war boom years. The number of spindles in 1922 at 3.117 million was only a shade higher than in 1914 when it was 3.009 million, though progress in loomage was more satisfactory. Every year from 1914, the industry was able to install more looms, raising the capacity from 48,845 in 1914 to 59,162 in 1918 and 65,521 in 1922. However, it so happened that fresh orders for machinery placed in the boom years arrived late because of supply bottlenecks. During this period, spurred by high optimism at least 30 mills changed hands on 'considerably inflated valuation', and were over-capitalized as a result. The exchange rate also declined and made it expensive to renew machinery. Several deep-seated problems confronted the industry and a relatively long phase of crisis began.[51]

India enjoyed a monopoly position in jute and the entire capital and ownership was predominantly British. Most of the market for jute products was abroad so mills worked for exports, though periodically, production was in excess of world demand and prices of jute goods declined. The industry was well organized to face such situations and nearly always succeeded in curtailing production to restore the balance between supply and demand. In 1913–14 jute mills had 36,050 looms and 744,289 spindles which rose to 40,639 and 834,055 respectively in 1918–19. The industry found the war immensely profitable and managed to expand its capacity steadily.[52] The end of the war saw further expansion, practically without a break, till 1939–40. The data depict a remarkably sturdy management in charge of the industry.

Nonetheless, an important change in ownership of capital occurred, first during the war and then later. Bagchi says,

> During the war Indians also seem to have captured a large part of the capital of the jute mills; the explanation cannot be that Europeans were keen to sell their shares in the companies concerned, for jute shares continued to carry very high dividends well up to 1926. One plausible explanation is that during the war a large proportion of the British businessmen of Calcutta were either out in the front lines or engaged in other war-work.[53]

Thereafter, corresponding to every European trade association, Indians set up parallel bodies. Indian interest succeeded in penetrating an entirely British owned and managed industry, trade and finance. However, tension along racial lines remained, and in 1922 the Marwari Association claimed, 'that while Indians held not less than 60 per cent of the shares in jute mills, the European managers did not buy jute through Indian traders'.[54]

The industry decided to act in the common interest to curtail production in 1921 by agreeing to work only 54 hours a week and continued to do so for several years. The jute magnates knew that some day they would have to face world competition from two sources. One was the development of the jute industry in other countries and the other, more serious, was that substitutes for jute goods would cut into the market. Their response was to keep the price of jute goods low which would discourage investments in substitutes.[55] If jute prices were raised, this advantage would be lost and the search for a substitute stimulated, 'and one of these days Germany will find one and your industry will be in danger of following the path of indigo'.[56] This became the industry's survival strategy. However, low-priced goods were also often of low quality and lacked standardization. The scientific aspects of jute manufacturing though already developed abroad and known to the mills, were ignored. Technology remained stagnant while complaints about low reliability of finished products increased. The industry never cared to attend to such complaints, because it could not do what was needed, mainly, install new and more modern machinery, which would raise costs and lead to higher prices. It became a vicious circle which finally led to its inevitable decline.

A common dimension in the preference for relatively low production technology in cotton textile and jute manufacturing was the availability of as much cheap labour as the industry required, with more waiting at the factory gates for hire as substitute labour. This factor established a predetermined preference for production processes which were discarded in the industrialized societies. The search for improved technologies deepens as labour acquires value.

The First World War stampeded the British bureaucracy to think of an industrial policy for India. Clive J. Dewey says: 'The first total war showed the direct relationship between military capacity and the possession of an adequate industrial base. It enormously enhanced the perceived importance of "strategic" industries directly related to the war effort.' Industrialization was viewed for the first time as a military necessity. The war necessitated large-scale procurement of military supplies, but there was another threat perception. 'The terrifying possibility of a Japanese attack timed to coincide with Britain's involvement in a European war sent shivers down the imperial secretariat's collective spine.'[57] Militarist reasoning led to peace time industrialization as a preparation for the next war. Since Britain's rivals pursued interventionist policies, so should India because, in the final analysis, only Indian resources would enable the country to defend itself. The drive towards an industrial policy was also a compromising response to the nationalist agitation. So in 1916, the Industrial Commission was appointed. However, 'a clear majority of the members of the Government of India which recommended the appointment of the Industrial Commission to the Secretary of State believed industrialization would make it more difficult, not less, for their successors to govern India.'[58]

The policy which emerged strove to work the free market to develop new industries and to aid private enterprise rather than create a miniature public sector. Pioneer factories might be set up, operated for some time and then sold to private interests. It would be an import-substitution model with the government providing the initial inputs and organization to demonstrate that the new ventures could be profitably run. Unfortunately, the policy had only a short run and, before it could be given a forward long-term peacetime orientation, the 1919 Act was put in place and the department of industries was devolved on the provinces. It killed the policy.[59] The provincial governments 'were given neither the resources nor the incentives to pursue such an ambitious programme. The two central cadres of technical services that survived this change in policy were killed off by local jealousies and financial stringency in 1922.'[60]

Morris points to a deeper problem: that of underdevelopment, general poverty and low demand which obstructed speedier industrialization. 'The entrepreneur in India had to accept not merely a higher level of risk but also a much greater range of uncertainty in all his calculations. The consequence was a much higher level of real costs that needed the promise of much higher rates of return if the risk and uncertainty was to be borne.'[61] The information and technical skills were either not available, or scarce and costly. The colonial state could not perform miracles. Nonetheless in Madras, pioneer factories were set up but there was remarkably low interest in taking them over. Financial assistance was not forthcoming, nor was there an assured market for the goods produced by the factories. Dewey writes, 'It will not do to revive the old canard that industrialization did not take place because Indians were incapable of managing industries. However, neither will it do to replace the old canard with another, and to assume that whenever enterprise was required it was automatically forthcoming.'[62] There is, however, considerable evidence that over time the supply of entrepreneurial talent rose steadily, when the government adopted a more favourable attitude towards encouragement and protection of newly formed and struggling industries. These formed part of tariff and fiscal policies.

The rupee exchange rate and the way it was managed also produced great controversy. The government maintained a stable rate of exchange at 1S.4d by selling Council Drafts in London and Reverse Council Drafts in India. 'The Gold Exchange Standard did possess some merit in stabilizing the rate of exchange within narrow points. However, so far as the Indian economy as a whole is concerned probably stability of the rate of exchange was not so significant as making the monetary system adjustable and flexible to meet the seasonal requirements within the country.'[63] The imperial system which designed the system seemed more interested in maintaining stable conditions in foreign trade and meeting Indian obligations towards the Secretary of State or Home charges. The interest of British investors, especially in regard to remittances, also favoured a stable rate. Since the backing for Indian currency had to be gold and sterling held with the Bank of England, the government was required to maintain reserves and sell bills in India on London at a fixed rate. Facilities for encashment of notes into coins or gold were additional reasons for the government to maintain reserves in silver too. During the war, the circulation of notes increased and to maintain confidence in the currency the government sold Reverse Councils on London.

During the war, though the heavy foreign demand for Indian money strengthened the rupee, the steady rise in the price of silver led to raising the official rate to correspond to the bullion value of the rupee. The bullion price of the rupee was 43 pence per ounce and this corresponded to the exchange rate of 1S.4d. However, silver prices continued to rise, exceeding the intrinsic value of the rupee, so the rupee should appreciate, and it did to 1S.5d in August 1917, 1S.6d in April 1918, 1S.8d in May 1919 and thereafter to 2S.2d in November 1919 and 2S.4d in December 1919. This was an unprecedented climb and the government appointed a committee to examine all the related issues and make recommendations.

The Babington–Smith Committee argued that silver prices had come to stay and made the startling recommendation to fix the exchange rate at 2S per rupee. It also recommended that the sovereign be made legal tender in India and the import and export of gold should be freed from government control. These recommendations were accepted and the sovereign was made legal tender at Rs. 10. However, at this rate, the demand for remittances grew and imports suddenly spurted. Eventually, the government realized that the rupee was over valued. In September 1920, the rate was abandoned and the rupee was allowed to float down to a more realistic level. In early 1921, it fell to 1S.3d but steadily rose later to reach 1S.6d in late 1924. The government took recourse to deflating the currency to stabilize the rupee and the currency was contracted by almost Rs. 52 crores between January 1920 and March 1923.

Another deflationary effect was produced by farmers' behaviour. They held their savings in silver bullion, jewellery or hoards of coins, so a considerable amount of currency went out of circulation every year and never returned to the banks. Thus, governmental activity in the short-term loan markets and the contraction of currency by withdrawing it from the government balances held at the Imperial Bank had a disproportionately intense reaction on the financing of trade.[64] The actual movement of cash during the 'busy' and 'slack' seasons was impaired by the deflationary policy, and the supply of credit was squeezed. These were blamed on the government's monetary policy. However, deflation was required to facilitate remittances which were needed in London to bolster the money market.

The 1919 Act made several far-reaching changes in the management of the Indian economy. First, devolution of power occurred at two levels. The Secretary of State in Council was divested of several important functions and these were devolved on the central government, which meant the Viceroy would exercise his expanded jurisdiction through his executive council, and also directly, on his own authority.

This showed up on three issues on which divergent views were expressed respecting the imperial viewpoint and the Indian. On the use of the Indian Army, the former had extravagantly visualized 395 battalions of various classes, four regiments of cavalry and some supporting arms of sappers, miners and signallers for exclusive deployment and imperial duty. It could be more, because the idea was to cut back on British garrisons and replace them with the Indian. This was sharply opposed in the Central Legislative Assembly, with the Viceroy supporting the view that the Indian army should primarily defend India and not be deployed for the extensive duties of running the empire. In the changed circumstances the Viceroy's position was upheld in London and imperial pleas ignored.

The second issue was of fiscal autonomy and the Fiscal Autonomy Convention came into effect in 1921. The government adopted a policy of discriminating protection. The argument that the India office should be consulted before any decision was held to be constitutionally obsolete and ruled out. The India Office still had the power to interfere to advance imperial preference and later succeeded, but the political answer was that the Government of India would use its liberty 'to devise tariff arrangements which seemed best fitted to India's needs as an integral part of the British empire'.[65] The third issue pertained to the purchase of stores, where it was decided that purchase decisions could be effected in India rather than in London. This was official import substitution at the cost of British industry and commerce.

Following the inauguration of provincial autonomy and

the resulting allocation of several tax heads to the provinces, the Centre was somewhat poor on finance. Several committees deliberated on the issue and came up with the utterly unworkable idea that the provinces should make fiscal subventions to the Centre. The latter was reduced to the status of a fiscal dependency of the provinces. A major loss to the Centre was the land revenue. It provided almost 36 per cent of total tax revenues, including the provinces in 1817–18, though in 1921–2 it declined to 27 per cent.[66] On the other hand, the provinces complained of their shares of contributions to the Centre. One complaint was on the grounds of equity that the more developed Bengal and Bombay paid less, while the less developed, UP and Madras paid more to the Centre. The other complaint was that the transferred subjects of education and health needed more expenditure and the only way they could cope was to reduce their share of finance to the Centre.

Actually, if the Centre were to reduce overall defence spending, its budgetary balance would be restored. In 1921–2, defence accounted for 33 per cent of total public expenditure (Centre plus provinces). The alternative to provincial contribution was to return to divided heads between the Centre and the provinces but, in the 1919 Act, it had been given up as an unsatisfactory arrangement. 'The contributions were abruptly reduced whenever central finance afforded a lapse, in a few cases remitted in full or part, and the apprehension of the provinces of an emergency in which they could be raised never materialized.'[67]

The Genesis of the Labour Movement in India

In several recorded episodes, factory labour took part in collective action in the form of demonstrations and strikes. However, further development of collective consciousness into representative organizations, even at rudimentary stages, had to wait for the emergence of leaders who could transform spontaneous surges of shared emotions of anger and resentment at injustices into a desire to unite into a body and give shape to these stirrings. It is doubtful that at the preliminary stage either the workers or their informal leaders knew about trade unions or their functions.

One leader, Vadappuram Bava, emerged in Kerala. He started working at an early age as both his parents had died. He soon learnt the requisite skills as he drifted from one factory to another and became a *moopan* (labour contractor) as well as a social activist working for the social advancement of his community, the lower caste Ezhavas. At his initiative, the Travancove Labour Association (TLA) was formed in 1922. He sought the support of other moopans as well as factory proprietors and met with no opposition. A strike had taken place at a factory in Kollam to demand an increase in wages, reduced working hours, a shorter working day on Saturdays and the payment of bonus. A deputation met the employer and after talks, the agitation was called off. This is an instance of a union at work through social activists who were non-workers, intervening and mediating with the employer. This spontaneous union in action took the shape of the TLA.[68]

Elsewhere, the cause of labour was espoused by social workers and public men who thought more in terms of labourers' social upliftment than in their class struggles, though some of them took part in strikes and talked to employers in their name. Interesting cases of social intervention have been cited. A few British civil servants sympathized with workers and, in Ahmedabad, Chatfield, the District Collector, intervened in a factory strike. He is described as a friend of the poor and a well-wisher of workers in the textile and other industries in his district. He offered to serve as an umpire in a board of arbitrators and the proposal was accepted. In 1918, during a strike the weavers held meetings, 'where Mr. Gandhi, Bai Anusuya, a sister of Ambalal Sarabhai, who is doing some philanthropic work, and certain members of the Home Rule League give them lectures on economy, morality, sanitation, citizenship, social duties and other kindred subjects'.[69]

Among the oldest unions was the Madras Labour Union led by B.P. Wadia. In the second year of its existence Wadia told the gathering that someone should go to England to convey their message to the English Labour Unions to help 'fight our battles'. Wadia was appointed 'to represent us before the Labour Party Conference, the Trade Union Congress, the Parliamentary Committee of the Trade Union Congress and the Secretary to the Labour Party and enlist their sympathies to our cause'. Several other unions in Madras which Wadia helped organize joined in this endeavour. This needed to be done because, 'Indian leaders had so far neglected the interests of labourers'.[70]

In Bombay and Ahmedabad, there was a spate of strikes but the unions that sprang up in Bombay were hardly different from strike committees. Trade unions were non-existent, yet strikes spread from mill to mill as if guided by leaders at the helm. Actually, workers had learnt the value of concerted action as a collective voice, but no more. The idea of an organization to secure concessions took root in other, more developed segments of the economy, such as the railways, posts and telegraphs and seamen at the ports. Conditions were thus favourable for successful strikes; and when a number of strikes resulted in substantial increases of wages, a fairly general outbreak was an almost inevitable consequence.[71]

The organizational element, as Chandavarkar has meticulously shown, was the informal networking system in Bombay's residential quarters of predominantly Ratnagiri workers. The spirit of solidarity among mill hands forged by ethnic bonds probably explains the comparatively longer duration of strikes in 1920, though these were less successful than the short ones in 1918. Strikes spread to other industries including postal and dock workers. 'Lightning strikes were the order of the day. The operatives had adopted the general practice of going on strike first and formulating demands afterwards.'[72] The strikes were either successful in securing wage increases and other demands, or were met with resistance and ended in failure, but no consequences emerged from them.

By comparison, the Ahmedabad mill workers found able leaders in the initial stages and formed category-wise unions, which they later consolidated into the Textile Labour Association. Two factors of extraordinary importance bring out the distinctive quality of the Ahmedabad labour movement. One, the initial leadership was provided by Anusuyaben Sarabhai, sister of a mill magnate and a social worker active in the labour locality. The strike occurred in December 1917 and continued for 20 days. Gandhi was present and insisted on non-violence. He had Anusyaben impose a fine of Rs. 10 on a worker for assaulting the Secretary of the Mill Owners Association. Second, the method of work and style of agitation made all the difference. An important supporting element has also been noted. It is that the workers and the employers belonged to largely the same linguistic and cultural background and they may have shared a common view about the goals and methods of the larger political struggle.[73] The Ahmedabad mills could hire workers even when wages were cut. Their bona fides were not in question, nor would Gandhi allow such questions to be asked.

Education emerges as an important influence in the formation of unions. For instance, postal employees found outside leaders such as V.G. Dalvi, a barrister, and Ginwala, a solicitor. The latter acted as the Honorary Solicitor of the Bombay Postmen's Union. Even clerks formed unions and the Bombay Clerks Union completed one year in 1918. A union of press employees was formed in 1920. Later Lala Lajpat Rai, a prominent national leader from Punjab, was elected its president. The railway men were in the lead in organizing themselves, holding annual meetings, conducting elections, maintaining accounts and passing well-drafted resolutions. They found leaders who could discharge these functions and retain the members' trust. Though these were early unions, they demonstrated a remarkable grasp of wider issues. In June 1920, three unions—the GIP Railway Union, the Bombay Dock Workmen's Union and the Bombay United Textile Workmen's Union—held a joint meeting to elect delegates for the ILO Congress, to meet the representatives of the North Western Railway Association and to express public sympathy for its workers who were on strike.

Sending a workers' representative to the ILO was important and the government's decision to send N.M. Joshi was not proper because he could not represent the workers. The unions appealed to the Viceroy to intercede in the railwaymen's dispute and help bring about an early resolution in the interests of the country. The leaders who conducted the meeting were P.J. Ginwalla, who was elected to represent the workers at ILO with D. Chaman Lal, BA (Oxon) and Dr D.D. Sathaye as two advisers under the terms of the League of Nations Conventions.

Earlier in August 1919, at a meeting of the Madras Labour Union, a telegram was sent to the Viceroy to nominate B.P. Wadia as the workers' representative to the ILO. The union claimed to have 10,000 members and its meeting attracted a distinguished group of public men in the city. By this time, the Non-Cooperation Movement had been launched and the legislative councils were to be boycotted. However, the meeting of workers pleaded that as provided in the 1919 Act, there should be a labour representative in the Council. The chief spokesman combined this plea with a call to duty. 'Let labourers be true, be loyal to the King Emperor and walk in the footsteps of Mahatma Gandhi (Bande Mataram).'[74] In the labour leaders' perspective, labour's interests were best promoted by availing of every opportunity which presented itself, and it was entirely reasonable to affirm loyalty both to the King and Gandhi without noticing any contradiction.

During 1918–21, strike activities were at their peak. While unions were non-existent among the textile workers, the method often employed by the workers was to hold a meeting and elect delegates representing each mill to meet mill owners' representatives and negotiate a settlement or, at least submit their demands. The idea of arbitration was frequently aired though the names mentioned in this connection did not always inspire confidence. Even in Ahmedabad, where it was promoted as a concept, it was not readily acceptable due to non-availability of someone acceptable to both sides. Some mills took a principled stand that no third party should intervene in a labour dispute. Workers, too, showed lack of trust, partly for the reason 'that the management was not anxious to show strict regard for the terms of settlement'. Yet, third party intervention sometimes did produce results. In 1919, around 120,000 workers in one mill after another struck, till practically all the mills, joined in and no settlement was in sight, partly because the mill owners knew no one who could represent the men on strike. The Police Commissioner intervened and held a meeting with the mill owners in his office. He strongly recommended an all-round increase in wages of ten per cent to their workmen, and they agreed.[75] The Governor was approached by the strikers through the good offices of the Police Commissioner, and he met several head jobbers representing the men. He advised them to return to work and offered to persuade the mill owners to consider their demands and do them justice. Eventually, on the termination of the strike, the terms of settlement were announced by the Police Commissioner and the men received the news with vociferous cheers and shouts of 'Vincent Maharaj ki jai'. 'It was a memorable scene, the men following the Commissioner's car for over a mile.'[76] Men were heard blessing the Governor and the Police Commissioner for acting on their behalf.

In Jamshedpur, the labour force was systematically recruited on a heterogeneous basis. In 1921, over a fifth of the skilled workers were Muslims, around 18 per cent were Rajputs, 16 per cent Brahmins, 13 per cent Kayasths, 6 per cent Sikhs and over 5 per cent Goalas. The unskilled hands belonged mostly to other castes, though 13 per cent were also Muslims. Most of the Brahmins were from Bengal and were employed as white collar workers. On the other hand, most of the highly skilled workers were European, American and Anglo–Indian. The tribals comprised the largest single segment of unskilled workers. According to Vinay Bahl, 'the factor of caste and community played an important role during the Tata Iron and Steel Company (TISCO) workers' strikes in which Bengalis, all holding clerical positions, refused to join the strikes.'[77] However, other caste groups showed solidarity on a consistent basis. Both Hindu and Muslim workers were able to show leadership qualities by the 1922 strike.

The 1920 strike had resulted in the framing of service rules for the monthly-rated and weekly-rated workers. The daily rated workers also started receiving leave benefits. Other leave rules were standardized and implemented more properly. However, among unskilled workers the turnover was high and to control this, the company introduced a bonus of two days wages for 27 days of consecutive work. It had introduced a Social Welfare Policy in 1918, which may be viewed as a pioneer in this field. However, sharp divisions developed between the educated and uneducated workers.[78]

The strike in February 1920 was led by a recently formed, largely unorganized union; yet, workers remained peaceful, orderly and maintained decency. Later, they picketed the factory gate and prevented cars and lorries from carrying workmen inside. They pelted stones at cars and assembled in large numbers at the gates. Troops were called in and, at one place, they were fired on when 23 workers were killed. Soon thereafter in March, the strike ended.[79] There was a racial dimension to the conflicts. In June 1920, the company reported: 'The unrest is industrial and not political. It is widespread. The European staff cannot get the men under them to work and Indians also cannot get the Indians under them to work.' This was a problem of work organization which must have hampered the company's efforts to raise efficiency and lower costs. The company noted with satisfaction that production did not decline, 'but there is evidence of a new spirit of independence among the men'.

There were grievances of racial slurs and insults, and combined with the effect of inflation and economic hardship these became unbearable.[80] In September 1920, the covenanted European employees struck work on pay scales, but it ended soon with the company offering to sign a new contract, though the pay increase was selective. In Jamshedpur as elsewhere, once a strike began, workers started looking for leaders who would take charge, guide them and negotiate with the expatriate management. They found their leaders in Calcutta, mostly practising lawyers, who responded to the call.

In the post-war years economic unrest was widespread, even in rural areas. It is remarkable that the political agitation which Gandhi started in 1919 and which gathered momentum in 1920 and 1921, formed merely the general backdrop to the industrial commotion that occurred at the time. Gandhi consciously stayed clear of industrial action and never wanted to connect the two or three distinct currents of unrest, strikes and agitations into a larger mass movement. In Ahmedabad, where he got deeply involved in labour disputes, he made sure that the process of finding a settlement was within the capacity of the local textile industry and it would remain unflinchingly non-violent. The struggle for wages and improved conditions of work must be bounded by workers' understanding of the economic nature of the industry, its strength as well as limitations. These had nothing to do with the fight for Swaraj. Moreover, most of the strikes were local and specific to the industry or were job-related. Hence the strikes of textile workers even in a city like Bombay were independent of similar actions by railwaymen, postal employees, clerks and others. The forms of protest too varied greatly, from petitions and holding of general body meetings in which resolutions were passed or representatives chosen, to demonstrations and strikes. In practically every case, they affirmed their loyalty and commitment to work, though occasionally also gave expressions of disgust, even anger at expatriate managers and supervisors. The latter class was accused of racism which triggered conflicts.

However, the glaring facts that emerge in the detailed and varied descriptions of strikes are the absence of organization among industrial workers and their hectic, almost desperate search for leaders. Even in Jamshedpur where the manpower was educated, workers still thought of Gandhi, C.R. Das and other public men who might spare their time and energy for their cause. Yet, what workers had learnt was that though not organized it was still possible to unite to engage in collective actions on specific issues. Furthermore, in every city where strikes occurred and a threat to peace emerged, workers had to deal with the government and its law and order machinery collectively. They had to cope with the presence of police, the military with bayonets drawn, troops on horses charging into crowds and firing, then count their casualties. Every such encounter taught them the pressing need for organized consultation, systematic mediation, learning basic economic facts about cost, competition, profit and the manner in which wages were linked to them, as well as skills of negotiation to search for an honourable end to the disputes. It was a hard learning process, but they realized that only trade unions led by capable and trusted leaders could engage in costly strikes and find the means to terminate them.

The first stage of the labour movement, 1917–22, was characterized by the discovery of the potentiality of a strike by factory workers. This discovery rested on the informal local leaders' demonstrated ability to create unity in action to give expression to a shared collective grievance. These took the form of strike committees which disbanded soon after the strike was over. The experience was repeated in the Bombay textile industry without producing any durable organization. However, it produced the awakening which preceded the formation and acceptance of trade unions. The political turmoil of the times brought political and social activists into the fold of the labour movement and provided the much needed leaders to launch trade unions.[81] Echoing a widely held view, Sharma writes:

> In the main, the common background between them was India's political struggle against a foreign power. But at that time, when the trade unions came to be formed by the outside leaders in India in the immediate post-war period, the principal motivation of such leaders seemed to be assertion of racial equality. Support is given to this argument by the fact that B.P. Wadia, the founder of Madras Labour Union (1918), India's first regular trade union was an ardent Home Ruler, but he was attracted initially to the trade union work out of his sympathy for the Indian workers' harsh treatment at the hands of European officers in the mill.[82]

By comparison, in the jute industry, the paradox persisted over a longer period. There was 'so much militancy, yet so little organisation', and trade unionism remained in its infancy.[83]

The All India Trade Union Congress (AITUC) was founded in 1920. For Bombay workers, Tilak was the moving spirit and they rallied to the AITUC. Lala Lajpat Rai was elected its first president and Dewan Chaman Lal its general secretary. The ILO was founded in 1919 and the first nomination of N.M. Joshi, a social activist, made by the government in October 1919gave rise to protests. Joshi then proposed, 'the convening of an All-India meeting for a discussion of the same and for the formation of an All India body, which alone could claim the right of nomination'.[84] In July 1920, a convention was held in Bombay which resolved to form the AITUC. There were 101 delegates from all over India but the distinguishing feature of the first meet was the presence of many leading politicians in the country. The British Trade Union Congress (TUC) was also represented. In the presidential procession about 10,000 people took part. This may be due to Lajpat Rai's popularity as well as the agitated atmosphere in the city. Most of the office bearers elected in the first AITUC were political leaders. Among them, Annie Besant was elected as one of four vice presidents. Sixty-four unions affiliated themselves to the AITUC. The railway unions with 91,427 members out of the total membership of 140,854 were the preponderant unions. The shipping unions with 19,806 members came next.

The political leadership knew how to use the new organization. Workers should join the nationalist movement and advance their interests within it. Referring to the Jamshedpur Labour Association which had affiliated to the AITUC, Vinay Bahl says, that under the influence of the latter the former was not encouraged to call a strike, because its 'leaders were interested in two things: (a) to save a national industry and (b) to subordinate the workers' movement to the Nationalist Movement'.[85] Nonetheless, though the AITUC did not give its approval workers at TISCO went on strike in 1922. About 20,000 workers were on a peaceful strike, not to wreck the company which to them was like mother–father (Ma–Baap) but to get fair wages, which revealed the hiatus inherent between workers and the top leaders with their middle class backgrounds and attitudes.[86] On behalf of the AITUC, Chaman Lal interceded in the strike and advised the workers to call it off and return to work. Later, the union secretary was dismissed from service.[87]

The government developed a two-pronged policy towards labour. On the one hand, it was supportive of the trade union movement during its infancy and sent encouraging signals, such as, accepting the right of the AITUC to nominate delegates to the ILO conference but, on the other, it showed its coercive powers, and unhesitatingly used the police and the army to suppress strikes. In 1921, the strike situation worsened due to surging spontaneous outbreaks of workers' anger. However, the government's fears rested on the worst possibility of the two distinct streams of agitation coalescing into a common political upheaval endangering the security of the state, and on occasions this apprehension produced overreaction.

At the second session of the AITUC at Jharia in 1921, the employers of coal mines were frantic and the police and military were called in. 'The workers, once denied the right to attend the session, spontaneously went into action.' The strike was effective and in consequence about 50,000 workers attended the session. Decorations were in khadi cloth and people wore khadi and Gandhi caps. Political speeches were delivered and a call for Swaraj was made.[88] Upon the conclusion of the session, the delegates went their way, crowds dispersed and the mines returned to normal working. None of this enthusiasm survived and trade unions failed to develop for many more years. No leader appeared on the scene who would galvanize the collective mood for action into a concerted drive towards union formation. The strike was symptomatic of dissipated collective energy.

The reformist trade union leaders were generally opposed to calls for strikes for political reasons. Gandhi was foremost in opposing workers in political agitations, so did not desire the Non-Cooperation Movement to reach out to workers or even indirectly to acquire the character of a class struggle. Yet, political strikes did take place in 1920 and 1921, the worst example is that of the desperately poor and helpless plantation workers who struck against heavy odds and ended in a human disaster. Gurkha troops were deployed, once again (as at Jallianwala Bagh in 1918), in an outrageous act against them.[89] In 1922, the post-war boom ended and it appeared that economic depression had set in.

The surging waves of strikes in 1921 gradually petered out and the workers' mood began to show waning interest in collective action. The labour markets in several industrial centres were weakened by the influenza epidemic. The withdrawal of the non-cooperation movement and virtual defeat of the Khilafat agitation resulted in a total absence of thrust in politics, and a sullen mood settled among the formerly active workers. Labour was on the defensive even where it had acquired rudiments of organization. One of the factors which produced withdrawal of active interest was the outbreak of communal riots in Bombay on the occasion of the Prince of Wales's visit between the Parsi community and the non-cooperative Muslims and Hindus. However, mill hands stayed away. In 1921, two positive developments, due entirely to government's initiative, furthered workers' interests. In January, N.M. Joshi was nominated to one of the two labour seats in the Central Assembly giving him access to official thinking on labour for several years. The Bombay government set up the Bombay Labour Office though mainly to gather statistics and conduct special inquiries and publish the Labour Gazette. It appeared that the government had at last opened itself to enlightened thinking on the subject.[90]

Though Indian labour was barely articulate, yet the fledgling AITUC drew considerable attention of trade union movements in Europe, UK and the newly established Red International Trade Unions. At the founding Congress in 1920, it received messages and greetings from the British trade unions. In 1921 another body, the International Federation of Trade Unions (Amsterdam) sought the affiliation of the AITUC and instead the AITUC decided to send fraternal delegates to the British TUC. International connections were opening up at ILO conferences too. The apex body of the AITUC reminded the government that it had not ratified certain ILO conventions, particularly those pertaining to hours of work, seamen's codes and unemployment insurance. It also expressed opinions on the recently enacted Factories Act, 1922, and the bill on workmen's compensation in 1922. The issue of international affiliation was repeatedly delayed due to the strong ideological positions of the rival bodies. However, the AITUC did pass a resolution, 'conveying messages of sympathy to the starving millions in Russia and calling upon the workers of the world to help Russia in her struggle for peace.'[91]

Whether international developments influenced government thinking, either in India or in London, is debatable because economic issues received notice rather directly and labour aspects were at best subordinated to these concerns. In India, it was the political aspect of the labour turmoil which was of primary interest, though Lord

Chelmsford prodded the mill owners and other employers to develop mechanisms for early resolution of disputes. Newman puts it in perspective:

> The bureaucratic leviathan was by no means insensible to external stimuli, but it sometimes took an unconscionably long time for reforms to work their way through the bowels of the monster. The India Office and the Secretary of State were often lobbied on industrial matters and embarrassing questions might be asked in the House of Commons, especially if troops were used to control strikers. The British labour movement kept a watchful eye on the rights and conditions of its Indian counterpart.[92]

The Swadeshi movement impacted the cotton textile industry directly and labour employed in it indirectly. Imported cloth suffered a setback and production of mill-made coarse cloth increased.

However, by 1922 international competition in the cloth and yarn trade increased. Japan became an active exporter. During the war, 'the import of Japanese yarn and piece goods increased exponentially. After 1918, Japanese yarn of counts 31s to 40s not only gained steadily at the expense of Lancashire but, by the mid-1920s, equalled the total volume of Indian yarn production in this range.' It was superior in quality to the Indian product and could be sold at prices equal to the cost of manufacture of this count of yarn without any allowance for depreciation or profit. Indian industry, never technically up-to-date and dependent on cheap unskilled labour for its technological choice, fell back and never recovered ground. The Japanese imports forced upon the industry a whole range of mill production. In 1922 while the Japanese exports of yarn to China rose steadily that of India fell to about half the level in 1920.[93] This would form the background to labour agitations which developed soon after the economic decline in 1922.

II. 1923–7

Bonds Undone, The Swarajya Party and a Weakened Gandhi

The withdrawal of the Non-Cooperation Movement and Gandhi's imprisonment resulted in disorientation among the participants and considerable disillusionment among the leaders. During the previous two years, the Congress and Khilafat committees and the local bodies that organized satyagraha, often around Kisan Sabha promoted issues, had practically become indistinguishable. For the Hindus, Khilafat was generally interpreted as opposition to foreign rule and rarely in its pan-Islamic significance. Although the Muslims, usually led by their clergy, understood more clearly its importance and were enthused by it the Hindus viewed satyagraha as a morally uplifting engagement in public life, more so because Mahatma Gandhi led the movement and explained it in Hindu religious phrases. Further, for both Hindus and Muslims going to jail and suffering punishments at the hands of tyrannical rulers, demanded moral courage and strength of character. Respect and admiration flowed from all quarters, including the bureaucracy whose diehard members for the first time saw the discipline and forbearance of satyagrahis in action.

At the popular level, people, perhaps for the first time, learnt the importance of the principles of aggregation in politics and unity of purpose

> Satyagraha was a new bonding action and ideology in Indian political life. Under its impetus, the Congress became a new way. A bonding institution functioned compared with its older role as the informal talking-shop of local political notables from restricted areas and social backgrounds. Gandhi was determined that Congress, if it was to be an instrument of Swaraj, must be representative of the whole nation in terms of geography and society, rather than of an educated minority whose politics he believed were denationalizing India. ... Under Gandhi's leadership Congress aspired and succeeded in becoming the representative organization for the whole nation

> and for all the people of India. It became a regular political institution capable of mobilizing masses. These gains outlasted the setback which followed when non-cooperation was given up. But a great deal was lost. Hindu–Muslim amity receded rapidly and gave way as communal riots increased in number and ferocity, reinforcing their separateness. Among Muslim leaders the belief gained that as a religious community the Muslims were a distinct political interest which could not be merged with the aspirations of Hindus. As a result, the first remarkable demonstration of religious unity and as a common political force could never be repeated.[94]

Such prospects steadily diminished as Muslim membership in Congress declined and become minuscule within a few years.

In the meantime, elections under the new Constitution were held, councils were formed and no one, once elected, appeared eager to resign. Moreover, in several provinces, ministers holding transferred subjects found the responsibility of functioning in partly-elected legislatures not just a learning process but also an opportunity to confer tangible benefits on particular sections of society. In Gandhi's absence, leaders like C.R. Das and Motilal Nehru hoisted the banner of loyal dissidence within the Congress on the issue of entry into the councils. It was pointless to stay outside, reject councils and do nothing. There were few takers for Gandhi's programme of spreading the message of khadi, removal of untouchability, promotion of Hindu–Muslim unity and other constructive activities which would take Congress closer to the masses.

Das, elected President of the Congress in 1922, used the occasion to deliver a powerful plea for entry into the councils, if for nothing else, to wreck the Constitution or disrupt normal functioning. As elected members, they would expose the bureaucracy, demand an end to diarchy and push for the establishment of truly responsible governments in the provinces. However, he failed to carry the delegates and the proposal for entry was rejected by a majority. Das resigned from the presidentship and with Motilal Nehru and Tilak's followers, who believed in responsive cooperation floated the Swarajya Party, but without leaving the parent body. Eventually, working within Congress, Das succeeded in winning over the delegates at the next Congress in September 1923. The Swarajists issued their manifesto and contested the elections for the councils which were to reconvene in January 1924.[95]

Gandhi was released on health grounds in 1924. He acquiesced in the decision and conceded an honest and fundamental difference of political perspectives. However, his objections to entry were more principled. First, the elected members would have to take the oath of allegiance which precluded a general policy of obstruction. They could promote constructive programmes, requiring the governments to buy khadi, impose a prohibitive duty on imported cloth, abolish the drink and drug revenue or enforce prohibition of liquor, etc. Second, if they failed, they should be prepared to resign their seats and prepare for civil disobedience.[96] This ruled out a permanent change of course from non-cooperation to responsive cooperation or responsive non-cooperation or some other expression which would admit of participation in the running of government. So, the only option the Swarajists had was to contest the elections and, even if voted to a majority in the House, to refrain from taking the oath of office and accept ministerships in the government, et cetera. This meant that only one option was left, and that was to cause obstruction and produce a failed system, which did not go down well with Gandhi.[97]

The second round of elections for the Central Legislative Assembly at Delhi and the provincial councils were held in November–December 1923. The main contest was between the Swarajist and the Liberals. The Central Assembly comprised 145 members, of whom 40 were nominated. The Swarajists won 45 seats, the remaining were taken by the Liberals and independents. A coalition party was formed by the Swarajists with several independents and named the

Nationalist Party. In the provinces, only in the Central Province did the Swarajists secure a clear majority. In Bombay and UP, they did not constitute the largest group; in Bengal they did, but were either weak or very weak in Madras, Punjab, Bihar and Orissa.

Their political doctrine was that the new Constitution was an obstruction to Swaraj and they must resist it. They would reject the votable parts of the budget to deny ministers their salaries and the bureaucracy of resources for their departments. The Liberals pointed out that these tactics were futile and would not harm the government. In fact, if the popular element was weakened, the government would revert to the old bureaucratic system and continue to rule with tyranay. Actually, several positive gains were claimed by them:

> During the years 1924-26, the Swarajists successfully opposed all proposals for additional taxation and 'unpopular legislation'. They successfully fought for reduction of taxation and had reduced the tax on salt, abolished the cotton excise duty and the import duty on sulphur. They passed resolutions on questions of national importance: on improvement to the condition of labour; protection to native industries; removal of racial distinction in the railways; grievances of Indians abroad; and subordinate services. They successfully fought for the repeal of several repressive laws, i.e. the Bengal Regulation III of 1818; the Criminal Law Amendment Act of 1908; the Bengal Ordinance I of 1924; the Bengal and Madras State Prisoners Act of 1850 and the Prevention of Seditions Meetings Act of 1921.[98]

The Swarajists could reasonably claim that they had prevented the misuse of legislature by the bureaucracy against Indian interests. The colonial government had already moved at least half-way to act as the nationalists wanted on a number of issues, to provide more protection to labour and discriminatory protection to industries. However, there was no response to the political demands, such as an end to diarchy, the convening of a round table conference, speeding the progress towards dominion status and several others. Politically, the Swarajists at the Legislative Assembly demonstrated that the voice of elected members was easily disregarded since any budgetary proposal or bill presented by the government and rejected by the House could be certified by the Viceroy and duly enacted. The same experience was often repeated in the provinces where the Swarajists were able to block grants or bills. These were then exposed as a sham and an obstruction toward Swaraj. Yet, council entry had its charm and soon it showed up as dissidence surfaced and gathered strength.

C.R. Das was the chief spokesman and unquestioned leader of the party. He followed Gandhi but did not subscribe to the various tenets of Gandhism. He combined practical pragmatism with lofty idealism and knew the art of making political compromises to achieve practical unity in action, and he demonstrated his skills in Bengal. He died suddenly in June 1925 and left a great void which Motilal Nehru and other distinguished leaders could not fill.

By this time, the policy of obstruction was getting tiresome and the coalition partners in the Nationalist Party began to express genuine doubts about its continued usefulness. Leaders of the eminence of Madan Mohan Malviya and Lajpat Rai saw that tactics of indiscriminate opposition were counter-productive and were hurting Hindu interests, more so as the government was eager to rebuild political support and responsiveness with the Muslims. The Swarajists failed to realize the significance of the counter viewpoint.

Among the Swarajists, the demand for a further change in policy towards responsive cooperation gained strength and, in 1925, the change was in place. V.J. Patel accepted office and was elected Speaker of the Assembly while Motilal Nehru joined the Skeen Committee appointed to examine faster Indianization of the army. V.J. Patel's election was solidly opposed by the government benches, but once elected he accepted the position and soon commanded the respect of all sides. In the Central Provinces (CP), the governor offered S.B. Tambe, leader of the Swarajya Party, membership of the Executive Council, which he accepted. This was in furtherance of Tilak's line of responsive cooperation but great criticism followed. This faction had rejected the established policy of boycott and the party suffered a split. The right wing stood for responsive cooperation and that all positions of power, influence and constructive responsibility should be taken for the good of the country. Most Maharashtrian members supported Tilak's line and would not yield to the official Swarajists' mandate.

Later in 1926, a new party, the Responsive Cooperation Party was announced and it contested the forthcoming elections on a separate mandate. In September, Madan Mohan Malviya formed the Independent Congress Party to contest the elections in cooperation with the Responsivists. Now the Swarajya Party was split into three. Lajpat Rai resigned from the Swarajya Party in disgust and joined hands with Malviya. Meanwhile, sensing the danger of splits in the Congress which the allurement of council entry had created, the Congress, in December 1925, decided that the legislatures be boycotted. In March, the Swarajists walked out of the Assembly and the same scene was enacted in the provincial councils. However, for them it was only a temporary withdrawal because later in the year they contested the elections again and, as expected, they performed far below the level of the previous elections. Though Gandhi did not approve of council entry, he virtually gave up the fight. There was a strong minority in the Congress which was no longer willing to follow his methods and doctrines. Gandhi accepted the facts of politics and sought practical compromises with those opposed to him.

In fact, Gandhi had little to offer. Congressmen had found an opportunity to engage in political action and believed that the councils provided worthwhile forums to hone their political skills and advance the cause of Swaraj. However, these were years of stagnation, and politics in the country was changing course. Moreover, most of them did not honestly believe that Gandhi's constructive programme, though entirely deserving of support, merited all their time and energy, nor that it was a necessary step to Swaraj. In fact, the Swarajists put council entry to good purpose. 'One was the problem of constitutional advance leading to self-government; the second of civil liberties, release of political prisoners, and repeal of repressive laws; and third of the development of indigenous industries.'[99]

On the other hand, the government played political games by creating dissension among the nationalists, and almost broke the ranks of the Swarajists. It also succeeded in separating the Muslims from the Hindus. The Muslims' cause was close to British interests. Though the Hindus accepted nationalism as their political creed, two opinions had already emerged on the matter of Hindu interests. The Hindu Mahasabha which had remained dormant, found new leaders within the Congress and revived. Madan Mohan Malviya and Lajpat Rai lent their voices to the Mahasabha. In 1925, a new organization, the Rashtriya Swayamsevak Sangh (RSS) was founded to create solidarity, unity and pride among the Hindus. The major trigger was the Moplah uprising and the savagery they had unleashed on the Hindus.

There was a string of Hindu–Muslim riots in which the Hindus, though often a majority community, came out worse. Hindu leaders saw their co-religionists not only hopelessly divided and incapable of uniting, but also lacking in martial qualities and given to cowardice. Gandhi studied the subject with great care and came to the conclusion that, while the Muslim was a bully, the Hindu was a coward, and this is what the riots showed.[100] An opinion had formed amongst the Hindus that Gandhi's championing of Khilafat contributed to strengthening the Muslims' aggressive trait. It gave the Muslim clergy a prestige they never had before and the awakened Muslim viewed Hindu nationalism as his main obstacle.

In 1924, the Muslim League, too, revived and in slow but

sure steps its right-wing leaders worked to restore mutual understanding with the British government and created a mandate to safeguard separate Muslim interests. Muslim leaders who joined the councils found it advantageous to administer transferred subjects in cooperation with the governors to promote schemes to spread education, health services and local government run services, no doubt for the benefit of the entire society but, more particularly, for their more backward fellow Muslims. The councils deepened political competition, and members of legislatures found themselves organizing and grouping along communal lines.[101]

The British played the communal card with skill. In 1924, the government told the Assembly, in response to Motilal Nehru's resolution for an early revision of the 1919 Act, that granting dominion status would mean entrusting the interests of the minorities to the majority, implying that it was their responsibility to protect them. Elections held at the end of 1926 for the councils showed that the Muslim electorate had mainly elected right wing reactionary elements who stood for cooperating with the British. The spirit of the Lucknow Pact was practically dead. Hindu–Muslim understanding was already under severe strain and suffered terrible jolts by the many riots that occurred in 1925 and 1926, particularly the assassination of Swami Shradhanand by a Muslim fanatic in 1926.

Instead of a united nationalist block, there were three political elements in the Assembly and the councils, that is, the Hindu Swarajists, the Muslims with a communal outlook and others including the responsive cooperators. This composition steadied the British position and they could more freely administer the 1919 Act with the support of ministers in charge of transferred subjects. The government no longer had to face defeat of its bills and budget proposals. It could count on the support of Muslim members, who for all intents and purposes sacrificed nationalist ideas to communal interests and took the view that 'Swaraj without communal representation and adequate safeguarding of Muslim interests was not worth having. On the other hand, even progressive nationalist Hindus firmly refused to have Swaraj at the cost of conceding excessive and unreasonable concessions to communal demands which cut at the very root of nationalism.'[102]

This fundamental difference confirmed the British view that India was not an entity but more a geographical space carved out by history for India's many religions and races to inhabit and that they would fight among themselves should the British withdraw by granting dominion status. Hindus and Muslims would fight it out for supremacy. India was not a nation. The British viewed the nationalists as a menace and used repression on them, along with favouritism towards Muslims, and other political tactics to weaken them. Yet, the demand for Swaraj could be logically pursued only on the basis of unity.

The 1919 reforms had effectively undermined any structure of nationalist unity by releasing other more latent forces in society. Judith Brown refers to provincialization of politics.

> Ironically there was occurring a 'provincialization' of politics, just at the time when opposition to the imperial regime was being voiced in the name of the Indian nation more powerfully than before. These were the two faces of the coin of political change, economic and social change, and the Raj's devolution of power through the reformed constitutional structures, generated deeper and wider political ambition and fear, focusing much of it on the new provincial structures of power.[103]

At the district level, new laws created elected bodies and, for the first time, local self-governments started functioning. Along with these the communal element also made progress. Separate electorates at the municipal level produced strong resentments.[104] In Bengal and Punjab, communal competition become stark and ominous. In UP, the land holders were the largest single group in the Council and mostly defended their landed interests.[105] For the nationalists, the principal focus of Swaraj-centred agitations dissipated owing to the rise of communalism. Provincial leaders like Fazlul Haq in Bengal masterminded communal politics, and the Congress challenge in the absence of C.R. Das never equalled his confrontationist style and charismatic appeal to the Muslim peasantry. He mobilized support around his newly founded Bengal Muslim Party which declared Congress to be a Hindu organization. In Punjab, the government found a strong ally in the landed interests. 'Both had equal status in maintaining the status quo. The British bolstered their interests and accommodated their claims in constitutional arrangements, because they were the chief source of recruitment to the army, made substantial financial contribution to the imperial coffers, and served as the instrument through which the sarkar exercised its authority in far flung areas.'[106]

Wherever feasible, the British formed an axis with the communal and landed interests and felt more secure. Gandhi agonized and despaired of politics. He decided to keep out of communal politics which had become a 'hopeless tangle'. The Hindus' latent communal consciousness became a discernible sub-stream in the nationalist movement and was justified as a natural reaction to the withdrawal of Muslims into separatist politics. Gandhi engaged more fully than ever before in propagating *charkha,* khadi, abolition of untouchability and Hindu–Muslim unity as much as was within his means.[107]

The Muslim League was a divided house. Nationalism still burnt bright in those who took part in the Non-Cooperation movement and had a rapport with the Congressmen with a broader outlook in life. The Khilafat cause over, the League devoted itself to constructive dialogue with the British as well as the Congress on the constitutional arrangement that would protect Muslim interests either before or on the attainment of dominion status. This was a controversial subject since Muslim interests in the Muslim majority provinces were entirely different from the provinces where they were in a minority.

There was also the question of the relative sharing of power between the Centre and the provinces. There was no support for a strong Centre, and the idea of a federation found ready acceptance with 'the functions of the central government being confined to such matters only as are of joint or common concern'. Each province should have full and complete autonomy. On the issue of representation in the legislature and all other elected bodies the League asked for a guarantee of 'an adequate and effective representation to minorities in every province subject to the essential proviso that no majority shall be reduced to a minority or even to equality'.[108] The other divisive issue was of joint electorates versus separate electorates. In March 1927, in a conference of Hindu and Muslim leaders at Delhi, 'a manifesto was issued in which the Muslim League accepted joint electorate with reservation of seats on a population basis in the provinces and with one-third of the total number of seats in the Central Legislature'. However, the League's leadership split on the issue, though the Hindu Mahasabha leaders had accepted this principle. The Punjab faction in the Muslim League, led by Sir Mohammad Shafi, broke ranks and they pressed their opposition to joint electorates.[109] They won in December 1928.

Once the Shafi league abandoned the idea of joint electorates the other demands made by the League, that is, separation of Sind from Bombay and introducing reforms in the North-West Frontier Province and Baluchistan were also questioned. Logically, there was no connection between an important principle and those of Sind, NWFP and Baluchistan. The premise was that in these provinces the Muslims were in a large majority, yet they would grant the same concessions to the Hindus which the latter would to the minorities in provinces where they were in a clear majority. Jinnah made it clear that the entire proposal had to be accepted, and it would not do to accept one part and reject the other. The matter of joint or separate electorates was directed towards an end.

> The end in view is that Mussalmans should be made to feel that they are secure and safeguarded against any act of oppression on the part of the majority, and that they need not fear that during the transitional stage towards the fullest development of national government the majority would be in a position to oppress or tyrannise the minority, as majorities are prone to do in other countries.[110]

The message failed as neither the Hindus nor the Muslims were sufficiently secure to move forward and enter into an abiding pact. In the end, the conclusion was that the Muslim must preserve his separate identity and not merge with the Hindu majority because joint electorates would result in an 'unequal combination, disadvantageous to the weaker side'.

The idea of giving up separate electorates was impracticable under the existing conditions. There was also the problem of representation of Sikhs in the Punjab who wanted it on a higher scale than their share in population. Under the 1919 Act the Sikhs already enjoyed the status of a separate interest with a corresponding separate electorate. This matter was left open to further negotiations but one which the League leadership did not systematically follow through. The Hindu leaders added a further dimension to the principle of joint electorates; in view of their strong economic positions in Punjab and Bengal, it was proposed that on the expiry of a fixed period of transition the system of joint or mixed electorates should be modified in consideration of such matters as voting strength and taxation.

It was on these criteria that the eligibility of inclusion in the voters' list was determined under the 1919 Act. These were treated as given, or as weighty considerations for determining the voting strength of each community. The Viceroy correctly judged that merely short-term political calculations had gone in the making of Delhi proposals, and if they failed, the Muslim leaders would attribute it to Hindu intransigence. Instead of narrowing the gulf it had widened it, and 'the eternal question of communal strife' was nowhere near resolution. 'The strain is undiminished and at any moment therefore we must continue to expect trouble'.[111] Khaliquzzaman later said: 'Had once joint electorates been brought into the Constitution it would have been impossible for the Muslims to secure Pakistan, because democracy was like a creeper which, if allowed to grow uncontrolled envelops every branch of political life.'[112]

The princes saw in the reforms a threat to their sovereignty and became apprehensive that, with further devolution of power to the elected representatives at the Centre and the provinces, the Crown may one day pass on imperial paramountcy, which was acquired by conquest and made secure by treaties, to the elected government and they would be left without any protection. They perceived a new dimension to politics in India and thought it opportune to open a fresh dialogue with the Viceroy on several issues. Following up on Lord Minto's idea to create a consulting chamber of princes, and use their power and influence to buttress colonial rule, the 1919 reforms led to the creation of a Chamber of Princes in 1921. The Viceroy was to preside over it when it met once a year. In his absence, an elected chancellor could preside. Not all princes joined this body; the larger ones stayed away since they were more certain of their rights under the treaties. However, the medium-sized princes used the chamber not only to define and protect their common interests, 'but also as the medium through which the demands for the limitation of paramountcy should be codified and secured'.[113] They drew up a list of 23 matters of internal administration on which the British government had interfered. In fact the paramount power had the power to depose a ruler if his conduct was met with strong disapproval. However the only issue on which the Viceroy concurred with the princes was to prevent the dissemination of printed matter calculated to incite disaffection against the princes. The Viceroy had to certify the bill to get its enactment in view of opposition in the Legislative Assembly.[114]

The Nizam of Hyderabad had opted out of the Chamber but found it expedient to raise the matter of paramountcy as well as the future of Berar in a strong representation to the Viceroy. Lord Reading reacted to it with an equally forceful affirmation of the supremacy of the paramount power going far beyond the terms of the treaty of 1800. The Nizam's claim to Berar was rejected on the grounds that the large Hindu majority of Berar was opposed to being placed under the rule of a Muslim sovereign. Moreover, Berar was part of the Central Province which was a seat, first of the Swarajists and later of the responsive cooperators and the Hindu Mahasabha. The Nizam had imagined the worst scenarios on Berar and 'Reading's refusal to restore Berar provoked the Nizam to challenge the supremacy of the Crown over the administration of any of his territories. His assertion was that paramountcy was limited to foreign affairs only. This was firmly rejected.'[115]

Far from acting as a counterpoise to the Congress, the princes were engaged in a more basic quarrel over respective rights with the Viceroy. The Nizam directly and all the bigger princes indirectly, were told that no ruler could negotiate with the British government on an equal footing. The British government enjoyed all the rights of paramountcy, whether ceded under the treaties or not, to decide all disputes solely at its discretion. However, the quarrel did result in the appointment of the Butler Committee in 1927 to review all connected matters and give advice on the matter of the fear, that unlimited paramountcy may one day result in their being subordinated to democratic British India and that the Crown would abandon their responsibility towards protecting their legitimate interests. Later, the questions were reviewed again and more basic reforms proposed.

Gandhi's Non-Cooperation Movement produced an unexpected affect in the dormancy in terrorist activities. In fact, several revolutionaries were won over by Gandhi's charisma and their ranks had thinned. Moreover, public support for them was withdrawn as people identified themselves with the agitation for Swaraj. However, following its suspension and alongside the Swarajya Party's obstructionist tactics in the councils the terrorist revolutionary activity also revived, mainly in Bengal and UP. In 1924, an Englishman, mistaken for the police commissioner, was murdered by a terrorist, Gopinath Saha. He was subsequently arrested, tried and hanged, and a wave of sympathy for his heroism and self-sacrifice swept over the Congressmen who, nonetheless, also joined hands to reject terrorism as futile and unacceptable. A resolution praising Gopinath Saha's courage and self-sacrifice was adopted by the Bengal Provincial Conference, and later C.R. Das raised it at the AICC meeting but met with more principled opposition.

In 1924, at the instance of the Bengal government, the Centre passed a new ordinance arming the executive with powers similar to the Defence of India Act and it bore striking similarity to the Rowlatt Act. The ordinance was an attack on civil rights and created deep apprehensions among many nationalists, particularly the Liberals, that if the obstructionist tactics were not ended the reforms may be suspended and the country once again placed under autocratic bureaucratic rule. Under the Ordinance, the government raided Congress offices, conducted house searches and arrested a large number of terrorists along with several Swarajists, even members of the provincial council.[116] In UP, the organization which promoted revolutionary politics was called the Hindustan Socialist Republican Association and it spread its influence in the Punjab. It produced several notable revolutionaries in the following decade. However, the larger part of India stayed out of their reach and influence, though in Bengal, Punjab and UP it continued to draw admiration and sympathy. Gandhi opposed terrorism as totally wrong and utterly unacceptable as a political doctrine and steadily under cut their support base. However, there is no denying that the two streams of nationalist agitation, one non-violent and the other violent, ran parallel to each other for a number of years.[117]

A small communist cadre had emerged in the early 1920s and they believed that Gandhi's spirituality was the political mask behind which the class interests of the capitalists and landed interests had organized themselves and found it convenient to use the language of religion and confused ideas of tradition and revivalism to misdirect the masses. On their part, the revolutionary youth failed to understand that terrorist strikes though productive of spectacular effects were no match to the resources of the violent state. On the pretext of suppressing terrorist activities, the oppressive state might give up the restraints of the new Constitution and let the bureaucracy and military deal with the nationalist forces. However, to the revolutionary youth it was shameful that a handful of foreigners should rule India. They held India in contempt and believed it did injustice to the masses. There was no way the imperialist rule could be terminated except by concerted violence against its perpetrators. Ram Prasad 'Bismill', who took part in a train decoity at Kakori near Lucknow, shouted while being taken towards the gallows, 'I wish the downfall of the British Empire'.[118] It is from the ranks of underground revolutionary organizations, like the Anushilan Samity and the Hindustan Socialist Republican Association (Army), that future leaders of communist and other Marxist parties emerged. They respected, indeed revered Gandhi, but never accepted his beliefs and methods.

Independently of Gandhi, Annie Besant pursued her agenda of Home Rule, now concretized as dominion status and as a unit of the British Commonwealth. On the tenet that the framing of the constitution should be done in India, she proceeded with the task of framing a bill for the purpose. At the All-Parties Conference held at Delhi in January 1925, she circulated the proposal of the bill among the participants. In February 1926, Annie Besant attended a private conference of about 40 members of the Central Assembly to consider the draft bill, called the Commonwealth of India Bill and it received wide support, including from Jinnah. Earlier in 1925, she had already received support and encouragement from C.R. Das just before his death. Gandhi encouraged her but without accepting sponsorship of the bill.

In April 1926, a large body of liberals and Congressmen agreed to become signatories to the bill. The sponsors said,

> We, the signatories to the present proposals, remain in our respective organizations, but unite in a common effort to obtain Indian freedom. We define Swaraj as full Dominion Status as claimed by the resolution of the National Congress of 1914. We accept responsive cooperation wherever useful for advancing the interests of the country, and all forms of constitutional agitation against proposals inimical to these. We support the Commonwealth of India Bill, now on the official list of the Labour Party in the British Parliament and recommend that any amendments thought desirable by the Council of the coalition parties, to be formed in consequence of the manifesto, should be sent to the Secretary of the parliamentary Executive Committee of the Labour Party, to be moved when the bill is in Committee of the Houses.[119]

The parliamentary Labour Party examined the Bill clause by clause, and supported it. It was read in the House of Commons and it was the first time a constitutional bill on India had been moved in the British Parliament, and Annie Besant deserved much credit for it.

Hopes were aroused in India when Ramsay Macdonald, the Leader of the Opposition, said on 2 July 1928: 'I hope that within a period of months rather than years, there will be a new Dominion added to the Commonwealth of our nations, a Dominion of another race that will find self-respect as an equal within this Commonwealth.'[120] However, nothing came of it and the initiative was not followed up. In fact, the Swarajya Party was fully engaged in a similar drive at the Central Assembly to secure the passage of its resolution asking the government, to take steps, to revise the 1919 Act, but the Labour Party government rejected this demand. Instead, a committee was appointed to review the working of the Act. This was about as far as the government was prepared to go. In the UK, the Secretary of State announced that, 'there will be, there can be, no reconsideration, until we see everywhere among the responsible leaders of Indian thought, evidence of a sincere and genuine desire to cooperate with us, in making the best of the existing institutions'.[121] The new Viceroy, inaugurating the Assembly in January 1927 was quite outspoken on how the British Parliament was likely to view the obstructionist methods employed in thwarting the work of the Assembly, that the application of Western constitutional methods in India might be mistaken.

Given these attitudes on a swifter advance toward responsible government, the announcement of a Parliamentary Commission headed by Sir John Simon in 8 November 1927 came as a total surprise. Political life in India was then marred by inertia. There were communal riots mostly on trivial matters, but they repeatedly showed the void in the essential unity; the people, needed to struggle for Swaraj and that Swaraj was a day dream. At the all-India level, the communal question dominated political discourse with everyone agreeing that genuine progress toward responsible government both at the Centre and the provinces was contingent on the leaders' ability to forge workable solutions to the pressing questions. The abrupt manner of appointment of a constitutional commission could not be construed to mean that parliament was either coerced or convinced of the need for setting the guide posts that led to Swaraj.

The Conservative government advanced the date to eliminate any possibility of the next government, which might be led by the Labour Party, doing so. It wanted to ensure that its verdict would closely fit its perceptions on the next round of reforms. The purpose was to retain full control over India on the straight grounds of imperialist-cum-racist logic that if dominion status was conceded, the next logical step could be full independence and this too would have to be ceded. In consequence, without India, the British Empire would cease, and Britain's position in the international system of balance of power would rapidly decline. This was anathema and had to be ruled out. Alternatively, the Tory government would not grant political legitimacy to Indian nationalism but would prefer to deal with the communal question and other identified interests as politically legitimate and grant them representation in elective bodies and government employment. This would provide the needed incentives to India's diverse interest groups and religious communities to manifest their roles and seek support from the alien government as their true well-wishers.

The government had already extended the principle of the 1919 Act of communal electorates to recruitment in government services. Perhaps this would mollify the Muslim and the Sikh interests and weaken Hindu nationalism further. Moreover, communal antagonism and other animosities, racial, ethnic and caste-based, were fundamental to India's numerous peoples, living as homogeneous groups while coexisting with others. Given this complex reality, there was no need to consider the 'the unsubstantial ghost of nationalism.' The British would no doubt respect the electoral verdict but, as Birkenhead viewed it, there was the greater responsibility towards the very large mass of unrepresented people, as the guardian of their interests.[122]

The appointment of the all-White seven member commission to review the progress made under the 1919 Act was received with total disbelief, though rumours were rife in the Assembly on such a possibility for several months and produced universal rejection due to its improper mode and unilateral nature. What the commission learnt and reported on India was meant to be an affront, an exercise of the imperial prerogative which rested in the Imperial Parliament, of unfettered power to understand on its terms of reference, what the commission learnt and reported on India. The decision was final and nothing which the British government later said by way of clarifications amounted to much. The commission was charged with the responsibility 'to inquire into the working of the Indian Constitution and to consider the desirability of establishing, extending, modifying or restricting the degree of responsible government'. The position of the Indians, who were assured a full hearing and due consideration, was that of petitioners and witnesses.[123]

The total omission of Indians was not just a psychological error of the first order, as averred to by Burke and Qurashi, but a systematic and purposive slight. Indians had already expressed their viewpoint, though still engaged in developing the basic principles on which they may produce an agreed draft of their future constitution. In the British perspective, the possibility of extending the reforms was as much on the cards as restricting them, and a freeze could also be considered. In fact, Sir Sankaran Nair had introduced a resolution in the Council of State on 16 March 1927, 'recommending to the Government that no further step towards responsible government be taken until Hindus and Mohammedans agreed to dispense with separate electorates'.[124]

Reforms and Economic Policy and Notable Changes in Economic Regime

The economic consequences of devolution of power from the Secretary of State for India to the Viceroy-in-Council started showing results in 1922. Following the grant of fiscal autonomy to India, the government announced a new policy of 'discriminating protection' in 1923. Under this policy, the government would appoint ad hoc tariff boards to examine the applications of industries for tariff protection. The first applicant was TISCO which was under great distress owing to low prices of imported steel. Worldwide, the production of steel was rising in excess of demand and prices of imported steel fell below the cost of production in India. The Tatas moved an application for 33⅓ per cent duty on all imported steel products. The Tariff Board granted a lower rate of protection of 15 per cent ad valorem on imported steel and 10 per cent on imported steel rail in 1924. It was estimated that at an average price of Rs. 180 per tonne TISCO should be able to recover costs and earn a fair profit. In addition, bounties were granted on steel rails. The company also had to rein in costs. The cost of production had peaked in 1922–3. It rose every year from 1919–20 but started declining in 1923–4, and in 1925–6 it had fallen significantly by about 20–25 per cent or more.[125] Rise in wage cost was a primary factor in raising the cost of production. Moreover, the strike in 1922–3 adversely impacted output per man. TISCO had undergone a high cost modernization of the plant but, in 1923, the same blast furnace which in India was priced at Rs. 5.575 million sold in the US at Rs. 4.310 million, and it was the same for other major mills and equipments. The advantages when the rate of exchange was 2S a rupee vanished as the rupee declined to lower levels, made worse when several European countries depreciated their currencies to find markets for excess production. The company complained of dumping of steel in India, while emphasizing the military importance of the steel it produced for the defence of the British Empire east of Suez. However, tariff protection was granted on the prevailing exchange rates, which meant that as European currencies depreciated further TISCO needed additional protection, in 1924 itself. The government granted a fiscal subsidy not exceeding Rs. 5 million to help the company tide over the immediate crisis. The Steel Industry (Protection) Act, 1924 granted protection for three years. The Swarajya Party took credit for this enactment, though TISCO had to lobby hard to get the votes for the Bill.

In April 1926, the government asked the Tariff Board to look into the conditions of the industry again and recommend appropriate protection. As a result, a new element in the tariff structure was introduced. Additional duties were imposed on imports from Europe, but exempted Britain. In 1927, a new steel enactment valid for seven years was adopted and the Indian iron and steel industry was saved from ruination.[126] However, right up to the Second World War the steel industry's need for protection continued without a break. In 1924, the two companies, TISCO and the United Steel Corporation, told the Tariff Board that 'without protection they would be unable to raise the capital for their enterprises'.[127] India had a comparative advantage in pig iron production but at the second stage other costs intervened, of which coal was important. The company could secure coal at a lower price from 1925 when the long-term contract for its supply at the higher contracted rate ended.

The availability of skilled and trained manpower was also a major problem. The expatriate staff was costlier, adding Rs. 2 per tonne to the cost of finished steel. They could be replaced only as trained manpower in India increased; TISCO thus set up the Jamshedpur Technical Institute. The semi-skilled and unskilled workers were cheaper but relatively inefficient and were employed in larger numbers than strictly required. Overall, the company reduced working costs in 1926–7 by more than the Tariff Board had demanded and still further in 1927–8. However, the company was over capitalized and overheads could not be reduced till it produced at the rated capacity.[128]

While in steel India faced tough competition from European producers, in cotton textiles it was from Japan. Rapid development of cotton textiles in Japan began in 1894 but it was able to oust Indian yarn, first from the Japanese market and later from China. In the early 1920s, Japanese competition gained at India's expense in the Far Eastern and domestic markets. The cotton textile industry experienced a decline from 1922 onwards. In 1924, the Bombay mill owners felt that due to severe erosion of profits they would not be able to pay the war time bonus, and a two-month strike followed. In 1922–3, while imports from the UK fell somewhat, those from Japan rose and this process continued for another decade.[129]

> Japan became a far more serious competitor of Indian mills than Lancashire because: (i) many Indian mills enjoyed an advantage over Lancashire mills in respect of wage cost per unit of output, whereas the position was reversed with respect to the Japanese mills, and (ii) Japan also sold the coarser varieties of cloth in which the Indian mills specialized before 1930.[130]

The Japanese feat is inexplicable except in terms of efficiency and drive for success, otherwise, it was way behind all the major cotton textile producing countries. Between 1923 and 1927, 'Great Britain possessed 35.0 per cent of the World's spindles and 25.3 per cent of world's looms; USA, 22.7 per cent and 24.5 per cent, Germany, 6.6 per cent and 7.7 per cent, France 5.8 per cent and 5.8 per cent; India, 5.3 per cent and 4.9 per cent, and Japan, 3.5 per cent and 2.1 per cent'.[131] In 1925, the Indian cotton textile industry was reeling before Japanese imports. The solution was to cut costs and improve competitiveness. Part of the burden was passed on to labour and, in addition, the mill owners demanded protection and abolition of excise duty. In 1922, the general rate of import duty was raised from 11 per cent to 15 per cent, while the duty on yarn imports was at 5 per cent. The government decided to help by suspending excise duty on cotton piece goods in 1925 and abolishing it in 1926. The excise duty had caused much political trouble earlier; the Assembly had refused to grant an additional countervailing duty from 3.5 per cent to 7 per cent due to political reasons. Now cotton piece goods were totally free from excise duty.

In 1927, the Tariff Board conducted an inquiry into the cotton textile industry. Japan was faulted for unfair competition. It had an advantage partly because it worked the double shift system and partly on account of employing women and children in the night shift. The choice of remedies was a bounty to the mills or an additional import duty. The government was disinclined to raise the import duty above 15 per cent, ostensibly to protect consumers' interests, but the more pertinent consideration was the interest of British exporters. The other consideration was that a protective duty on cotton textiles would impact customs revenue and adversely affect government finances. This was considered a fallacious argument. It was also pointed out that with increased production by mills and the imports the total cloth available for consumption during 1924–5 to 1928–9 surpassed the level before the war by a small margin (from the average of 3,582 million yards to 3,668 million yards); it was a beneficial development which should not be halted or reversed.[132] Yet, the Bombay mills reported losses in 1924 and 1925.

The Tariff Board found that the mills which produced only yarn suffered more, while the situation was better for the composite mills. The Ahmedabad mills continued to pay dividends, while the upcountry mills actually expanded between 1922 and 1926 when the Bombay mills were in the throes of a depression. It was also noted that the removal of excise duty on piece goods had not helped much and the competition of Japanese imports remained unabated. The main reason for Japanese success lay in its commercial organization which was exceptionally efficient. 'The large importers of raw cotton are also the principal exporters of piece goods, and are directly or indirectly interested in actual manufacture. Moreover, manufacturers concentrate on standard lines, thus obtaining the advantage of mass production to a high degree.'[133]

In 1927, the government opted for a mild protective duty on yarn within the range of 30s and 40s. However, the deeper problems which kept Indian industry at a low level of efficiency remained the greater obstacle to progress. Bagchi cites labour, its illiteracy, poor standards of physique together with the power of the unions as a competitive obstacle, which could not possibly be dealt with through protective tariffs. Additionally, the effect of imports favouring exchange standard at 1s6d to a rupee, against which the Indian capitalist class strongly but fruitlessly argued, should also weigh in the weakened long-term thrust of this industry for modernization and higher efficiency. Morris says that the industry could not reduce either wages or other costs because of the inflated capital burden of the post-war boom and 'the speculative mentality of Indian entrepreneurs. Unable to meet foreign competition, companies failed, mills were dismantled, great managing agencies collapsed. Always the emphasis has been on the burden of foreign competition, in this period

Japanese rather than British, with the analysis focused on the struggle for ever higher and more permanent protective tariffs.'[134]

This sums up the position over the inter-war period. 'The British industry was affected much more harshly than the Indian, and Japan's mills achieved their considerable gains only because many inefficient units were squeezed out and the industry underwent a major reorganization.'[135] Problems of industry got fused with the particular patterns of economic growth in different countries. Japan was comparable to UK but India stood apart despite its industrial development.

Problems of the low equilibrium trap were witnessed in several engineering industries which applied for protection and were inquired into by the Tariff Board. Most of them were dependent on local supplies of pig iron and steel and looked for secure demand from within India. In 1923, the government seemed to have projected an expenditure of Rs. 1,500 million on rehabilitation of the railways over the next five years. The Stores Purchase Rules could be relaxed if there were manufacturers of railway equipment in India who could compete with British companies. However, they had to be there with considerable experience to hold out the promise that in cost and quality, equipment manufactured in India, would meet the railways' requirements.

It was observed in 1923 that, on a recent tender for 3,132 wagons, the lowest Indian tender was 50 per cent higher than the British one. Clearly the company was in need of protection just to survive. In another example of attempted import substitution on private account without direct government sponsorship or support, the import price of bridgework was Rs. 250 per tonne while in India the average cost was Rs. 310. The government had already raised the revenue duty on all iron and steel products and raw materials from 2.5 per cent to 10 per cent in 1922, but manufacturers of bridgework needed protection on an added scale. The Indian Standard Wagon Co. 'found that it could not reduce costs to a sufficient extent to compete with British producers if it could not produce at least 1,500 wagons per annum, and it would not reach that target if it did not receive special terms from the railways in the initial stage'. The Railway Board refused to grant special terms.[136] The firm could not reach the breakeven points solely on the basis of Indian demand and the Tariff Board recommended bounties in place of protective duties over a period of five years; the bounty declined as production increased.

The problem of inter-industry linkages and macroeconomic imbalances impacting basic industries was also soon revealed. On the recommendations of the Inchcape Committee on Retrenchment, the government decided to cut capital expenditure on the railways and their requirements declined for the foreseeable period. Given the gap in the minimum scale of production of 200 locomotives per year, the railways' demand could not hold out hope for more than 180 locomotives, and the Tariff Board declined the request for protection. The Indian company, managed by a British company specializing in locomotives and wagons, could not possibly carry on because the problem of scale was further compounded by the existence of three gauges in India. On insufficient scale and high costs, which could not be lowered due to restrictions of low demand, protective tariffs, by themselves, would not have kept the manufacturers survive market uncertainties. However, in tinplates protective tariffs worked because the company, a subsidiary of Burmah Oil Co., was already on a long-term contract with TISCO, so the policy of inter-connected tariff protection and bounties worked.[137]

The jute industry continued to thrive on the strength of its exports and strict collective control over production. In 1922–3 the IJMA mills had 25,000 hessian looms and 16,400 sacking looms. These were the result of continuous advance in the last two decades. In 1927–8 these numbers rose to 31,000 and 19,200 respectively. In fact, expansion continued till 1930–1 when due to the onset of the Depression it ceased and some reduction in capacity took place. The total number of people employed in the IJMA and other mills correspondingly rose from 321,296 in 1922–3 to 335804, while the peak was reached at 343,868 people in 1928–9. The total value of exports of jute manufacturers shows a rise from 1922–3 till 1928–9 and thereafter they fell and lost half of their market by 1933–4.[138]

The industry complained of low labour efficiency which was not in accordance with the technical efficiency of the plants and the general organization of the industry as a whole. On the other hand, 'the method of recruitment of labour by "sirdars", who thereby obtain a strong financial hold over the workers', militated against progressive management. Yet, the advantage with the Indian mills over Dundee factories was that the manufacturing costs were lower in India.[139] By 1930, this advantage began to vanish. The industry prospered with the growth in the volume of international trade and during this period worked 54 hours a weak, thereby balancing its output with the demand. However, it dodged the question of long-term efficiency and international competitiveness of jute as a packing material and slowly lost the advantage to its competitors.

The coal industry reached peak production in 1919 and stabilized at that level. There were far too many companies with limited finances working the coal mines. They worked on uncertain profitability as is implied by the fact that nearly half the 132 coal companies which were quoted declared no dividend. The companies employed cheap, unskilled labour on shallow mining and showed low pithead prices of coal. In 1922 and 1923, the war time restrictions on exports were removed but the industry failed to regain its markets; indeed, in 1925, foreign coal was competing effectively with the Indian in Bombay and Karachi. It also faced competition from oil fuel and hydroelectricity. The industry needed protection but the government was not impressed and, instead, referred the technical questions of quality, cost of transport and other matters to an expert coal committee which reported in 1925. The Committee recommended that measures should be adopted to check rising costs, improve organization and reduce cost of transporting coal, for example by increasing the rebate by railways on exports.[140] Indian coal could not be satisfactorily transported to the west coast owing to lack of proper transport facilities and failed to compete in consuming markets at a distance from eastern India, where the coal mines were located. The industry experienced distress as the cost of mining rose, resulting in higher prices while the market fell between 1923 and 1925 in the face of imported coal.

Organizationally, the coal companies were trapped in the zamindari system of acquiring rights on land and at the same time securing abundant supply of cheap tribal labour for mining coal. The companies manipulated tenancy and debt relations with people who cultivated the rented land, borrowed money and also worked on mines. Moreover, labour was hired in gang strength through contractors who also engaged supervisors, foremen and clerks to take work, record output and pay wages. Even in large mines, 'the management had little knowledge or control over the production process'.[141] Corruption was unavoidable while long-term matters of efficiency, technological improvements and safety were neglected. These defects were hard to remedy.

There is a general lament among authors who analysed India's economic development in the inter-war period that rapid progress in industrialization was impeded by shortages in skilled labour as well as in trained manpower. A major explanatory factor is the overstocking of every industrial labour market by cheap, unskilled labour. Its ready availability led to choice of machines and production processes which unskilled hands with some instruction and under direct supervision could work. Though overmanning was the common feature of the factory system, wages were low and manufacturing costs stayed below other countries where technological equivalence was superior, labour more skilled, man–machine ratios at optimum levels but average unit costs were higher. These facts were known and the economic implications were well understood. As long as profits were earned and production assured, Indian manufacturers could face competition in a free market and felt no pressure either to invest in modern machines or to man them on the basis of training institutions.

Man and machine being complementary, any significant investment in the latter necessitated a prior commitment on training of skilled labour in sufficient numbers to be assured of a secure supply. Skill training forms the essential infrastructure of modern industry, and it was largely absent, because neither the government nor the industry spokesmen showed sufficient keenness to put it in place. A vicious circle was allowed to function over several decades and in part was responsible for the 'arrested' development of India. TISCO was an exception. It had to cut costs to survive and the only known method was to replace the costly expatriate manpower by an equally skilled and competent Indians so they were trained by the company at its expense on the facilities it had set up. But for this additional investment, even with the support of protective duties and fiscal bounties, the company would have found it tough to match imported steel on price and quality.

The vicious circle also extends to inter-industry effects. Cheap labour is initially attractive but it keeps the technology low and prevents industrial expansion by severely inhibiting inter-industry linkages and growth of complementary industrial and commercial ventures. Railways and coal mining were complementary industries and developed together but failed to generate wider spread effects.

John Hurd explains thus:

> India had ample reserves of coal, but the rates for transporting it by rail were so high and sea rates so low that railways in western India often imported British coal. At the same time, the labour-intensive methods used for mining coal in India continued. In other countries where the requirements of railways had stimulated expansion in the coal industry, increased production led to a greater use of machinery, economies of scale, increases in productivity, and consequently

> to lower prices. The lower prices in turn generated a greater use of coal in other industries and expansion of their output. In India this did not happen. The low price of labour prevented the processes of production from changing, and expensive transport costs kept the delivered price of coal high. As a result, the spread effects from the increased production of coal remained limited.[142]

Labour did not get the opportunity for training in the railways as it had happened in the USA and Europe. 'It is true that the shortage of Indians with technical and managerial skills presented an obstacle' to their recruitment but more to the point, they suffered from a basic disadvantage, 'a reflection of racial discrimination rather than labour market necessities'.[143]

Indian railways came in for extensive evaluation during the 1920s. There was no dearth of criticism, partly on the ground that the railways were quite insensitive to the voices of critics and showed little earnestness in removing the shortcomings which were pointed out. There were glaring defects either of a strategic nature or such design weaknesses that their rectification required large-scale capital expenditure with an entirely new focus on economic development. This was never put on the government's policy agenda and was hence systematically excluded from the review process.

The reforms that were put in place were in large part due to the deliberations of the Indian Railway Committee appointed in 1920 with Sir William Acworth as chairman. The Legislative Assembly lent the voice of the popular, nationalist opinion and asked for more basic changes. The Railway Board was reconstituted in 1922 and made responsible for the functioning of the railways system and answerable, if not accountable, to the Assembly. In 1924, a Rates Tribunal was appointed and in 1926 a Rates Advisory Committee was established. Around this time, the government accepted direct responsibility of state management of those railway companies whose contracts expired and the government had to decide one way or other whether to renew the contracts or nationalize them. However, a mixed system continued and unfailingly it met with unanimous condemnation. 'One of the main criticisms levelled against such companies at present is that they favour foreign trade and foreign merchants as opposed to internal trade and the interests of indigenous concerns.'[144]

On financial administration a major change was introduced. The railways would make a regular contribution to the central budget instead of amounts which fluctuated annually. In 1925–6 following the railway 'convention' of 1924 the railways budget was separated from the general budget.

> The Exchequer is entitled to receive from the railways a sum equal to 1 per cent of the capital at charge in the penultimate year plus one-fifth of the surplus profit in that year. This is the 'fixed contribution' from the railways. In addition, if after payment of the fixed contribution, the amount available for transfer to the railway reserves exceeds Rs. 3 crores, one-third of that excess is to be paid to the Exchequer.[145]

In 1921–2, due to commercial slump, the railways' earnings declined sharply and showed a deficit of Rs. 9.1 crores. The situation improved thereafter up to 1929. The idea was to turn the railways into real commercial undertakings and generate profits, only then would the tax payer get any benefit from them. It was also decided to progressively Indianize the staff, by recruiting 5 per cent of the positions in superior departments in India. Between 1925–6 and 1927–8, the proportion of Indians in permanent gazetted appointments rose from 32 per cent to 70 per cent.[146]

However, major economic reforms were either not considered or indefinitely postponed. The policy of 'discriminating protection' was in place and it was possible to restructure freight rates to reflect the working of this principle, at least to reduce the cost of shipment of coal to distant consuming centres which would have been an aid to the coal industry. This was not done. In fact, the government never attended to the strategic value of the railways in fostering interindustry linkages though it did promote linkages of agriculture with other sectors of the economy. 'It purchased consumer goods and supplied raw materials to industry and food to urban centres, and it earned a considerable amount of foreign exchange. But it did not have a large demand for inputs from other sectors.'[147]

In 1925, a Royal Commission on Indian Currency and Finance was appointed under the chairmanship of Hilton-Young and it reported to the Government in July 1926. Though described as gold exchange standard, the Indian rupee was directly linked to sterling and could more accurately be referred to as the 'sterling exchange standard'. The option of a gold standard with a gold currency was also available, but not accepted. What was considered feasible was to have a gold standard but without a gold currency. The commission decided that, in order to retain public confidence, the rupee must be linked with gold and it should be visible. So the rupee should be directly convertible into gold but without gold coinage. This meant that the Central Bank should be able to buy and sell gold at a fixed legal ratio and in predetermined quantities. Otherwise silver rupee coins and paper currency should circulate. It was estimated that to meet this obligation, India would have to import over a period of 10–11 years about $103 millions of gold. In practice, it meant a double linkage. Silver rupee coins would remain stable only as long as the price of silver remained below the bullion value of the rupee; it should never exceed the exchange value. This complication seemed unavoidable, given the necessity to have silver rupees circulate as legal tender.

The commission also decided on a controversial question, that is, fixing the rupee–sterling rate at 1s6d to a rupee. The sterling–gold parity was restored in summer 1925 and the exchange rate oscillated around this rate, so it became 1s6d to gold as well. On meagre evidence the commission concluded, 'that an equilibrium of Indian prices and exchange in relation to the world situation had once more been attained, and recommended stabilization at the new rate of 1s6d'.[148]

Sir Purshottamdas Thakurdas, in a minute of dissent, pointed out that it was erroneous to assert that the rupee had already reached an equilibrium in relation to world prices, since the government had worked to raise the exchange rate from 1s4d to the current rate. On 1914 = 100, the WPI at Calcutta had stood at 172 in 1923 and 173 in 1924 and declined sharply to 159 in 1925. Rothermund says,

> After the steep decline of the exchange rate in 1921–22 the British Indian government followed a long-term policy of deflation in order to support the exchange rate. The reverse council drafts had failed as an instrument for this monetary policy so the alternative course of contracting the Indian currency had to be pursued systematically. There was no new coinage after 1922 and old coins returned to the government were put into the melting pot and sold as bullion in the world market. This even helped the government to improve its budgetary position. The coins that had been taken out of circulation were not replaced by bank notes either. From 1919 to 1929, a total amount of coins worth 1 billion rupees was taken out of circulation, while the amount of bank notes was kept more or less constant.[149]

The dissenting opinion averred that the government had deliberately missed the chance to fix the exchange rate at 1s4d, which was prevalent before the war, because it now suited it to fix it to the sterling gold standard. Moreover, the gold price might fall and would render the exchange rate too artificially high and difficult to maintain. Deflation would be needed for this purpose which would hurt Indian producers. Most of the economic transactions in agricultural produce involved circulation of cash in the busy and slack seasons and needed much less credit. The contraction of currency 'had a disproportionately intense reaction on the financing of trade'.[150] In the ensuing controversy, it was pointed out that the higher exchange rate would increase the debt burden on the already indebted peasants while, at a lower rate, government expenditure would rise. 'The Bombay interests claimed that the government wanted a high exchange to cheapen its remittances to London and give a boost to imports.'[151] The evidence, as Rothermund explains, is to be observed in the function remittances served in strengthening the London money market.

The Rupee Ratio Bill fixing the new ratio at 1s6d was enacted into law in 1927 in the face of strong opposition in the Assembly. The Currency Commission also recommended the creation of a central bank for India to be known as the Reserve Bank, and it should be a shareholders' bank like the Bank of England and independent of political control. The Assembly disagreed and preferred a state bank. It also opposed the exclusion of political influence; instead it should be provided for by electing three directors by the Central Assembly and an equal member by the provincial councils. The bill for enacting the Reserve Bank was withdrawn by the government due to non-reconciliation of its views with those of the Assembly.

On the higher exchange rate, a telling point was made by industry spokesmen. The foreign manufacturer was given an indirect bounty of 12.5 per cent which more than neutralized the advantage provided by protective duties, and in cotton textiles there was no protection at all and it could lead to ruin. The grim forecast rested on the assumption that the purchasing power of the agriculturists would decline by 12.5 per cent as the initial impact was felt by them and they adjusted their expenditure for fixed costs like land revenue, debt and interest charges. These fears were close to realization. Deflation had caused financial stringency and bank rates were at 6 to 8 per cent. 'Further, government borrowing at high rates (another method of reducing money supply) drained the money market of investment funds and, in the words of a broker, made it "exceedingly difficult for industrial concerns to raise money either by way of debentures or preference shares" causing "a serious check to industrial expansion".'[152]

Continuing the debate, Sir Purshottamdas argued in 1928, that while the capital issued in Britain between 1913 and 1927 increased from $56 million to $126 million, in India it declined dramatically.[153] Less tenable was the plea for gold coinage and a gold exchange standard, since to operate the system the combined backing of the US and the UK was required. In fact, the rupee was more firmly tied to sterling though it was freely convertible in gold. Rothermund also referred to foreign trade and India's excess of exports over imports to Britain. Between 1923 and 1929, the annual average exports to the UK were 3.5 billion rupees while imports were only 1.2 billion. The negative balance of trade was compensated by the transference of Indian reserves to the London money market.[154]

Federal finance was an important limb of the 1919 Act. However, it was beyond the principle of rational allocation of tax heads to leave the Centre as a financial dependency of the provinces. By 1924, the railway finances were separated from the central budget and this reduced an element of uncertainty. Public debt was another problem area. It stood at Rs. 261 crores in 1922 but declined to Rs. 228 crores in 1924. 'Out of this, Rs. 98 crores represented the accumulated deficits, about Rs. 10 crores was due to the building of New Delhi, and Rs. 120 crores was India's war debt. To this must be added the productive debt of Rs. 5.78 crores.' The unproductive debt could be redeemed in 50 years and the productive debt over a longer period. The annual provision on account of compound interest at 5 per cent was Rs. 3.66 crores.[155]

Redemption of public debt was possible only if the budget was in surplus. The government eliminated budgetary deficits in 1922 and produced surplus budgets thereafter every year up to 1929, except 1928 when there was a small deficit. Debt charges rose from 1923 onwards from Rs. 19.2 crores to over Rs. 21 crore but later levelled off at lower levels. Defence expenditure, which was pointed at by the nationalists as an unwarranted military commitment to the defence of Biritish Empire east of Suez, was systematically marked down from Rs. 87.4 crores in 1920 to Rs. 65.3 crores in 1922 and to lower levels during the next 15 years. In 1927, it was Rs. 54.8 crores, which was still disproportionately high considering that the total outlays on education, public health, civil works and agriculture together were only Rs. 35.7 crores.[156]

Education, medical and public health, agriculture and industry were allotted to provinces and the popular ministers were responsible for these. They complained of shortage of funds. Given the financial constraints in 1925–6, Bombay spent most on education, followed by Madras, UP, Punjab and Bengal. Madras preferred to spend the most on medical and public health; Punjab prioritized agriculture. However, none of these items could be raised to a level where they would impact the population in any major way because revenues were low and general administration and police claimed large chunks of provinces' resources. Nonetheless in Madras, in steady steps it was possible to spend more on education than on general administration from 1928–9 to 1930–1, though thereafter, the old pattern was re-established.

There was considerable variability among provinces, though a glance at the fiscal data over 1921–2 to 1939–40 shows that the basic conflict of fund allocation between administration and police as one category and education, and medical and public health as the other remained, though over time the former managed to reassert their claim.[157]

Vera Anstey adjusted the totals for revenue and public expenditure in 1925–6 to the price level of July 1914 and this provide a long-term perspective in real terms. Thus viewed, the aggregate revenues of the Centre and provinces in 1925–6 were at Rs. 93.86 crores compared to Rs. 76.50 crores in 1913–14, while in nominal terms it stood at Rs. 149.24 crores. On expenditures, in real terms, the aggregate of the Centre and provinces rose from less than Rs. 75.61 crores in 1913–14 to Rs. 90.72 crores in 1925–6 while, at current prices, the total was Rs. 144.26 crores. In real terms, the debt services, justice, police and jails and superannuation declined, while that of military services and defence, general administration, education and medical and public health rose. The sharpest increase happened to be in general administration which rose from Rs. 2.97 crores in 1913–14 to Rs. 8.23 crores in 1925–6.

Much of the fiscal politics was federal in nature, centred on the respective contributions made by the provinces to the central budget. Whenever a budgetary surplus emerged, one of the two claimants was the provincial contributions and the other the salt tax. The latter won in 1924–5 due to the Assembly's declared preferences. In the next year, the provincial contributions were lowered. In 1926–7 the cotton excise duty was repealed and there was a further reduction in the provinces' contributions. This factor contributed to the efforts of the provincial governments to produce balanced budgets by 1925–6. In 1927–8, the provincial contributions were stopped on an experimental basis, and in the following year, the system was finally terminated.[158] According to Thomas, 'India owes a great deal to Sir Basil Blackett. He thoroughly overhauled the Indian financial system. He was intensely interested in the development of India's resources and he believed that Indian economic life could be quickened and enriched by exploiting the dormant capital of the country.'[159] Perhaps, he was thus praised, but the deeper problems were more basic, linked partly no doubt, to the sterling exchange standard but for the larger part to the absence of an overall developmental perspective for the Indian economy.

Labour Finds Leaders: Recurring Strikes, New Laws

Between 1917 and 1927, the Bombay textile workers had mainly depended for leadership and guidance on a small band of political workers and social activists who along with other activities also found time to organize workers and attend to their problems. By 1927, the communist cadre, though very small, became active in organizing and leading the working class in Bombay. They started working in 1923 and received active financial support from the organizations sponsored or controlled by Moscow. S.A. Dange received money for his paper, *Socialist*, and also to support allied organizations. The British government soon discovered that Bolsheviks were active in India and imagined the worst. In the Kanpur Communist Conspiracy case in 1924, several of them including S.A. Dange and Muzaffar Ahmed were convicted with jail sentences and it slowed their organizational activities. The fledgling movement received more than financial support from abroad; a number of British communists came to India to lend a helping hand in putting together the basic organizational nucleus towards a Communist Party of India as a section of the Comintern. Indian communists were also recruited abroad and sent to India. M.N. Roy was already a known international communist and the principal accused in the Kanpur Conspiracy case, though he was still abroad.

Dange was released from prison in 1927, while Muzaffar Ahmed was released in 1925 and they became the foremost Indian communist leaders based in Bombay and Calcutta respectively. They attracted young intellectuals who had taken part in the Non-Cooperation Movement and, on its suspension in 1922, were disillusioned by Gandhi's leadership style and looked for a more active alternative forum than his constructive work in villages, against untouchability,[160] et cetera. The underground revolutionary movement also searched for an ideology and found it in communism or socialism, and the example of a revolution leading to the birth of the Soviet Union provided the needed inspiration. It is important to note that the origin of communist ideas 'sprang from the urge for national liberation and not as a result of a positive appreciation of the inevitability of social change according to Marxian analysis, which during Lenin's time was further enriched to suit the era of the "moribund state of capitalism" '.[161] In India, the national bourgeoisie was admitted to play a revolutionary role though of a limited nature. So communism in India was born out of the national movement for Swaraj led by Gandhi. However, the British believed that Indian communists were

Bolshevik agents; they received money from Moscow and were trained at Tashkent to create unrest in India.

In Bombay, the communists took part in the 1924 strike and in 1925 they formed the Labour Swaraj Party of the Indian National Congress. The idea was to wage the struggle for independence by organizing workers and peasants and their participation in the working class movement began to register growth. Strikes were led by local communist leaders in 1927 in the Buckingham and Carnatic mills of Madras as well as in the South Indian Railways.[162] Their small cadre was augmented by left-wing labour leaders and included a few British communists. The British TUC supported the labour movement in various ways. Its left wing included militant trade unionists who believed that communists in India should have the same legal right to form a Communist Party as they do in other dominions. They were unsuccessful, partly because the government was sensitive to the charges from the conservative benches, of permitting revolutionary violence in India. In February 1925, the Dundee jute workers sent money to P.C. Joshi to organize jute workers in India.[163] Other helpful ideas did not materialize. 'Nevertheless, Joshi used his personal contacts to get copies of rules and regulations of various British Unions (in the textile and railway industry for example), their journals, and details of labour legislation all of which he hoped to use as possible models for work in India'.[164]

In 1925, a British communist, Percy Gladding, spoke at the AITUC Congress and reported back that the number of communists in India was negligible but they could infiltrate the AITUC. However, Indian trade union leaders were more moderate than radical in their views and did not accept mixing political ideologies with trade union work. In Bombay, the British communists are credited with greater achievement in labour circles.[165] However, progress was slow because most of the industrial workers showed complete unfamiliarity 'with even the basic idea of organization' and failed to understand the practical difference between the moderates who approached the employers 'with faith in the goodness of the system whereas the communists believed that conciliation, or even the redress of grievances, was valuable only as a tactical expedient when labour was weak'.[166]

The Bombay workers accepted the moderate, welfare-oriented leaders as freely as the communists. They were mostly middle-class leaders with strong social consciences 'nourished by Western education or Western examples and were far removed socially from the workforce.'[167] The moderate leader, N.M. Joshi, had the advantage of a well-equipped office at the Servants of India Society and able assistants. 'Joshi also enjoyed a privileged position as a member of the Central Legislative Assembly. He used that position effectively for ventilating workers' grievances as well as for helping unions in their clashes with employers and the Government.'[168] There were others who aspired to rise to social prominence on the strength of their trade union work according to Chandavarkar:

> For trade unionists who also operated as vakils and pleaders in the mill district, writing notices, pursuing wage arrears and filing claims in the small-causes courts on behalf of the workers, their acceptance by employers and the state was good for business. For publicists, championing the workers' cause, it could also advance political careers. Workers too, sometimes found that they could secure their needs or resolve minor grievances through their offices.[169]

By comparison, in Ahmedabad, the pathway to trade unionism was far smoother and marked by a continuity of leadership.

> In 1922, Shankar Lal Banker, one of the powerful leaders of the Labour Association, was imprisoned for taking part in the non-cooperation movement. In his absence, the work of the Association was greatly handicapped. Therefore Kalidas Zaveri, one of the founder members of the Majoor Mitra Mandal, gave up his practice as a lawyer and devoted himself fully to the textile labour association. At the same time in 1922, Gulzarilal Nanda, who had given up research during the non-

> cooperation movement, and Khandubhai Desai joined the Textile Labour Association as full-time paid officials on a meagre monthly salary of Rs. 25. Under the guidance of Banker and Miss Sarabhai, they developed the Association from a small institution into a powerful one and made efforts later after Independence to spread the concepts of a Gandhian labour movement in other parts of India, through the agency of the INTUC.[170]

Rules were strict and enforced. In 1922, workers in the throstle departments of 21 mills went on an unauthorized strike. When arbitration proceedings were pending, Miss Sarabhai decided to dissolve the throstle workers' union, but recognized it again after the workers apologised for their conduct. Such events never happened in Bombay and the two cities represent two distinct stages of the development of trade union movement. The Ahmedabad textile workers understood the importance of craft-based organizations as the most efficient form of trade unionism to defend their interests. 'The craft unions that were formed were the Weavers' Union, the Winders' Union, the Throstle Union, the Card Room and Frame Department Union, and the Drivers', Oilmen's and Firemen's Union.' They formed a federation in the name of the Textile Labour Association and it later evolved into an industrial union.[171] It was on the strength of their organization that the unions agreed to let arbitrators decide disputes and accept Gandhi's guidance and leadership. Bombay workers were far behind in their collective consciousness.

In 1923, the textile mills were in a crisis and decided on a wage cut of 15.5 per cent. A strike followed and continued for three months. Ultimately, the union leadership gave in and agreed to the wage cut. It demoralized the workers and they started deserting the Labour Association. It took Gulzarilal Nanda and Khandubhai Desai nearly one year of painstaking work to get back to workers and redress their manifold grievances, to win back their confidence and rehabilitate the union. The special feature of the union's functioning was the system of personal complaints.

> Every conceivable type of complaint appears on the counterfoils, from an allegation against a jobber or mukadam of having smacked the complainant's head to a complaint that the other workmen hamper the complainant in drawing water from a tap or well. Each complaint receives personal attention; and the mills appear to afford a surprisingly large degree of power to the Secretary, who enters the premises, records statements, and passes orders, much as a District Officer might do.[172]

Later, it expanded into a wide range of welfare activities including a cooperative bank with 40,000 shareholders. Nothing comparable to it happened in any other industrial centre. However, most of the Muslim weavers stayed out of the union.

For the cotton textile mills in India, 1923 onwards were years of adversity and the mill workers had to bear a part of the cost of adaptation and adjustment which mills had to go through in their struggle to stay afloat. The years, 1923, 1924 and 1925 were particularly bad as is borne out by data on labour disputes and man days lost. Karnik describes the strikes as primarily defensive while the employers were on the offensive. In 1923, there were a total 213 disputes which took a toll of 5.05 million man days. In 1924 there were fewer, 133 disputes, but the loss in man days at 8.73 million was higher, while in 1925, the 134 disputes imposed the staggering cost of 12.57 million man days. Thereafter, the incidence of work stoppages declined. The most prominent causes are listed as pay, bonus and personnel. 'Among the industries the worst affected was the cotton spinning and weaving industry. It accounted for 339 out of 737 strikes which took place during the period, giving the percentage figure of 46. The next affected was the jute industry which accounted for 173 strikes being roughly 15 per cent of the total.'[173]

In 1923, the cost of living was lower than 1922 but workers still demanded higher wages. Actually the employers wanted to lower them and the Ahmedabad strike was triggered by the employers. In 1924 there was a major strike in the entire cotton textile mills in Bombay on the issue of the customary bonus which the mills refused due to economic depression. There were also other demands, such as a workday of eight hours instead of ten. Workers held out for more than two months, and then, realizing the futility of the strike, returned to work. The government set up a committee of inquiry, and it helped.

In 1925, the general strike in Bombay was the result of the mills' decision to enforce a wage cut of 11.5 per cent. There was little difference between these strikes and those which preceded them. According to Morris, 'there was unrest without discipline, strike without organization. When the mill hands returned to work all that remained was the memory of common action on a city-wide basis.'[174] There was nonetheless a new feature in labour relations. A demand was made by the labour spokesmen to raise broader economic and management related issues. In 1924, they submitted a memorandum to the Governor which, 'called for removal of freight and excise duties, better management and marketing, less speculation in the raw cotton trade and the reorganization of production on a more rational basis'.[175] In 1925, the central government actually intervened, abolished the excise duty of 3.5 per cent and the announced wage cut was restored. This terminated the strike.

At the end of the 1925 strike, the Bombay Textile Labour Union was formed at the initiative of N.M. Joshi. This was the work of a number of labour welfare groups aided by a handful of workers. N.M. Joshi, who had primarily engaged in relief work during the 1924 and 1925 strikes, became more involved in trade union work. In 1925, he presided over a Committee of Assistance to help the strikers. As a result of public sympathy, for the first time, the Bombay Municipal Corporation sanctioned one lakh rupees for workers' relief. It was widely believed that the wage cut was not justifiable. In this case, the opinion of the Legislative Assembly also weighed with the government as well as the mill owners. It is possible to trace the beginning of tripartism in India in the events of 1924 and 1925. At this stage, the government's involvement appeared to complement the policy shift towards discriminatory protection and the acceptance of a positive role in promoting the industrial development of the country. However, there was no consistency in government actions.

The attitude of the workers in Bombay appears to show some enthusiasm in support of a union which would advance their interests and project them before the larger public. This was the lesson of the successful strike in 1925. It was a significant step forward, in as much as they began to recognize the difference between welfare work and a union. In the 1924 strike, 'the workers of the Bombay Workingmen's Institute of the League helped the Strikers' Family Relief Committee, the Central Labour Board and the Mill hands' Children's Relief Fund Committee in distributing relief'. The League did laudable work in reducing the scale of distress and starvation in the families of striking workers. Indeed, N.M. Joshi was a committed leader of the League and stepped in to pay attention to the urgent problems of workers as often occurred in a general strike, but only because there was no union. His moderate views soon brought him in conflict with the communists.[176]

In 1925, the Communist Party of India was founded with the active help and guidance of several British communists who were sent to India for this purpose. About communists in Bombay, Karnik writes: 'They had no interest in life except their work in trade unions and the Communist Party. They organized a number of new unions, they revived some old unions, they captured same others from the older moderate leaders. In 1926 and 1927 they organized a number of strikes, some of which were successful'.[177] In 1926 the Indian Trade Unions Act was passed and it gave immunity to the union activists from civil and criminal conspiracy and facilitated the formation of new unions in relative safety. The level of activity among workers rose and 'a new spirit of militancy also became evident'.[178]

The jute mills workers worked and lived in pathetic conditions. In theory to organize around 300,000 workers concentrated in a narrow range of about 20 miles north and south of Calcutta should have been easy, 'yet a striking feature of the history of the jute workers' movement was the absence, relatively speaking, of strong and enduring trade unions'.[179] Actually, a large majority of jute workers never accepted trade unions as their organizations. They were there for them to support and follow, but not to belong to or establish membership-based claims. However, throughout the 1920s industrial relations in the jute industry remained disturbed and a tradition of militant and well-organized strikes appeared to exist. Between 1921 and 1929 there were 201 recorded strikes. These were mostly organized by short-term strike committees. Most of the strikes took place in individual mills and on immediate issues. In 1923, one mill decided to work single shift and dismissed 2,000 workers. A strike followed. In this year there were 32 disputes in the jute mills, 20 in 1924, 15 in 1925, then a spurt to 32 in 1926, followed by a sharp decline to 11 in 1927. All of them were local strikes in various mills and never took the form of a general strike in the jute industry. Workers took recourse to strikes as the only way they knew of conducting their protest and resolving disputes.

Industrial relations are a power relationship. In eastern India, more particularly in the jute industry, economic and political power was totally in the hands of the expatriate mill owners, and exercised as often as necessary by the expatriate personnel who managed the factories, supervised and took work from the mostly unskilled and illiterate workforce which was predominantly non-Bengali. They were desperately poor, lived in wretched conditions and invited contempt and disgust from the more affluent Bengalis who lived in Calcutta and looked down on factory work as well as factory labour. They were utterly powerless, as much due to the social distance that separated them from the racially cocooned white mill owners and the expatriate staff, as the religious and ethnic differences which additionally always divided them.

The weavers were mostly Muslim. They looked for Muslim leaders to guide them, and they flocked to mosques. The Hindu workers were naturally segmented and lived accordingly, though they could be roused on communal grounds. Still trade unions were formed but could not shed their 'frail and nebulous character'. 'The groundswell of labour protest in the jute industry during the two general strikes of 1929 and 1937 was accompanied by the same phenomenon: quick flourishing and wilting of trade union organization.'

In two regions unions were formed. 'In both these areas, the leadership of the unions was in the hands of a group of young Bengalis, committed by their ideology to the cause of the working class.'[180] Their entry made a vital difference. The middle class Bengali communists gave the jute workers a collective voice and capacity to exercise power in strikes. They were educated, understood law and the way the administration worked; so they could function as the leaders-mediators and convey the sentiments, anger and mood of desperation of the workers to the owners in English. The young leaders mitigated the power imbalance and endeavoured to compensate for the illiteracy and backwardness of workers, but they could never overcome their deep-rooted weaknesses as a people. The workers had gone through the experience of factory employment; they accepted the new nomenclature and status of the working class, but experienced great difficulty at the subjective level of group consciousness in making the transition. They were and remained alien to the bourgeois-democratic traditions in which Western-style trade unionism flourished. The jute workers stayed outside it. There were additional factors unique to Bombay, and which were all the more unique in Ahmedabad, which explain their specific of development.

The jute workers seemed unable to develop the minimum prerequisite of social consciousness appropriate to industrial culture to be able to fashion something like a trade union.

The government was willing to act its part in improving the life and working conditions of industrial workers. The assumption of additional responsibility can be related to three sources of pressure and actuation of public concern. The most direct was the 1919 Act which conferred the status of interest on 'labour' and provided them, with a political voice in the legislative bodies and the ILO. There were labour leaders as highly motivated and well meaning as N.M. Joshi who were keen to play their part to improve labour laws and frame rules of governance which would reduce anarchy and distress in the lives of the working class. It appears the government needed them in two roles, as advisers on labour policy and as spokesmen of labour's interests. The second was the ILO and the government's responsibility towards its conventions and recommendations. India's infant trade union movement discovered in the ILO a very important agency to voice their opinions, demand action from the government and find international connections to gain support and strength.[181]

The third was British public opinion which was sometimes directly aimed at the Secretary of State for India. The British TUC played this part fully convinced that what it was demanding from the government in India was also in the best interests of Britain.[182] In the UK, the attitude of the TUC was greatly influenced by the weight exercised by the left wingers. While there was willingness to press the claims of the labouring classes in India for greater protection, there was no consensus on more pressing political questions. In the mid-1920s, British trade unions made concerted efforts to elicit reliable information on wages and working conditions in India, while the government sought to present a more agreeable picture.[183] These matters also came up in the Central Assembly and in press comments and led the government to conduct an inquiry into such issues as the practice of imposing fines on workers or making deductions from wages on various grounds. Nevertheless, the habit of slow motion persisted and legislative measures took longer to materialize.

Though fines were not the most efficient method for ensuring discipline and orderliness at work places, the unions did not ask for a law to prohibit the practice. The Ahmedabad Textile Labour Union said: 'Owing to the particular circumstances under which Indian workmen are situated, the union does not consider it advisable to advocate a wholesale legal ban on every system of fines, and it recognizes the inadvisability of completely depriving the employers of their power to fine.' The Girni Kamgar Mahamandal of Bombay was of a similar opinion.[184] However, the law should lay down that foremen and labour contractors cannot exercise this authority, and it should vest only with the heads of departments. In Bombay it was observed,

> that it is the jobbers, head-jobbers, foremen and the mukadams who fine the worker and their action in this matter is more often than not confirmed by the heads of the department. The practice in some of the Ahmedabad mills of entrusting this power to detectors who obtain percentage of the deductions made in respect of spoilt cloth must be acting very adversely upon the operatives.[185]

Later, these abuses and other shortcomings were systematically investigated by the Royal Commission on Labour.

Objective conditions showed surplus of labour, on one hand, and adverse market conditions, on the other. The British trade union observer found to their astonishment, that: 'Four times the number of operatives per loom or spindle are employed in mills in India than are necessary in Lancashire. The Indian textile operative lacks the skill, stability and stamina of our work people.' They also learnt that, 'although the engines run ten hours per day, the operative does not work continually the whole of the day, time being allowed for prayers, bathing, smoking, etc. It is questionable if more than eight hours' productive labour is obtained from the individual operative. In order that the spindles and looms may be kept running the management must employ extra labour.'[186] Given these objective constraints, the finding was: 'Trade unionism is not at the moment making progress, and is at a very low ebb. Their work is more political and social than industrial. We did not find any textile trade union that was managed and controlled by the operatives. The lack of education of the worker prevents him from taking responsible positions in his trade union.'[187]

The AITUC held its sessions though the audiences were small, participations of workers dismally low and the sessions were generally lack lustre. C.R. Das presided over two sessions and delivered political speeches. In 1924, the session at Lahore attracted,

> a variegated assortment of delegates and visitors, who represented practically every class in Indian society except the working class. Labour leaders there were in abundance, and perhaps one or two among them may at one time have swelled the ranks of the proletariat, but with the solitary and distinguished exception of Mr. Miller, Irish railway guard and organizer of the North Western Railway Union of Punjab, there were present in that social and intellectual galaxy no worker or peasant who earned his bread by the sweat of his brow, and who had nothing to lose but his chains.[188]

The AITUC held another session in Calcutta soon after the Bombay textile workers' strike in 1924, but failed to make any mention of it. There were internal quarrels and factional fights and the meeting broke up in a rain of abuse and all-round fisticuffs. However, a number of resolutions were adopted pertaining to railwaymen, protection of trade union rights, on retrenchment and organizational matters.[189] Apparently at the Calcutta session, there was 'the beginning of a clash between the old and the new leadership of the AITUC. In the former category came the old guard of the Indian National Congress and the Moderates, and in the latter came the communists. Thus the fourth session of the AITUC proved the "baptism" of communism in the Indian labour movement.'[190]

N.M. Joshi, who led the moderates, did not lose heart and stayed with the AITUC. In 1925, he was elected Joint Secretary, and two years later, the General Secretary. He built the organization along conventional lines with provincial committees and organized provincial conferences. However, the old guard of the Congress leaders gradually withdrew from the AITUC. In their place the younger, left-oriented, socialism-inspired leaders stepped in and the AITUC for a short while came under the influence of Jawaharlal Nehru and Subhas Chandra Bose.

III. 1928–31

Simon Commission, Civil Disobedience and the Round Table Conference

Communal riots had become all too common an occurrence in 1926 and 1927 and vitiated the political currents and cross-currents in the country. For the British, the only alarming aspect was the revival of underground revolutionary activity and an occasional outbreak of terrorist violence. Otherwise there was a lull in the nationalist camp. Both forms of violence, exhibited during communal riots and attempts at assassination of prominent British officials were strongly deprecated by the nationalist leaders as much as by the government which, however, lacked the support of a strong public opinion in dealing with them. This was partly due to inertia in the nationalist camp but also because the Muslims and the Hindus were adrift and busy with the immediate task of consolidating their respective positions on political issues of far-reaching importance.

The Hindu Mahasabha emerged as a political party in March 1926 and received the support of prominent Congress leaders like Madan Mohan Malviya, Lala Lajpat Rai, Swami Shradhanand, Choitram Gidwani and Jairamdas Daulatram along with several others. It approved of the *Shuddhi* Movement, of opening the doors of Hinduism to others who wished to return to the fold. This was strongly opposed by the Khilafat Conference which met in June. 'Mohammed Ali declared that it was the right and duty of Muslims to convert every Hindu and even Gandhi to Islam; but they were not ready to allow that right to the Hindus from among the Muslims and the Christians. Muslim leaders like Dr Ansari and Azad kept aloof from this controversy, though they also attended the conference.'[191] This was no doubt the immediate cause that separated the two communities, but communal separation was gifted by the 1919 Act and it grew in the provinces and at the district levels at elections, generally on power sharing. Between 1924 and 1929 due to the play of political forces at the all-India, province and the district levels, communal separatist politics became more inwards, seeking solidarity within the religious communities, moving towards institutionalized political forms.[192]

In India, there was a broad consensus of political opinion that the 1919 Act suffered from inherent defects, it was wholly insufficient and needed to be reviewed to speed up the pace toward Swaraj, or at least the guide posts which unmistakably lead to the goal. In the UK too, the viewpoint in political circles, especially Tory opinion was becoming hostile towards reforms. According to Lajpat Rai,

> From the very outset, the British Government in England and in India have been trying to wriggle out of the dilemma in which they were placed by the reforms. Even the letter of the law has not been always observed. The whole history of the working of the reformed governments, whether in the provinces or in the national sphere, betrays an anxiety to prove (a) that it was a mistake to have given the reforms; (b) that the reforms have failed; (c) that there was not only no case for an advance, but that there were reasons for taking back what had been conceded.[193]

These perceptions received support from the sustained propaganda against India as an entity, though mostly centred on the numerous failings and shortcomings of the Hindus. Katherine Mayo's book, *Mother India*, which was freely distributed in England formed part of the campaign to arrest any possibility of reviewing the working of the reforms to make them more acceptable to Indians and secure their cooperation in administering them. From the British standpoint, as provided in the 1919 reforms, a review would be required at the end of 10 years. The Act was implemented in 1921 and the total experience of working it was five to six years. At the end of 1926, the Swarajya Party was much weaker than it was in 1923, and the era of boycott was unlikely to last much longer. There was no doubt some residual pressure on the British government to demonstrate their goodwill, a change of heart, a willingness to cooperate in return for cooperation, but nothing that dictated a faster pace, a swifter move, indeed, a rush to institute a statutory commission for the purpose.

On political grounds, it was decided to undertake a Tory review of the reforms, since once a review report was in place it would mould future thinking, and it better be a unanimous report, or the majority in the Commission should be such men as would give it a strong body and texture. Accordingly, the Simon Commission was announced in November 1927. Birkenhead, who made the announcement of a parliamentary commission had not shown any respect to India or its subject people ever, and could not have possibly given a contrary impression. Lord Irwin later regretted it, but said that when he was asked for his opinion, his advisers had agreed that the commission should have only white Members of Parliament and this is what he conveyed.

An avalanche of adverse comments, sharply worded criticism and rejection of the Simon Commission followed. Sir Tej Bahadur Sapru as the leader of the moderates was most disappointed and announced: 'Neither our self-respect nor our sense of duty to our country can permit us to go near the Commission.'[194] The Congress decided on mass demonstrations on the day of the Commission's arrival with similar demonstrations in every city visited by them, and the refusal of legislatures to elect their committees to meet and cooperate with it. There would also be a social boycott of the members of the Commission. The government never anticipated this, and the veritable storm which the Commission's tour in India produced led, contrary to the Viceroy's appeal for cooperation, to more recriminations and several rounds of repression and police violence. On the other hand, the European community was opposed to the setting up of a commission or to consider any further advance over the 1919 Act.[195]

Police violence produced a major casualty. Lala Lajpat Rai received blows on his chest and head while demonstrating against the Simon Commission's visit at Lahore, and he later died, the death attributed to the injuries he had suffered. It produced a terrorist act of revenge. Saunders, the S.P. of Lahore was shot dead as he was suspected to have delivered the blows.[196] Despite these setbacks the Commission continued to meet the Central Committee, the provincial committees and Indian witnesses including,

> the Muslim and the Hindu communalists, the non-Brahmins, the Marathas, the depressed class representatives, the advocates of European, Anglo–Indian, Christians and Sikhs, and land, labour and other interests. Obviously these narrow particularistic groups, singly or collectively, did not represent the deep, permanent present as well as future material and moral good of the people of India as a whole. They naturally laid stress upon their separate claims, and were unmindful of what they owed to the country as a whole. At one stage the Chairman of the Commission had to administer a rebuke to the extravagant claims of a communal deputation.[197]

The Commission took long to deliberate and signed the two parts of the Report on 12 May and 27 May 1930. By this time, much had changed. In the UK, the Labour government was formed; Irwin went to England to hold discussions with the new government and issued a conciliatory statement on his return. 'The statement affirmed the right of parliament to form its own judgement of the Indian constitutional problem, but conceded the importance of reaching a solution which might convey the assent of Indian political parties.'[198] He also announced the decision of the British government to set up a Round Table Conference where India's representatives would confer with His Majesty's Government and seek the widest possible area of agreement for the final proposals which the government would place before parliament, etc. Irwin also referred to the 1917 declaration that the purpose of constitutional progress was the attainment of dominion status. It was more ambiguously worded, but carried this impression.

Irwin found the Assembly's work very frustrating. The government sponsored Public Safety Bill and the Trade Disputes Bill met with strong opposition, in fact the President of the Assembly ruled the Public Safety Bill out of order and the government was censured. He was convinced of the need for a fresh initiative, to give an assurance on the goal of India's advance, and to remove the affront to India's self-respect. On the other hand, both Birkenhead and Simon had nothing but contempt for Indian nationalists. The former wrote to Irwin, 'I cannot imagine any more terrible fate in the world in the present situation in India than to hack out a new constitution with such talkative and incompetent colleagues.'[199] Earlier, talking to Annie Besant in London on hearing of protests in India on the appointment of the Commission, he said, 'you dare not reject anything that we offer you, and if you dare do it, we shall see.'[200] Irwin had assured him that it would be possible to break the boycott of the Hindu Congress with the help of the Muslims, the Liberals and the Indian states. On Muslims, he wrote to the Secretary of the State, 'they are after all, our best friends, and however impartial it may be our duty to be, we are not called upon, as I see it, to throw over our friends for new allies whose friendship has been a very uncertain quality.'[201]

Shortly after the announcement of the Simon Commission, two important initiatives were taken in India to settle the differences on communal representation, distribution of powers between the Centre and the provinces in a federal constitution and other political matters. An All-Parties Conference met in February 1928 to work towards unity, but its proceedings were marred by endless wrangling. Strong positions were taken and there was a deadlock. The Hindu Mahasabha took a firm stand on practically every issue on which the Muslim position had already hardened. These were: separation of Sind from the Bombay presidency and reservation of seats for Muslims in the Punjab and Bengal councils. The Muslim League withdrew from the conclave. Slowly all chances of reconciliation vanished. It was a great setback. As the Hindu leaders saw it,

> the Indian minorities were religious groups and therefore, though their religious rights might be safeguarded, no political or administrative rights need be safeguarded. The Muslims, on the other hand, considered themselves a nationality with a distinct religion, culture and traditions, and therefore a distinct individuality, which demanded recognition in constitutional and administrative arrangements. From this it followed that the Indian government ought to be federal in character and the Muslim share in legislative, executive and administrative organs of government ought to be clearly provided in the constitution, at the same time their religious and cultural rights should be protected.[202]

Lajpat Rai was so disheartened that he virtually gave up the Swarajya Party and identified himself with the Hindu Mahasabha.[203]

This was followed by two moderate leaders, Motilal Nehru and Sir Tej Bahadur Sapru, setting up a working group on constitution making. It is called the Nehru Report published in August 1928. It made out a case for dominion status, not as an accomplished fact but more as a declaration of rights which in due course would produce a political entity, independent and totally free of the British Parliament's overriding powers. The declaration of rights guaranteed religious liberty and cultural autonomy. There would be joint and mixed electorates with reservation of seats for Muslims in the Central Legislative Assembly and in the provincial councils where they were in a minority, with a similar reservation for Hindus in the NWFP, but no reservation for Muslims in Punjab and Bengal. Reservation would be for a fixed period. There would be adult franchise for men and women without any discrimination on any grounds. Sind and Karnataka would become separate provinces and any further reorganization of provinces would be on a linguistic basis. The respective powers of the Centre and provinces would be provided in the schedules.

Jinnah raised an objection on Muslim representation at the Centre which, he said, should be one-third. If adult suffrage was not introduced or was delayed, Muslim seats in Punjab and Bengal should be reserved at their share in the population. All the residuary subjects should vest in the provinces; it should be a weak Centre while the provinces should govern themselves as autonomous units of a federal India. Sapru agreed with Jinnah on 33⅓ reservation for Muslims at the Centre but Jayakar strongly opposed it. Jinnah lost the vote in the All-Parties Conference held in December in Calcutta.[204]

The Nehru Report was accepted by the Congress. The Muslim position gradually hardened as far too many senior leaders found faults in the Report and virtually rejected it. In UP, criticism grew in vehemence. A variety of fears were aired, some of them quite wild: 'Muslims will disappear from all legislative bodies unless separate electorates are guaranteed to us.'[205] Ultimately, nothing came of the Nehru Committee Report, and even the Congress declared in 1929 that it had lapsed. In fact, the political fallout was more serious. In place of friendship and trust a wide gulf separated the Ali brothers from Gandhi. They rejected Gandhi's leadership and together with other Muslim leaders decided to withdraw from the nationalist platform and agitation for Swaraj. They would side with the British to further Muslim interests.

In 1930, the Simon Commission's Report was made public. It gave separate electorates to the Muslims though in principle they were opposed to it. The Commission conceded that nationalism was a growing force in India though sectional interests still absorbed much of the energy of a majority of Indians and seemed unwilling to surrender their claims to the common good: 'Division by creeds and classes means the creation of political camps organized against each other, and teaches men to think as partisans and not as citizens, and it is difficult to see how the change from this system to national representation is ever to come.'[206] Yet, communal representation to Muslims was assured and they could not be deprived of this protection The British government had given pledges to the Muslims in 1909 and 1919 and these were incorporated in Acts of Parliament. These must be maintained. However, it barely took notice of the principle that in a democratically elected government there must be coherence among ministers and a commitment to exercise collective responsibility. The system is unlikely to work if in a ministry some owe allegiance to one section and others to another. 'Such a government can neither be stable nor effective, nor a government.'[207] Apparently, they were convinced that India could not advance much faster towards self-government; yet the experience of associating elected ministers in a system of provincial autonomy was a success.

While diarchy had failed and should be scrapped, there was no reason for not substantially expanding the powers of elected ministers as responsible to the councils. Irwin rejected the report as lacking in objectivity and made constructive suggestions to undo the mischief it had already caused. He was for complete provincial autonomy, some devolution of authority to the representatives of people, that is, some form of diarchy at the Centre, and safeguards for certain subjects like defence, foreign affairs and minority rights. 'This will resolve the impasse in which Simon had left them, with an elected assembly and an irresponsible executive.'[208] According to Moore, 'Irwin's immediate aim in defining Britain's purpose was to transform the Indian political scene. Throughout October Irwin's initiative seemed likely to win

Indian liberal and moderate Congress support for a Round Table Conference.'[209]

Irwin's announcement amounted to bypassing the Simon Commission, if not its virtual rejection. In subsequent political developments, the Report hardly played any part since other more momentous events were taking shape. The boycotts had energised political life and this was reflected in the Congress's acceptance of full independence as the goal. However, it needed a political sanction which Gandhi decided on later. In the meantime, the debate in parliament proved to be a great damper. Later the Labour government's spokesman made it clear that dominion status was the goal for India, but not in the immediate future; progress would have to be in stages and at the sole judgement of parliament.

Gandhi met Irwin and pointedly asked if the Round Table Conference would proceed on the assumption of dominion status and produce a blue print toward its realization. Irwin could not give this assurance and negotiations broke down. The die was cast, and at the Lahore session of Congress in December 1929 it decided that the term Swaraj shall mean complete independence. Also that nothing would be gained by attending the Round Table Conference. The central and provincial assemblies would be boycotted and AICC would decide when to launch the civil disobedience movement and non-payment of taxes. 'The flag of independent India was unfurled and a feeling of solemn dedication settled upon the hearts throbbing with inexpressible emotion. The incubus of the mind had at last been removed, what remained was its disappearance from practice.'[210] Gandhi decided that 26 January should be observed as Independence Day and the country should take a pledge announcing the decision to work for Purna Swaraj. Pledges were taken all over the country in solemn silence.

Then Gandhi hit on the idea of the Salt Satyagraha. On 2 March 1930, he wrote a letter to the Viceroy announcing his decision to start the satyagraha and explained the grounds on which it rested. On 12 March at 6.30 in the morning,

Gandhi set out on the march. He was 61 years. This was the famous Dandi March to the seashore where Gandhi would break the salt law. It was a 241 mile march, at the end of which, on April 5 at sunset, Gandhi reached the seashore, and on the following morning broke the salt law. The Civil Disobedience Movement commenced and spread from breaking the salt tax to boycotting foreign cloth, British goods, liquor and drugs. In several places there were campaigns for non-payment of land revenue and other taxes.

On 5 May, Gandhi was arrested. 'Mass satyagraha followed during which at least 60,000 persons were imprisoned. A large number of satyagrahis were assaulted by the Police.'[211] On police repression Tara Chand quotes Louis Fischer, 'The British beat Indians with batons and rifle butts. The Indians neither cringed nor retreated. That made England powerless and India invincible.'[212] At the physical level, the formidable challenge to British power could be and was met, so that by early 1931 the government had re-established its control; in fact, in November there were less than 30,000 people still in prison. Others had been released. However, at the psychological level the effect was much deeper and the government's moral authority to rule over its unwilling subjects was fundamentally undermined. The British claim to be guardians of India's voiceless millions lay in tatters, and Gandhi demonstrated his power by using an extraordinarily novel weapon of wresting authority.[213]

The civil disobedience movement ended in a truce in early 1931, and was viewed as a sell-out by the more active campaigners who expected it to continue longer. However, it was losing steam and the moderate nationalists were keen on ending it in a manner which both sides would find acceptable. In March 1931, the famous Gandhi–Irwin Pact was signed. According to its terms the civil disobedience movement would be withdrawn; matters being discussed at the first Round Table Conference would be considered further, and Congress would take part in it; all kinds of defiance of laws would cease including the boycott of British goods but picketing would be allowed; the ordinances promulgated to deal with the movement would be withdrawn, prisoners released, fines, et cetera. would be remitted, additional police withdrawn and immovable property seized by the government would be returned. As a result of the Pact, the Congress, again a legal body, was able to hold its annual session in the last week of March.[214]

In a critical review, Rothermund states that depression had already hit India and businesses as well as farmers were hurt by the severe credit contraction that had taken place, and Gandhi realized that with empty coffers it would not be possible to support the thousands of volunteers who enrolled to conduct the movement. 'An honourable peace treaty after a valiant non-violent fight was Gandhi's immediate aim, and when Irwin seemed to be willing to grant him this boon, he was prepared to go a long way to meet his demands and to reduce his own conditions on which he had appeared to insist very firmly.' Accordingly, 'Gandhi had yielded all and gained nothing'.[215] Irwin's main objective was Gandhi's participation in the Round Table Conference, another was to avert a peasant uprising similar to one in Burma which was crushed after tying down British troops for over a year.

Perhaps in a technical sense the Gandhi–Irwin pact was just a little short of capitulation on Gandhi's part, but he entered it knowing fully that principally what nationalist India had gained was political recognition of Congress as a power centre and its capacity to mobilize the masses as a demonstrated fact. However, more importantly, Gandhi needed it, since the movement had already lost momentum. Moreover, the business community was keen on a speedy return to normalcy and sent him strong signals on their economic desperation and the necessity for some effort at alleviating the effects of the world Depression.[214] Gandhi needed to retain their support and was keen on preserving the character of the Congress as an organization of national aggregation to which all or anyone may belong and accept his moral leadership.

Within the Congress he had to make sure that whatever he did also had the support of the radical wing led by Jawaharlal Nehru as well as the moderates and the responsivists. In mid-1930, Tej Bahadur Sapru and M.R. Jayakar worked hard at mediation and Irwin was willing to respond but Gandhi was not keen on it and it proved abortive. Irwin's role was to act expeditiously on reconciliation as was foretold by the British Prime Minister in his concluding address at the first Round Table Conference on 19 January 1931. He said that in any future constitution the government would ensure that the reserve powers are so framed and exercised as not to prejudice the advance of India through the new constitution to full responsibility for her own government. 'He also appealed to those engaged at present in civil disobedience' to cooperate in the future work of the Round Table Conference.[217] Several leaders who returned from the conference were inclined to support the outline of the scheme which was presented there. They were anxious for peace.

> It was significant of the eagerness of Gandhi and the CWC for peace that during the Gandhi–Irwin talks little difficulty was experienced with the constitutional issue. Gandhi agreed that Congress should cooperate in considering further the scheme for the constitutional government of India discussed at the Round Table Conference, of which federation was 'an essential part', as were 'Indian responsibility and reservation or safeguards in the interests of India, for such matters, as for instance, defence, external affairs, the position of minorities, the financial credit of India, and the discharge of obligations.'[218]

For Gandhi, the basis of future cooperation was established, though at the ground level what effect the Pact produced on the bureaucracy had to be seen. However, he agreed to the suspension of the civil disobedience movement, not its abandonment. So the Pact was in effect a truce to give him a chance to discover the likely outcome of the next Round Table Conference. Congressmen could still reassert their demand for complete independence. Gandhi had achieved national unity in action, but there was little sign of a consensus emerging on the national demand to be put before the Conference. His main difficulty lay in the fact that the badly needed Hindu–Muslim unity was lacking. The Muslims had by and large stayed aloof from the civil disobedience movement, and the Muslim leaders' position on constitutional questions had hardened; and it was the same with the leaders of the Hindu political opinion.

Rothermund points to another aspect of the movement which did not please Gandhi at all. He did not like the North Indian no-rent campaigns which pitted the peasants against the landlords and thus led to a class struggle among Indians'.[219] According to him, 'Gandhi found out about the real sufferings of the peasants only after he had concluded the Pact and then toured the most affected areas. He learned to what extent the revenue authorities had made use of their rules and regulations to inflict as much damage on revenue registers as possible.'[220]

Actually there was an acute cash problem in rural areas of UP where peasants needed money to pay the land revenue. The landlords had filed 8,246 suits in 1929–30 for enhancement of rents and there was no relief forthcoming from anywhere. However, the local Congress leaders were unwilling to unleash rural radicalism because many of them were small zamindars, moneylenders or connected to trade.[221] In Gujarat the no-rent campaign took a heavier toll; tenants lost their lands. As a result of the Pact those lands which were not sold were returned to the tenants. The tangible gains were the release of prisoners and return of forfeited properties. More was not possible but the general reaction was one of relief.

However, the youth groups viewed the settlement as a betrayal. At the Karachi Congress the settlement received the endorsement Gandhi asked for, though he had to put in considerable effort to secure it. The Karachi Congress decided that Gandhi alone should speak for Congress in London, mainly to ensure that Congress spoke with one voice at the Round Table Conference.

In mid-April 1931 Lord Willington replaced Irwin and government policy hardened. It appeared prepared to hit hard and hit at once, if civil disobedience was restarted. The new Viceroy was determined, 'to work the settlement only on condition that they should not again subject the services and their allies to the strains of renewed civil disobedience'. The government seemed convinced that the Congress was preparing for another struggle, while the settlement had lowered the morale of officials and loyalists. Gandhi understood this and worked to save the settlement.

> In deciding whether to go to London, Gandhi had to weigh the obvious importance of 'converting' British opinion if he was to gain permanent, constitutional results, against the probable futility of trying to attempt this if events in India were simultaneously working to nullify his British campaign, either by Congress alienating British opinion or by government action in his absence implicitly denying the Congress claim to speak for Indians.[222]

On the other hand, Gandhi said at Karachi, 'it would be useless for the Congress delegation, if we cannot possibly arrive at a proper communal solution, to proceed to England.' He told a British correspondent, 'my coming (to England) is contingent upon certain circumstances, two of which are satisfactory working of the settlement and solution of the communal question.'[223]

Under a new Viceroy in India and a new government in UK, a shift further to the right in political parameters took place whose significance Gandhi and those close to him failed to grasp. Willingdon had been governor of Madras and Bombay and also in Canada. He was a liberal in British politics though conservative in India. The new British government was 'conservative, imperialist, doubtful of India's fitness for self-government' and had little use for the policy of accommodation followed by Benn and Irwin. The new Viceroy immediately rejected the Pact and disapproved of Benn's anxiety to get Gandhi over to London; nor could he be treated as a plenipotentiary negotiating terms of peace with the Viceroy as an equal. Unknown to Gandhi a marked shift in political direction had already been worked out at London.

The possibility of advance towards self-government at the Centre was made crucially dependent on the accession of the princes to the proposed federation; it would be voluntary, consequently subject to further negotiations and could not be taken for granted. With a hostile bureaucracy, this vital link, needed for the inauguration of the proposed federation, could not be hastened and might become indeterminable. The Muslims, too, had to accept it. Hence, the nationalists, if they were keen on it would have to cope with two vetoes—of the princes and the Muslims. Gandhi was not at all prepared to deal with such Machiavellian tactics and diplomacy. He had barely followed the political nature of parliamentary debate on the issue of dominion status with safeguards for India, which Irwin in good faith held out but had met with trenchant comments and outright disapproval by the Tory MPs.

For one thing, there could not be such a thing as dominion status conditioned by binding safeguards. Dominion status implied, as was the meaning put on the term Swaraj, that the British Parliament's jurisdiction over India would lapse and cease thereafter. Nor should Irwin have assumed that parliament would abdicate its right to legislate on India on the general assurance that if Indians should succeed in resolving their problems and reach a settlement among themselves it would be accepted and followed by the grant of dominion status. Clearly Irwin had overstepped his powers; he was subordinate to the Secretary of State who represented parliament and was responsible to it. The cabinet alone could enter on such a binding assurance.

In early April, Gandhi met Muslim leaders in Delhi to secure a consensus on a composite constitutional demand acceptable to both Congress and Muslims. He met with a rebuff in the form of Jinnah's 14 points and insistence on separate electorates. Shaukat Ali had in his speech reiterated this demand along with, 'special weightage in the provincial and federal legislatures which would protect Muslims where they were minorities and secure their dominance in areas where they had small majorities—the latter being an important concern of the Punjabis, Fazl-i-Hussain and Feroz Khan Noon, who were prime movers of the gathering'. The 14 points were packaged with the sole motivation of shielding Muslim interests from the threat of Hindu domination in any constitutional arrangement which may bring Congress into power in a shared arrangement with the British. These included the demand that Muslim representation in all cabinets, at the centre and provinces was essential, also that no legislation on communal matters should be proceeded with if three-quarters of the members of the community objected.[224] In response, the Congress made a statement on fundamental rights, which concept was already incorporated in the Nehru Report.

For all practical purposes, the Congress conceded most of Jinnah's demands, but insisted on joint electorates and rejected the claim to 33 ⅓ per cent representation to Muslims in the Central Assembly. However, the Congress formula failed to satisfy the untrusting Muslim leaders who were now completely alienated.[225] They had already rejected the Prime Minister's declaration of 19 January. In Shaukat Ali's view, the Muslims had ruled India for 850 years and he asked them 'to realize that the future must be worthy of their past'. Muslim leaders were apprehensive that once the princely states joined the federation the number of Hindu majority provinces and states would increase substantially. This needed to be counter-balanced with a larger northern block of provinces where Muslims were in a majority and were in power. In short, Gandhi failed in his mission on this dimension of the Round Table Conference.[226] He had already given up the hope, or was mentally prepared, that the Second Round Table Conference would occupy itself on framing the basic structure of the next constitution resting on the premise of dominion status.

The third dimension was the working of the settlement. If it crumbled, Gandhi would lose hope of achieving anything worthwhile in London. He was keen on saving it, but complaints on its terms being flouted by officialdom were steadily reaching him. He had positioned himself as an intermediary between the government and the people, and he frequently wrote to the Home Secretary and the governors on the subject of sundry violations of the terms of settlement by the government. He was keen on involving local Congress leaders in representing the peasants' complaints, but the government would not yield on it.

He appealed to the zamindars to be more reasonable with their tenants and not to insist on their questionable perquisites. He tried to reconcile incompatible interests, and with his ambivalent attitudes on the fundamentals of agrarian relations failed to satisfy either the government on land revenue and remission of rent, the zamindars in UP, or secure the fair and reasonable claims of the tenants. The government was anxious not to permanently lose the rent it claimed as revenue. At one point, Gandhi declared that if the government failed to keep its part of the settlement and allowed complaints to go unattended he would not attend the London Conference. However, it was saved with a second settlement on 27 August; so the Delhi Pact continued and Gandhi would attend the Second Round Table Conference. Yet, Congress held out its option of defensive direct action if inquiry into genuine grievances was denied, and this would not be held violative of the Delhi Pact. Altogether, the second settlement was needed to facilitate Gandhi's departure to London.[227]

From Shimla Gandhi travelled to Bombay and sailed on 29 August, accompanied by Mahadev Desai, Pyarelal, Devdas and Miraben. On the same ship were Sarojini Naidu and Madan Mohan Malviya. His mood was one of despair but he believed that God had made the way to London clear through the second settlement. He arrived in London on 12 September 1931 and stayed in the East End.

The communal question dominated the Conference; various community leaders made the resolution of the communal tangle as the condition precedent to constitutional advance. At one stage, the delegates of the minorities—Muslims, Anglo-Indians, Indian-Christians and Scheduled Castes—produced a 'Minorities Pact' claiming separate electorates and weighted representation for each minority. To Ramsay MacDonald their claims added up to 46 per cent of the total population.[228] Congress rejected the idea and it failed to make progress. 'Gandhi had to drink many a bitter cup of humiliation to the dregs during these days. The interminable bargaining, the controversy on the secondary issues, the tactical manoeuvres, the behind the scene alignments disgusted and disillusioned him.' He felt isolated: 'Gandhi realized that he had underrated the forces arrayed against him and the Congress. It was almost with a sense of relief that he saw the conference trail off to a formal conclusion.'[229] He had worked hard and proposed a number of possible solutions to the communal problem but failed. The Muslims accepted no solution; only a decision by the government on their 14 points demands would satisfy them.

Gandhi failed in his principal mission to secure the acceptance of Congress as the political representative of the entire people of India and to negotiate a settlement with Britain on this basis. Rothermund makes a far-fetched assumption that, 'he wanted to bypass the conference and aimed at an encounter with the Prime Minister so as to reproduce his Pact with the Viceroy at a higher level. He was prepared to make many concessions if he could make a pact with the Prime Minister.' These are listed and it is asserted that, 'after his symbolic revolution Gandhi would have been satisfied with a symbolic transfer of sovereignty. A skilful prime minister in full control of his government could have made a deal with Gandhi who would have successfully defended it in India, just as he had defended the pact with

Irwin in spite of severe criticism.'[230] This assertion may be true as a possible strategic device to get over the complexities of Indian politics and find a solution to the festering political disputes which otherwise might never be resolved. However, if such an outcome was at all realizable the Second Conference was not the occasion for it. Moreover, he should have never gone alone with the restricted mandate of the Congress Working Committee. Nehru with radical views was the Congress President and he should have been present at the negotiations and concurred with Gandhi's perceptions. Gandhi knew the limits to his power which the Muslim opposition had imposed; this he credibly granted at the Conference and would have yielded ground on it if any settlement with the British was possible. However, there was no reciprocity by other minorities, and none whatsoever by the Muslim delegation.

Gandhi knew his weakness and had forebodings that, for him and the Congress, the Second Conference would be fruitless. As it happened, the Muslim delegation, as staunch allies of the imperial government, used the tactics of political intransigence to great effect. They easily won on issues on which the Simon Commission had already made recommendations, and defined the safe limits to political concessions the Tories were prepared to make. The NWFP and Sind would be separated into distinct provinces and the reform process would extend to them. These would create a solid bloc of provinces with Muslim majorities constituting Muslim India. The Commission had given full support to increased provincial autonomy though the Centre remained strong with considerable reserve powers, while the concept of freed provinces with a weak Centre in a fragile federation was viewed as so much kite flying and not followed.

Muslims demanded full provincial autonomy and they got a large part of it. As approved by the Commission, the demand for separate electorates was also granted to the Muslims. The Secretary of State, Hoare, estimated that the British government had 120 million allies in India who had stayed away from the civil disobedience movement and Muslims 'comprised the largest, compact bloc in it'.[231] The government decided to reward the Muslims who had allowed it to use the crescent card to inflict defeat on Gandhi, and placate other minorities in other ways. The Tory majority government which was formed in late October 1931, while the Second Conference was still in session, decided to return to the Simon Commission Report and otherwise practically wreck the conference.[232]

Simon was a member of the new cabinet and he was totally opposed to the British government negotiating a political advance with the Indians; the farthest he would go was to allow consultations on a predetermined agenda. Parliament must remain supreme, and it could not be bypassed; nor could the racial aspect of the British Commonwealth of free nations which was in the offing be ignored. In fact the Commission he led had not used the words, dominion status for India, even once. The Muslims never wanted it to be granted prior to their rights and claims being conceded as the statutorily defined safeguards in the next constitution. These safeguards should form part of powers of provinces in a future federation, and guaranteed. Hence a federation without the Crown at the helm was unthinkable for them.

Hoare proposed two bills, one on provincial autonomy and the other on the proposed federation. Willingdon strongly opposed the move—that such a course would lead to a catastrophe—so the idea was given up. A single Act with two parts was accepted as much better. It was admitted that before provinces agreed to ceding powers to the Centre on national grounds they should have several years of experience as autonomous entities; the pace could not be hastened. Moreover, Indian princely states were expected to voluntarily join the federation, thereby uniting the two Indias, but they too were keen on safeguards for themselves and a weak Centre, so that a future democratic government would not whittle down their internal autonomy, or address them in the style of a paramount power. The Congress was no less keen that the people of India under the princes should not lag behind in democratic rights, and should be enabled to enjoy the same level of democratic rights and aspirations for self-governance as in British India.

However, the princes were not thinking of sharing power with their people; if at all, the princes would cede powers to the federation, keeping all the powers granted to the autonomous entities to themselves; they were the states.[233] On such anomalies rested the future of the proposed federation. The Tories also quashed the idea of the Viceroy functioning as a constitutional governor. He must continue as the executive head of a subordinate branch of imperial Britain. Meanwhile, a new power axis was being formed. 'A Tory-bureaucratic–Muslim alliance was at hand. An era of reaction was opening. Events in India towards the end of 1931 confirmed their (the Hindus) suspicions of Britain's determination to break the freedom movement.'[234] On 17 December, in an Order-in-Council, Willingdon declared that the Delhi Settlement was no longer operative and in UP, on the no-rent campaign, there should be no correspondence with Congress. The Viceroy would not meet Gandhi while the no-rent campaign continued and direct action should be taken if any agitation is started.[235] 'The Delhi pact was dead and gone.'

Economic Depression, Deflation, Rupee Ratio, Spreading Distress

During the 1920s, the major long-term factors working on the economic life of the people were growth in population at a steady rate of over one per cent per annum, increase in literacy, expansion in irrigation and the rise to prominence of Indian industrial and commercial classes. Between 1921 and 1931, the industrial workforce grew annually at one per cent. Urbanization also picked up and in 1931, 2.86 per cent of population lived in cities of 100,000 people or over. In 1931, the population was over 33.8 crores compared to 30.57 crores in 1921. The major contributory cause was the success of government efforts at controlling epidemics and reduction in child mortality. However, most of the increase in population had to be absorbed in agriculture which was already under pressure. The labour markets in industrial cities had to cope with a large number of new arrivals looking for jobs or work and they tended to depress the wage structure.

The economy continued to grow though at a slow pace.[236] It had moved cyclically in the past, the 'net value added by the secondary sector at 1938–39 prices' show the peak at Rs. 2,534 million in 1912–13. This figure was exceeded for the first time in 1924–5, at Rs. 2,561 million, but thereafter it generally climbed to reach Rs. 3,426 million in 1930–1. This was over 66 per cent higher than the 1920–4 level of Rs. 2,062 million showing a growth rate of a little above 6.6 per cent annually. The largest contribution to the growth in this sector was made by 'small-scale and cottage industries', from Rs. 1,178 million in 1920–1 to Rs. 2,274 million in 1930–1, and without any protection. Manufacturing showed growth but at a lower pace. Mining too grew but at a still lower pace.

Corresponding figures for the primary sector, comprising agriculture, livestock, forestry and fishery show similar trends. At 1938–9 prices, the peak level of 'net domestic product from the primary sector' was reached in 1910–11 at Rs. 11,520 million. It grew at an unsteady pace in the previous decade. In the following decade, 1910–11 to 1920–1, excepting 1918–19 when famine conditions prevailed, agriculture advanced slowly and exceeded the previous peak in 1919–20 when it was Rs. 11,750 million. Agriculture declined in 1920–1 and this sharply reduced the total for the sector. However, thereafter, it showed erratic fluctuations over a rising trend. In 1930–1, the NNP from the primary sector reached a new peak of Rs. 11,779 million.[237] During the two decades, 1910–11 to 1930–1, the total area under 26 crops listed in Sivasubramanian's study increased from 125,609,000 acres to 134,078,000 acres.[238] These figures show that extensive cultivation was largely responsible for raising agricultural production, and point to the manner the increased population found work. Population growth also exacerbated the problem of subdivision and fragmentation of holdings and increase in the number of subeconomic tenant farmers. The landless searched for work.

In 1928, the Royal Commission on Agriculture brought out its report, which was heeded and a number of reforms were introduced by the provinces and the centre towards implementation of its recommendations. The government was asked to enact laws to promote consolidation of holdings, to prevent cattle diseases from spreading, to establish regulated markets in agricultural produce and consider whether trade associations or cooperative sale societies could be promoted. The Commission emphasized 'the dependence of agricultural progress upon the population problems, and the improvement of the general standard of village life, education, and health', as well as the important principle that, 'no lasting improvement in the standard of living of the mass of population can possibly be attained if every enhancement of the purchasing power of the cultivator is to be followed by a proportionate increase in population'.[239] However, nothing was done to start a birth control movement and this centrepiece of Indian poverty and agricultural backwardness generally went unattended.

The total cropped area increased from 212 million acres in 1920–1 to 226 million acres in 1925–6 and 229 million acres in 1930–1. However, total irrigated area increased only marginally from 48.9 million acres in 1920–1 to 49.6 million in 1930–1. Irrigation provided by government works remained static at 13 per cent of the cultivated area while the share of private and public works declined slightly from 23 per cent to 22 per cent. However, government continued to spend increasing sums on irrigation. Total capital outlay on irrigation (in lakh rupees) rose steadily from 72,35 in 1920–1 to 84,53 in 1924–5, 112.32 in 1928–9 and 139,58 in 1932–3 and the overall trend was maintained up to the commencement of the Second World War. Considering the low margins of sufficiency of food supplies in India and the threat of famines in local areas due to low precipitation in one or successive years, this cost was no more than the bare insurance cover against much higher famine relief expenditures which necessarily would have to be incurred.

A majority of people ate a poor diet and lacked the stamina to ward off diseases which acute malnutrition caused. This was an endemic problem, but it became life threatening if sudden shortage of food supplies occurred. For agriculture, the 1920s were relatively lucky. There was a good harvest in each year between 1921 and 1924 and thereafter economic revival continued till 1929. However, the Indian people needed to eat more protein and fat and not more cereals, and on this dimension the vicious cycle formed by low demand and chronic supply shortage stayed unbroken. People needed more information on dietary principles, more education to improve general understanding of the importance of a balanced diet for good health, as well as to wean themselves from the established grooves and traditional habits pertaining to foods and prevention of diseases. The Royal Commission brought out the vital interconnectedness of agriculture with social mores, people's values and their reluctance to accept progress based on science and self-effort as well as birth control. However, little progress followed. The figures on cropped area are official and referred to by Vera Anstey in relation to data on irrigation. However, they differ greatly from Sivasubramanian's data on the total cropped area. The two sets may pertain to gross and net areas under cultivation or to entirely different methods of estimation.

Agriculture was already connected to world trade in primary commodities. The second half of the 1920s saw the weakening of world demand and a move toward the termination of the bullish conditions which had received impetus after the First World War. Baker points out,

> The bullish atmosphere which had prevailed since the 1860s (despite several short-term slumps) was abruptly terminated.

> In brief, where once demand had been increasing faster than supply and where this had pushed up the prices in the characteristically speculative primary produce markets, there now seemed to be more supplies than demand. This position was reached earlier in the case of some commodities than others, but the slide of these particular prices managed to prick the bubble on which all markets were floated. This stage had been reached by mid-1929.[240]

The weakening of demand occurred earlier in those commodities which were also produced in the industrial countries. As production in the latter revived, competition became more intense.

In 1928–9, the world stocks in wheat were already ample, there were good harvests in the United States and Europe and it started the downward spiral of prices. Thereafter, the US moved towards protectionism and Europe toward deflation of respective currencies and economies. Baker says that, 'in the South East Asian rice market, there were also signs of increasing competition. India had long ago been replaced by Burma as the major trader and from the First World War onwards, Thailand, Indo–China, Taiwan, and Korea placed increasing amounts of rice in maritime trade.'[241] The collapse of wheat prices impacted other prices of primary goods and by 1927–8 these started tumbling in the unstable markets.

Elsewhere in the world, competitive deflation lowered output and employment, but not in the inelastic peasant agriculture of India. Groundnut production rose in 1930–1 compared to the previous year, then fell but rose again in 1932–3. In cotton, 1925–6 was the year of peak production but, thereafter, it declined erratically, to revive in 1935–6 and 1936–7. In jute, 1926–7 marked the highest level of production but in 1931–2 it was at less than half of that level. The market value of groundnut was highest at Rs. 387 million in 1927–8 but fell catastrophically to Rs. 194 million in 1930–1. Though it revived in the following year when output was lower. Cotton fetched the highest value of Rs. 1,770 million in

1923–4 but declined to Rs. 1,032 million in 1928–9 and fell more sharply thereafter to Rs. 548 million in 1930 and Rs. 442 million in 1932–3; decline in output was much less. In rice, the peak value was registered further back in 1919–20, at Rs. 5,730 million but stayed below this level in the following decade; and in 1928–9 it stood at Rs. 4,819 million, then fell every year to reach a low of Rs. 3,057 million in 1930–1, Rs. 2,734 million in 1931–2 and still lower during the next three years. In wheat, the most prosperous year was 1921–2 when it touched Rs. 1,750 million, but was already at a low level of Rs. 1,059 million in 1927–8, and in 1930–1 it declined to Rs. 681 million and Rs. 628 million in the following year. This was the lowest value fetched by wheat since 1900–01.[242]

Severe shrinkage of demand and inelastic supply together contributed to the decline in the value of agricultural commodities in India. The shock effect of the worldwide depression weakened confidence, and the overvalued rupee hampered revival as it encouraged imports, while the deflation of the currency pursued for other reasons essentially wiped out prosperity. 'The general level of primary produce prices halved between 1929–30 and 1931–33, while manufacture prices declined around 30 per cent. Prices dropped so dramatically that primary produce remained cheap and continued to find a reasonable market in the depressed economies of the West.'[243] In 1929, the government was faced with budgetary problems as well as on balance of payments. What it did made the economic conditions worse. Foreign firms withdrew credit, while the expatriates in India stepped up remittances.

The ex-post data provide a basis for surmises on the responses of the average tenant farmers in the country. Wherever possible, farmers cultivated more of the same crop, believing that the decline in market realizations would be reversed in the next year, or they switched over to other crops, but this depended on diverse factors, such as, availability of seeds and other inputs and they may have had to borrow money to meet the costs. Rural indebtedness increased and became a heavy burden. Estimates of rural indebtedness by provincial banking inquiry committees during 1929–30 provide a basis for evaluating the seriousness of the debt burden. In Bombay, the average debt per family came to Rs. 329, but it was also reported that the percentage of families free from debt was 13 per cent in Sind, 21 per cent in north Gujarat, 23 per cent in south Gujarat and 29 per cent in the Konkan. By comparison, in Madras it was reported that the debt was Rs. 19 per rupee of assessment, and the figures for the latter were not given. In Bengal, the average debt per agriculturist family was placed at Rs. 160. In Punjab the reporting was more informative, total agricultural debt in 1921 was estimated at Rs. 90 crores, which rose to Rs. 135 crores in 1929. 'The debt's multiple of land revenue was 27 in 1929 as compared to 19 in 1921. The debt per head of those supported by agriculture was Rs. 104 in 1929 as compared with Rs. 76 in 1921. The debt per cultivated acre rose from Rs. 31 in 1921 to Rs. 45 in 1929.'[244]

Similarly, data for other provinces, based on varying methods of inquiry, are given. The economic significance of the debt as reported for CP and Berar was that the total debt of Rs. 36.5 crores came to about 49 per cent of the normal crop value in gross terms, while the interest charges amounted to two and a half times the total revenue demand, and to one-third of the normal agricultural income. The total debt represented Rs. 227 per cultivating family.

The size of debt was important since it directly impinged on the welfare of tenants. Rent and interest were charged to current income and if it was low it might lead to greater indebtedness, or loss of family assets, or even destitution. Moreover, once a debt was incurred for unproductive purposes it could not be repaid and would become cumulative. As prices fell in the following decade the burden of debt increased and peasant households lost gold and land as they helplessly coped with adverse conditions. There is no doubt that agricultural land was good security for incurring the debt, but with unpaid debt the security of the land was lost as tenants were evicted and the ownership transferred to money lenders. During the 1930s, this problem received priority attention of the provincial governments as they worked hard to give some relief to the oppressed tenant cultivators.

Rothermund analysed rack-renting and money lenders' grip on peasant agriculture in the context of laws such as, the Punjab Land Alienation Act, 1901 which practically prohibited the transfer of land to non-agriculturists. It further stipulated that a tenant could not be evicted as long as he paid the rent, and that the rent could not be raised beyond the permitted level, which might be one per cent per year. 'In periods of rising prices, this meant that the occupancy right of a tenant was soon much more valuable than the landlord's right with regard to the same unit of land.'[245] However, in periods of falling prices arrears of rent could not be paid and conflicts with landlords ensued.

In 1930–1 in UP, Nehru witnessed many such conflicts, just at the time the Second Round Table Conference was in session and he was dismayed that the Congress, with a strong presence of zamindars, could not openly support the peasants. An economic reason for the intensity of agrarian conflicts may be observed in the paradoxical behaviour of land prices remaining stable though prices of crops were declining. This was because of two reasons. First, the effect of population increase on land resulted in subdivision of land and sharecropping. The sharecroppers received half or less of the produce and so focussed on maximizing production per sharecropper rather than the yield. Higher yield would have led to the same beneficial result but that was dependent on increased investment per acre. This no one did, partly owing to low economic capacity to save and invest, partly on scarcity of credit and for the remaining due to prevalent risk aversion. However, demand for land would either rise or prevented from falling with the growth in the number of cultivators, including sharecroppers. 'Land as security and as a source of rental income was much more in demand than the precious metals. A rising population would guarantee that the value of land was bound to rise.'[246]

The policy of deflation adversely impacted the farm economy though it took several years for the effect to be felt. It appears that for reasons not connected with the fiscal autonomy of India, the government took recourse to contracting money supply through an administrative device. Its reverse council drafts exceeded the council drafts and the effect was the withdrawal of money from circulation. Apparently this did not suffice, so the government decided, to deflate the currency by other means. This policy raised the velocity of circulation and increased interest rates. Shortage of rural credit could have been anticipated, but was apparently ignored by the government owing to other priorities.[247]

Baker views the shortage of rural credit as an autonomous factor occasioned by the Depression and does not blame the government's deflationary policies. 'The immediate effect of the Depression was to inhibit the flows of credit within the village with the result that there was a definite drop in the acreage under cultivation in the plains in the three years after 1928–29. The commercial crops suffered most.' He refers to the groundnut crop, 'which peaked in the late 1920s and then petered away'. The cotton acreage also followed the same course.[248] He expounds the theme further:

> Local credit was not so freely available after the Depression. Cultivators who had prospered in the 1920s, and had immediately lent out their profits to their neighbours, fared very badly between 1929 and 1933 when the steady contraction of prices made it impossible to gain any reasonable return from the form of moneylending. In the aftermath, there was much less competitive moneylending and consequently a much greater chance of dependence on a few sources of credit.[249]

Peasant cultivation was put to further strain by the unrelenting demand of the government for increased revenue. In the Bombay presidency the original revenue demand was raised from Rs. 43.79 million in 1929–30 to

Rs. 45.325 million in 1932–3. Suspensions and remissions also increased, nevertheless actual collections rose steadily. This hurt the land owners directly and not the tenants and labourers. 'The landlords and the rich peasants, so often seen as the beneficiaries of economic change over the British period, were apparently the very groups most adversely affected.'[250] The manner in which the land-owning classes adapted to the strains of lower cash incomes and higher cost payments can be conjectured, probably an increase in the number of chronically deficit households resulting in alienation of lands or sale of assets.

The rupee exchange controversy developed when deflation of currency had been going on for five years. It did not directly feature in the debate due to non-availability of information on this subject. The government was keen that the price level should adjust downwards to be in equilibrium with world prices. This was needed to maintain the rupee–sterling parity and also to stimulate exports. It resulted in a contradictory pull on policy because the British government was keen on protecting exports to India. In fact, Britain was heavily involved in multilateral currency flows due to repayment of war loans to the USA on one hand, and receiving reparations for war damages from Germany on the other. Its international reserve position was precariously balanced and indirectly helped by the considerable US loans and investments in Europe, of which Germany was a major beneficiary. Germany in turn used the foreign exchange earnings to make annual repayments to Britain and France.

Indian exports in excess of imports were badly needed since the export surplus was kept in the form of monetary reserves in London and not used for financing domestic investment in India. Contraction of money supply was needed to maintain the exchange rate at 1s6d, which discouraged exports while encouraging imports, but lowered the price level which would have the opposite effect. Consequently, between 1922 and 1931, the total monetary stock comprising notes in circulation and silver rupees declined from Rs. 5,090 million to Rs. 3,790 million.

The contradiction between the need for India to build up both exports and imports in steps with a faster pace of development and use of export surplus towards this end and the pressing requirements of the British economy were resolved almost totally by sacrificing India's concerns and interests. The many arguments then advanced in support of the official policy were mostly contrived, pretentious or false. Sir Purushottamdas Thakurdas had made a prophetic warning on the disastrous effect of an artificially bolstered exchange rate in the event prices fell. The argument that the prices showed a declining trend and were already too low for the economy, was ignored, since it had been decided that in the drastically altered position of post-war Britain, India must play a supportive role and not insist on fiscal autonomy. India's new Finance Secretary, Schuster, understood better: that India faced grave peril owing to the unrestricted flow of remittances to Britain conjointly with the problem of dwindling exports. The latter resulted in low earnings in foreign exchange, so the next problem was how to meet the demand for remittances along with the Home Charges. Schuster sought a major credit to be provided by the Bank of England to prevent flight of capital from India, but the Bank refused. He then argued for lowering the ratio to 1s4d, but this too was refused. For the British government, it was an unthinkable proposition and could not be conceded.

The slump had a most baneful effect on the finances of the government. The average annual value of exports in the decade ending 1929–30 was Rs. 326 crores which fell in the next two years to Rs. 136 crores. The value of raw cotton, piece goods and twist-end yarn were at Rs. 81.47 crores per annum for the period 1924–5 to 1928–9 and these came down to Rs. 41.37 crores during 1929–0 to 1933–4. Jute, raw and manufactured, used to earn Rs. 86.68 crores per annum in the former period, which declined to Rs. 44.14 crores per annum. Likewise, the slump affected every item of export.

In quantitative terms, raw cotton and raw jute were exported in smaller quantities and fetched still less due to fall in prices. However, ores were exported in larger quantities, yet earned less.

As the Depression deepened, exporters started exporting more, perhaps because at lower prices demand had picked up but the country continued to lose. These impacted government finances adversely. Customs revenue declined from Rs. 50.30 crores in 1929–30 to Rs. 45.91 crores in 1930–1, excise revenue fell from Rs. 18.22 crores to Rs. 14.51 crores in these two years, and the total tax revenue fell from Rs. 107.37 crores to Rs. 95.57 crores respectively. The grand total of all revenues showed a decline from Rs. 146.50 crores to Rs. 128.32 crores between 1929–30 and 1930–1. However, the grand total of public expenditure resisted cuts and actually rose from Rs. 141.90 crores in the former to Rs. 143.62 crores in the latter year. Debt services rose along with general administration and several other less important heads.[251] The yield of import duties declined as imports, principally of sugar and cotton, were in lower quantities. As profits of companies sank to lower levels, so did income tax revenue. The railway finances showed deficits in every year for six years starting with 1930–31. According to Thomas,

> The situation was not brought about solely by the trade depression. There were important aggravating factors like the economic boycott, frequent hartals and so forth. These political disturbances weakened confidence in India as a field for investment both at home and abroad, and led to the decline in the price of Indian securities and a large withdrawal of capital from the country. This meant increased expenditure on loans, and the Government of India was forced to take measures to protect their position. High money rates prevailed, and this increased the difficulty of traders. The rapid decline in the price of government securities disclosed the true state of public credit.

The 3.5 per cent India sterling stock fell from 69 in 1929 to 60 in April 1931 and then to 43.5 in September.[252] This was when the British government went off the gold standard. In India, the government issued an ordinance abandoning the obligation to sell gold or sterling under the Currency Act, 1927 and three days, 22–24 September, were declared public holidays. However, banks functioned normally on 25 September onwards, and the restrictions on foreign exchange transactions were soon removed.

The pound was set to float and logically the rupee could also have been set on the same course. This would have ended the ratio controversy as the rupee would have found a market-determined relationship with sterling. Instead, the ratio of 1s6d was reaffirmed and the rupee was re-linked to sterling but without gold. As prices fell, the currency was further contracted. This looked very strange, because the government borrowed money even as it destroyed part of the money in circulation as unwanted in real terms. The British government decided that the only option India had under the circumstances was to draft an emergency budget in the current Assembly session. As directed, the emergency budget was presented at the end of September. Earlier in the month, Schuster had recommended to float the rupee and, on being countermanded by the Secretary of State, Samuel Hoare, he advised the Viceroy to submit the resignation of the government. However, this was described as 'desertion' before the enemy and rejected. Schuster argued,

> Linking of the rupee with an unstable currency is derogatory to India, it is the most signal proof of India's subservience, it has been done not in the interest of India but of England, one object has been to retain financial control and particularly of India's gold reserves, and it may prevent the recovery of trade which might otherwise be anticipated. It will be said that at a time of unprecedented agrarian depression government deliberately prevented a rise in Indian prices which would have followed a free rupee.[253]

This too was ignored.

In the emergency budget, the government showed action by way of retrenchment and increased taxation. A 10 per cent cut in pay was imposed on all government servants drawing a salary above Rs. 40 per month. The Viceroy accepted a cut of 20 per cent and members of his Council took a deduction of 15 per cent in their salaries. Custom duties were enhanced and surcharges imposed. Income tax rates were raised and a general surcharge of 25 per cent on the existing rates was announced. Higher taxes immediately raised a storm of protests by the business classes, both European and Indian. The government was balancing its budget but unbalancing the budgets of business concerns.[254] On the positive side, India's credit was restored. At the same time, capital expenditure was drastically slashed and it impacted the purchasing power of the people. The government followed a pro-cyclical policy though owing to the low weightage of the government budget in the economy, the macro effects may not have been large. Together with the demonetization policy of the previous decade, the load of additional taxation and sharp reduction in civil works produced adverse conditions which, by themselves, looked irreversible.

The money supply had declined by 6 per cent in both 1929–30 and 1930–1. Interest rates now rose and exacerbated the problem of raising working capital. As the depression deepened and farm households struggled to find cash to meet the debt and land revenue or rent obligations, and avert the threat of eviction from their lands, they started selling gold ornaments. 1931 happens to be the year India's gold began to appear as an export item. According to Tomlinson,

> The most striking development of the period was the export of substantial amounts of privately owned gold from September 1931 onwards, which turned India into a net exporter of previous metals for the rest of the 1930s. The flow of imported gold which had been such a feature of the Indian economy before the depression was now reversed; between 1931 and 1939 net exports of the treasure were worth Rs. 349.41 crores.[255]

Economic distress led to primary dis-hoarding of gold ornaments. These were then melted and turned into bullion.

However, what led it into the London money market was speculative trading profit. Rothermund provides data on the differential rates of depreciation of the rupee and the pound in terms of gold, relative to the value in August 1931. In October, November and December 1931, the rupee depreciated by 15.8 per cent, 17.7 per cent and 26.5 per cent respectively, while the pound depreciated at a faster pace of 19.8 per cent, 22.5 per cent and 31.2 per cent respectively. This differential made it possible to buy gold in India and sell it in London. 'Both the push and the pull factors originated from the deflationary policy of the government, because the contraction of money supply precipitated distress sales and also maintained the exchange rate of the rupee at a level which was higher than the statutory rate.'[256]

Perhaps by some short-term reasoning, a relative appreciation of the rupee was viewed as a desired development, inasmuch as it reinforced the government's commitment to adhere to the statutory rate of 1s6d as a matter of foremost importance. Moreover, London was craving for gold, excessive withdrawal of gold reserves had already commenced and the sudden announcement of abandonment of the gold standard was made to protect existing reserves of about 130 million pounds sterling. For several years, a feeling of scarcity of monetary gold was felt, as the USA had used the gold inflows, caused by balance of trade surpluses, to build its gold reserves rather than let the money supply increase and the price level rise. Hoarding of gold built up pressure on gold standard currencies as speculators stepped in with withdrawal of gold from the weaker currencies and heightened the vulnerability of the entire world system based on gold.

The arrival of gold from India into London reversed the pressure and the stability of the pound appeared more secure. 'The combined effect of the push and pull factors was advantageous for the new sterling bloc and, therefore the British had no reason to interfere with the process which was a windfall to them.'[257] However, in India, it measured the extent of disinvestment in agriculture and trade, hence the impoverishment of the people. Those who had saved earlier were forced by conditions beyond their control and logical grasp to dissave and somehow protect their lands as the only source of livelihood and survival. At the macro level, the sale of gold released purchasing power to build up the sagging aggregate demand. It also represented the distressed transfer of savings from one section of the population to the traders and speculators in gold who made profits and built up bank balances.[258]

In 1930 and 1931 several other problems rose. In 1929–30 the wheat crop yielded 10.828 million tonnes, a sharp increase over the previous year's output of only 8.88 million tonnes, and in 1930–1 it was lower but still a good crop of 9.635 million tonnes. The weighted average price declined from Rs. 136.6 per tonne in 1928–29 to Rs. 102.1 per tonne in 1929–30, Rs. 70.7 per tonne in 1930–1 and further to Rs. 67.2 per tonne in the following year.[259] This was partly due to the low purchasing power of the people but what led to the sharp drop in prices was the arrival of Australian wheat, resulting from a bumper harvest in that country. Moreover, in January 1931 the Australian pound was devalued by about 25 per cent to overcome the balance of payments crisis of 1929–30. India exported wheat and that would have helped in some manner but it was difficult to stabilize the market with Australian wheat competing in India. In 1931, the government imposed an import duty on wheat. The adoption of the Wheat Import Duty Act, 1931 is credited to the influence of Fazl-l-Hussain, the Punjab Unionist Party leader who was then a member of the Viceroy's Executive Council. Wheat imports declined by more than half between 1930–1 and 1931–2. Meanwhile, along with the pound, the rupee too stood devalued relative to gold in September, 1931 when Britain gave up the gold standard.[260]

Rice suffered in a different manner. Indian rice was exported to Japan but its production in that country had been stepped up and Japan became self-sufficient around 1928.

Thereafter, rice imports from India were blocked. According to Rothermund,

> in October 1930, a plentiful harvest reached the Japanese market and prices fell by one-third. This could have remained a purely internal matter, but in a world market that was already apprehensive of falling price trends, the news of the price fall in Japan had an immediate impact on the London price market, where the price of Indian rice fell drastically in November 1930. There was no immediate reaction to this in India; it was only when the winter rice harvest reached the market in January 1931 that the Indian rice price fell very steeply.

The weighted price declined in 1928–9 and 1929–30 from Rs. 162.6 per tonne to Rs. 146.8 per tonne. In the following year the price was Rs. 103.9 per tonne and a year later, in 1931–2 it fell further to Rs. 88.1 per tonne. The price continued to fall for another two years before stabilizing at higher levels.[261] The sharp setback to rice indicated the extent to which Indian agriculture was buffeted by speculative forces connected to world trade. Tight credit in India must have been a primary cause because there was no glut in the Indian market, nor was imported rice a factor that governed domestic prices. A likely cause may have been panic sales shortly after the harvest mainly due to the drying up of credit.

The immediate impact of the depression was such that 'the local traders and moneylenders were completely flabbergasted and did not know how to manage the market any longer'.[262] Yet, the subsistence farmer carried on and took his losses as fated. Conflicts arose because the government with its revenue demands, the landlords with claims on rent, and moneylenders charging higher interests and insisting on stricter terms for loans, had to depend on the cultivators' ability and willingness to pay and if their position was deeply eroded the others who had earlier profited at the expense of the cultivator also suffered. The moneylenders who were also traders experienced total disruption of their business because losses mounted as the stored grain declined in value. It is possible to connect this phase with the sale of gold. When

Britain went off the gold standard, the price of gold suddenly spurted by about 20 per cent, 'and this was a signal for all moneylenders to force their debtors to surrender their gold ornaments'.[263] Soon gold reached the London money market:

> Schuster could hardly believe it when he saw heaps of beautiful gold ornaments piled up in the currency office. When faced with the option to part with these ornaments or to sell their land indebted peasants all over India must have handed over these necklaces and bracelets to the moneylenders who were quick to make a profit by selling them.[264]

Communists in Unions, Powerful Strikes, AITUC Splits

The development of the labour movement in India is inseparable from the role of the active communist organizers. Among the mill workers, the trade union in the mid-1920s was an external element for them, but not necessarily of them. Though employed in factories with formal organizations, most workers in Bombay, Calcutta and other major industrial cities were rural in upbringing and outlook and frequently visited their villages to renew their ties and perhaps restore depleted energy. They understood unity in action as well as the cost and consequences of strikes. These were painful but necessary to voice collective grievances and so were often unavoidable. However, trade unions required a dedicated core of activists, imbued with idealism, free from the stranglehold of jobbers and not subject to the mercy of the employer.

At the initial stages, a few communists organized workers and peasants parties at the provincial level. These parties, mainly in Bengal since 1926 and Bombay since 1927, were not communist parties with a camouflaged name. They included a broader cross-section of left-leaning Congress workers who were disillusioned with Gandhi's style of leading and inexplicably withdrawing movements. They were also disenchanted with the obstructionist tactics of the Swarajya Party politicians, yet found unacceptable the method of revolutionary terrorism. They looked for another way of taking forward the broad based nationalist struggle against foreign rule. To this agenda were added the more basic but longer-term struggles against all forms of exploitation and tyranny, principally Indian feudalism and capitalism. In such gatherings were included Marxists, leftists with a broadly secular and humanist ideological positions, as well as left Khilafatist radical Muslim activists with a communal outlook. However, the small bands of self-educated Marxists formed the unifying and leading elements of these parties. They also understood the Leninist version called Bolshevism or communism and accepted the international leadership provided by the Comintern.

Enrolling as members of the Congress or the Peasants and Workers (PW) Parties the communists were directed to work in trade unions and bring the AITUC under their influence to turn it into a class organization capable of taking the initiative or responding to political agitations for India's independence. The AITUC must be wrested from the control of reformist leaders like N.M. Joshi and Diwan Chaman Lal who did not believe in class war and were unwilling to train workers to view themselves as the grave diggers of capitalism. Beginning in 1925, the communist influence in the organization reached a stage in 1927 where they could alter its programmes and introduce new features. One of them, S.V. Ghate, secured election as a Secretary of the AITUC in March 1927. At the next session in November 1927, another communist, S.A. Dange, who was convicted and jailed in the 1924 Kanpur Conspiracy case was elected as an Assistant Secretary. Under their influence the organization moved steadily toward a leftist and more political course. However, they failed in steering it towards Moscow and affiliating with the Red International of Labour Unions or in ousting the moderates and Gandhian nationalists from leadership roles.[265]

The AITUC had also made a call for the boycott of the Simon Commission and, in February 1928, a workers' demonstration was organized in Bombay with the Workers and Peasants Party (WPP) cadre in the leading and organizing roles. For the first time red flags and festoons displaying the hammer and sickle were carried in the procession. A political hartal was observed. According to the communists, 'The February 3 demonstration was the beginning of a new stage of development in which the masses entered the political field as an independent political force under the leadership of their own party and organizations.'[266] In January 1929, the Bengal Peasants and Workers Party (PWP) led in organizing a rally to boycott the visit of the Simon Commission. Workers were politicized and learnt about the weight they could carry in the ongoing nationalist agitation for Swaraj. In Bombay, the mill workers appeared to be preparing for the prolonged strikes that followed.

The Bombay cotton textile mills faced adverse economic conditions and the Tariff Board asked the industry to raise its efficiency and cut costs including the wage bill. 'So far as costs of production are concerned, it is in labour costs that it is to be found the main reason why the depression in the industry has been felt so much more acutely in Bombay than it has elsewhere.' The Tariff Board recommended 'internal economies' and suggested that 'in a time of depression, the most obvious method of effecting an economy in the cost of production is by reducing the wages of labour.'[267] The mills had tried this in 1925 and there was a strike. This time the solution lay in introducing rationalization and increasing the workload. Fewer workers would be employed. It worked. Output was diversified and between 1925–6 and 1931–2, 'the average number of hands daily employed in Bombay fell by 13.5 per cent, but the industry's output of yarn increased by 23.4 per cent and of woven goods by 32 per cent.'[268]

One mill put up a notice that with effect from 1 January 1928 spinners who worked two sides of the spinning frame would earn 50 per cent more. Retrenchment was seen as the next step and 500 spinners struck work on 2 January demanding continuance of the existing system of one spinner manning only one frame. The dispute ended in a compromise.

Another dispute arose in about eight mills on the issue of the proposed reduction in wages and the new system of work. Workers were asked to work three looms in place of two as hitherto and the strike spread. Workers agitated, displayed anger by stone throwing, while the two moderate unions counselled them to exercise restraint and boycott only those mills which had introduced three looms per weaver and two frames per spinner. In one mill the workers were told that as the majority of them had not joined the union, it was not possible for it to negotiate a settlement with the management. Slowly, a number of mills started working as workers who had gone on a spontaneous strike returned to work. Other mills remained closed. By the end of March, the strike ended, the mills worked the new rationalization scheme and the employers came out as winners.

In April, a number of strikes continued from the previous month, but there was no way a compromise could be worked out on the main issues, which were connected to the introduction of the rationalization scheme involving higher workload and reduction in the workforce. The unions and the WPP workers organized a huge procession of mill hands asking all workers to join a general strike. This was followed by stone throwing at mills forcing them to close down. By 26 April, all but two mills had to close their gates. 'Communists took an active part in organizing meetings and processions and in campaigning for the general strike.'[269] The strike was conducted by a joint strike committee which had 30 members comprising an equal number of moderate and militant wings. They raised 17 demands, to which the mill owners responded by publishing the terms on which mills would be reopened. These were not acceptable to the strike committee and it asked workers to continue the strike. Later, efforts at mediation were made and negotiations were conducted but proved futile. Then the government stepped in and a settlement was reached on the appointment of a Committee of Inquiry.[270]

The mills reopened on 6 October and workers returned

to work. As agreed, the government appointed a Committee of Inquiry with Justice Fawcett as the Chairman and published its report in March 1929. The remarkable part of the strike was the manner in which workers flocked to the communist-led Girni Kamgar Union (GKU). It was formed in May and soon attracted thousands of members. With 54,000 members the GKU dwarfed all other unions and emerged as the unrivalled custodian of workers' interests. Under the leadership of the communists the union created a structure of factory committees. It was a self-conscious workforce which responded to the GKU's organizational efforts. However, from this it could not be inferred that the newly enrolled membership understood the logic of discipline of unionization or the lasting imprint of their commitment to the union. The spontaneous response of workers to a most genuine threat to their jobs was to go on a strike, not to turn to the union, hold discussions and decide on a strategy of action, including negotiations and a compromise. Their eagerness to flock to the most militant elements conducting the strike showed that they were keen to carry on the battle, which, but for the government's intervention and the mediating role played by the moderates, would have ended in exhaustion and sullen abandonment of the cause by workers, who by now would be hungry and tired and eager to return to work. A great strike must aim at a settlement, else it would end in a collapse.

The government intervened with a purpose; the strike was actuated by genuine causes, but no less genuine was the mill owners' case and the despairing nature of problems they faced and wished to overcome. Hence there was a need for a via media or a devise which would lead to a settlement. The government was also interested in shielding the trade unions to help them grow along constructive lines, more or less on the model of the British trade unions. And it would not let the communists take over the unions still in their infancy.[271]

It was a costly strike. 'The total time lost to the textile industry on account of this strike amounted to nearly

22 million working days and the loss in wages to the labourers is calculated at approximately 3.5 crores of rupees.'[272] The city played a benevolent role; the Mayor's Relief Fund Committee took steps to feed nearly 10,000 children every day. The international working class rallied to lend support to the strikes and sent thousands of rupees in financial aid. The British TUC sent money, as did the Soviet Union and others.[273] The Strikers' Relief Fund was used to issue rations to workers and also to pay boat fares to workers to return to their villages. Though the general strikes ended on 6 October 1928, other disputes continued to occur in different mills and the cotton textile industry in Bombay remained in ferment.

Bombay was not the only trouble spot. In Jamshedpur there was a sectional strike in the Sheet Mill and the Boiler Department of the Iron and steel works, but it soon turned into a general strike and led to a lockout. In June 1928, nearly 25,000 workers were locked out. The crane drivers had struck earlier in February and in March, 700 to 800 men went on a strike in the New Rail Finishing Mill. Following this, there were several departmental strikes, all of which disorganized the efficient working of the company. The two observed features were: '(1) that the men consistently adopted the unconstitutional and, in a steel works, the harmful method of stopping work without giving any previous intimation whatever to the management; and (2) that the labour association was neither consulted nor its sanction obtained before direct action was taken in each case.'[274] In September, TISCO resumed normal functioning following a settlement in which Subhas Chandra Bose played a leading part.

In the railways too there were strikes at different places due to large-scale retrenchment, ill-treatment and assault on the workshop men, demands for higher wages and recognition of the union as well as against victimization. In the NGS Railway negotiations were conducted by V.V. Giri. In March, 1928, the municipal workers of Calcutta struck work and ended with a small increase in pay.[275]

In Bombay, following the Fawcett Committee report in March 1929, trouble resumed. In April, another strike started. 'Over a lakh of workers employed in the 62 mills in the city were involved in the strike. It resulted in a loss of about 8 million man days. The strike continued for about four months "and then ended disastrously."'[276] The issue was dismissal from employment due to absence from duty. It was viewed as victimization and resented by the GKU. Moreover, new hands were employed while the union wanted the dismissed workers to be reinstated, which implied dismissal of new hands. This, the mill owners refused to grant. About 6,000 workers were involved on the issue of dismissal. However, the second general strike failed to enthuse the workers; the strike dragged on and slowly workers abandoned the favoured union, the GKU, and returned to work.

Meanwhile, the Trade Disputes Act, 1929 was passed and enforced; so the government referred the dispute to a Court of Inquiry, under the provisions of the Act in July. 'The strike ended in a complete disaster. The workers did not gain any economic advantages. They had to accept willy-nilly the rationalization system. More and more mills brought it into force. However, the greatest defeat that the workers suffered was the smashing of their union which, until a few months back, was a powerful organization.'[277] The mill owners decided to put an end to the Mill Committees which interfered in the everyday functioning of mills, sometimes dictating terms to managers. The second strike gave the mill owners a chance to fight the union system and they came out the winners. One by one the active workers were dismissed or discharged on disciplinary grounds. Workers retaliated with strikes, but these gave the owners the opportunity to deliver further crippling blows to the union.

In the jute mills, workers formed unions mainly to conduct strikes and later forgot about them. The Whitley Commission observed:

> The attitude of mill hands towards the labour union is more or less indefinite. Membership grows very rapidly, during strikes

> or temporary excitements and falls equally rapidly after the termination of disputes. To some of them especially those who struck work through the instigation of officials of a particular union and had to resume without any satisfaction, the name of Anjuman or union has got into a bad odour. Their attitude, however, towards the union is fully recognized by employers who listen to the grievances placed by the union.

The office bearers of the union were honorary workers who had little time to attend the union office or enrol new members.

Referring to the spate of strikes in 1927, 1928 and 1929, the Commission said,

> The underlying cause of these stoppages was the growing consciousness of labour, but the immediate cause was partly economic and partly personal. The most deplorable factors in the strike situation were bad leadership, most careless handling of the strike situation by the employers or their agents and the preaching of Bolshevism. It is a matter of profound regret that few of those who conducted these strikes have any experience of negotiations for a settlement, and they unconsciously did a great disservice to the infant labour movement in India.

The Commission pointed out that employers do suffer huge losses, 'but the blow to the employees, who surrender unconditionally after weeks of semi-starvation and exhaustion of their slender resources (the strikes of Lillooah, Bowreah, Tatanagar are included in this category) is stupendous and crushing.'[278]

The jute mills had increased hours of work from 54 to 60 per week. It produced many strikes because, the Bengal government informed the Centre that, 'in each of these disputes there invariably was a complaint on the part of workmen concerned that the change which was accompanied by the lengthening of the working week, resulted in a decrease in their weekly earnings.' This was the economic basis of the general strike in 1929.[279] The jute mills laid off about 6,000 workers and followed it with a cut in wages. The industry was in the grip of depression and struggled for survival. The only method known to the jute industry magnates was to stay competitive by lowering cost of production. This included retrenchment or lay-off to cut the wage bill. The same mechanism was followed in the railways. The government stopped setting up courts of inquiry because these would be of no avail.

It may have been sheer coincidence that, in 1928–9, the political line of the Comintern took a left turn. Karnik is of the view that the Bombay general strike in 1929 was conducted by the young and inexperienced communist leaders mainly to conform to the Comintern's directive to intensify class struggle and prepare the masses for a revolutionary confrontation with the capitalists and British imperialism. All the senior communist leaders had been arrested in the Meerut Conspiracy case and were not there to lead the GKU.

> The arrests took place in March 1929. By that time Indian communists had received their new directives from the Communist International. The directives were according to the ultra-left line that was adopted at the Sixth World Congress held in Moscow in September 1928. According to the new line, the revolution was just around the corner and everything was to be done to hasten its advent.[280]

The GKU was no doubt a red flag union and it pushed workers to continue with a strike which was failing, but the general strike of jute mill workers in 1929 was entirely in the control of moderate leaders. The Muslim weavers in the jute mills were closer to their mosques than to any political leaders and it was a straight fight for working hours, wages, the manner piece rated work was calculated and fed by mistrust. There was no communist hand in Calcutta in 1929.

The AITUC was badly hit by the new line because though the communists were dominant, the moderate leaders were unwilling to be commanded by them and refused to toe the line on class war. A major question was to determine the AITUC's attitude towards the Royal Commission on Labour. N.M. Joshi and Diwan Chaman Lal had agreed to be members of the Commission, while the left wing wanted to boycott it. Joshi stood his ground; he would also not agree to the left's position to withdraw from the ILO. At the tenth session in November 1928, hot words were exchanged. On ILO and the Whitley Commission, the left-dominated AITUC managed to pass boycott resolutions.[281] The moderate group then decided to withdraw from the IATUC and float another organization, by the name of, the Indian Federation of Trade Unions.

Jawaharlal Nehru was the president of AITUC but he simply watched the great split and could do nothing to prevent it. It could not have been prevented because the left's voting strength had increased enormously on admission of the GKU as an affiliated union with the supposed membership of 40,000 men. The communists were determined to boycott the Whitley Commission, reject the Nehru Report, denounce the Round Table Conference, forge links with international organizations sponsored by Moscow, and they left no scope for compromise.[282] Actually, Nehru sympathized with the left and thought that the seceding of the right wing was unnecessary and avoidable. N.M. Joshi said, 'Some of us were not willing to boycott the Whitley Commission, and if the Congress wanted our cooperation, no resolution on non-cooperating with the Commission should have been passed. The same is true regarding the resolution on the Round Table Conference. We welcomed the idea of a Round Table Conference.'[283]

As a result of the split, the AITUC became a much weakened organization. Yet, in 1930, it thought of calling a general strike of a political character. Little is known on whether any action could be taken on it. There were a number of strikes of an industrial nature in which, wherever feasible, the communists participated. However, a much bigger civil disobedience movement was in progress and it dwarfed all other protest activities.

The 1929 split was followed by further dissensions in the AITUC. Most of the senior communist leaders were in detention in the Meerut Conspiracy case, so it was left to the younger and relatively inexperienced communists to interpret the directives of the Comintern and act accordingly. Outside the WPP, the communists had no political presence. It was not even known whether a Communist Party of India existed. The Comintern had no evidence that other than on paper it was at all there. The only mass organizations in which the communists functioned were the unions which they had brought into existence or revived. In Bombay, the leading unions were the Girni Kamgar Union and the GIP Railwaymen's Union. However, practically in every mass organization they had to work together with the militant nationalists and the moderate responsivists. Adherence to the new left line of the Comintern could not be complied with in such organizations where few would concur with the denunciation of Gandhi's style of leadership in the Salt Satyagraha, or the Gandhi–Irwin pact which followed.

Though the sources of dissension were in the politics of the new communist line, to prepare every mass organization toward a revolutionary class war, the second split in the AITUC was triggered by a minor dispute as to who between the two contenders actually represented the GKU, so may sit in the General Council. The AITUC's president, Subhas Chandra Bose, decided it one way, by casting two votes, then faced the unpleasant experience of a vote of censure against himself, which was lost by 26 to 24 votes. The second split occurred in 1931 because, 'not being successful in getting the whole AITUC to agree to their line, not prepared to give up their left sectarian approach, the communists broke away from the AITUC.'[284] In 1929, Jawaharlal Nehru was a passive spectator of the split and in 1931 Subhas Chandra Bose was directly involved and unintentionally acted in a manner which precipitated the second split. The N.M. Joshi-led organization became known as the National Trades Union Federation (NTUF), earlier the IFTU, while the communist-led secessionist group called itself the Red Trade Union Congress. Now the AITUC represented only a minor section of trade unions, mainly because many unions preferred to stay aloof and unaffiliated. In January 1931, the GKU (Red Flag) leadership took an initiative to prepare the ground for unity based on its platform that: 'The trade union is an organ of class struggle.' Further, no union can work for the object of reconciling the interests of capital and labour, 'or to foster friendly relations between the employer and the employee'.[285] This was rejected by the NTUF.

The Trade Disputes Act, 1929 was criticized by the proponents of class war, but it was little noticed that by this enactment the government took on itself certain responsibilities to produce settlements in industrial disputes. The only parts of the Act which were used in extremely few cases pertained to Courts of Inquiry on the assumption that the findings of an impartial inquiry into the causes of the dispute and the manner it had been conducted would result in public pressure on the disputing parties and lead to an amicable termination of the dispute. However, in the case of the Fawcett Committee an unrealistic objective that the report would result in a permanent settlement was not realized. The Committee did make several valuable suggestions, which could not be implemented due to the breakdown in negotiations between the parties.

The part of the Act which the unions were agitated about was that no strike unconnected to the industry could be permitted and they may attract fines and imprisonment. This meant that sympathetic strikes were illegal. Similarly, lightening strikes or lockouts in the public utilities were made punishable. Prevention of general strikes was a feature of the Act which created much alarm. However, the government rarely depended on these provisions in dealing with a strike, though legal yet threatening to go out of control, or illegal; it used the punitive measures of other laws, including the Public Safety Act, 1929 to deal with them. Both laws were enacted, though they were strongly opposed in the Assembly. The latter was actually defeated when the Bill was put to vote, but was nonetheless enacted by certification. Its aim was to curb communist activities in the country. In 1927, the AITUC had passed a resolution rejecting and condemning the Trade Disputes Bill as a menace to the existence of the trade union movement, because it deprived workers of the right to declare strikes of a political nature and the employees of public utilities to air their grievances in the form of strikes without prior notice. The Act required that a notice be served before starting any industrial action.[286]

ENDNOTES

1. Sir Verney Lovett, *A History of the Indian Nationalist Movement*, London, Frank Cass and Co. Ltd., First Edition, February 1920, New impression of Third Edition, 1968, p. 172, also Ch. VII.
2. Judith Brown gives a detailed account of Gandhi's work in Champaran as well as the response of the government. See *Gandhi's Rise to Power, Indian Politics 1915-1922*, Cambridge, At the University Press, 1972, Chapter 3, 'Satyagraha, 1917–18', Quote on pp. 71–2.
3. Ibid., p. 106.
4. Ibid., p. 165.
5. R.C. Majumdar, *History of the Freedom Movement in India*, Vol. III, Calcutta, Firma K.L. Mukhopadhyay, 1963, p. 21. According to Ram Gopal,

   > The Punjab was a paradox. On the one hand it alone supplied more than half the recruits to the army and was the only great province which made a really serious war effort. On the other, it had been one of the storm centres of revolutionary activities. On the tyrannical methods employed there, a typical example is of a revenue officer (Tehsildar), who used to prepare a list of all men in a village and ask each family of three or four brothers to provide one or two recruits for the war. If the fixed number was not made available voluntarily, he would resort to cruel punishment.

   How India Struggled for Freedom (A Political History), Bombay, The Book Centre Pvt. Ltd., 1967, pp. 304–5.
6. Ibid., pp. 305–6.
7. A.K. Majumdar, *Advent of Independence* (Foreword by K.M. Munshi), Bombay, Bharatiya Vidya Bhavan, 1963, pp. 79–80.
8. Ram Gopal, *How India Struggled for Freedom* (loc. cit), 1967, pp. 307–14.

9. In a letter to the King, Chelmsford praised Sir Michael O'Dwyer for acting 'with his accustomed courage and promptness, and we must be grateful for the fact that we had him at the head of affairs in the Punjab when this outbreak took place.' In another letter he said that deep racial feelings were at the root of the disturbance. However, 'there can be, I think, no doubt that we were faced with disorders that might well have resulted in another mutiny if they had not been promptly and vigorously suppressed.' On Gen. Dyer's action at Jallianwala Bagh he said that, 'it was impossible to get over the fact that his action at Jallianwala Bagh went far beyond the necessities of the case and that we could not acquit him altogether of a lack of humanity in connection with his neglect of the wounded whom he left uncared for on the spot.' He also referred to the Hunter Committee's finding that there was no conspiracy behind the disturbances and said: 'While we could not disagree with the finding, I cannot help thinking that there was more in the theory than the committee found. The simultaneous nature of the disorders, the widespread interference with communications and the similarity of the excesses committed in the various areas of disturbance to my mind all point to preconcerted action. We shall probably never know the real truth, just as we have never known it in the case of the mutiny of 1857.' *Secret Papers From British Royal Archives*, Chief Editor P.N. Chopra, New Delhi, Konark Publishers Pvt. Ltd. Letter 121, p. 197 and Letter 122, p. 199.
10. See the textbook by Dr. Rama Nand Aggarwala, *National Movement and Constitutional Development of India*. Third Revised Edition, Delhi, Metropolitan Book Co. (P) Ltd., 1961 Part III. Ch. XI, XII and XIII.
11. R.C. Majumdar, *History of the Freedom Movement in India*, Vol. III, (op. cit.), pp. 78–85 and Ram Gopal, *How India Struggled for Freedom* (loc. cit.), pp. 315–6.
12. Brown gives a detailed review of the two movements in *Gandhi's Rise to Power* (op. cit.), in Ch. 6, 7 and 8.
13. The text of the treaty as published in India together with the background and the position Gandhi took may be seen in S.R. Bakshi, *Indian National Movement and the Raj*, Vol. 1, New Delhi, Criterion Publications, 1989, Ch. IX. 'The Khilafat.'
14. Mushirul Hasan (Ed.), *Communal and Pan-Islamic Trends in*

Colonial India, New Delhi, Manohar, 1981, article by the editor, 'Religion and Politics in India. The Ulema and the Khilafat Movement.' Quote on p. 15.

15. Ibid. See Prabha Dixit's, essay, 'Political Objectives of the Khilafat Movement in India.' Bimal Prasad refers to the Muslim expectation that the temporal power of the Khalifa was related to their political importance in India.

    The fact that the Indian Muslims take a deep interest in the fate of their coreligionists outside India and that the collapse of the Muslim powers of the world is bound to have an adverse influence on the political importance of the Mussalmans in the country, and that the annihilation of the military powers of Islam in the world cannot but have far-reaching effects on the minds of even the loyal Mussalmans in the country

    was the message that was strongly conveyed by the Muslim League in December 1919. *A Nation Within Nation* (op. cit.), pp. 156–7.
16. Ibid. pp. 165–8, also Tara Chand, Vol. III (op. cit.), pp. 496–7. He cities a different set of figures on Moplah casualties.
17. Ibid., Tara Chand provides a short comment on Gandhi's action. 'The question was why did Gandhiji not realize the far-reaching consequences of his admission. For if the success of civil disobedience was apprehended to unleash uncontrolled forces of evil, there remained no justicaction for the movement unless chaos was regarded as preferable to order enforced by foreign rule.' Vol. Three, p. 499.
18. S.M. Burke and Salim Al-Din Quraishi, *The British Raj in India, A Historical Review*, Karachi, Oxford University Press, 1995, p. 235.
19. Ibid., p. 236. According to Burke and Quraishi:

    It obviously was a failure so far as the achievement of concrete goals was concerned. Swaraj was not achieved, the Punjab and Khilafat wrongs were not redressed. But, the campaign had woken the spirit of the people. Though the subscribing members of Congress never exceeded six million, its actual sympathizers began to number many times that figure. It had proved itself to be a country-wide fighting machine. Government repression had succeeded only in making prison and punishment more honourable. There was a greater realization by the people of their rights and more consciousness that they must rely on their own efforts to win them. Their faith in the bona fides of the foreign government was considerably reduced. The country on the whole became more Swaraj conscious.

Bisheshwar Prasad evaluated the results with reference to the philosophy and principles of the Non-Cooperation movement. He makes a strong defence of Gandhi. See, *Bondage and Freedom: A History of Modern India (1907-1947)*, Vol. II, Freedom, 1858–1947, New Delhi, Rajesh Publications, 1979, pp. 351–7.

20. Bimal Prasad, *The Foundations of Muslim Nationalism*, New Delhi, Manohar Publishers and Distributors, 1999, p. 200. He writes:

    However natural the exercise of power in the interest of the Muslim majority on the part of ministers drawing their support from it, the Hindus could not but feel deeply resentful, especially as they had, in spite of their smaller number, enjoyed a privileged position in the pre-reform era because of their educational and economic superiority. The result was acute communal tension. (p. 201).

21. Ibid., p. 219.
22. Ibid., pp. 219–20. The author gives a lengthy quotation from Annie Besant's speech in 1922. Lajpat Rai also thought along similar lines.
23. Dr Rama Nand Aggarwala (loc. cit.), p. 141.
24. Burke and Quraishi (loc. cit.), p. 239.
25. Ram Gopal, *How India Struggled for Freedom* (op. cit.), cites the agitation in Oudh (UP), where the peasants rose against their exploiters in January 1921, while their demonstration in Rae Bareilly was quelled by police firing. Another demonstration of the same kind took place in Fyzabad district where the property of a taluqadar (a big landlord) was looted and people thought that it had Gandhi's sanction. In Andhra Pradesh the Congress committee decided on stoppage of government taxes, pp. 321–31.
26. Bipan Chandra, *India's Struggle for Independence, 1857-1947*, New Delhi, Viking, Penguin Books (India) Ltd., 1988, p. 193.
27. Brown (op. cit.), pp. 331–5. 'Gaol saved the Mahatma's face and preserved the illusion of his power. The outstretched hand of the Raj rescued him from the embarrassment of having to admit that the Hindu–Muslim alliance which he had seen as a condition of Swaraj was not a rock but a quick sand.' p. 337.

28. D.R. Gadgil, *The Industrial Evolution of India in Recent Times, 1860–1939,* Bombay, Oxford University Press, Fifth Edition, 1971, Ch. XV, 'The Agriculturist, 1914–39', quotes on p. 207.
29. Ibid., 'Agricultural Statistics of British India,' p. 209.
30. Sivasubramanian refers to this view of Ashwini Saith and also another opinion that the yields in all likelihood remained about the same, citing data deficiency.
    See his, *Annual Estimates of National Income of India, 1900–1 to 1946–7.* New Delhi, Oxford University Press, 2000, p. 64.
31. Neil Charlesworth, 'Trends in the Agricultural Performance of an Indian Province, The Bombay Presidency, 1900–1920' in K.N. Chaudhuri and Clive J. Dewey (Eds.), *Economy and Society, Essays in Indian Economic and Social History,* Delhi, Oxford University Press, 1979, quotes on p. 120.
32. Ibid. The Bombay farmers preferred cotton over millets, 'Cotton was the success story of early twentieth century Bombay, continuing the expansion of the late nineteenth century.' Its total area rose by more than 15 per cent during the first half of the 1920s, p. 125. According to Charlesworth the ability of Japan to step up export of cotton goods between 1910 and 1920 by four times was based largely on Indian cotton.
33. R.D. Choksey, *Economic Life in the Bombay Gujarat (1800–1939),* Bombay, Asia Publishing House, 1968. p. 87
34. Ibid., Table 25, p. 99.
35. Christopher John Baker, *The Indian Rural Economy 1880–1955, The Tamil Nadu Countryside,* Delhi, Oxford University Press, 1984, p. 227, also pp. 227–30.
36. Ibid., see the instructive Table 8 on p. 229.
37. Ibid., p. 230.
38. B.R. Tomlinson, *The Political Economy of the Raj 1914–1947, The Economics of Decolonization in India,* The Macmillan Press Ltd. 1979, p. 10.
39. Choksi (loc. cit.), pp. 105–6.
40. Ibid. pp. 101–10.
41. Charlesworth (loc. cit.), pp. 122–4.
42. Choksi (loc. cit.), pp. 44–5. For West Bengal, Thorner gives census data to show that between 1911 and 1921 the total male population declined as did the working force, those engaged in agriculture, fishing, mining, construction and transport.

By comparison the workforce in manufacture increased. See Daniel Thorner, *The Shaping of Modern India*, New Delhi, Allied Publishers Pvt. Ltd., 1980, Table 1, p. 131.

43. Tomlinson (loc. cit.), pp. 86–7.
44. Mridula Mukherjee, 'Commercialization and Agrarian Change in Pre-Independence Punjab' in K.N. Raj, Neeladri Bhattacharya, Sumit Guha and Sakti Padhi (Eds.), *Essays on the Commercialisation of Indian, Agriculture*, Delhi, Oxford University Press, 1985, pp. 65–6.
45. Amiya Kumar Bagchi, *Private Investment in India, 1900–1939*, Cambridge University Press, 1972, p. 79, including the footnote.
46. Ibid., Table 3.2, p. 80.
47. Ibid., p. 83.
48. Rajnarayan Chandavarkar, *The Origins of Industrial Capitalism in India, Business Strategies and the Working Classes in Bombay, 1900–1940*, Cambridge University Press, 1994, p. 26.
49. Ibid., p. 62. The discussion of the emergence of Indian capital is inclusive of the communal aspects though the author shows that the development of the Parsi enterprise demonstrates more clearly that their acceptance of greater risks in the export trade or factory industry was largely a function of their narrowing options elsewhere. p. 59, see the section, 'The Evolution of Capitalism in Western India.' pp. 44–67.
50. Ibid., p. 250.
51. Ibid., pp. 252–3.
52. A.K. Bagchi (loc. cit.), pp. 276–7, especially Table 83.
53. Ibid., pp. 278–9.
54. Ibid., see the footnote on p. 278.
55. Dipesh Chakrabarty, *Rethinking Working-Class History: Bengal 1890–1940*, Delhi, Oxford University Press, 1989 (in arrangement with Princeton University Press), pp. 40–1.
56. Ibid., p. 41 (extracts from IJMA Report 1914).
57. Clive J. Dewey, 'The Government of India's "New Industrial Policy", 1980–1925. Formation and Failure' in K.N. Chaudhuri and Clive J. Dewey, *Economy and Society, Essays in Indian Economic and Social History* (loc. cit.), pp. 232–3.
58. Ibid., p. 236.
59. Ibid., See the discussion of the key recommendations of the Commission and the role the Centre had to play; pp. 240–2.

60. B.R. Tomlinson, *The Economy of Modern India 1860–1970*, Cambridge University Press, 1993, p. 132.
61. Morris D. Morris, 'The Growth of Large-Scale Industry to 1947', as Ch. VII, in *The Cambridge Economic History of India, Vol. 2, C.1757-C.1970* (Ed. Dharma Kumar), Cambridge University Press, 1983, p. 556; also 554–8. He says:

    No single act of policy or single change of behaviour could have made for much more rapid progress than did occur. It is not that India was caught in a low-level equilibrium trap from which, once liberated, development would be cumulative. When a great array of evidence is put together, the image that emerges is rather of a web of relationships which dampened the absolute level of performance and inhibited the rate of change. (p. 558).

62. Clive J. Dewey, 'The Government of India's "New Industrial Policy", 1980–1925, Formation and Failure' in K.N. Chaudhari and Clive J. Dewey (Eds.), *Economy and Society, Essays in Indian Economic and Social History* (loc. cit.), p. 251.
63. M.D. Joshi, 'Currency' as Ch. 17 in V.B. Singh (Ed.), *Economic History of India, 1857–1956*, Bombay, Allied Publishes Pvt. Ltd. 1965, p. 301, For a detailed review of the question, see B.R. Tomlinson, 'Monetary Policy and Economic Development: The Rupee Ratio Question 1921–1927' in *Economy and Society* (loc. cit.).
64. Ibid., p. 201.
65. B.R. Tomlinson, *The Political Economy of the Raj* (loc. cit.), pp. 174–9. Quote on p. 119. 'The Fiscal Autonomy Convention, which was part of the 1919 Act, laid down that if the Government of India and the legislature were in agreement on protective tariffs, the Secretary of State would avoid interfering with tariff policy as far as possible.' 'The Fiscal System', as Ch. XII, by Dharma Kumar in *The Cambridge Economic History of India* (loc. cit.), p. 922.
66. Ibid., Table 12.7, p. 929.
67. Shailendra Singh, 'Inter-Governmental Fiscal Relations', as Ch. 21 in V.B. Singh (loc. cit.), p. 547.
68. A rich account of the labour movement in Kerala has been meticulously presented in the only study of its kind in K. Ramachandran Nair, *The History of the Trade Union Movement in Kerala*, published by the Kerala Institute of Labour and Employment, in association with, New Delhi, Manak

Publications Pvt. Ltd., 2006, pp. 53–64.

69. A.R. Desai (Ed.), *Labour Movement in India*: Documents: 1918–1920 (Indian Council of Historical Research, New Delhi), Bombay, Popular Prakashan, 1988, p. 47; also see pp. 45–70, dealing with strikes and lockouts and arbitration of disputes. To cite a notable opinion on Gandhi, a mill owner who negotiated with Gandhi did not wish to enter into a controversy, 'with a personage like Mr. M.K. Gandhi, who has implicit confidence in himself and who regards himself as infallible in the assertion he makes'. p. 64.
70. Ibid., pp. 32–5.
71. V.B. Karnik, *Strikes in India*, Bombay, Manaktalas, 1967. Also G.K. Sharma, *Labour Movement in India*, Jullundur, University Publishers, 1963, pp. 73–6.
72. Ibid., p. 75.
73. A.K. Bagchi (loc. cit.), pp. 141–2.
74. A.R. Desai (loc. cit.), p. 38, also p. 40.
75. Ibid., pp. 108–14. The police commissioner also addressed workers' meetings. Addressing them in Marathi he asked them to deal directly with the owners. The newspapers pleaded for the workers. In 1919 the *Times of India* wrote: 'In these days of epidemics and famine of unprecedented severity, it was impossible for them to make two ends meet. They had to incur debts in order to keep body and soul together.' p. 129; also pp. 145–7.
76. Ibid., pp. 133–5.
77. Vinay Bahl, *The Making of the Indian Working Class. A Case of the Tata Iron and Steel Company, 1880–1946*, New Delhi, Sage Publications, 1995, Ch. 2, Table 2.4 and the text.
78. Ibid., p. 144.
79. A.R. Desai (loc. cit.), pp. 224–35 and Bahl (loc. cit.) pp. 210–8.
80. Vinay Bahl (loc. cit.), Ch. 4, pp. 204–8.
81. G.K. Sharma (loc. cit.), pp. 78–80.
82. Ibid., p. 78, also Vinay Bahl (loc. cit.), p. 139.
83. Dipesh Chakrabarty (loc. cit.), p. 123.
84. Prem Sagar Gupta, *A Short History of the All-India Trade Union Congress (1920–1947)*, AITUC Publications, September 1980, p. 13.
85. Vinay Bahl (loc. cit.), p. 248.

86. Ibid., pp. 251–8.
87. V.B. Karnik, *Strikes in India* (loc. cit.), pp. 90–2.
88. Prem Sagar Gupta, *A Short History of the All-India Trade Union Congress* (loc. cit.), pp. 24–33.
89. V.B. Karnik, *Strikes in India* (loc. cit.), pp. 81–5.
90. Richard Newman, *Workers and Unions in Bombay 1918–1929, A Study of Organization in the Cotton Mills,* Australian National University, Canberra, 1981, Ch. V, 'The Political Microcosm.'
91. Prem Sagar Gupta, *A Short History of the All-India Trade Union Congress,* (loc. cit.), p. 35.
92. Richard Newman (loc. cit.), p. 87.
93. Rajnarayan Chandavarkar, *The Origins of Industrial Capitalism in India* (op. cit.), Ch. 6, 'The Development of the Cotton-Textile Industry: A Historical Context.' pp. 254–7. In relation to the steel industry and the threat posed by Japanese imports, see, Vinay Bahl (loc. cit.), pp. 157–9. There were also political fears.
94. Judith Brown (op. cit.), pp. 220–1.
95. For a detailed review see S.R. Bakshi, *Swaraj Party and the Indian National Congress,* New Delhi, Vikas Publishing House Pvt. Ltd., 1985, Ch. 2, 3 and 4.
96. Ram Gopal, *How India Struggled for Freedom* (loc. cit.), pp. 340–1.
97. S.R. Bakshi (loc. cit.), pp. 66–8.
98. Ibid., pp. 74–5.
99. Bipan Chandra (op. cit.), p. 241.
100. Bimal Prasad (op. cit.), Ch. IV, 'The Communal Backlash and Resurgence of Muslim Nationalism, 1922–1927', esp. pp. 187–9.
101. Ibid., pp. 195–218.
102. R.C. Majumdar, *History of the Freedom Movement in India,* Vol. III (op. cit.), p. 261.
103. Judith Brown (loc. cit.) pp. 226.
104. Mushirul Hasan, *Nationalism and Communal Politics in India, 1885–1930,* New Delhi, Manohar, 1994, Ch. 7, 'The Communal Breach'.
105. Ibid., pp. 184–6.
106. Ibid., pp. 199–206; quote on pp. 199–200. Hindu communal politics is discussed on pp. 207–10. In 1924, Lajpat Rai wrote on the communal representation in Punjab: 'Practically all social relations between Hindus and Muhammedans, and

Sikhs and non-Sikhs have ceased. All three communities have their separate clubs, separate organizations and separate colleges. Even in sporting clubs or social functions all three communities insist on communal representation.' Bimal Prasad (op. cit.), p. 223. He predicted a Muslim India and a non-Muslim India; p. 224.

107. Ibid., Prasad discusses at some length the attempts made by the leaders to create communal unity by arranging another political pact. See pp. 225–43.
108. Chaudhry Khaliquzzaman, *Pathway to Pakistan*, Orient Longmans, Pakistan Branch, 1961, pp. 76–7.
109. Ibid., pp. 89–91. In December 1928 the League reversed its stand on the subject, see pp. 99–100.
110. Bimal Prasad (op. cit.), pp. 262–6.
111. Ibid., pp. 268–9.
112. Khaliquzzaman (loc. cit.), p. 100.
113. R.J. Moore, *The Crisis of Indian Unity 1917–1940*, Clarendon Press, Oxford, 1974, p. 28.
114. Ibid., p. 29.
115. Ibid., pp. 30–3, Brown says: 'Reading's dismissal of the Nizams' claim might suggest a Viceroy arguing from an impregnable position. But the British were themselves making, or being forced to make, significant adjustments in their relations with the subcontinent, beyond the obvious major policy shift incorporated in the Montague Chelmsford Reforms.' (loc. cit.), p. 236.
116. R.C. Majumdar, *History of the Freedom Movement in India*, Vol. III (loc. cit.), Ch. VII. He describes the terrorist activities in Bengal and UP; also Bipan Chandra (loc. cit.), pp. 239–40.
117. Ibid., pp. 524–8.
118. Dr Sukhbir Choudhry, *Growth of Nationalism in India (1919–1924)*, Vol. II, New Delhi, Trimurti Publications Private Ltd. 1973, is based on a Ph.D. dissertation at the Jawaharlal Nehru University and treats the subject from the Marxist perspective. The section, 'Young Revolutionaries', pp. 163–289 deals with their ideas, methods and the effect they produced among the masses. The Kakori case is described on pp. 209–11.
119. B. Shiva Rao, *India's Freedom Movement. Some Notable Figures*, New Delhi, Orient Longmans, 1972, pp. 48–50.
120. Kanji Dwarkadas, *India's Fight for Freedom 1913–1937.*

An Eyewitness Story, Bombay, Popular Prakashan, 1966, pp. 300–9; the main features of the Bill are included therein. Quote on pp. 304–5. R.C. Majumdar, *History of the Freedom Movement in India*, Vol. III (loc. cit.), pp. 265–71, conveys the impression that it was more a gesture on the part of the Labour Party and carried little political weight. However, Annie Besant thought that India would soon get Swaraj unless she acted stupidly, and Kanji Dwarkadas agrees that this is the way it happened. Tara Chand in his *History* chose to ignore the theme entirely.

121. R.C. Majumdar, *History of the Freedom Movement in India*, Vol. III (loc. cit.), p. 292.
122. Birkenhead was an articulate spokesman of British interests and produced many quotable sentences quite contemptuous of India. His name and utterances keep popping up in practically every work done on India covering his tenure as the Secretary of State for India. See Daniel Thomer, *The Shaping of Modern India* (loc. cit.), pp. 54–5. Also S.M. Burke and Salim Al-Din Quraishi, *The British Raj in India. An Historical Review* (loc. cit.), Ch. 12, 'Communal Antagonism' and Ch. 14, 'Appointment of the Simon Commission and its Repercussions', Tara Chand, Vol. IV (loc. cit.), the sections, 'The Conservatives and Reforms', pp. 57–60 in Ch. 1 and 2, pp. 61–7.
123. Burke and Quraishi (loc. cit.), pp. 260–1.
124. Tara Chand Vol. IV (loc. cit.), p. 106.
125. A.K. Bagchi (loc. cit.), Table 9.3, p. 309.
126. Ibid., pp. 313–4.
127. Vera Anstey, *The Economic Development of India*, London, Longman, Green & Co., Fourth Edition, 1952, Footnote on p. 245.
128. Ibid., pp. 251–4.
129. A.K. Bagchi (loc. cit.), Table 7.5, p. 238.
130. Ibid., p. 239.
131. Vera Anstey (loc. cit.), Footnote on p. 262.
132. Ibid., Table XIV, p. 621.
133. Ibid., p. 272, see pp. 268–72. It is an excellent review. Also A.K. Bagchi (loc. cit.), pp. 253–61 for a similar review over a longer period.
134. Morris D. Morris, 'The Growth of Large Scale Industry' in *The Cambridge Economic History* (loc. cit.), p. 610.

135. Ibid.
136. A.K. Bagchi (loc. cit.), pp. 337–9.
137. Ibid., pp. 341–6.
138. Ibid., Tables, 8.3 p. 277 and 8.4 on p. 280.
139. Vera Anstey (loc. cit.), pp. 281–2. According to her the problem of efficiency was part of the problem of the method of labour recruitment. 'The jute mill hands are drawn mainly from a distance, very few Bengalis being employed as they are too prosperous to work in the factories. Hence the jute industry does not obtain full advantage of its situation in the heart of the most populous and advanced districts in India.' p. 281.
140. Ibid., pp. 237–8.
141. B.R. Tomlinson, *The Economy of Modern India* (loc. cit.), pp. 125–6.
142. *The Cambridge Economic History* (loc. cit.), Ch. VIII, para. 2, 'Railways', pp. 749–50.
143. Ibid.
144. Vera Anstey (loc. cit.), pp. 135–43. Quote on p. 138.
145. Ibid. Footnote on p. 140. The Retrenchment Committee feared that 'the Railways might at any time become a heavy liability on the national resources. The earnings were unsteady and varied according to the nature of the season, so that the inclusion of those earnings in the general accounts made the central budget a veritable gamble in rains.' The result was, as Blackett put it, an alternation between raids by the railways on the taxpayer and raids by the tax-payer on the railways. P. J. Thomas, *The Growth of Federal Finance in India. Being a Survey of India's Public Finances From 1833 to 1939*, Humphrey Milford, Oxford University Press, 1939, p. 338. The reference is to budget statement (1924–25); also pp. 338–9.
146. Vera Anstey (loc. cit.), footnote on p. 141. Of the 736,888 staff strength the Europeans were 5,036, the Anglo-Indians, 14,312 and the rest were described as Indians. The principal beneficiaries were the Anglo-Indians whose staff strength increased markedly. See Table VIII, p. 614.
147. *The Cambridge Economic History* (loc. cit.), 'Railways', p. 759. On economic grounds, the main line of criticism was directed at the primary function of the railways. 'In the actual management of the railways in this country, the freight policy has not been conducive to the interests of this country. It has encouraged more foreign trade than the internal trade of the

country, and has been instrumental in helping foreign industries often at the expense of Indian industries'. C.N. Vakil, Lecture delivered in October 1937, reprinted in *Poverty and Planning*, Bombay, Allied Publishers Pvt. Ltd., 1963, p. 79.

148. Vera Anstey (loc. cit.), p. 427, also pp. 424–32.
149. Dietmar Rothermund, *An Economic History of India. From Pre-Colonial Times to 1986*, London, Croom Helm, 1988, p.78.
150. B.R. Tomlinson, 'The Rupee Ratio Question' in *Economy and Society* (loc. cit.), p. 201. He offers a flimsy excuse that 'the monetary authorities in India were ill-equipped to take decisions about the optimum level of circulating currency.' The government followed a deliberate policy on deflation and was not concerned on its effect on the supply of credit and domestic prices. See the text of the article, pp. 201–9.
151. Ibid., p. 207. Indian capitalists were well informed. In a resolution adopted by an industrial organization,

    The government was accused of deflating or contracting Indian currency to the tune of about Rs. 450 million between 1920 and 1924 and another 160 or 170 million up to 1927 in an effort to push up the rupee–sterling exchange. While the normal pre-war expansion of currency was over Rs. 200 million per year, the average expansion between 1921 and 1925 was nearly half that figure, i.e. 111.2 million per year.

    Aditya Mukherjee, *Imperialism, Nationalism and the Making of the Indian Capitalist Class, 1920–1947*, New Delhi, Sage Publications, 2002, p. 85, also pp. 81–95.
152. Ibid., p.94.
153. Ibid.
154. D. Rothermund, *An Economic History of India* (loc. cit.), pp. 80–1.
155. P.J. Thomas (loc. cit.), pp. 339–40, Quote on p. 339.
156. Ibid., Table 3, p. 497 and Table 6, p. 502 in Appendix F.
157. Ibid. Appendix F, Revenue and Expenditure of the Provincial Governments for 1921–22 to 1939–40; also Vera Anstey (loc. cit.), Statistical Tables XX and XXI.
158. Ibid., pp. 396–9.
159. P.J. Thomas (loc. cit.), p. 341.
160. V.B. Karnik, *Indian Trade Unions. A Survey*, Bombay Manaktalas, 1966, Ch. 7, 'Emergence of Communists', the role of British communists was decided in 1922 by the Comintern,

that the British party should launch a well organized movement in India. Also see, K. Seshadri, 'An Assessment of the Communist Party's Role in the National Movement for Independence and Socialism up to 1939' in *Proceedings of the Seminar on Socialism in India, 1919–1939*, Part I (Memeo), Nehru Memorial Museum and Library, New Delhi, 1970.

161. *Proceedings of the Seminar on Socialism in India, 1919–1939*, Part I, pp. 391–2
162. Prem Sagar Gupta (loc. cit.), pp. 92–4
163. Ibid., see Partha Sarathi Gupta, 'British Labour and the Indian Left' in *Proceedings*.
164. Ibid., pp. 273–4.
165. Newman names George Allison, Philip Spratt and Ben Bradley in 1926 and 1927 doing organizing work in Bombay and Calcutta, Richard Newman (loc. cit.), p. 108.
166. Newman, Ibid., also pp. 109–10.
167. Ibid., p. 119. Newman profiles the leaders of their individual traits, the factions they led and their potential as future labour leaders on pp. 138–42.
168. V.B. Karnik, *N.M. Joshi, Servant of India*, Bombay, United Asia Publications, June 1972, pp. 54–5.
169. Rajnarayan Chandavarkar (loc. cit.), pp. 405–6.
170. Makrand J. Mehta, 'Origin and Growth of the Trade Union Movement in Ahmedabad, 1917–1939' in *Proceedings*, Part II (loc. cit.) (Mimeo).
171. V.B. Karnik, *Strikes in India* (loc. cit.), p. 91.
172. Ibid., p. 95. It is an extract from an article which appeared in the March 1925 issue of the *Labour Gazette*, see pp. 94–5, also pp. 98–9.
173. V.B. Karnik, *Strikes in India* (loc. cit.), p. 132.
174. Morris D. Morris, *The Emergence of an Industrial Labour Force in India*, Bombay, Oxford University Press, 1965, p. 182.
175. Richard Newman (loc. cit.), p. 143.
176. V.B. Karnik, *N.M. Joshi, Servant of India* (loc. cit.), pp. 38–47. Quotes on p. 43.
177. Ibid., p. 51.
178. Ibid.
179. Dipesh Chakrabarty (loc. cit.), p. 116.
180. Ibid., pp. 124–8. Chakrabaty also propounds his views on the broader cultural aspects of labour which do not blend with

the bourgeois democratic traditions of the trade union movement. Quote on p. 125.

181. *The Labour Movement in India, 1923–27*, Vol. IV, 2004, published by the ICHR is largely devoted to 'India and International Organizations'. The documents bring out the negative voice of the government's nominees in rejecting the proposals for adopting ILO conventions in India on various grounds.
182. Partha Sarathi Gupta's article (loc. cit.), describes the TUC role on matters concerning India. These include the pressure exerted on the government to enact the Trade Union Act. In March 1924 Lord Olivier, Secretary of State of India, sent a telegram to the Government of India to expedite this proposal.
183. *Labour Movement in India, Documents*, Vol. 5, 2004, pp. 324–7. The United Textile Factory Workers' Association of Great Britain published a report of an investigation made on its behalf in 1926 by J. Hindle and M. Brothers. It says: 'Fining is excessive. In some cases the whole of the workpeople are subject to fines, even though they have produced good cloth; in other cases cloth examiners depend upon money received as fines for their wages.' p. 326.
184. Ibid., p. 372; also pp. 371–95.
185. Ibid., p. 394.
186. Ibid., p. 325.
187. Ibid., p. 327.
188. *Labour Movement in India* (loc. cit.), Vol. IV, 'Where Are the Masses?' by E. Roy, p. 257.
189. Prem Sagar Gupta, *A Short History of the All-India Trade Union Congress*, (loc. cit.), pp. 41–8.
190. G.K. Sharma (loc. cit.), p. 90.
191. A.C. Guha, *India's Struggle Quarter of a Century, 1921–1946*, Part I, Publications Division, Government of India, June 1982, p. 97.
192. *Nationalism and Communal Politics* (loc. cit.), Ch. 7, 'The Communal Breach'. Also see Lajpat Rai, *Unhappy India* Calcutta, Banna Publishing Co., 1928, Ch. XXVIII, 'Divide Et Empera'.
193. Lajpat Rai, p. 457, also the following pages and the next chapter.
194. R.C. Majumdar, *History of the Freedom Movement in India*, Vol. III (op. cit.), pp. 309–10.

195. A.C. Guha (loc. cit.), pp. 118–22.
196. Ibid. According to Guha, 'The year 1928 saw the reorganization of violent revolutionary groups. The Hindustan Republican Army and Jugantar and some other groups were preaching and preparing for violent activities. The Murder of Saunders was the first overt act of the former; the bomb thrown in the Assembly by Bhagat Singh and Batukeshwar Dutta was the second act.' pp. 133–5.
197. Tara Chand, Vol. IV (op. cit.), pp. 73–4.
198. Ibid., p. 72.
199. Ibid., p. 118.
200. A.C. Guha (loc. cit.), p. 113; also Annie Besant's rejoinder.
201. Tara Chand Vol. IV (op. cit.), p. 66.
202. Ibid., pp. 106–11; Quote on p. 109.
203. Ibid. In 1925 Lajpat Rai gave this solution to the insoluble issue of communal politics:

    My suggestion is that the Punjab should be partitioned into two provinces, the Western Punjab with a large Muslim majority to be a Muslim governed province, and the Eastern Punjab with a large Hindu–Sikh majority to be a non-Muslim governed province ....Under my scheme the Muslims will have four Muslim states. (1) The Pathan Province or the North-West Frontier; (2) Western Punjab; (3) Sind; and (4) Eastern Bengal.'

    Tara Chand Vol. IV (loc. cit.) says, 'The partition of India was not the product of the fertile imagination of Muslim undergraduates at the Cambridge University, nor even poet Iqbal's fancy, but the brain-child of a hypersensitive Hindu stalwart', p. 110.
204. Tara Chand (ibid.), pp. 112–3, also R.J. Moore, *The Crisis of Indian Unity*, pp. 35–40 Moore has interpreted Jayakar thus:

    If progressive concessions were made to the Muslims then nothing would remain of Indian unity by the time that dominionhood was achieved. If, on the other hand, immediate freedom were assured then communal provinces could be conceded safely. Here, in embryo, was the conflict between the bargaining positions that the Muslim and the Hindu communalists were henceforth to assume. The Muslims would make the assurance of safeguards the condition of their acceptance of Muslim demands. These bargaining positions left little room for communal agreement.' (p. 37).
205. Mushirul Hasan, *Omnibus* (loc. cit.), pp. 261–3, also

the discussion which follows in the next few pages, esp. pp. 266–70.

206. Tara Chand, Vol. IV (op. cit.), p. 75. Quote is from Montagu-Chelmsford Report.
207. Ibid., p. 81.
208. Ibid., p. 137.
209. R.J. Moore, *The Crisis of Indian Unity 1917–1940* (loc. cit.), p. 94. He devotes several pages to behind the scene discussions with prominent leaders on the subject. 'The omens remained favourable after Congress leaders had received advance notice of the contents of the declaration.' p. 95.
210. Tara Chand (op. cit.), pp. 123-124.
211. A.K. Majumdar, *Advent of Independence*, Bombay, Bharatiya Vidya Bhavan, 1963. p. 114. According to Tara Chand, 'salt making, salt peddling, courting arrest, suffering brutal attacks, going to gaols handcuffed or bound with ropes, forcible breaking of meetings, shootings, confiscation of property, were the order of the day. Some 100,000 are reckoned to have been imprisoned.' p. 126, also on pp. 126–32.
212. Ibid., p. 127.
213. Judith Brown (op. cit.), pp. 268–72; also Ram Gopal, *How India Struggled for Freedom* (loc. cit.), pp. 375–80.
214. Ibid., pp. 382–5 and Tara Chand Vol. IV (op. cit.), pp. 161–2.
215. D. Rothermund, *Mahatma Gandhi: An Essay in Political Biography*, New Delhi, Manohar, 1991, Ch. 11, 'The Pact with the Viceroy.' Quotes on p. 68 and p. 70. Also see the more balanced summing up by Judith Brown (op. cit.), p. 273.
216. Moore observes,

    In August, leading merchants and industrialists began to divide over the need for a truce in order for business to recover. Sir H.P. Mody urged the Mill Owners Association of Bombay, of which he was Chairman from 1927 to 1935, to review its political policy in the light of economic conditions. Trade and industry were at a standstill, credit was largely destroyed, and unemployment was widespread. In Bombay there was a paralysis of the economic structure. Continued civil disobedience would spell economic disaster.

    The Crisis of Indian Unity 1917–1940 (loc. cit.), p. 180.
217. Burke and Quaraishi (loc. cit.), p. 285, also R.J. Moore, *The Crisis of Indian Unity* (loc. cit.), pp. 181–2. Moore says that on January 22, Irwin replied to Benn on the possibility of an

amnesty, that the Congress Working Committee had been legalized and the government had unconditionally released the members and ex-members of the Committee.

218. R.J. Moore, *The Crisis of Indian Unity,* (loc. cit.), p. 184. These subjects formed part of the text of Settlement published on March 3, 1931.
219. D. Rothermund, *Mahatma Gandhi* (loc. cit.), p. 63.
220. Ibid., p. 71.
221. Judith M. Brown, *Gandhi and Civil Disobedience, The Mahatma in Indian Politics, 1928–34,* Cambridge University Press, 1977, Chapter 3, 'Mass Civil Disobedience.'
222. Ibid., p. 216.
223. Tara Chand, Vol. IV (op. cit.), p. 163.
224. Ibid., pp. 165–8 and Judith Brown (loc. cit.), pp. 221–2.
225. Ibid., pp. 230–41. Brown provides a number of details and the distinct possibility that not only would Gandhi not have gone to London but was preparing to pull Congress out of the conference path to Swaraj.
226. B.R. Nanda, *Mahatma Gandhi, A Biography,* London, George Allen and Ruskin, 1958, pp. 314–5.
227. Ibid., pp. 316–7. On the positions taken by the Muslim, the Sikh and the depressed classes see R.J. Moore, *The Crisis of Indian Unity,* (loc. cit.), pp. 218–23.
228. D. Rothermund, *Mahatma Gandhi* (loc. cit.), p. 73.
229. R.J. Moore, *The Crisis of Indian Unity,* (loc. cit.), pp. 235–6.
230. D. Rothermund, *Mahatma Gandhi* (loc. cit.), p.73
231. Tara Chand, Vol. IV, pp. 171–4. Also Philips and Wainwright (Eds.), *The Partition of India,* 'Policies and Perspectives', London, George Allen and Lenwin, 1970, pp. 64–8.
232. R.J. Moore, *The Crisis of Indian Unity,* (loc. cit.). He also narrates the princes' position at some length, pp. 127–44 and pp. 220–33.
233. Ibid., p. 232–6.
234. Ibid., pp. 232–6
235. Ibid. See the text on pp. 246–9. The policy of 'Hit Hard and Hit at Once' was approved by the Secretary of State on December 19; also Willingdon's view of the Pact and Irwin.
236. S. Sivasubramanian, *The National Income of India in the Twentieth Century,* New Delhi, Oxford University Press, 2000, Table 4.44, p. 293.

237. Ibid., Table 3.24, p. 149.
238. Ibid., Appendix Table 3(a), pp. 154–5. (These pages are not numbered).
239. Vera Anstey (op. cit.), p. 180.
240. Baker (loc. cit.), p. 116.
241. Ibid., p. 119.
242. S. Sivasubramanian, *The National Income of India in the Twentieth Century* (loc. cit.), Appendix Tables 3(b) and 3(c).
243. Baker (loc. cit.), p. 120.
244. G.B. Jathar and S. G. Beri, *Indian Economics. A Comprehensive and Critical Survey*, Vol. One, Eighth Edition, Geoffrey Cumberlege, Oxford University Press, 1947. (The first edition was published in 1928). pp. 251–3.
245. D. Rothermund, *An Economic History of India* (op. cit.), pp. 44–7, Quote on pp. 46–7.
246. Ibid., p. 48. On the value of land, Baker (op. cit.) has the following to say:

    > Given the questionable character of land as a form of surety; it was dangerous for an outsider to lend money directly in plains villages. The only people who were really capable of assessing a villager's credit worthiness and compelling repayment were other villagers who could rely on personal pledges for security and who could use the village's internal government to sort out any dispute.

    p. 154. Land prices rose at a later period, pp. 163–5.
247. Baker, (loc. cit.) p. 78.
248. Ibid., p. 164.
249. Ibid., p. 165.
250. Neil Charlesworth, 'The Impact of the Interwar Depression on Agriculture in the Bombay Presidency. A Case for Further Arrested Development', in Clive J. Dewey (Ed.), *Arrested Development in India: the Historical Dimension*, New Delhi, Manohar Publications, 1988, p. 290 also Table 2.
251. Vera Anstey (op. cit.), Statistical Tables, Table XX, pp. 632–3.
252. A.J. Thomas (op. cit.), p. 360.
253. Dietmar Rothermund, *India in the Great Depression, 1929–1939*. New Delhi, Manohar, 1992, p. 44.
254. A.J. Thomas (loc. cit.), pp. 361–3.
255. B.R. Tomlinson, *The Political Economy of the Raj* (op. cit.), p. 37.
256. Dietmar Rothermund, *India in the Great Depression* (loc. cit.), Table 2b, p. 49 and the quote on p. 48.

257. Ibid. Tomlinson's explanation is a contrived one and rest on non-plausible reasoning. 'Indian gold could be sold abroad for considerably more than had been paid for it even one year before. The fall in internal prices increased these returns in real terms.' The farm households had bought gold earlier for security reasons and for raising their credit standing; they hardly acted on a profit motive. B.R. Tomlinson, *The Political Economy of the Raj* (loc. cit.), p. 37.
258. Ibid., pp. 37–9.
259. S. Sivasubramanian *The National Income of India in the Twentieth Century*, (loc. cit.) Appendix Table 3(b); also *India in the Great Depression* (loc. cit.), pp. 80–2.
260. Ibid. pp. 81–4.
261. S. Sivasubramanian, *The National Income of India in the Twentieth Century* (loc. cit.), Appendix Table 3(b). The quote is from *An Economic History of India* (loc. cit.), pp. 98.
262. Ibid., p. 99.
263. Ibid., p. 104.
264. D. Rothermund, *India in the Great Depression* (loc. cit.), pp. 47–8. The reference is to George Schuster, *Private Work and Public Causes, 1881–1978*. Cowbridge, 1979, p. 115.
265. V.B. Karnik, *Indian Trade Union* (op. cit., Ch. V, 'Emergence of Communist') and *N.M. Joshi, Servant of India* (loc. cit.), Ch. VIII, 'Union, Strike and AITUC.'
266. *History of the Communist Movement in India: The Formative Years*, Vol. I, 1920–1933, New Delhi, CPI-M Publications in association with Leftword Books, 2005; p. 121.
267. Rajnarayan Chandavarkar (loc. cit.), p. 273.
268. Ibid., p. 274.
269. V.B. Karnik, *Strikes in India* (loc. cit.), Ch. VII, 'The General Strikes'. Quote on p. 185.
270. ICHR, *The Labour Movement in India 1928–1930*, Vol. 7 (Eds. A.R. Desai and Sunil Dighe), 2003, pp. 321–53.
271. Ibid., Vol. 8, pp. 820–22. It is based on the findings of the Royal Commission on Labour, 1930.
272. Ibid., Vol. 8, p. 822.
273. A list of donors and the amounts received find a detailed mention in Prem Sagar Gupta, *A Short History of All India Trade Union Congress* (op. cit.), pp. 121–2.
274. *Labour Movement in India*, Vol. 7 (loc. cit.); A report in the *Labour*

Gazette, July 1928, pp. 505–516; Quote on p. 505. The dispute is narrated further in pp. 517–31 and pp. 532–6.

275. *A Short History of the All-India Trade Union Congress*, (loc. cit.), pp. 118–21. The Railway Workers' fight for their rights is narrated in *Labour Movement*, Vol. 7 (loc. cit.), pp. 595–736.
276. V.B. Karnik, *Strikes in India* (loc. cit.), p. 194.
277. Ibid., p. 198.
278. *Labour Movement in India*, Vol. 7 (loc. cit.), pp. 481–82, also V.B. Karnik, *Strikes in India* (loc. cit.), pp. 234–49.
279. Dipesh Chakrabarty (loc .cit.), p. 119.
280. Ibid, V.B. Karnik, *Strikes in India* (loc. cit.), p. 169 and pp. 199–200.
281. *A Short History of the All-India Trade Union Congress*, (loc. cit.), pp. 149–57.
282. Ibid., pp. 150–82.
283. Ibid., pp. 177–8.
284. Ibid., p. 195.
285. Ibid., 198, also pp. 198–207. The document, ''Platform of Thirty', was drafted by M.N. Roy, the dissident communist, who with his followers, had acquired considerable influence in the AITUC. See *Indian Trade Unions* (loc. cit.), pp. 76–8.
286. *A Short History of the All-India Trade Union Congress*, (loc. cit.), pp. 141–2.

Chapter 3

BRITISH POWER AND WORLD WAR TRANSFORM INDIAN POLITICS, 1932–45

India was turbulent during 1928–33. The defining political event was the civil disobedience movement which was fully suppressed and the British capacity to rule India was unassailed. The second instalment of reforms through greater provincial autonomy under the 1935 Act was put into effect. Congress re-emerged as a parallel power centre, and this was a shock to the new Viceroy. By the end of the decade the separatist Muslims also engaged in political contests. For consent and support, the British could count on the several communal and interest identities which had acquired institutionalized political bases under the 1935 Act. The princes were also propped up as blockers to the extension of reforms at the Centre and as a counterpoise to the Congress. Together, they made British rule in India secure. However, the depression had gnawed deeply into the peasant economy which needed deeper reforms and remedies. So did industry and business interests. The super-structure of alien rule was getting deeply eroded. The Second World War weakened the economy, while the Bengal famine exposed the hollowness of the power base of foreign rule. Yet, the most material change occurred in the UK. With the ascendance of labour to power in 1945, politics changed course in India.

I. 1932–6

Repression, Gandhi in New Roles: The Swarajists and Elections

Gandhi could never have imagined that boiling seawater to make salt would unseat the King–Emperor or even that the Gandhi-Irwin Pact presaged a wider settlement with the British. Yet, the salt *satyagraha* broke India free from the grip of inertia and political stagnation. Gandhi asked the country to take the plunge into civil disobedience, hoping thereby to unite the Congress and energize people into action to make the battle for Swaraj more directly relevant to the politically articulate masses. This form of political action resulted in a truce preparatory to the Second Round Table Conference, and there it ended. Gandhi returned on 28 December 1931 and, on the following day, the Congress Working Committee met and decided to resume civil disobedience. Gandhi wrote to the Viceroy asking for a meeting, which was refused. Immediately thereafter, battle lines were drawn.

On 4 January 1932, Gandhi was arrested and the Viceroy Willingdon promulgated several ordinances which amounted to the imposition of a civil martial law. Civil liberties were extinguished and the authorities were given powers to seize people and property at will. Within a short spell the government showed the level of its preparedness to strike hard immediately, by arresting thousands of Congressmen all over the country.[1] The government viewed the re-launch of the Civil Disobedience Movement as a virtual declaration of war and decided to handle it with an iron fist. A 'Civil Disobedience Manual' was prepared for the guidance of the officials with the aim of crushing the movement before it got underway.[2]

An important development that preceded the making of the new Constitution was Lord Willingdon's decision, with full support from the Secretary of State, Sir Samuel Hoare, to repudiate the Gandhi–Irwin Pact. Full authority was restored to British officials down to the lower ranks of police officers to use as much repressive measures as they thought fit and needed for crushing the nationalist movement. The earlier announcement of the Labour government that Parliament would formulate proposals for the new Constitution on the basis of the agreement reached at the Round Table Conference was also politically repelled and undone. The Viceroy had not just refused to meet Gandhi; every effort was made to make up for the humiliation suffered by British civil servants at the signing of the Gandhi–Irwin Pact in 1931.

At lightning speed the government declared the Congress and all the organizations connected with it or sympathetic to the nationalist cause as illegal and forfeited their resources. Press freedom was eclipsed and stringent measures were taken to deprive the civil disobedience movement of any publicity. Collective fines were imposed on villages, cultivated lands were seized and sold as deterrent punishment, and in the rural areas where the civil disobedience movement had reached and peasants had rebelled on the issues of land revenue and rents payable to the zamindars, lands and cattle were sold beyond recall. In nine months, the government counted 6,155 convictions, though the rate was steadily declining. In the first four months more than 80,000 *satyagrahis* went to jail though many of them were released without facing convictions. The government was anxious that the prison capacity should not be over-stretched; instead it was better to impose fines, or still better to secure an apology and release the detenues. The repressive measures proved effective and decisive in securing an unquestioned victory for the government at the end the year. In a few more months, in 1933, there wasn't any life left in the civil disobedience movement, and to the government's satisfaction the Congress lay shattered. However, what was not realized was that so was the people's faith in British rule.

The Third Round Table Conference ended without any positive outcome, though before concluding, most of the participants agreed to let the British government resolve the problem of communal representation and the perplexing question of safeguards for the minorities, so that the new constitution would receive the largest measure of support. Ambedkar demanded that for electoral purposes the depressed classes should be treated as a separate community. Muslim representatives were forthright in asserting that without adequate safeguards at the Centre and the provinces no constitution would be acceptable to them. These matters were then decided by the British government with the announcement of Prime Minister MacDonald's Communal Award. It was followed by a white paper outlining the main features of the new constitutional arrangement which would be proposed before Parliament.

In the communal award, which was designed to undo any assertion of composite Indian nationalism, the following communities and interests were accorded minority status: 1. Muslims, 2. depressed classes, 3. backward classes, 4. Indian Christians, 5. Anglo-Indians, 6. Europeans, 7. commercial and industrial classes, 8. landholders, 9. labour, 10. universities and 11. Sikhs. Hereafter, each minority would have designated electorates to elect a fixed number of seats allotted to them in the provinces. In the new Constitution, every recognized minority would be expected to champion its respective causes and promote its interests through bargaining with other interests. With considerable powers still vested in the Viceroy and the governors, most of them might find it expedient periodically to extend support to the colonial government's policies and its initiatives, though these might hurt the national purpose. Political intransigence may be practised on a broader basis and not remain the characteristic feature of Muslim politics as hitherto. Every group could now expect to be treated as a distinct entity separate from the broad national movement which alone was striving for self-government in the form of the dominion status, or full independence.

The British could never accept India as capable of remaining a unified state on its own strength, or even under a representative form of democratically elected government, to exercise the rights of majority rule with restraint and due recognition of the rights of the minorities. India was manifestly too heterogeneous and diverse to merit recognition as one nation, not even as a nation in the making that needed support and strengthening. This attitude belied the hope the liberals had in the direction and purpose of British policy on reforms. They were disappointed at the wholly negative assertions of the Churchill-led diehard conservatives that India's progress towards self-government should be systematically checkmated.

The August 1932 announcement precipitated a crisis which Gandhi had anticipated. He knew that the Communal Award was in the making and wrote from prison to the Secretary of State in March 1932 opposing the proposal of granting a separate electorate to the depressed classes. 'He recalled, what he had said at the Second Round Table Conference, that he would resist with his life the grant of separate electorates to the depressed classes.' This was not said, he assured Sir Samuel, 'in the heat of the moment or by way of rhetoric'.[3] On 13 September 1932, Gandhi, still at Yervada prison, announced a fast unto death from 20 September, to annul the grant of separate electorates to the Hindu depressed classes. Soon after the commencement of the fast, negotiations began between Dr Ambedkar, supported by his colleagues, and a few top-ranking nationalists who were also orthodox Hindus and, on 24 September, the Poona Pact was signed. Immediately the agreement was cabled to London, where MacDonald and his ministers accepted it and modified the Award. On the twenty-sixth, Gandhi broke his fast. Ambedkar gave up on a separate electorate but, as a counter-balancing advantage he got 148 seats instead of the 71 seats earlier in the Award.

According to Brown:

> Gandhi envisaged his fast and the pact as inaugurating a new era in India's public life, one of social reform and a new approach to Indian realization of a fundamental nationhood

> uniting not only castes but communities. He also saw it as a beginning for himself, and intended to embark on a new public role even though he had not been released.[4]

Gandhi's mind was focused on the question of untouchability as inseparable from Swaraj. However, he was told by his well-wishers that if he wanted to pursue this matter, he would have to suspend the civil disobedience movement. It was aimed at Hindu orthodoxy, a matter that did not involve a foreign role at all. However, according to Gandhi, India would not be able to demand Swaraj if society did not eradicate this evil. At this stage, the civil disobedience movement was still active, though showing signs of weariness and tapering-off.

Independence Day was celebrated on 26 January 1933. On 31 March, the Congress held its session in Calcutta which was broken up by a brutal assault by the police. About 256 delegates including 40 women were arrested, though most were released later. Majumdar writes: 'But while the Congressmen continued their fight with grim determination and held aloft the banner of freedom, Gandhi had no heart in the civil disobedience movement and his mind was fully occupied by the anti-untouchability campaign.'[5] In fact, at the end of September 1932 the moderate leaders had argued with him to accept a settlement with the government provided it was as between equals. They did not know that Willingdon was obdurate and would not consider releasing Gandhi; not even for campaigning against untouchability. At the end of October, the entry of visitors to the prison was barred again and all interviews were refused; Gandhi was boxed in by the prison authorities. These restrictions were later relaxed and he could again receive visitors.

In March 1933, the British government published a white paper containing the reform proposals. For the reform-minded nationalists the pressing issue was whether Congress would agree to work the reforms or, forced into opposition, wreck them. Gandhi broke the logjam by announcing on 30 April that he would fast for 21 days starting on 8 May, in an inner response to the Harijan issue, for self-purification. Now the government thought afresh on whether to wait any longer and take the unacceptable risk yet again of Gandhi fasting for 21 days and risking his life, or to just let him free and see what he did on release. On the first day's fast Gandhi was released and he went through the 21 days' ordeal in a friend's house.

Immediately on his release, on Gandhi's advice, the Civil Disobedience Movement was suspended for six weeks and several leaders were clearly annoyed at this decision. Later, it was decided that since the government did not seek a settlement, to continue the movement at a lower level of intensity as individual civil disobedience. Perhaps this was the only way out for the Congress because the Viceroy had rebuffed Gandhi's request for an interview yet again and instead had asked for a total abandonment of the civil disobedience movement.[6] Gandhi opened the new campaign by commencing a march to a village on 1 August, but was rearrested along with 340 of his followers. He was released on 4 August and ordered to stay in Poona. He disobeyed the order and was arrested again and this time sentenced to one year's imprisonment. He was not allowed to work on anti-untouchability; in protest, Gandhi decided to start a fast yet again on 16 August. At the end of seven days, his condition became critical and he was unconditionally released on 23 August.

By this time, while the mass campaign had ended with nothing to show for it, most Congressmen were weary and politically bewildered. The individual civil disobedience movement needed an organization and resources to sustain itself. These were wanting partly due to the repressive measures and, for the balance, whatever existed was voluntarily wound up by the acting Congress President while announcing the suspension of the larger movement. Gandhi disapproved of secrecy as antithetical to satyagraha, 'yet so pervasive was the repressive apparatus that the alternative to functioning secretly was not to function at all'. Nanda summed it up thus:

> The movement was at a low ebb even in the autumn of 1932 when Gandhi's fast on untouchability diverted attention from it. The Harijan work opened safer channels for activity which not a few Congressmen were glad to use. The temporary suspension of mass civil disobedience in May 1933 nearly killed it; the revival of individual civil disobedience was to the government little more than a minor nuisance. It is, therefore, neither the fact of withdrawal nor its timing which fully accounts for the anger or sorrow expressed by prominent Congressmen at that time. The harsh repression by the government had temporarily numbed the country, but many Congressmen felt that if their leader's strategy had been determined less by moral and more by political considerations, the government could have been embarrassed to a greater extent.[7]

On his unconditional release Gandhi decided that given the Court's sentence of one year in prison, he would not resume individual civil disobedience. Instead he would devote all his energy on the anti-untouchability campaign. 'Slowly and silently the movement faded away, and during the upheaval caused by the great earthquake at Bihar on January 16, 1934, it passed away unnoticed into the limbo of oblivion.'[8]

For Gandhi, the question of untouchability amongst the Hindus and denial of entry in temples to the untouchables became a matter of overriding importance, more pressing than any political issue, such as, the scheme of the new constitution, or the civil disobedience movement. In November 1933, when he was fully recovered in health, he started on a long tour on the new mission. It ended in August 1934 and by then Gandhi had travelled 12,300 miles devoted to Harijan uplift and securing for them permission of entry into temples. At a few places he met orthodox Hindus in a violent mood. In Poona, in June 1934, a bomb was thrown at the car and occupants were injured but Gandhi was not in the car. For all practical purposes, Gandhi had withdrawn from active politics. Now the social uplift of the Harijans claimed all his attention.

The policy of repression received solid support from the non-official European community. In 1931, the Bombay branch of the European Association wrote to the Bombay government, to take stern steps to counter the civil disobedience movement, declare Congress an illegal body and it was suggested, 'that all those who are known to have been responsible for the organization and financing of the last civil disobedience movement should be at once brought under control, and, if necessary, put under restraint. It is suggested, in fact, that they should be treated in the same fashion as enemy subjects interned during the war'.[9] In 1932, the Council of the European Association asked the government to make sure that the main provisions of the Ordinances remain operative, and further, that Congressmen and women should not be released from prisons till they recanted. There should be no weakening on the part of the government-indeed, there may be need for stronger action. Apparently, the government did exactly as it was advised. It is not surprising that in the Communal Award the Europeans in Bengal were given sufficient seats in the legislature to safeguard their interests and also maintain the balance of power between the Hindus and the Muslims. Muslims had, by and large, abstained from the movement, and had not expressed open hostility to it.

By 1934, the ascendancy of imperial power in India was once again established. Lord Willingdon had not only defeated the civil disobedience movement but left no option to the Congress leadership other than that they should first suspend it and later give it up entirely. The Swarajya group then revived and rekindled political interest in taking part in the forthcoming election to the Central Assembly. They hoped to carry the nationalist message into the Assembly on two electoral planks. These were: (i) repeal of all repressive ordinances and (ii) substitution of Congress's scheme for self-government in place of the one presented in the white paper.

The Tory opponents of reforms had effectively introduced

several safeguards in the Bill at every stage before its enactment as the 1935 Act, such that the concept of ministerial responsibility to the legislature would become a chimera or an illusion. Parliament totally abandoned the promise of dominion status as the goal, and deleted any reference to it in the preamble, retaining the same parts from the preamble of the 1919 Act. Domestic politics in Britain determined on a priori imperial considerations that reforms must be confined to the provinces, together with the reserved powers of the governor. Though diarchy was abolished in principle, yet governors were accorded special responsibilities to rein in the ministers and prevent misuse of majority rule to enact any legislation that could harm minority rights and interests. The Congress formally announced entry into the legislatures as part of its overall programme of action. The government responded by lifting the ban on Congress organizations—except in Bengal and the NWFP—and announced the release of civil disobedience prisoners expeditiously. Now the entire initiative rested with the government and it prepared the ground for the next important step with respect to the inauguration of provincial autonomy as proposed in the White Paper, on the enactment of the Government of India Bill already with Parliament.

Elections to the Central Assembly in November 1934 were held under the 1919 Act and elicited a keen contest between the nationalists and others. The issues raised by the Communal Award caused a split in the Congress and resulted in the formation of another group, called Congress Nationalists. Muslim representatives managed to secure 18 seats and, together with the Independents, held the balance between the combined strength of nationalists who secured 55 seats as against the government's totalling 50. The liberals failed to secure any seat.

The Viceroy never expected this and had imagined that the policy of repression had truly crushed Congress. Now three centres of power clearly emerged on the basis of the severely restricted franchise under the 1919 Act. These were:

the government which despite being in a minority was all powerful and could enact even the defeated bills on the basis of Viceroy's certification; the nationalists who would work for larger political objectives and secure such concessions from the government as might be conceded for securing passage of bills; and the political voice of the Muslims which, though broadly communal, often lent its weight in defence of landed interests. Jinnah emerged as the unquestioned leader of the Muslims and he powerfully projected political Islam as the third force in Indian politics. Hereafter, if any advance was to be made on the provincial autonomy aspects of the 1935 Act, the consent of Muslims as articulated by the Muslim League under his leadership would be a prerequisite, else there would be a stalemate and the nationalists' cause either checkmated or totally thwarted by the politics of intransigence. This assured an upper hand to the government.

Before its enactment, the White Paper and the Bill received much adverse comment in India. Suggestions by Indians at the Round Table Conference and also subsequent to it formed no part of the final Act. The British, alone, were responsible for preparing the scheme and later modifying it at every stage of its deliberations. The Bill had to satisfy Tory diehardism before it could be enacted. Perhaps the political purpose for the conservatives' attack on the Bill was to ensure that the federal part of the Constitution should never materialize, thereby ensuring that the power of the empire would not lose its glory; and this critically rested on the hope that the princes' India would stay aloof from the federation. However, the idea of provincial autonomy was well regarded and this may be traced to the Montague–Chelmsford Report which had envisaged the future of India in terms of progressive constitutional development of self-government in provinces under a responsible Government of India. As it turned out, while the provincial autonomy was duly inaugurated under an expanded electorate and communal representation, the federation concept remained on paper. Consequently, a unique dyarchy emerged; while the 1919 Act operated at the

Centre, the new Constitution of 1935 was implemented in the provinces.[10]

In the provinces, along with the principle of dyarchy, the distinction between the reserved and the transferred subjects was abolished and the subjects earmarked in the new Constitution came under the legislature's jurisdiction, hence to the ministers' control. The total number of seats in the provinces was 1,585, which were grouped into 16 different classes. The general constituencies numbered only 67. Landlords got 37 seats. Commerce and Industry were allotted 56 seats and labour, though poorly organized, got 38 seats. Securing a clear majority through elections appeared to be an improbable feat not designed in the 1935 Act. The government, while luring the Congress to contest the elections on the basis of a considerably expanded franchise, reasonably expected it to lose and thereby demonstrate the correctness of Willingdon's style of hard-line governance.

However, the new Viceroy, Lord Linlithgow, was keen to implement the Constitution in letter and spirit. Addressing the Legislative Assembly in 1936, he said:

> My heart-felt plea to every man and woman of goodwill and public spirit is that they should give these reforms a fair and reasonable trial, and that they will join with me and with the Governors of Provinces in an earnest endeavour to work the new Constitution in a spirit of tolerance and cooperation, for the honour and good of their motherland.[11]

Linlithgow was not a stranger to India. About a decade earlier, he had led the Agricultural Commission and toured India extensively. As the new Viceroy, he now asked for trust and promised to extend the same to the leaders of political parties with whom he hoped to remain in touch. He appeared to be eager to start a new political chapter in India and, though a conservative himself, did not consider the autocratic style of high-handed governance of his predecessor appropriate. However, as Tara Chand noted: 'In the field of politics the position was extraordinary. The British rulers had prepared a Constitution for India which the political parties had either totally rejected or reluctantly acquiesced in.' Moreover, 'the economic situation was deplorable. The unsatisfactory condition in agriculture which resulted from the world depression showed no improvement.' The team had changed. There was a new Viceroy and Secretary of State at the India Office, but this meant no real change in the policy of the government.[12]

Gandhi had accepted the plea of the Swarajist and given a go-ahead to prepare for elections and enter the legislatures. It was not at all clear, however, whether the Congress would accept office. Nehru, leading the left-wing in the Congress expressed himself clearly on the subject: 'We go to the legislatures not to cooperate with the apparatus of British imperialism but to combat the Act and seek to end it and to resist in every way British imperialism in its attempt to strengthen its hold on India and its exploitation of the Indian people.'[13] There were others, among them K.M. Munshi, who studied the Act and explained it in considerable detail to Gandhi and sought his opinion. To this, Gandhi said that perhaps they could do something with it. He was not averse to Congressmen following the constitutional path. Both the Congress and the Muslim League had rejected the federation part of the Constitution but were willing to work the provincial autonomy. In Britain, the Churchill-led conservative opinion had already expressed the hope that they would endeavour to make sure that the princes did not agree to accede to the federation and, hence, it might never get off the ground. So the best prospect for the new Constitution lay in the scheme of provincial autonomy, though, as Constitutional experts and political observers had already noted, the governor's role and powers were the very negation of the concept of ministers' responsibility.[14]

No one knew how the governors and the British civil servants would respond to the pressures generated by the electoral process and expectations were aroused in the people that the ministers would achieve as much as was promised in the election manifestos. Much would depend on the goodwill and understanding displayed by the governors and civil servants in the everyday conduct of government business, especially in the event of decisions being taken by the popular governments with which they truly disagreed. Moreover, could cabinet meetings be properly held with the governors presiding over them? At the same time, the important change over the 1919 Act couldn't fail to be noticed. It rested, 'in the full liberation of the Provinces from the superintendence, direction and control of the Central Government and the Secretary of State except for certain specific purposes. The freedom conceded in 1919 in the transferred field now covers practically the whole government of the Provinces.'[15] The Act provided the safeguard that whenever the governor acted in his discretion, on the exercise of his individual judgement, he would be under the general control of the governor-general who in turn was endowed with requisite power of discretion and direction in the matter.[16]

The Swarajists in the Congress claimed that they would use the legislatures to enact laws to remedy the defects of existing legislation, to improve the economic conditions of the people (particularly of tenants and debt-ridden rural households), to promote the cause of Harijan uplift, discourage the consumption of liquor and promote the cult of *swadeshi*, among many other things. They believed that the constitutional path must always be kept open to complement the pressure exerted by the civil disobedience movement and advance the country's progress towards full-fledged self-government and independence. Indeed, according to Coupland, the only difficulty that hampered the realization of dominion status was the unwillingness of the Hindus and the Muslims to subordinate their communal interests to the greater welfare of the whole; and if they could actually do so, there would hardly be any place for safeguards. 'And, if in the event the Act were so used as to demonstrate that India was capable of national self-government, the British Parliament could hesitate no longer to surrender what was left of its "trust" to the Indian Parliament.'[17]

Linlithgow expressed positive sentiments of trust and good faith for working the Constitution without, however, providing any opening for the possibility of political negotiations to improve the Act. He had opened the doors for consultations and discussions and followed it up with invitations to Gandhi and other leaders for talks. On his meeting with Gandhi, he wrote to the King: 'I thought Mr. Gandhi attractive and extremely shrewd. He is courteous in his approach and frank in his expression of opinion. But I judge him to be implacable in his hostility to British rule in India, to the destruction of which he had dedicated every fibre of his mind.'[18]

In fact, only the Liberals defended the Act though they too realized that, for the success of provincial autonomy, the governors would have to be men of wide sympathies and common sense and ministers, 'who will not seek deadlock'. The premise being that, 'its success must ultimately lead to a vast expansion of powers, equal to those enjoyed by the dominions.'[19] Their political weight had declined considerably, though the party still carried prestige, mainly due to the individual stature of liberal spokesmen than for any following in the newly franchised electorate. Nonetheless, the governors and the civil servants had thought and hoped that the liberals and other moderates would do well in the forthcoming elections while the Congress, as the party of revolt, was already so badly beaten in the defeat of the civil disobedience movement that it might as well be viewed as finished. There are no indications that the new Viceroy shared these perceptions; actually, he was keen to learn on his own.

An extraordinary feature of the 1935 Act was the division of subjects into three lists: central, provincial and concurrent. Labour and related subjects were included in all three lists. At the federal level, the subject number 34 is described as 'development of industries, where development under federal control is declared by federal law to be expedient in the public interest'; and the number 35, as 'Regulation of labour and safety in mines and oilfields'. In addition, the subject number 36 is described as: 'Regulation of mines and oilfields and mineral development to the extent to which regulation and development under federal control is declared by federal law to be expedient in the public interest'. Clearly, all the three subjects were of interest to labour. In addition, the provincial list also included relief of the poor and unemployed. The concurrent list under which both the federal government and the provincial governments could legislate, included factories, and welfare of labour, conditions of labour, provident funds, employers' liability and workmen's compensation; health insurance including invalidity pensions, old age pensions and unemployment insurance. The subjects described as trade unions, industrial and labour disputes were also on the concurrent list. The classification of the subjects in the three lists showed that, as with labour, the federal government should have the power of coordination and unifying regulation throughout British India. The subjects in the concurrent list were essentially provincial in character and so it would be administered by the provinces in accordance with provincial policy. However, in the event of a conflict between a law enacted at the federal level with one in any provinces, it is the former that would normally prevail. A safety provision was made in the Act to overcome the hazard of an overactive federal legislature to enact on a concurrent subject so as to oust the provincial jurisdiction.[20]

The political importance accorded to labour may be traced to the government's anxiety on the increasing influence of communists in trade unions and the scale of industrial disruption that was already caused. The plan was twofold: to induct organized labour into the constitutional process and to enable its elected representatives access to legal forums to record their assent and dissent in law-making that affect labour's welfare or standing in the society. The other part was to upgrade labour's status in society by granting it near parity at the federal level (10 seats), with commerce and industry (11 seats). In the provincial assemblies, where most enactments on labour were expected to be done, it was allotted a total of 38 seats. Moreover, the seats which were to be filled by the representatives of labour would be elected by the labour organizations.

Thus in one stroke, the 1935 Act gave the trade unions formal political representation and an importance they could never have expected on the basis of their actual strength. The colonial state accorded organized labour a political weight comparable to commerce and industry, hitherto exclusively enjoyed by them even on matters affecting labour. With this move, the colonial state demonstrated a political wish to expand the social base on which it would aim to rest. The premise was that the more power centres that were co-opted into the political management of the country, the more secure would be its long-term interests. It was hoped that all the leading power centres might view the continuation of India's connection with the British empire as generally advantageous and British presence as the controlling power at the federal level one that would continue to be needed to maintain overall political balance and order under a democratic constitution, along with the steady progression of provincial autonomy towards self-government.

The 1935 Act made ample provisions to protect the realm from violent activities and extremist agitations that became a threat to law and order. First, the supremacy of parliament over British India and its power to legislate in connection thereof was reasserted in the Act. Second, there was a list of forbidden subjects on which no legislature in India may enact any law or derogate the rights of the Crown. At the provincial level, the governor's sanction to introduce the finance bill was required and similarly on several other matters which covered the subjects in the concurrent list. No law could be enacted which would have an adverse affect or discriminate against British commercial interests in India. Third, though free entry of British commercial interests in India was assured under the Act, there was also a provision for exclusion or deportation of persons deemed undesirable, indeed, 'the governor-general or governor in his discretion in view of grave menace to tranquillity or to combat crimes of violence may suspend the operation of the law for such time as he thinks fit. This, of course, would enable entry of British communists to be barred who might seek to enter India to stir up communal strife.'[21] There was of course hardly any basis for connecting the British communists with communal violence in India, though there was ample evidence that they came to India to promote the influence of communism in the trade unions and to fashion the labour movement along lines laid down in the Comintern's directives. The Meerut trial had arraigned three British communists; and the British intelligence in India was following their activities and concern. The Communist Party was already banned in 1934 and alongside, five organizations connected to it.

Global Depression, Deepening of Distress, Arrested Development

The most alarming feature of the sub-period of the Great Depression was the uninterrupted decline in most indicators of the economy, particularly in agriculture and foreign trade. (The subject was touched upon briefly in Chapter 2; it merits forther elaboration.) In these years the impact of worldwide depression was most severe and it spread wretchedness among people. The severity of the depression may be viewed in the context of the low participation of India in the growth of the world economy between 1925 and 1929. Principally, agriculture had stagnated. The quinquenium average of rice production in 1925–30 was 30.3 million tonnes and of wheat 8.8 million tonnes. Both showed some growth in the next five years, to 31.4 million tonnes and 9.3 million tonnes, but while wheat output remained steady, that of rice plummeted. In 1935–6, the former was 9.4 million tonnes and the latter only 23.2 million tonnes. The very basic food output data suggests that India's rising population faced hunger on a mass scale over an extended period of time. Prices were on a declining trend for a decade before the onset of the depression, which wiped out any economic motivation to produce more per acre and gave rise to a collective experience of economic distress, poverty and indebtedness as an unbroken trend. Vera Anstey wrote:

> From 1920 to 1929 the general price index (based on 1914) fell from 202 to 141, and fell continuously each year. Although prices of particular commodities fluctuated, they were lower in all cases in 1929 than in 1920 or in 1921. Even during the boom years, 1925 to 1929, the general index fell from 159 to 141, and so did the price indices of cereals, sugars and of raw and manufactured jute and cotton. It will be noted that throughout the period since 1920, the fall was much greater and more continuous for food stuffs than for industrial materials (for which the peak price years come sometime after 1920–21), whilst the price of manufactured jute attained its peak in 1925 and remained high up to and including 1928. Hence, even during the boom, a larger agricultural population in India was selling an unexpanded total output at substantially lower prices than in the earlier twenties.[22]

On a long-term basis, the all-India index of retail prices of food stuffs was on a declining trend. With (1873 = 100) an old base year, the index declined from 375 in 1921 to 311 in 1929 and further to 148 in 1934.[23] The index number of wholesale prices (1914 = 100), of cereals showed a decline from the peak figure of 153 in 1920 to 135 in 1925, a rise to 139 in the next two years and continuous decline thereafter to 125 in 1929, 100 in 1930, 78 in 1931, 68 in 1932, 66 in 1933, followed by a rise to 69 in 1934, 75 in 1935 and 79 in 1936. The WPI of pulses showed a similar trend.[24] Purchasing power dwindled rapidly and it had to be replenished somehow. Peasants sold gold ornaments and these acts prevented imports from shrinking even more drastically than they did during those years.

Vera Anstey's account receives further support from

Sivasubramanian's study. The data on gross value of output from agriculture at current prices show the low figure of Rs. 11,033 million in 1930–1, which was a sharp decline from Rs. 18,553 million in 1924–5. It fell to Rs. 9,981 million in 1931–2, Rs. 9,494 million in 1932–3, Rs. 8,954 million in 1933–4, then rose to Rs. 9,916 million in 1934–5, to drop marginally to Rs. 9,884 million in 1935–6. In 1936–7, the turn-around began and the value of output rose to Rs. 11,397 million. At 1938–9 prices, the output as well as the NDP series show less variability, though this is a statistical construction. At higher prices in 1938–9, the real value of output showed a steady trend since the output variability was less. It hides the scale of calamity the farmers suffered from the decline in current prices year after year.[25]

The absence of choice is further indicated by the data on acreage under various crops. No matter how much the prices declined, the peasant households had to cultivate and grow stable food crops for their own consumption. The need for producing marketable surpluses every year depended on the scale of fixed financial obligations they had to discharge and these were mostly required to be paid to the zamindars and moneylenders. The acreage under the rice crop in the period 1930–1 to 1937–8, varied between a little over 30 million acres and a little less than 31 million acres; it couldn't have been more stable. For wheat, the data show a slight upward variance, between the low figure of 13.280 million acres in 1930–1 and 14.677 million acres in 1937–8. This may be the effect of increase in irrigation facilities in wheat-growing areas.[26]

India became deeply poor, perhaps more in these years than in the previous two decades. At current prices, the national income declined from the high of Rs. 34,693 million in 1924–5 to Rs. 32,748 million five years later and thereafter it fell from one year to the next, to reach Rs. 22,783 million in 1931–2, Rs. 22,014 million in 1932–3, Rs. 20,846 million in 1933–4, then rose to Rs. 21,952 million in 1932–3 and steadied over the next two years. Growth in population on such a bleak economic scenario led to per capital income settling down at lower and still lower levels. In 1933–4 it was Rs. 59, on a steady decline from Rs. 110 in 1924–5.[27] However, on levelling the outputs to 1938–9 prices, the per capita figure was steady at Rs. 64–5. Having weathered the combined effects of a prolonged period of deflation and the Great Depression, the economy appeared to be in a stable state of pitifully low equilibrium, moving neither up nor down. As far as agriculture is concerned, Rothermund summed up the situation thus:

> The Great Depression was caused and perpetuated by a worldwide contraction of credit. This contraction was perhaps even more severe in India than in the industrial countries of the West. As far as the general mode of agrarian production was concerned, India had not progressed much beyond the level of subsistence agriculture, but due to the prevalence of rent and revenue payments in cash, even the smallest peasant was compelled to sell a good deal of his produce and was also involved in credit relationships. At least half of the peasantry was more or less permanently indebted. Rent, revenue and debt services could not be easily adjusted to the low level of agrarian prices. Moneylenders now tend to foreclose mortgages and to buy up land rather than to extend credit. They also profited from the sale of distress gold which they extracted from their debtors.[28]

Over more than a decade, the experience of slowly descending output prices would have sapped the economic viability of any new investments in agriculture. In fact the entire net output after meeting the revenue demand of the government was barely sufficient to meet current expenditure on consumption. The data on per capita consumer expenditure relative to per capita income pose insurmountable problems of estimation and reconciliation. It is hazardous to put them together and draw meaningful inferences. Clearly, consumer expenditures are over-estimated and fall outside the series on per capita income. Between 1931–2 and 1936–7 the former exceed the latter in every year by a substantial margin. Nonetheless, at current prices, both show a tendency to decline. In 1931–2 the per capita consumer expenditure is shown to be Rs. 82.5 which declined to Rs. 68.9 in 1936–37, while the per capita income was Rs. 66.8 and fell much less to Rs. 62.7 in the two years respectively.[29] These point to zero net savings, perhaps even some net dis-saving, as people sold or alienated their assets to buy goods for current consumption.

The scenario is also suggestive of a grotesque probability, that, even as peasant households suffered immense privations and went through unmitigated distress, there occurred a transfer of real income and economic resources to the urban industrial and tertiary sectors, of which a part was used in repatriation of foreign capital and savings, mainly to the UK and the balance in industrial investment of all kinds, including rice and dal mills. In consequence, the salary earners, professional classes and businessmen enjoyed relatively augmented levels of standard of living. The entire agricultural produce which was put on sale was available at low or still lower prices year after year. The real value of rent and interest earned rose in terms of rice or wheat, but not wages paid to labour.[30] For a small class of property owners, particularly absentee landlords, it was possible to engage in conspicuous consumption in an effort to enhance their already secure status in a deeply class differentiated society. There is some evidence that cash rents declined in volume and a part of wages was paid in kind. These were due to low levels of liquidity resulting in lowered volumes of aggregate cash flows in the economy, in payments of all kinds and settlements of trading transactions.

Agriculture as an economic activity survived mainly due to the flexibility of cost of inputs. The ratio of net domestic product to the gross value of output remained at over 82 per cent. It varied by a small margin which indicates that total deductions varied or declined in the years of depression by nearly as much as the gross value of outputs. All factor incomes declined with great speed to keep in step with the market prices. This of course happened partly due to the methods used for estimating costs as given percentages to the value of output, so the relationship is defined to be true; else, if costs had declined less than the gross value of outputs, a marked decline in agriculture as an economic activity should have occurred. However, in a deeper sense, in a subsistence economy, there existed no genuine choice or little that could be exercised. Farmers had to produce for self-consumption and also supply most of the inputs themselves without recourse to purchases. In a non-cash economy even the relationship between the landowners and the sharecroppers is defined in kind, as a share in the produce, without any recourse to the market. The burdensome exploitative element enters at the stage when transactions, mostly obligatory, must be settled in cash. Wherever this factor was important, it produced resentment, even rebellion against the claimants, the government, the landlords and the moneylenders. However, Charlesworth shows that there was little difficulty in realizing the demands for land revenue perhaps because commercial cultivation generated the cash income sufficient to meet the demand.[31] Moreover, farmers were not bereft of choices.

> In the long term, though, there was no panic retreat from commercial crops into the foodgrains because this was not necessary. Instead, the retreat could be made into methods and types of commercial agriculture which were cheaper and, in particular, less labour-intensive. This helps to explain the presidency-wide trends in the cultivation of various crops. Cotton cultivation declined overall because the largest cotton producers in Gujarat and the southern districts of Maharashtra enjoyed limited opportunities for adjustment within cotton cultivation and therefore switched crops.[32]

For Punjab, Mridula Mukherjee writes, that during a period of falling prices, as in the Depression, the cost of cultivation being less elastic formed a high proportion of gross income and after adjusting for land revenue and water rates might have exceeded it, leaving the farmers with losses and it either wiped out their accumulations, thereby reducing the value of their capital or sharply lowered their standard of living.[33] In respect of Tamil Nadu Baker produced considerable evidence, on how in the face of falling prices credit dried up as the credit providers withdrew or vanished. Those who were saddled with unsold stocks suffered losses. 'the valley's rice trade stumbled through the 1930s. There was nothing like a complete collapse but there was a general shrinkage.' Increasingly, there was a tendency not to produce more than the local demand and 'the valleys were feeding just themselves and their neighbouring areas'. This was the result of the shrivelling of the complex marketing network which had existed before the Great Depression.[34]

In the case of groundnut, the acreage declined. 'Over one-third of the groundnut acreage disappeared between 1928-29 and 1934-35. On the Arcots plain, the groundnut acreage was almost halved in this period.' This was because the price had fallen so low that cultivation of groundnut was not worth the trouble. Cotton performed better owing to the fact that, 'the simultaneous expansion of a local cotton industry sustained demand for Tamil Nadu's cotton and throughout the 1930s the cotton markets were active, even if the price was depressed'. Consequently, the acreage average of the 1930s was at the same level as in the 1920s.[35]

However, overall, the conditions described by Baker were very bleak.

> Once it was clear that the depression was not merely a short-term cycle, there began a series of desperate and hopeless attempts by all those in the credit pyramid to retract the funds lent to those below them and to get out of the produce market. By 1929, the Imperial Bank had virtually stopped providing any credit to the Nattukottai Chetties (who were one of the most speculative elements in the market and were also more encumbered than other bankers because of their South East Asian connections), and by 1931, when the combined attempts of Delhi and London to deal with the international aspects of the financial crisis resulted in a rapid contraction of Indian

> currency, the Imperial Bank had become very sticky about lending to any of the bazaar bankers.[36]

Gold was sold and exported by Madras to the extent of Rs. 8 crores between 1932–3 and 1934–5.

Before the depression, rural credit was a profitable business. Credit suppliers were able to attract agricultural profits to themselves in various ways and plough it back in rural trade and farming. The depression wiped out profits and produced bankruptcy for those who stayed. The result was that given the downsize, such current savings which the traders and moneylenders could still generate or mobilize were transferred into financing small-scale industries in urban areas. Profits made in the sale abroad of distress gold became an identifiable source of new capital formation. 'From the mid-1930s onwards in Madras, for example, landlords and others began to invest increasingly in industry, especially in sugar and cotton, the Chettiars and Naidus diversifying from trading and indigenous banking into cotton mills, company floatations boomed and a stock exchange was established.'[37] This is how in UP and Bihar sugar mills were financed.

The British rulers contributed to the deepening grip of the depression by making it worse. They defended the fixed exchange rate of 18d = 1Re as an imperial law though it defied reason. 'The only way of maintaining the ratio in a period of falling prices was by means of severe contraction of currency.' Rothermund refers to perverse arguments such as:

> If ... prices fall and the country requires less currency and if on top of that, large quantities of redundant silver currency are returned from hoards, the currency authority must meet the situation by cancelling currency. Otherwise, an inflated condition exists, internal prices would keep unduly high in relation to external prices, and internal rates for money unduly low. The result would be that the material flow of exports, which is necessary to maintain the country's balance of trade would be restricted ...[38]

The total money in circulation fell from Rs. 5,090 million in 1922 to Rs. 4,230 million in 1929 and further, rather sharply, to Rs. 3,300 in 1935 and Rs. 3,070 million in 1938. Monetary policy was conducted in a pro-cyclical manner to keep internal price levels sufficiently low so that a surplus of exports over imports was maintained. This was the essential condition for paying Home Charges, meet debt obligations and allow repatriation of capital by the expatriates.

The deflationary policy succeeded in maintaining a favourable balance of trade but mainly due to export of gold as merchandise. However, the terms of trade moved against India. Though both export and import prices reached lower levels the former stayed below the latter.[39] The surprising change that took place in the structure of foreign trade was the relative decline in British exports to India, though it remained the single largest exporter. The United States and Japan raised their shares despite imperial preference. India emerged as an important earner of dollars and this was of intrinsic value. In this role and as an exporter of gold, India played a role in stabilizing the international position of the British economy.

It took a perverse monetary policy to perform this desired helpful colonial function toward shoring up Britain's balance of payments in the adverse conditions of world trade. The massive repatriation of British capital from India to the UK may be placed in this context. Overall, it weakened Britain's economic position in India, which gave rise to the theme of decolonization. Britain appeared to be engaged in reversing the flow of capital before 1914 in the adverse conditions created by the world war and the depression. Tomlinson put the data in perspective.

> In each year from 1919 to 1930, Britain had a visible surplus with India totalling £79.5 million. This new development was the result both of the decreasing importance of Britain as a supplier of Indian imports and of the increasing importance of Britain as a market for Indian exports, despite the attempts of the British government, at the 1932 Imperial Economic

> Conference and elsewhere to increase the share of British goods in the imports of other imperial countries.[40]

As against a trade surplus with Britain, India ran up trade deficits with Japan and Germany and this marked the change in the relative position of British manufacturing among the industrialized countries. It showed the improved competitive position of Britain's trade rivals in the Indian market. Britain also lost on account of the modest growth of import substitution industries which reached out to the Indian consumers at lower prices. The decline of UK's exports to India formed part of the overall reduction of British exports in world trade during the 1920s and 30s. 'By 1939 the Indian economy was a good deal less complementary to the British one than had been the case in 1913, for the destructive impact of world demand for Indian produce had severely affected India's place in the imperial economic system.'[41]

This argument, though far-fetched, implies that outside the imperial trading bloc the scope of Indian exports was largely dependent on the initiative other countries took in building trade ties with India. On their own, both Indian exporters and importers were too tied to Britain in diverse commercial links to move out of the British orbit. What is not in question is that India was primarily engaged in export of agricultural commodities and the demand for these in the industrialized West, including Britain, was steadily falling. The depression produced a sharp decline in prices and, but for the export of gold, might have led to trade deficits. This is largely a matter of surmise because export of gold released more purchasing power mostly in urban centres which was partly expended on imports. Without this, the aggregate demand would have been still lower and may have resulted in greater contraction of currency.

Rothermund has analysed the phenomenon of gold exports extensively. He says:

> If we take the export of distress gold from India as an index of the impact of the depression we can divide the years from 1931

> to 1939 into three periods. The first one ending in February 1935 is marked by a very large outflow of gold (annual average Rs. 600 million), the second one ending in February 1937 shows a reduced outflow (average Rs. 340 million) and in the last one ending in February 1939 the outflow is even further reduced (average Rs. 100 million). In the first period gold exports constituted between one-third to one-quarter of total exports, in the second one they amounted to one-sixth and in the last one they receded to 8 per cent. If we remember that India normally used to import treasure on private account even the outflow of the last period is remarkable. The sale of gold was still required to compensate for the reduction of purchasing power on the eve of the Second World War.[42]

These formed part of the 'fundamental shake out of capital and liquid funds from the agrarian economy'.[43]

Along with heavy disinvestment in agriculture, there was some disinvestment in industry and other sectors as well. Bagchi refers to A.K. Banerjee's estimates that 'about Rs. 1,492.3 million of India's external public debt was repaid during 1921 to 1938–9; Rs. 1,000 million were repaid during the five years from 1931–2 to 1935-6'.[44] The probable reasons for the relative withdrawal of British capital have been put down to:

> (a) political uncertainty connected with the gathering strength of the nationalist movement and the concessions made by the British Government to it; (b) the greater attractiveness of investment in the Far East (illustrated by the pulling out of the Sassoon interests from India), and (c) the difficulties faced by the British economy which led to a massive repatriation of British capital (mainly public) in the early 1930s.[45]

The immediate economic factor which might have generated a mood of pessimism was the fall in export earnings and the difficulty government faced in making normal remittances of about £35 million per year to meet the Home Charges. In 1931, the government's effort to raise a sterling loan failed and it may have been feared that the system of remittances was on the verge of a breakdown. The money market was very tight and bank rates shot up to about 7 to 8 per cent.

> FICCI repeatedly complained that the government in order to maintain and cheapen remittances was persisting with a high exchange, despite the fact that it exacerbated the economic crisis in India, as it led to the depressing of prices, pushing up of the value of taxes and debt, depletion of gold resources, flight of capital and a rapid growth in national debt and debt services.[46]

Gold exports enabled the government to pay the Home Charges, meet interest and debt repayment obligations and provide enough foreign exchange to allow for remittances. The government also had to raise finances to administer the state machinery and bear the cost of a large army. The overall direction of economic policy no doubt was of laissez-faire, as modified by the policies of discriminating protection and imperial preference. To the pleas that the government should reflate the currency, raise the price level and lower the farmers' burden of indebtedness, there was no response.

The government was reconciled to living with the reality that India was a very poor country; indeed, it would do nothing to alter the balance of economic forces in any particular direction or pursue any policy that ran the risk of adversely affecting India's credit rating. In theory, even in a laissez faire economy, monetary policy is one tool the government possesses to increase/decrease liquidity, lower/raise interest rates and thereby expand or contract the volume of credit to influence the levels of output and employment. This presupposes flexibility in the conduct of monetary policy which is ordinarily assured by granting sufficient autonomy to the central bank of the country to act on its own judgement without being unduly influenced by the government or the course of political opinion. In India, this flexibility was non-existent, indeed denied by law, which stipulated that the exchange rate of 1s6d to a rupee must be maintained to meet the primary obligations of the government. The net result was a frozen response and total inability to take any worthwhile economic initiative to deal, first, with the adverse economic consequences of the Great Depression India imported from the world economy; second, to speed up the pace of recovery when it began and, third, to control the inflationary process, particularly the exceedingly harmful consequences of hoarding of goods in short supply, made worse by speculation and profiteering, during the first stage of the Second World War. The government did finally act and abandon the policy to do nothing or do as little as possible by the inexorable logic of war finance and laid the foundation of a planned economy during 1942–5.

The colonial political economy is best summed up in the instruction Montagu Norman as Governor of Bank of England gave to Sir George Schuster who was the Finance Member for India, on the course of economic policy the government should follow to alleviate the depressed condition: 'Do nothing, stand fast.'[47] Then the ratio controversy was flaring and gold was flowing out and the question was, should something be done about these very uncomfortable phenomena. Tomlinson describes the inertia of the colonial mind in the following way:

> The colonial Government of India rarely acted within the domestic economy as the agent of metropolitan or expatriate business interests, although officials were even less disposed to assist Indian entrepreneurs or to bring about conditions that would encourage them in dynamic industrial programmes. The Government of India worked hard to uphold a particular system of political economy in India, but it was one in which administrative concerns took precedence over development initiatives. The advances that were made in business organization in India, including the slow spread of the mechanized industrial manufacturing sector, were largely achieved in spite of the inertia created by an administration that ruled in economic matters by a mixture of benign and malign neglect. The result, especially in fiscal and financial policy, was to create tensions between British wants and Indian needs, both official and non-official, that eventually compromised the basis of imperial rule as well as the future progress of the South Asian Economy.[48]

The single most important policy initiative the government took was to enact the Reserve Bank of India Bill 1933, which had been in the making since 1927 and was currently in the midst of a major controversy on constitutional reforms pertaining to the question of where the ultimate control over fiscal and monetary policies should rest. The conservative opinion in England was very clear that the Finance Member of the Governor General's Council should be a white member of the civil service and the ultimate control should rest with the Secretary of State for India. However, it was equally clear to the reform-minded British politicians that devoid of transfer of power over financial and monetary policy matters the new Constitution would be bereft of significance and would fail to satisfy any form of nationalist opinion in India. This then centred on the question that if the Finance Member was to be an Indian, what might be the administrative arrangements for the control of the proposed Reserve Bank of India, so that it remained free from his influence. The solution lay in the idea that the governor, though nominally free of government counsel, should be appointed by the Governor General in the exercise of his discretion. Later, this provision was changed in the Bill and the appointing power rested with the Governor General in Council after consideration of the recommendations made by the Central Board on this matter.

The compromise reflected the acute dilemma faced by the imperial masters as to what India might do, once it controlled economic affairs, regarding the very important Indian obligations to the UK in respect of debt, interest payable and Home Charges, the British element in the Indian army and the future of British trade and investments in India. Tomlinson records that, 'one Treasury official reviewed the problem literally in black and white terms and concluded that, with a "white man's" Reserve Bank and proper safeguards, even a "black finance minister" could do no harm.'[49]

The Reserve Bank of India Act was passed in 1934 and it

started functioning in 1935. The Bank was legally obligated to uphold the exchange ratio of 1s6d to a rupee even if it meant disregarding the expressed opinion of the Legislative Assembly to devalue the rupee. The Governor, Sir Osborne Smith found to his dismay that even in such a matter as lowering the bank rate he could be out of step with the Finance Member. The ensuing controversy resulted in his being replaced by the more pliant J.B. Taylor.

Smith also clashed with the Finance Member on the ratio question and was popular with the Indian members of the Board. However, the Finance Member Grigg was a hard line conservative who would permit no reform and viewed the lowering of the bank rate, against his wishes, as an act of war.[50] Osborne Smith supported cheap money policy. Actually the market anticipated the lowering of the bank rate.

> It reflected a marked easing of monetary conditions and a sharp decline in money rates during the latter part of 1935. Call money rate in Bombay, for instance, was quoting at 0.25 per cent in November compared to 2 to 4 per cent in January–June 1935; the Treasury Bill auction rate was quoted at about 1 per cent as compared to 1.5 to 2 per cent in January–June 1935. There had also been a marked contraction of scheduled bank credit since July.

Yet, the reason the Finance Member was opposed to it was its impact on the rupee-sterling exchange rate.[51]

In terms of GNP, the estimated figures show that the pre-depression peak year was 1928 when it was Rs. 35.02 billion. The trough was reached in 1933 when the GNP declined to Rs. 21.92 billion. However, despite the setback to the economy during this period, the bank rate first rose from 6 per cent in 1928 to 6.50 per cent a year later, declined to 5.6 per cent in the next year and then rose a year later to 7 per cent. However, in 1933 it was brought down to 3.5 per cent and lowered further to 3 per cent in 1936. Thereafter, it remained unchanged till 1940. During the revival years there was spare liquidity in the banking system and the price level started rising slowly. However, the severely battered agricultural production was still stagnant and real income per head, owing to the increase in population, was settling down to a very low level of about Rs. 108–110 per year.[52]

Disunity Weakens Labour, Impact of Depression, Unity Moves

Labour in industry had learnt the practice of industrial relations during the formative period of the trade union movement in the preceding decade. Though there is little evidence that they had learnt to use the unions for collective bargaining, the Ahmedabad's Majoor Mahajan stands out as an example of formal industrial relations based on the principle of mutual recognition and reciprocal respect. This is in marked contrast to the workers' behaviour in the cotton textile centres at Bombay, Kanpur, Sholapur and the jute workers in the Calcutta area.[53] Nowhere in India could one see trade unions of the quality and durability of the Majoor Mahajan, during this decade in any employment segment. In most places workers' industrial relations and behaviour usually went through two phases; short spells of strikes and, if led by the communists, sometimes one mill strike was connected in a concerted way to a planned general strike. This was followed by the longer phase of their withdrawal from the unions and any form of organized activity. This may be a period of sulking, a sense of defeat or submission to the employers on their terms for such periods as the need for militant action did not again become the dominant mood. They may then return to the union and rally round the leaders who, though being present and available all this while, were clearly not needed and were actually neglected.

A part of the explanation for this dichotomous behaviour lay in the continued presence in their midst of informal cohesive cultural formations which met their basic needs for solidarity, belongingness and articulation and it may be traceable to the rural origins and the ethnic or communal orientation of workers. On a daily basis, workers employed in a particular mill, with a common background of shared rural connections and village ties, speaking the same dialect or language and professing the same religion, hardly needed a trade union or the educated, English-speaking, urban middle class leaders, who provided leadership, unless the workers themselves felt a need for action.

Ahmedabad's Majoor Mahajan and Bombay's Girni Kamgar Union met this need by spending considerable time and attention on attending to individual work-related grievances of the workers, which included problems of personal lives of such members as sought the union's involvement. However, even they, particularly the latter, experienced near abandonment in the aftermath of failed strikes. The other part of the explanation is reflected in the hypothesis formulated by Chandavarkar,

> that the terrain upon which the Indian working class, perhaps any working class, fought its battles was determined by its opponents and, therefore, their forms of action reflected not their level of consciousness, but the range of options available to them inside a particular economic and political conjuncture. The mill owners undoubtedly influenced the structural characteristics of the workforce, but it is the outsider, the politically inclined trade union leaders who decided, mostly on ideological grounds, the range of options that were supposed to be available to workers in the colonial milieu, and the battles they should wage.[54]

The trade union attitude, whether acquiescent or militant, may be expected to display diverse traits in the widely dispersed conditions of industrial development and proletariat formation. As already noted, no two industrial centres like Bombay and Ahmedabad in this respect could be farther apart. The Congress government brought out the difference, owing to non-interference by the government in the settlement of industrial disputes. This is reflected in the fact that between 1926 and 1934 in the Bombay textile industry 32 million man days were lost, whereas in Ahmedabad the loss was only 138 days. As a result, the Bombay textile operatives suffered a loss of Rs. 427 lakhs

(Rs. 42.7 million) whereas the corresponding figure for Ahmedabad was only Rs. 2 lakhs (Rs. 0.2 million).[55]

The marked difference between the Bombay textile workers proneness to conflict and those of Ahmedabad is also reflected in the strikes data for the quinquennium 1931–6. The total number of disputes in Bombay was 138 but 96 of these were in the cotton textile mills. They also accounted for 205,409 workers out of the total of 221,967. Ahmedabad mill workers did raise disputes, but settled them faster and at a lower cost to themselves and the mills. While the man days lost in the Bombay mills were 4,335,204, in Ahmedabad these were only 300,617. The impact of the depression was of course greater on the Bombay mills and their response was to effect rationalization and enforce wage cuts. The workers fought back against this offensive. 'But it had no effect. In the period employers were not afraid of strikes. Many a times they welcomed them as a convenient method for reducing production.'[56]

Communists played a notable role in building workers' resistance to employers' policies though they were committed more to the doctrine of class struggle than in conducting industrial disputes. Usually the workers' fight was in sheer desperation and they could not have expected to win in a hopeless struggle. Yet, the communists appear to have imagined that the given strikes were merely a prelude to the next stage, which would be a revolution against both capitalism and imperialism. As a result, in the 1934 strike of the Bombay textile workers, which spread to Sholapur and Nagpur, the response of the police was excessively harsh. In Ahmedabad too, the communists led the strike in 1935 partly to restore the wage cut of 6.25 per cent to which the Textile Labour Association was a party and also to discredit the TLA. The mills refused to deal with them and proceeded to enforce the wage cut. The TLA engaged in an anti-strike propaganda. The strike predictably failed, but it did show that the Muslim weavers were not with the TLA.[57]

The Bombay mill owners response to the depression was

piecemeal and anarchic. According to Chandavarkar,

> During the early 1930s as prices fell and demand slumped, most mills began to nibble at piece rates, retrench their workforce and increase workloads ... Twenty-six out of 49 mills admitted to having cut their basic rates, but four of these claimed to have restored them. A further eight mills reported having increased their rates due to changes in the character of production, but this did not necessarily mean that earnings would have risen as well. The overwhelming majority of mills made several and substantial cuts in their dearness-of-food allowances, and they varied widely in extent. But in the case of nearly half the mills, they were reduced from the original level of 80 per cent of the basic wage for piece workers and 70 per cent for fixed wage workers to below 35 per cent.[58]

This information was collected by the Bombay Labour Office and published as 'The Wages and Unemployment in the Bombay Cotton Textile Industry, 1934'.

The disorderly conditions were productive of strikes, but collective bargaining which would have produced more orderly conditions on wages, rationalization and standardization of work and output was unlikely to be accepted as it would have required the mill owners to accept the communist Girni Kamgar Union as the sole bargaining agent. The government had ordered the enquiry and would have appreciated if the unions had waited, but as it happened, the report was published just about the time the strike failed in its purpose. Driven by hunger, workers started reporting to work. Thus the two-month-old strike ended. The government did its part in breaking the strike, by prohibiting workers' meetings, banning picketing, arresting all the principal leaders and using police force to overawe the workers.[59]

At Jamshedpur, due to the intrinsic national importance of TISCO, the management usually enjoyed the support of the government as well as the national leaders including Gandhi, Subhash Bose and Rajendra Prasad. The relationship between the management and the labour associations was mostly adverse, even hostile. However, owing to the recurring fight between them on class lines, the association often invited national leaders to come over and intervene and the management nearly as often heeded their advice. Consequently, TISCO at Jamshedpur developed industrial relations, with traits not found elsewhere, namely recognition of a union and its withdrawal later, agreements followed by disputes, which were sometimes mediated by national leaders; yet subsequent to their intervention there were more disputes. The company was not averse to employing unfair means to break the union; it promoted a rival union which enjoyed its confidence and other such tricks. The story finds parallel tales in the American labour movement, but not in India.[60]

Yet another pattern is observed in the railways, its principal characteristics defined by their European managements and the large number of Anglo-Indian employees who jointly opposed the unions and strove to defeat them. This was particularly severe when agitations were led by the communists and the colonial government ordinarily stood solidly with the railway managements. The more serious problem with the railways was its openly racial and blatantly communal employment and promotion policies. These were fully backed by salary/wage differentiation and in the provision of housing and other facilities.

The British Railway Administration published data on the racial and communal structure of railway employment for 1934–4. The table showed distribution by Europeans, Hindus, Muslims, Anglo-Indians and domiciled Europeans, Sikhs, Indian Christian's and others. On superior posts, the data was grouped in three classes—European, Anglo Indian and Asiatic Indian.

> The communal discrimination in regards to recruitment, pay and promotion and facilities for the education of the children to the European and Anglo-Indians was not confined to the superior posts only. In the lower services too a great deal of

> preference was shown for Europeans and Anglo-Indians. They were paid higher salaries and were allowed better amenities and privileges than Indians for the same work. The principle of equal pay for equal work was denied. In promotions also the Anglo-Indians received partial treatment.[61]

According to the author, Mahesh Kumar Mast, 'the policies of communalism and racialism had an evil effect on the development of the trade union movement in the railways. This led to the division of the movement on communal and racial grounds'.[62] Hindus and Muslims organized into separate unions, though taken together the railways unions organized the fastest and were better than those of other industries during the post-1919 reforms. Industrial relations were seldom cordial and unions often agitated or called strikes against victimization or unfair transfers of union activists and supporters.

With the onset of the Depression, matters suddenly turned adverse. The management started a policy of cost reduction by effecting retrenchment and pay reductions. The financial position of the railways deteriorated year after year as the interest charges exceeded the net revenue and it became impossible to make any contribution to general revenues. The steep fall in prices resulted in severe curtailment of passenger and goods traffic. The railways had their back to the wall and, even as the impact fell on workers, they fought hard though mostly in vain. Consequently, the union membership declined from over 39,000 in 1930 to little over 22,000 in 1934. In 1935, revival began for both the railways as well as the unions. Altogether, the railwaymen paid a heavy price mostly by way of retrenchment since the government had permitted the railways to remove about 10,000 men from employment. The unions could do nothing to stop retrenchments and strikes were of no avail.

The diverse strains in India's labour movement essentially reflected the technological and economic characteristics of the various industries, but also, the compositional features of the labour force. Since the latter differed greatly, both by industry as well as region and, to a considerable degree, these were consciously influenced by employers' policies, the industrial relations developed along decentralized lines often marked by local strains. The unifying and standardizing influence was in the larger employers' organizations, of which the foremost were the Railway Board and IJMA for the jute workers. This element was noticeably absent in the cotton textile industry. The only place the employers functioned with a group spirit and strove to regulate industrial relations at the local textile industry level was Ahmedabad. In this respect too, the Ahmedabad cotton textile industry emerged as wholly unique. By comparison, the Bombay Mill Owners' Association though older was always handicapped by the prevalence of individualism among mill owners, almost to the anarchic level and, while it endeavoured to achieve greater uniformity in the decade, 1924–34, the Association's effectiveness at the mill level was nearly always uneven, on occasions quite low.

The class of trade union leaders which emerged in this decade had two major traits. First, it was predominantly of middle class background and had the advantage of formal education; the educated leaders made ample use of their knowledge in building trade unions along the British pattern. This was perhaps more in the belief and spirit that working in the workers' midst, educating and convincing them would enable them to convey the message that the union was for their overall good and, that they backed their efforts with sincerity, service and sacrifice. Second, this class of trade union leaders was deeply political in its attitudes and perceptions; for most of them, the trade union work was actuated by political beliefs and became inseparable from the larger goals set for the country by the national leaders and political parties. Though, ideally, trade unions should be kept separate from political affiliations, it couldn't be done in practice.

The handful of moderates like N.M. Joshi were highly valued as selfless leaders but usually had few followers. The entire class of trade union activists and leaders later developed the all-India industrial federations and affiliating centres. This achievement deserves to be acknowledged as a major success of the labour movement in India; and with them the leaders also won for themselves recognition and esteem, even among the employers. With such leaders trade unions could strive to promote solidarity and unity among workers and, at the same time, strengthen political links with the ideologically committed parties. To the communist trade unionists this was the foremost objective.

The 1934 general strike in Bombay conveyed a powerful message to the government that the policy of non-intervention in industrial disputes had to make way for a more purposive though moderate policy of intervention. This was mainly to inhibit industrial disputes from producing work stoppages which could be prevented and also to shorten the duration of unstoppable strikes. In August 1934, the Bombay government enacted the Bombay Trade Disputes Conciliation Act, 1934, applicable to the textile trade or industry which could be extended to other industries by notifications. The government was empowered to appoint a special or chief conciliator, assistant conciliators and a labour officer to discharge particular duties. The conciliators' duty was to mediate, once a trade dispute came into existence or was apprehended. The labour officer's duty was to watch the interests of the workmen with a view to promote harmonious relations between employers and workers and to represent the grievances of workmen to employers to obtain their redress. For conciliation purposes, the parties to the dispute could appoint delegates, but an extraordinary provision was made, 'that the labour office may be appointed as a delegate on behalf of the workmen'. While the Act received a general welcome, this particular provision met with criticism.

The government also expressed an uneasiness at the possibility of the wrong set of delegates attending the conciliation proceedings and added a proviso that, 'a person shall be disqualified from acting as a delegate, if such a person is not, in the opinion of the conciliator, after the conciliation proceedings have started, a fit and proper person to be a delegate'. An order to this effect was made final or non-appealable. Conciliation proceedings could produce settlements but also make reports.[63]

The government's motive as explained by the Home Member in the Council was

> to prevent communists and extremists from interfering in the affairs of the textile industry in Bombay. Trade unionism in Bombay was not a spontaneous development, but had been superimposed on the working class by outsiders. The moment the leaders were arrested the workers were leaderless and on such occasions the labour officer would fill the gap. This officer would, in the first instance, function as a welfare officer, and would try to negotiate and act as a conciliator only if necessary.[64]

The Act was a soft measure to weaken the hold of communists on labour, but could not be used to prosecute communist leaders for causing prolonged and grave hardship to the public. The government's attempt to prosecute them on this charge failed because the High Court was not convinced that the Act could be employed to achieve such results. A number of other beneficial legislations were enacted during this period. The government paid heed to the Whitley Commission's report and upgraded several labour standards by amending the existing legislation as well as enacting entirely new laws. The Factories Act was substantially amended in 1934. The Children (Pledging of Labour) Act, 1933 was a notable move towards outlawing the vicious practice of giving advances to secure child labour. In the same class may be placed the Tea Districts Emigration Labour Act, 1932 which came into force in October 1933. The Bengal Workmen's Protection Act, 1935 was enacted to prevent recovery of debts from certain classes of workmen by moneylenders on pay days or to engage in violence against the debtors. In the Central Provinces, the Central Provinces Adjustment and Liquidation of Industrial Workers Debt Act,

1936 was placed on the statute book. On this subject, N.M. Joshi had moved a private bill in the Legislative Assembly in 1933, but it was not proceeded with though it did receive considerable notice. However, a major central law, the Payment of Wages Act, 1936 to regulate the power to make only authorised deductions from wages and to ensure proper payment of wages on the due dates, was passed. This Act prohibited the practice of arbitrary imposition of fines on workers, though fines could still be imposed for such acts or commission as were specified by the employers and approved by the local government or the prescribed authority. This Act went a long way in establishing the rule of law in factories and protected workers receiving less than Rs. 200 per month.

The creation of labour constituencies under the 1935 Act provided an effective platform for politically ambitious leaders to carve out power bases for themselves as trade union leaders. The development of local self-government, first under the 1919 Act and further strengthened during the 1930s, produced an unintended effect on the politicisation of unions. Murphy explains the phenomenon thus:

> The shock results of the 1927 Madras municipal elections made very clear to the political parties in the South that they either had to come to terms with the existing labour leaders, or to promote their own unions if they were to win the industrial worker's vote. In the meantime, however, the success of labour in the municipal elections and moves to grant labour seats in legislatures, as well as disillusionment with the existing political organizations, encouraged the disparate group of political workers in the south to form their own independent labour party. The Madras case merely demonstrates how politics and trade union work became deeply intertwined; it also shows the diverse nature of political responses of trade unions depending upon the local circumstances and ideologies of leaders participating in the fray, and the particular lessons they learnt to keep themselves in prominence.[65]

At the all-India level, the political involvement of trade union leaders became gradually more delineated by ideology and party affiliations and was not necessarily conditioned by local circumstances. The AITUC had split solely on ideological lines in 1929, the communists having captured it. The moderates then floated their own organization though there is some question whether this was unavoidable. Five years later, one could legitimately enquire as to which of the two had more unions affiliated to it, or commanded the greater allegiance of the workers. In 1934, the AITUC secured a marginal accretion of numbers when the sectarian left communists took their Red Trade Union Congress back to the parent organization. It is suggested that the rise of Hitler as a fascist dictator in Germany led to a rethink in the Comintern and the change in political line now strongly encouraged the communist parties to work through broad-based popular fronts. The Red TUC obediently following this line decided to reunite with the AITUC. In any case, the pressure for reunification of labour organizations was growing among the affiliating unions since circumstances had turned adverse and it was often painful to lead strikes with labour clearly divided in rival camps.

Nevertheless, the issues that caused the schism in the labour movement were unbridgeable as instanced by one very basic issue: should the trade union become an organ of class struggle? The moderates accepted the premise that the basic task of trade unions was to organize workers to defend and advance their interests and to engage in struggles against the employers. However, to emphasize that the trade union was an organ of class struggle or that the interests of capital and labour were irreconcilable would be wrong.

Responding to pressure from below, the AITUC floated a platform of unity drafted by M.N. Roy though the conditions for unity were tough. Among the 13 points were included such items as: 'xi. No representative of the Trade Union movement shall accept the nominated seat in the Central or Provincial Legislatures, nor serve on any official committee.'[66] N.M. Joshi was willing to agree only that nominated members would not act as the representatives of the movement, but no one could be barred from accepting a nominated position. He further clarified, 'if the cause of the split is to be removed, there must be a clear definition made of the right of the majority to assert its right to coerce the minority in its views and actions and if the minority is to be given freedom, as it must be, it must be defined to what extent the freedom must be given and in what respects.'[66]

A little later, another moderate leader Jamnadas Mehta, while deploring the perils of a divided trade union movement, was categorical in laying down a precondition: 'An essential condition of success is the absolute independence of the movement. We should not be open to the suspicion of being the antechamber of the government on the one hand or the dupes of Moscow on the other.' He showed the difference in the methods used by the socialists and the communists in these sharp words. 'The Socialist loves to enlighten and inform, the communist prefers to inflame and incite.'[67] The rival positions on unity were made clearer and the distance between the moderates, who saw themselves as a minority and the aggressive communists could not be bridged. This was at the all-India level.

By contrast, among the workers there was increasing pressure to take effective action in self-defence against the employers, hence the need for greater unity in action. Yet, despite laudable intentions to promote unity moves, there was little progress. Meanwhile, the railway unions formed a central body called the National Federation of Labour. In April 1933, this new body, held a joint convention with the Indian Trade Union Federation. The two created a new body called the National Trades Union Federation and this strengthened the forces of the moderates. However, the politics of labour blocked the unity moves as witnessed by the communists call for a general strike in the cotton textile mills; it was led by the communist unions to the unfortunate exclusion of moderates in the united strike committees, who were then forced to form a parallel strike committee. Not only did the two groups lead a common strike from separate forums, they also ran each other down.

In July 1934, the government found the communist menace so great that it declared the Indian Communist Party along with its committees, subcommittees and branches illegal throughout the country. The Bombay government took further preventive action under the Special (Emergency) Powers Act to intern six prominent communist leaders, thus preventing them from taking active part in union work. At the same time, the Mill Mazdoor Sangh, representing mainly Muslim weavers in Ahmedabad and led by communists was outlawed. Furthermore, despite being registered, nearly a score of trade unions led by communists forfeited their legal status. The principal result of government repression was that the AITUC now came under the control of other Marxist trade unionist followers of M.N. Roy. Roy, a dissident communist, was expelled by the Comintern and was politically active in the Congress. Another result was that the newly formed Congress Socialist Party opened a front for the joint participation of the communists with the socialists. Hereafter, the communist cadre worked mainly in the Congress, sometimes holding important organizational posts therein. Functioning within the Congress and the CSP the communists steadily grew in membership.

In 1935, the unity moves received considerable impetus. The Red TUC had already merged with the AITUC and some progress was made towards consolidating the combined forces of the AITUC and the NTUF. The basis of unity was created by an agreement between the two groups on five principles: (i) class struggle (ii) one union in one industry (iii) no foreign affiliation (iv) representation to Geneva to be decided every year and (v) the AITUC to be the central organization. However, structural unity was not yet in sight because issues that needed to be sorted out were principally ideological and political. The moderates demonstrated their ascendance by practically dominating the All India Joint Labour Board headed by V.V. Giri. In a resolution of the

Board, the 1935 Act was criticized as retrograde and reactionary. The representation given to labour was found to be utterly inadequate; moreover, the Act was faulted on the grounds that it held, 'no prospects of the Indian masses and the working classes ever securing an adequate and effective voice and control in the legislatures and administration of the country and is, therefore, unacceptable to them'.[68]

Following this, the AITUC yet again redoubled efforts to achieve structural unity and formulated a more reasonable and helpful formula which might be acceptable to the NTUF leaders, This was welcomed by them in a formal resolution. Meanwhile, the AITUC leadership found collaboration with the Congress Socialist Party a source of strength. The AITUC was keen that organized workers should find direct representation on Congress committees and for this purpose working within the CSP would be a useful.[69] At the May 1936 convention, the political message of revolutionary trade unionism overrode any economic question that needed to be met.

> We have to maintain our class identity and class outlook without which we will not be able to fulfil our role as the leaders of the struggle and secondly we have to become an integral part of the Indian National Congress machine. This two-fold task can only be achieved by the method of collective affiliation, i.e. by affiliating our trade unions or class organizations to the Indian National Congress.[70]

In this respect, the illegal CPI was still pursuing the united front line promoted by the Comintern. However, this wish was not granted and Congress declined to accept any class organization as an affiliate, though it continued to allow communists to function through its committees and organs. Collective affiliation would weaken the Congress as a united platform of the national struggle and render it into a loose federation of affiliating mass organizations.

II. 1937–41

Elections Under the 1935 Act, Provincial Autonomy, The War

The bulky Government of India Act, 1935 was described by K.M. Munshi as 'a great feat of political acumen and constitutional draftsmanship. It had many commendable features, and I had little doubt that, if the act was worked properly, the transition to full-fledged Dominion Status for the whole of India would have been easy with the executives in the provinces being made responsible to their respective legislatures.'[71] He read the Act and explained its key features to Gandhi and succeeded in securing a complete reversal of the Lahore resolution of the Congress, on the complete boycott of the central and provincial legislatures and which called on Congressmen to abstain directly and indirectly, from participating in future elections. The leaders who sponsored the Council Entry Programme visualized the revival of the Swaraj Party or another party within the Congress and, enlisted those whose hearts were not in the civil disobedience movement but still wanted to engage in worthwhile political activities. Gandhi gave his blessings to the idea, though the thought of floating a separate party was given up.

Meanwhile, the AICC decided that the Congress should directly enter the fray and engage in parliamentary activities. A Parliamentary Board was constituted to carry out the Council Entry Programme. The Congress had already contested the election to the Central Assembly in 1934 and now the elections to the provincial legislatures as well. Nehru, as the left's spokesman, argued that 'the withdrawal of the Civil Disobedience Movement and Council-entry and the recourse to constructive programmes represented a "spiritual defeat" and a surrender of ideals, a retreat from the revolutionary to the reformist mentality, and a going back to the pre-1919 moderate phase.'[72] Despite these views, Nehru took an active part in the election campaign and emerged as a popular leader of masses.

In the expanded franchise, 35 million voters were eligible

to vote, a fact of considerable importance to all the political parties since representation in the assemblies would be based on numerical strength. This was a major advance over the 1919 Act and the franchise now represented more than 12 per cent of the adult population in British India. In the last few years the Congress had become increasingly mass-oriented and in December 1936, at the Faizpur session, it was decided to work for more effective mass contact. In the party manifesto the new Constitution was rejected and the principle affirmed that only a Constituent Assembly could frame a constitution on the basis of India's independence, while the scheme of the federation was rejected outright. Inside the legislatures, the Congressmen 'will work for the establishment of civil liberties, for the release of political prisoners and detenus and to repair the wrong done to the peasantry and to the public institutions in the course of the national struggle'. The Congress would work for the removal of rural indebtedness and unemployment, the provision of agricultural loans at low rates of interest and to improve the standard of living of the industrial labour and many other things. However, it was not yet clear whether, if elected, the Congress would hold office.

The question of political prisoners and detenus was bound to become a constitutional issue because, on this matter, governors had reserved powers, though they could use personal discretion in deciding individual cases. Elections were held in January-February, 1937 and the Congress entered the fray with great force. Perhaps more than one hundred thousand workers who participated earlier in the civil disobedience movement and were now out of jails worked enthusiastically for Congress candidates. The remarkable thing about the elections was that no one defended the government and every party criticized it. The Muslim League, whose manifesto was drafted under Jinnah's direction, did not mention either Urdu as the language of the Muslims or the separate electorate. In UP, an informal alliance was arrived at on the assumption that, in the event the Congress would be allowed to hold office, the two parties might join hands to form a coalition government. It didn't work out this way because, unexpectedly, the Congress secured a clear majority in the UP Assembly and moved away from the idea of a coalition; however on this event an entire political hypothesis in respect of the Muslim League's behaviour has come to rest.[73]

There was considerable hesitation in the Congress High Command on the question of holding office. However, once the British Prime Minister, Neville Chamberlain, explained the constitutional position all the difficulties were removed in a step-by-step manner.

> The main point which emerged from Chamberlain's reply was that with the introduction of provincial autonomy, the British Parliament's control over the provincial governments would come to an end, except in the rare circumstances in which a provincial Governor felt obliged to exercise his statutory powers in disregard of the advice of his ministers. This was followed by an assurance by Lord Linlithgow, on June 22, 1937, that the Governors would exercise their special powers with extreme introspection.'[74]

Thereafter, taking note of senior Congress leaders like C. Rajagopalachari's strong inclination to form the government, the Congress Working Committee (CWC) gave the go ahead signal. On the attitude of Congress ministers, K.M. Munshi says,

> To my knowledge, no Congress Ministers ever made any effort to combat the new Act; this was implicit in our acceptance of office. Only on one occasion, in February 1938, a serious conflict arose over the release of political prisoners in UP and Bihar, but the impasse was tactfully surmounted. From my experience of office as the Home Minister, I can also say that the Governors of Bombay never gave any cause for conflict.[75]

An extraordinary unity of purpose was displayed toward working the new Act.

Though the expected difficulties with the governors did not occur to the extent anticipated, the unexpected did; barely eight months after the assumption of office by the Congress ministries, the Muslim League passed a resolution on the hardship, ill-treatment and injustice meted out to Muslims and appointed a committee to make a report on the same. On the publication of the report in November 1938, the Congress ministers made enquiries and gave detailed replies. This was a sharp political move on the part of the Muslim League to chart an independent course. The complaints were found to be without basis but the political damage had been done and paved the way for a total separation of Muslim politics from the nationalist movement.[76] Neither the Viceroy nor the concerned governors took any action on Jinnah's demand for a Royal Commission to enquire into the charges. Though Jinnah did not press them, at a later stage he did tell the Viceroy to dismiss the Congress governments; it didn't matter to him that this would be an undemocratic act, perhaps because he never did believe that India's problems would be solved through democratic politics.[77]

Two political objectives seem to be uppermost to Jinnah. First, to prevent the inauguration of the federation until the Act was suitably amended to provide for adequate safeguards to the Muslims. Second, to consolidate the considerable gains Muslims had already achieved under the leadership of Fazl-i-Husain of Punjab and so well reflected in the 1935 Act. Fazl-i-Husain is credited with most of the gains that accrued to the Muslims. The gains are listed by his son and biographer.

'Muslims had gained nearly as much as they had asked.' These are summed up in Fazl-i-Hussain's biography and Moore agrees.

> The Muslim position under the new Constitution was adequately safeguarded, and the demands put forward in the Delhi Resolution (1929) were to a large extent secured. The NWFP became a Governor's Province. Sind was separated from Bombay and declared to be a Governor's Province. The Muslim share in the public services was fixed at 25 per cent of all Imperial appointments. With regard to residuary powers, it is

> true that the Muslim demand that they should be vested in the provinces was not accepted, but as desired by Muslims they were not vested in the Centre, but were to be exercised by the Governor-General at his discretion. The demand for $33^{1/3}$ per cent representation in the Cabinet, Central and Provincial, was not met in the Act, but provision for giving effect to it was made in the Instrument of Instructions issued to the Governor-General and the Governors. Muslims were to be represented by separate electorates without prejudice to the weightages obtained by Muslim minorities under the Lucknow Pact; Muslims in the Punjab were given a statutory majority. The only demand in this respect which was not conceded was in the case of Bengal, because of the necessity for providing representation for Europeans ... All this put the Muslim mind at rest and it also concluded the labours of Fazl-i-Husain for five years in the Government of India.[78]

Jinnah planned the next political moves to secure more gains to the Muslims. He rapidly acquired decisive power in the Muslim League and became more popular. 'Jinnah became convinced that parliamentary government would mean Congress "totalitarianism" in India. The demand for safeguards of equal rights to India's Muslims lay in their achievement of equality of power through their solidarity within the All India Muslim League. Under his organization the League's membership grew from a few thousand to several hundred thousand in 1937–38.'[79]

Though the facts pertaining to 'atrocities' failed completely to face the scrutiny, yet the Muslim opinion found a rallying ground based largely on anti-Congress sentiments. Within a year of Congress governments taking over in the provinces, major developments took place in Muslim politics. Sir Sikander Hyat Khan, the Premier of Punjab and leader of the Unionist Party, advised the Muslim members to join the Muslim League and similar declarations were made by Fazl-ul-Haq, Premier of Bengal and Sir Muhammad Saadullah, Premier of Assam. Jinnah became the leader of the Muslims in the country as never before and he used his popularity to spread the influence of the Muslim League in the rural areas.

The by-elections that took place between 1937–43 demonstrated beyond question that the Muslim League had captured the loyalty of the Muslim electorate and the wider support of the masses.[80] Jinnah became more intransigent than he had ever been and demanded that Congress should cease representing the Muslims, that it should publicly acknowledge the Muslim League as their sole representative, followed by the demand for parity in any constitutional arrangements between the Congress as the party of the Hindus and the League as the party of the Muslims.[81]

Writing about Indian problems in 1941, George Schuster observed:

> concurrently, The Moslems, alarmed by the experience of provincial government under Congress ministries have been organizing themselves more closely and in more hostile opposition to Congress and while making it clear above all that they cannot agree to entrust their fate to Constituent Assembly of the kind demanded by Congress, have moved towards plans for protecting Moslem interests by some form of political segregation of Moslem areas.[82]

The Congress never could gauge the depth of Muslim segregationism, which rested on the antagonistic premise that the Muslims were a nation in their own right and entitled to assert their rights on the grounds of religion, language, culture, even racial distinctiveness and demand that these be conceded. Jinnah led the segregationist Muslim politics with unreserved commitment and found the British as his strongest ally.

Political alignments in the assemblies increasingly grew along communal lines; this was a development no one could have anticipated. In the Congress ruled provinces, the Hindu majority was on the side of the government while the opposition comprised Muslim legislators. Gradually, the non-League Muslim members either joined hands with the League or actually got affiliated to it. This was the case in UP. In Bihar too, the non-Congressmen were excluded from ministry formation, so the Muslims formed the majority in opposition, 'consequently the legislature was divided into the Congress Party (Hindu) against the Muslim opposition.'[83] The same picture was reflected in Punjab and Bengal, though Muslims were in a majority in these provinces. Congress was weakest in Punjab and sitting in the opposition it had mostly Hindus on its side. Yet, these two governments worked satisfactorily, having few problems with the governors and lasted the longest (actually till independence) with changing leaders and ministers but with a stable political structure.

This was the direct result of the separate communal electorate. Additionally, though the Congress fielded a large number of Muslim candidates for the provincial assemblies, most of them lost. To begin with, the Muslim League no doubt fared poorly and other Muslim parties showed better results but, later under Jinnah's leadership, the Muslim legislators agreed to unite under the League whether on the side of the government or in opposition. This, however, had more to do with Muslim separatism which was taking root in the minds of Muslim intellectuals and leaders independently of Jinnah and its progress could be directly traced to the intellectual influence of the Aligarh Muslim University. The work of Syed Ahmed Khan may also be acknowledged, as the founder and principal spokesman of the doctrine that India never was and could never be a nation and furthermore, that Muslims must develop the political consciousness to function as a block, as an ally of the British, and claim their fair share in power, jobs and commercial opportunities.[84] Jinnah nurtured it to achieve the political objective of a communal partition of India.

The strength of the Muslim League was mostly in the northern provinces where Muslims were in a minority even though the Muslim elite enjoyed considerable social status and political clout. In October 1938, at a conference in Karachi, the League could applaud the achievements of the provincial League ministries. This was indeed quite remarkable for a party which failed to carry any Muslim majority province in 1937. By December 1938, the League could denounce the Congress as an enemy worse than British imperialism. This political line was pushed further and was reflected in the League's working committee resolution, adopted at Patna in 1938, to resort to direct action if necessary.

Talk of civil war was in the air for the first time ever.[85] The Congress-Muslim League feud had all the making of a deeper communal conflict. Brailford writes on the mood prevailing among the leading members of the Muslim community. 'The Muslims can never forget that they are a race of conquerors, and in their more romantic moods some of them in my hearing have talked of restoring their former ascendancy by the sword.' Further,

> if Muslims were content to draw their inspiration from the tolerance and justice of the Emperor Akbar, their love of the past would be a blessing. But more often it is their military exploits that they think. The worst consequence of this habit is that it arouses answering chauvinism in the Hindus, who also have their martial races and their military pride.[86]

From the threat of direct action to the adoption of a formal resolution on Pakistan, it was just one logical step that followed at the Muslim League convention at Lahore in March 1940. It had an audience of over 100,000 people who heard Jinnah speak to them in English for over a hundred minutes and responded with thunderous applause. He asserted that Muslims were a nation by any definition.[87]

In the Congress ruled provinces, the people welcomed the formation of popular government 'as if they were breathing the very air of victory and people's power, for was it not a great achievement that khadi-clad men and women who had been in prison until just the other day were now ruling in the secretariat and the officials who were used to putting Congressmen in jail would now be taking orders from them'.[88] The British civil servants were a disciplined cadre and obeyed the ministers, even as they complained to their immediate superiors of the very great change that had taken place at the district level in running the administration; for quite often the local Congress legislators interceded in administrative matters and influenced the implementation of government policies in ways that suited them, thereby undermining the authority of district-level officials.[89] This opinion travelled to the Viceroy's Council and produced a stiffening of attitudes. At one stage in 1939, the Viceroy consulted his British advisers on what attitude he should take towards the Congress. Sir P. J. Grigg thought the time had come to hit Congress hard and the Commander-in Chief, General Cassels, was inclined to agree, but the Home Member, Sir Reginald Maxwell, disagreed and so did the Chief Justice. The Viceroy pursued the policy of compromise and conciliation.[90] The immediate issue that arose then was whether Gandhi should be dissuaded from a fast which might result in his death over a political storm in the native state of Rajkot, though the real issue was that the civil service was ill at ease in the Congress ruled provinces in the north, particularly UP.

The Congress governments lasted for two years and four months. Their tasks were already set out by the High Command, foremost being the extension of civil liberties and release of political detenus and prisoners. The emergency powers acquired earlier by legislation such as the Public Safety Acts were repealed and bans on political organizations lifted. Nothing could be done, however, about the ban on the Communist Party since the appropriate authority was the Central Government, though communists could now function freely through the Congress organizations. The press was freed and cases of prosecution against them were withdrawn.

However, even as the prevailing mood was one of freedom, there were too many instances of Congress leaders interfering in the day-to-day administration of local officials and sending complaints, however petty, directly to the ministers. In September 1938, the Congress Working Committee passed a resolution advising, 'Congressmen not to interfere with the new course of administration. In June 1939, another resolution was passed asking Provincial Congress Committees not to interfere with the discretions of ministers, and if there were differences on policy mattes to raise them at the Parliamentary Sub-Committee'.[91]

In agrarian reforms, Madras took the lead; the legislature adopted a resolution to drastically modify the land and revenue settlement in areas under the permanent settlement though it could not be implemented by an enactment. In Orissa, a Bill was passed reducing all rents in the zamindari areas to the levels prevailing in the ryotwari areas. A small compensation was payable to the zamindars. Later, on the question raised around this bill, Premier Biswanath Das had to resign and the bill was reserved by the governor for the consideration of the Governor-General. In UP, an Act was passed for further security of tenure, fixation of rents by the government agency, abolition of a number of abuses and easing numerous restrictions on the tenants.[92] In Bihar, all increases in the rents effected since 1911 were abolished; likewise the concept of damages realizable on arrears of rent was abolished and so was the interest payable on them. Moreover, the arrears of rents were substantially lowered and,

> the land which had been sold in execution of decrees for the payment of arrears between 1929 and 1937 was to be restored to its previous tenants if they paid half the amount for which the land had been put up for sale. The landlords' power to realize rents was so greatly curtailed that he had now less rights than any other kind of creditor for exacting what was due to him.[93]

Though the landlords were well represented in the two assemblies, more in UP and less in Bihar, the pro-tenants legislation reflected a spirit of conciliation and compromise and adherence to the Congress's election manifesto. Relief of peasant indebtedness was affected in every Congress ruled province; and registration of moneylenders was enacted in both Congress and non-Congress led provinces.

According to Coupland,

> of the two declared intentions of the Congress, to work the Act and to combat it, the latter fell more and more into the

> background. The dispute over the 'safeguards' in the spring of 1938 was the only major constitutional crisis; and most of the Congress ministries would have been as reluctant to resign on that issue at that time as they were to resign on a wider issue in the autumn of 1939. They all worked the Constitution—they might be said, indeed, to have overworked it by trying to do too much too quickly and they acquiesced accordingly, for the time being, in such checks as still remained on the exercise of complete self-government.[94]

However, the non-Congress governments worked the Constitution better. Punjab demonstrated the highest level of stability and this may be partly due to the strong position of Sir Manohar Lal and Sir Chotu Ram in the government. Sir Sikandar was determined to keep Punjab as free of the contagion of political agitation as possible and, in this, he was largely successful.

In the Congress governments stability was ensured by the disciplinary control of the High Command, though there was much factionalism and on occasions instances of misuse of authority could be cited. In all provinces, the problems of law and order were dealt with strongly and this included the use of repressive measures often similar to the practices of the autocratic colonial governments they had replaced. The Congress, as an organization of national aggregation was totally clear that in the name of civil liberties no one could advocate murder, arson, looting and class war by violent means or incite communal conflicts. The Congress governments were expected to take effective measures for the defence of life and property.

The Congress ministries resigned following the outbreak of the war due to the failure of the British government to declare their war aims as far as India was concerned. The nationalists, led by Nehru, were deeply sympathetic to the cause of defence of democracies against the Nazi onslaughts. However, on 3 September 1939, when Britain declared war on Germany, India followed suit. There were no consultations and this was viewed very adversely by the Congress. As early as in 1934, when Indian troops were sent to China in its defence against Japanese aggression, the Congress had strongly protested on the issue of using Indian manpower and resources for imperialist purposes. In March 1939, at the Tripuri Congress the AICC 'resolved upon resisting the imposition of war on India, and cautioned the provincial governments against the acceptance of the dictatorship of the Centre. The Congress observed April 23 as the anti-war day.'[95] Yet, in August, the Congress Working Committee (CWC) announced its support in defence of democracy and freedom, but simultaneously protested against the exploitation of India towards imperial ends.

These protests were totally ignored; instead, the Viceroy declared that a grave emergency existed, the security of India was threatened and followed the declaration with the promulgation of a number of ordinances. The Government of India clearly anticipated resignations and made preparations for bringing into operation Section 93 of the 1935 Act, by which provinces would be directly governed by the governors. It was now prepared to declare a lightning war against the Congress and any organization which impeded the war effort. At the same time, on 8 October 1939, proposals were made to secure the participation of the Congress and the Muslim League in running the government. These would be: (a) the expansion of the Viceroy's Executive Council (b) the establishment of a War Council to advise the government and (c) the setting up of a body to revise the 1935 Act after the conclusion of the war.

These failed to produce any move by the Congress which might be viewed as conciliatory. Just then Linlithgow took a stiff stand and rejected the Congress demand on the declaration of Britain's war aims. He also proceeded to simultaneously wreck the effort being made by The Labour Party leaders to reconstruct the Central Assembly, 'so as to reflect the current disposition of political power in the provinces, and to appoint selected members of the new body to the Viceroy's executive'. In fact, Cripps had advised Nehru to accept nothing 'short of action which proves conclusively the faith behind words'.[96] Nothing came of these moves and on 22 October, the Congress rejected the Viceroy's proposals and asked the Congress ministries to resign. A week later, Cripps denounced the government's policy on India and asked for a declaration without reservation that its object should be self-government for India after the war. A key issue was the convening of a Constituent Assembly to write India's Constitution, but the Tories would not budge on it. This went totally against the Tory position that parliament must remain supreme on all aspects of India's constitutional progress.

On the subject of Congress ministries' resignations and the return of Congress to its role as a party of protest, unswervingly committed to full independence, two sharply contrasting opinions have emerged and are sometimes still discussed several decades after independence. First, the 1935 Act was rejected by everyone and by the Congress, root and branch. Yet, it was also an undeniable fact that the provinces were given considerably greater autonomy than before and, even the limited experience of administering the 1919 Act showed that, at the hands of capable leaders, it could be put to serve the people. These formed the basis of the pleas made for the Council Entry Programme which received strong support among Congress leaders. Eventually, the rebels took the reins of office and performed creditably.

On the resignations, R.P. Masani says,

> It was a grave error, a tactical blunder, abruptly terminating one of the most promising experiments in responsive cooperation known to history. By pulling out its provincial ministries on its own initiative and flinging itself once more into the wilderness the Congress weakened its bargaining power. Had it left it to the British Government to find ways and means of arriving at a peaceful solution the history of India might have taken a different turn.[97]

The CWC met for five days and discussed British actions for 30 hours. Three political antecedents might have been considered and found quite galling. Within a few hours of

Britain going to war, the Viceroy declared India a belligerent country. In quick succession several political decisions were taken. The government of India Act, 1935 was amended by parliament in eleven minutes, empowering the Viceroy to override any provisions of the Act. 'The same day, the Defence of India Ordinance was issued by the Government of India, which provided for curtailment of liberties.'[98]

Undoubtedly, the Viceroy was technically right in acting within his powers and, since the Central Government was still governed by the 1919 Act, he was not accountable to any legislature in India. Yet, his actions were of all-India importance; they had far reaching political implications and he could have initiated political consultations earlier, rather than later. Linlithgow was on good talking terms with all the key political leaders, but he had not received any signal from London to prepare India politically for war, even as, in secrecy, he was gearing the administrative apparatus and preparing the governors to do so. Inexplicably, the Viceroy and the governors acted deliberately in stopping short of bringing the popular ministries into the picture. Actually, the hard-headed British members of the Viceroy's Executive Council were keener on hitting the Congress hard, rather than attempting anything as inconceivable as securing its cooperation in exerting itself to victory in the war. Linlithgow knew that his main job was to commit Indian resources to the war and, towards this end, he would ask for collaboration from national leaders on his terms, which he spelt out. The new Act was already drained of democratic content and all powers, as detailed under any legislation or otherwise, were vested in him. The Congress could still run the governments where it was in power but hereafter they must follow him or take the command from the war cabinet in London. In the event, the resignations were actually a riddance much desired by the imperial masters.

What was possibly a riddance though, proved disastrous for the British conduct of war, while it was a source of joy to the Muslim League which decided to celebrate 22 December as 'Deliverance Day'. Jinnah ridiculed the idea of the Constituent Assembly and assured the Viceroy of full support of Muslims in return for securing their interests by him. In 1940, the Muslim League steadily moved towards political separatism and received sustained encouragement from the Viceroy as well as the Secretary of State for India, Zetland. Muslims were praised for joining the army in a fitting affirmation of their martial tradition and politically cajoled. The League adopted the Pakistan resolution in full knowledge that it had the tacit support of the British conservative opinion. The Muslims were already given the right of veto on all constitutional proposals. There were few indications, if any, that among the Congress leaders the full implications of the strong political axis being formed between the British and the Muslim League were grasped. Linlithgow understood better the long-term consequences of the widening of cleavage with the Congress. Instead of moving closer, the Congress too took its stand as a rebel movement in full recognition of the fact that differences with the British government were irreconcilable.

The resignation of Congress ministries threw the political situation back into the melting pot. The Congress had little option but to revert to its role as a party of revolt and several Congress leaders declared that the time was opportune for Gandhi to again call for another round of civil disobedience movement. However, as Gandhi saw it, the situation obtaining in 1940 was far more complex and perplexing. First, India was already at war and all powers pertaining to the conduct of the war were vested in the Viceroy. Moreover, there was a strong political opinion within the Congress leadership, that the allied cause merited support and, if this was not politically possible, nothing should be done that would give comfort to the Axis powers. Furthermore, a part of India under non-Congress ministries, including Punjab and Bengal, was lending full support to the British government. So the political context was not only vastly different from the previous civil disobedience movement, it now had several active forces that might strongly oppose it and produce conditions of domestic confrontation.

Second, the Muslim League was presently a much stronger political force, it had adopted the Pakistan resolution and demanded 50 per cent of the seats in the Viceroy's Executive Council. In addition, from the nationalist perspective, communal tensions in the country had increased considerably and this factor weighed with Gandhi on deciding against launching another mass movement at this stage. Gandhi admitted in so many words that though the Congress had much greater support in the country, it lacked the backing of the Muslims.

Third, the possibility of the Congress returning to the constitutionalist path was still open, though the obstacles were increasing. Neither Gandhi nor the Viceroy, echoing the viewpoint of senior British civil servants, wanted popular governments to be restored, though for very different reasons. Gandhi knew that, willy-nilly, the Congress governments will have to support the Viceroy and the British military command in all crucial policy matters, since mobilization for war would have the highest priority. From the British perspective, 'Congress cooperation, it was felt, would take the form of daily and exasperating obstruction to which "non-cooperation" even active hostility would be preferable. A section of British opinion was, therefore, not at all keen to have members of Congress in office during the war and secretly welcomed their departure soon after its outbreak.'[99]

Gandhi overcame the political impasse in the Congress by inventing the new devise of individual civil disobedience against the war but without causing too much unrest in the country. Selected satyagrahis would make a public declaration that it was wrong to help the British war effort with men and money, but would not obstruct either recruitment or any particular policy of the government in this regard and would court arrest and accept prison sentences, if convicted. Nehru was given a four-year sentence and this shocked even Churchill. However, they were all released a few days before the Pearl Harbour attack and paved the way for the Cripps Mission.

The Last Phase of the Depression, War, Economy Under Strain

By the beginning of 1937 the economy showed signs of revival as the Great Depression the world over bottomed out. In the West, it appeared that a mini-boom which had developed was beginning to peter out. However in India, in the vast agricultural sector, no such things happened, though the financial future in the view of both debtors and creditors looked more promising. The important change that had occurred meanwhile was the passage of laws in provinces one after another to provide relief to the indebted farmers. For Madras, Baker has this to say following the enactment of the Agriculturist's Relief Act in 1938.

> This measure, by far the most important piece of all debt legislation, was contrived to scale down the arrears of interest that had been accruing during the depression. It ruled that all arrears of interest dating from 1932 and before should be wiped out, that all interest from 1932 till October 1937 should be calculated at five percent and all interest thereafter at six and a quarter per cent, and that any debt on which the interest paid already accounted to twice the original loan should be deemed discharged. This was a serious measure. In the first fourteen months of the Act's operation over 100,000 cases were filed, relating to more than Rs. 200 lakhs of debts.[100]

This law was obviously a considerable legislative success.

In Punjab, a number of agrarian reform measures were enacted by the legislature. The Punjab Alienation of Land Act, 1900 was amended thrice to prevent transfer of agricultural land to moneylenders and mortgagees, to annul alienations whenever made and to restore their possession to the alienor. The Restitution of Mortgaged Land Act, the Agricultural Markets Products Act, the Registration of Moneylenders Act and The Relief of Indebtedness Act were popular measures which preserved broad-based public support for the National Unionist Party government. In UP and Bihar, political difficulties slowed enactment of progressive legislation, mainly owing to the fact that in the upper chamber, the Congress was in a minority while the majority of members represented propertied classes including landlords and moneylenders.[101] The progress made in UP and Bihar has been already noted.[102]

The depression touched the lowest point in 1933–4 when the net domestic product from primary sectors, comprising agriculture, livestock, forestry and fishing, at current prices was the lowest ever at Rs. 10,445 million, it rose to Rs. 11,164 million in 1934–5 but in 1935–6, declined to Rs. 11,047 million. By this time, the vast majority of the population which earned its living in these sectors had lost the accumulated gains of the previous two decades. Agriculture declined the most; in 1933–4, the net domestic product derived from it was a mere Rs. 7,336 million which was less than half of the value in 1928–9. However, thereafter, a revival occurred at a slow and uneven pace; in the next two years, 1937–8 and 1938–9, the NDP was lower than recorded for 1936–7. In fact, prices did not move up till the outbreak of the Second World War.[103]

Vera Anstey says,

> The benefits of revival accrued chiefly to the better-off sections of the population and to those directly dependent upon mining and modern large-scale industries. The position of the agriculturists remained precarious, as is shown by the continued export of gold, although it was estimated that per capita consumption of certain essentials returned roughly to the pre-depression level.[104]

Actually, the per capita income at current prices declined throughout the depression years. It started declining quite early, from the highest level reached in 1919–20, when it was Rs. 123, slowly to Rs. 116 in 1924–5, Rs. 112 in 1926-27, Rs. 108 in 1928–9 and Rs. 82 in 1930–1, touching the lowest level of Rs. 64 in 1933–4. Thereafter, it rose to Rs. 67 in 1936–7 and held at this level for the next two years up to 1938–9, and moved up to Rs. 74, Rs. 79 and Rs. 94 in the following three years. The pre-war figure of Rs. 67 marks the last stage of the Great Depression. At 1938–9 prices this was lower by Rs. 4 compared to 1929–30, though surprisingly in 1919–20, at constant prices, the per capita income was only Rs. 67.[105] Per capita income figures undoubtedly show the combined effect of the growth in population and a stagnant economy. The Great Depression made it a particularly painful experience.

Unlike agriculture, significant progress was made by several industries. In the cotton textile industry, a series of bilateral negotiations were conducted between Indian interests and Lancashire and Japan to produce mutually agreed trade arrangements, which, on the whole, worked to the advantage of the textile industry as well as the cotton growers. With Britain, a new agreement, the Indo-British Trade Agreement, 1939 was signed which further qualified the scope of imperial preference and provided for reduction in preferential duties if British textile exports fell below the allotted quota. The government simultaneously raised import duty on long staple raw cotton the mills used for producing finer counts of yarn. This was strongly resented by the mill owners. The question was whether it provided some protection to Indian cotton growers and encouraged them to grow long staple cotton or was it to weaken the competitive ability of Indian mills against Lancashire interests. Altogether, the textile industry was doing better and the Bombay mills were earning profits. For cotton growers, an adverse development was the decline of cotton imports by Japan after 1936–7. Raw cotton remained depressed till its revival in 1939.

The cotton textile industry was under pressure to introduce structural changes, improve efficiency and defend its position in the Indian market in the face of severe competition from Lancashire and Japan. On the cost-price-quality dimension the Lancashire textiles were losing out to Japan, while due to the political boycott of imported textiles, their demand in India also declined. The overall domestic demand for mill cloth grew slowly and the Indian mills took advantage of it. According to Bagchi,

> The adjustment to the challenge of Japanese competition, and to the opportunities afforded by the increase in the size of the domestic market open to Indian mills and a result of the loss of competitive power by the British industry, took place along two broad directions. First, there were improvements in efficiency in established centres such as Bombay and Ahmedabad. There was also a general growth in multiple-shift working in all the major centres in the 1930s right up to 1939, when mills were faced with increasing stocks and falling sales, and closed their night shifts, until the war came to the rescue. Second, there was a spread of the industry to new locations which were nearer to the local markets and which also had lower wage costs.[106]

The Ahmedabad mills had a distinct advantage over Bombay in that they were relatively smaller in size and also better managed. They were focussed on the domestic demand for piece goods and performed better when opportunities developed for increased import substitution. However, in comparison to the efficiency and labour productivity in Japan, the Indian textile industry prospered under a backwardness syndrome which bound together the mill owners and the workers, with their low skills, weak physical stamina, their poor learning aptitude and the obsolete technologies employed. The industry may be threatened with extinction one day, the mill workers become unemployed and disperse, the government may watch the proceedings and say one thing or the other, but still no initiative at any level would be taken as may overcome the inertia and break the syndrome.

The raw jute market remained weak and prices declined in 1937 and 1938 but revived in 1939. Jute was of special importance to Bengal's economy. It was grown and sold by a large number of peasants. While in India it had a monopolist buyer, the jute mills, exports also influenced the market trends. The jute mills and the export firms dominated the market. One possible solution for the mills was to restrict output, but Bengal's peasants had hardly any choice. Rice was no less depressed; so the average peasant could decide to grow more jute, yet earn the same income. Jute acreage and output were largely determined by the prices fetched in the previous year and the weather. 'The second Bengal Jute Enquiry Committee, 1939 recommended compulsory restriction, and the Government of Bengal instituted a system of licensing of jute acreage under the Regulation of Jute Area Act, 1940.' It was not needed because there was a spurt in prices in 1939 and this trend was maintained. Under the circumstances, if government orders were put into effect, it would reward any rational peasant to increase the jute acreage in violation of orders since jute prices were rising.[107]

The jute industry showed puzzling features. The industry was highly organized and in the throes of the depression. Yet, looms per mill during 1936–7 to 1938–9 were higher at 621.1 compared to 553.9 during 1926–7 to 1928–9. This may be put down to increased informal competition between the IJMA mills and the non-member mills. However, profits were either low or very low, while the workforce had declined, raising labour productivity. As a result, in 1938, the jute industry faced chaotic conditions because: 'Each mill faced different problems. Each company was a separate legal and financial entity and had its own body of shareholders whose interests had to be satisfied. Even if a Managing Agent held important blocks of stock in each of the units it managed, the differences in appropriate market policies had to be compromised.'[108]

The industry was no doubt highly organized, yet very individualistic. The West Bengal government decided to intervene and issued an ordinance in September 1938 limiting hours of work to 45 per week and control over the use of machinery. This removed the fear of over-production and the jute mills agreed to regulate production on a voluntary basis. Meanwhile, the demand for jute manufactures rose as rearmament in 1938 gathered pace and, by the end of the year, the war demand raised prices and profits. It temporarily solved the problems of low efficiency and indifference toward quality of goods produced; but there was still a general lack of preparation on the long-term threats posed by the substitutes for jute packing, among others.

The sugar industry and sugarcane growers were the two classes which benefited most by the policy of discriminating protection. In 1931, the sugar industry was granted tariff protection. It was argued that protection to the industry needed to be granted to develop improved varieties of sugarcane and their cultivation in India and this was required to maintain a reasonable standard of living of the cultivators. Protective tariffs would support both the sugar mills and the cane growers. The Sugar Industry (Protection) Act, 1932 visualized the protective cover to be maintained for 15 years and it produced results. In 1929–30 the consumption of white sugar was estimated at 1,046,000 tonnes while imports were 933,000 tonnes. Revenue tariff duties were already conferring some protection, so in 1931–2 imports declined to 510,000 tonnes. Thereafter imports declined every year and ceased in 1936–7.[109]

During this period, there was also a marked decline in total sugar consumption and it may be put to the effect of the depression on the economy and the people's consumption levels. While domestic production of white sugar rose at a steady pace imports declined faster, lowering the overall availability of white sugar in the country. By 1935–6, the domestic production at 932,000 tonnes was sufficient to meet the domestic demand, while imports were the lowest thus far at 198,000 tonnes. Soon, a new factor intervened on Indian sugar; in May 1937, the International Sugar Agreement was signed. The British government pledged that India would not export sugar in the next five years and instead it could be viewed as a sugar importing country. This was much resented in India since it was totally uncalled for and ignored India's interests. In 1937, there was overproduction of sugar in India. 'In the spring of 1937 a rich harvest and a collapse of the market led to a crisis. In some areas the peasants burnt their cane in the fields because it was not worth harvesting it any more.'[110] An international sugar restriction scheme had been in operation since 1931, to which India was not a party.

By 1937, it appeared that India might enter the exports market to ease the problem of overproduction. Vera Anstey says,

> But the International Scheme of 1938 aimed at including all countries interested in international trade in sugar and at preventing the undue expansion of production by importing countries with the aid of protection and or subsidies. By this time, India, by means of protection, had become practically self-sufficient and the possibility of exporting was envisaged. According to the agreement, the consuming (importing) countries undertook not to expand output further, whilst India undertook not to export sugar (except to Burma). In return, the existing preferential arrangements were permitted to continue within the Empire.'[111]

The agreement caused great discontent in India mainly because it declared India to be a free market for sugar where any country may sell sugar up to a maximum of 50,000 tonnes per annum. The agreement was totally one-sided. It imposed a restriction without any corresponding benefits and, as an imperial obligation forced on India, it barred the export option.

In 1937, it became necessary to check further expansion of factories and to ensure at the same time that the cultivators got a fair price for cane. Accordingly, the government decided to lower the protective duty while imposing an additional cost on the mills in the form of a higher excise duty. With restricted production India must still remain an open market for imported sugar. This required a concerted response. A sugar syndicate was formed which fixed minimum selling prices and maximum sales quotas for the member mills. While the UP and Bihar governments made membership of the syndicate compulsory, a number of mills preferred to stay outside it. The non-member mills prevented the emergence of an all-India body exercising monopolist power. Yet, sugar prices rose in 1939. Earlier, the prices had not risen despite the excise duty, because it was shifted to and borne by the sugarcane growers. In June 1940, the UP and Bihar governments repealed their respective laws requiring the mills to become members of the Sugar Syndicate and it led many mills to withdraw from it. The government soon realized that it would not do to just provide protection to the mills, while leaving the cultivators totally unprotected. It stepped into the business. The plea of the Sugar Syndicate for restoration of recognition 'was granted on condition that the release of stocks and fixing of sugar prices would be controlled by the governments'.[112]

The growth in the sugar industry occurred at a very fast pace. The number of factories increased from 31 in 1931–2 to 112 in 1933–4 and 140 in 1938–9. The unchecked pace of growth led to overproduction and yet complaints increased about mills reaping undue profits by not paying a fair price to the cultivators. The government's response for checking an excessive number of factories being erected was to raise the excise duty in 1934. The Sugar Cane Act was passed, authorizing the provincial governments to declare particular districts as a 'Controlled Area', in which mills had to pay the minimum price for cane as well as make their direct purchases from the cultivators or the licensed purchase agents. The UP government put it into effect. In 1936–7, this policy did not obviously work to expectation since the actual cane prices fell below the prescribed minimum and the government had to lower the controlled minimum to get the factories to lengthen the crushing season.[113]

Market imbalances impacted the behaviour of mills toward cane growers. According to Bagchi, 'in many cases the minimum price became in effect the maximum price. The cultivators were also cheated by dealers under-weighing their cane and deducting too large an amount for the alleged dryness of cane. They were made to pay commissions or tips to dealers, cane managers or the subordinate staff of the mill.'[114] There were more complaints of the same kind and showed the fundamental conflict of interest between the powerful mills as buyers of cane and the weaknesses of the large number of cane growers who brought the cane to the factory gates and could not return without selling it. Only the government could control the rapacity of mills. The experience of protection was undoubtedly beneficial but also showed that an assured home market attracted, 'too many resources into both the cultivation of cane and the refining industry, threatening the profitability of cultivator and the mills alike. This seems clear evidence of substantial underemployment of resources in India.'[115] In the sugar industry, the combined effect of protection and international trade agreement necessitated the intervention of the government as the controller of outputs and prices.

Prices started rising in 1939 and the value of agricultural output rose from Rs. 10,035 million in 1938–9 to Rs. 12,813 million in 1939–40. At constant prices, the rise was nominal and the price level started correcting itself. In fact, the costs of inputs rose faster, so the net output showed a marginal decline. In 1941–2, the value of output rose to Rs. 15,033 million which was largely inflationary since at constant prices there was a decline, from Rs. 11,015 million in 1940–1 to Rs. 10,535 million in 1941–2.[116] The Indian economy had no doubt changed course, it was no longer trapped in the vicious circle of deflation and depression. However, this was just the beginning of the war finance induced inflation and it would get worse with every year. Farmers responded by increasing the acreage wherever it was possible to do so, this being the only method known to them to raise output and earn profits resulting from higher prices. However, the method of extensive cultivation had severe limits which could not be stretched. The farmers could switch from one crop to another, depending on price differentials in the previous season, but, with the food crops needed for household consumption, the stretchable margins were necessarily very low. It showed up as the problem of low elasticity of supply and the protracted deficiency in growth of output, despite a steady rise in prices caused by excess demand in war conditions.

By comparison, industrial output expanded faster though further expansion was blocked by the fixity of the physical stock of machinery already installed in the factories. The first impact of the onset of war, which could be anticipated but for which the government made no preparations, was the abandonment of the fetish of balanced budgets. The doctrine of laissez-faire, which was compromised repeatedly on one ground or another in the previous decade but never rejected for reasons of principled adherence, was given up in the face of practical difficulties. It also showed an utter lack of intellectual preparation on the dimensions of a war economy.

Between 1923 and 1940, over a period of 18 years, the Indo-British economic relations changed markedly. The British presence in the Indian economy diminished, mainly because Britain was disinvesting more than it was investing and British capital steadily lost its hold on Indian industry and other non-British interests over one sector after another. This may be the inherent logic of capitalism together with the long-term effects on the British economy of the First World War, changes which occurred in world trade and finance during the 1920s and finally the Great Depression. Politically, India changed so much that the British had difficulty visualizing a stable, colonial-style dominance over any length of time. Every time a new batch of reforms were proposed there was opposition from European interests in India along with the weakening of resolve among the British civil servants and was followed by unmistakable signs of diminished collective self-confidence, even demoralization. In as many ways as one could observe, India seemed to be slipping out of imperial grip.

On the sequential effect of the several liberalizing steps, the government took to enable Indian economy to diversify and grow, Tomlinson has this to say:

> These changes in central government policy in the 1920s and 30s created some new opportunities for Indian manufacturers of consumer and intermediate goods. However, the emasculated remains of the new industrial policy, coupled to revenue tariffs, amended stores purchase rules, and discriminating protection did not represent, together or

> separately, a major new economic strategy. State factories and industrial intelligence had a minimal impact; educational reform was neglected; stores purchase rules affected a very limited area of enterprise; revenue tariffs were imposed to meet fiscal, not developmental, criteria; protective tariffs were subject to stringent tests and stiff conditions. In the important area of monetary policy the government lost control of the rupee exchange and the money supply in 1919–20, and could only re-establish its influence on the money market and financial systems by ruthlessly following its own deflationary policies in the post-war slump. During the depression of the 1930s the Government of India found that any attempt to mitigate local difficulties by an independent exchange and monetary policy was impeded by its weak reserve position, or blocked by the British Treasury in London.[117]

Workers Struggle, Trade Unions Unite, then Divide on War

During the preceding five years, workers had faced adverse conditions as industry struggled to survive in the face of low demand, increased competition and high cost of production. Most of the load of adjustment toward increased efficiency had to be borne by labour, resorting to agitations and protests, even strikes to protect jobs, which were unsuccessful and, as a result, demoralization among workers set in. By 1935 the worst of the depression was over and it showed up in the companies' performances and profits. Improvement in the economy had a positive, enlivening effect on trade unions and workers' attitudes towards them. This was aided by the several legislative measures which were presented to the Legislative Assembly. These dealt with amendments to the Trade Disputes Act, the Indian Factories Act and the Indian Mines Act; and there was a new law, the Payment of Wages Act.

Labour members were active participants in the Assembly, delivering speeches asking for the desired changes, which were often ignored, or moving cut motions to secure a more definitive reply or assurance from the government. N.M. Joshi pleaded for some protection to workers from forced unemployment and reduction of wages. V.V. Giri took an active part in defending workers' interests. Along with others who were sympathetic to the cause of labour, they engaged the government on the ILO conventions when they came up for discussion and on occasion successfully moved resolutions which, duly amended, were carried. Labour representatives voted against the Criminal Law Amendment Bill which was to be used to suppress the communist movement but could be used against any popular movement or organization.[119]

Following the elections in 1937 and the formation of popular governments in the provinces the trade union movement regained its momentum.

> New unions were formed and old ones were revived and reactivated. AITUC was the main gainer of the new accession of strength to the trade union movement. The National Trade Unions Federation (NTUF) of Joshibua (N.M. Joshi) and his friends did not register any gains. It continued to languish. That compelled him and his friends to think in terms of unity with AITUC.[120]

The latter was energized by the communists who now had the new Comintern direction of working through united fronts and asked to shed the ultra-left line which had led to splits in AITUC and weakened the organization. Besides the communists whose organizations were already banned, the Congress Socialist Party was also active in the field. It signed an agreement with AITUC, 'according to which the former undertook to affiliate its unions with the latter and the latter pledged to support the Party as the political party of the working class. The socialists had come to the AITUC with a strong bias in favour of unity in the labour movement.'[121] This line suited the communists as well; the communists were active in AITUC as a mass organization, while in the Congress Socialist Party (CSP) they engaged in faction work, which was so successful that it nearly wrecked the party. The AITUC's attitude towards the Indian National Congress, was to seek affiliation, but the move was rebuffed and Nehru had to hear from the dominant right wing leaders, not to take them for granted and to act with restraint on organizational matters. He resented this message deeply but gave up the effort.

Around 1935–7 AITUC was the third largest political organization in the country, the first and the second being the Indian National Congress and the Muslim League. In 1935–6, the AITUC had 71 unions with a membership of 93,750, distributed in 11 classes of industries and activities over eight provinces and one in the Indian states. It was a growing organization with an active cadre. The AITUC passed resolutions on the premise that with the triumph of Nazism in Germany another war would break out sooner or later. Among the 33 resolutions adopted in 1936, one was on war. This resolution called upon, 'all organizations immediately to set up local joint committees for agitation against imperialist war and for the defence of Soviet Union so as to prevent the exploitation of Indian money and resources by British Imperialism in such a crisis and to utilize it for intensifying the struggle for National Independence.' [122] It also urged all the radical parties to work for a Peoples' United Front. The political programme laid particular emphasis on common action: (i) to reject the new reforms (ii) to oppose the impending imperialist war (iii) to defend the Soviet Union (iv) to defend civil liberties (v) to safeguard and advance the interests of the working class and (vi) to contest the elections under the new reforms.[123] These resolutions clearly show the influence of Comintern in AITUC and its political concerns steadily advanced, though the Communist Party was illegal and many communists were in jail.

The M.N. Roy group, though expelled by the Communist International, was now strongly represented in the labour movement and, despite expulsion followed the same line and propelled AITUC in the direction set by Moscow. In 1939 when war became imminent, the AITUC working committee adopted resolutions, against rationalization schemes in the textile industries, criticizing the jute industry for resorting to extensive retrenchment and demanded unemployment insurance to prevent starvation that existed on a large-scale. AITUC helped to organize the unemployed and propagate their cause by means of demonstrations, rallies, et cetera. Responding to one such call, the Bombay unions decided on a one-day protest strike on 2 October and held a rally in which an anti-war resolution was adopted, though with no reference to the defence of the Soviet Union.

The AITUC was a pronouncedly leftist organization. On its platform, the Congress policies were denounced and Gandhi's leadership rejected. The political focus of the AITUC was markedly different from that of the rival NTUF and it came in the way of the much desired unity between the two. By January 1938, the AITUC was much stronger with 98 unions and a membership of 133,050 distributed in seven provinces and nine classes. All it needed to achieve unity was to practise moderation, which in practical terms meant that it should refrain from passing resolutions denouncing others whose actions it disapproved. The formation of Congress governments in several provinces created the right political mood in the AITUC and impelled it to accept the rather stiff conditions for unity proposed by the NTUF. In December 1937, the NTUF passed a resolution on unity with certain conditions. At a Joint Negotiations Committee a decision was taken that while the constitution of the NTUF would be accepted and come into force, NTUF must apply for affiliation to the AITUC. Thereupon a special joint session of the two organizations was held in April 1938 to implement the agreement and form one central organization. Complete merger took place in 1940.[124]

The attitude of Congress ministries towards the unions was very favourable, but they resented labour militancy and strikes. The governments were reminded of the policy announced in 1931 to secure to industrial workers a decent standard of living, shorter hours of work and improved conditions of labour, in conformity, as far as the new economic conditions in the country permitted, with international standards, et cetera. These tactics yielded little, mainly because there was nothing specific about practical measures that should be taken as part of the governments' larger responsibility towards the development of the economy and uplift of the masses. Instead of cooperation from the unions, what the governments had to face was a fresh upsurge of unrest and big strikes in 1937–8 itself. In the very first year, there was a sudden rise in industrial disputes, as if workers, tired of their passivity and having suffered losses in the last three to eight years, were desperate to correct previous wrongs.

The Congress government in Bombay gave the clearest expression on labour policy. The government would be actively involved in maintaining industrial peace and to ensure a fair deal for the workers

> It is the intention of Government to promote legislation aiming at the prevention of strikes and lock-outs as far as possible. The basis of this legislation would be the requirement that no reduction in wages or other changes in conditions of employment to the disadvantage of workers should take effect till they had sufficient time and opportunity for having the facts and merits of the proposed change examined through the channels of voluntary negotiations, conciliation or arbitration or by the machinery of law.

A corresponding obligation would rest on the workers. The government desired that the working class should acquire organized strength, the trade unions should run on proper lines and no legislative programme should be viewed as a substitute for strong trade unions able to engage in collective bargaining. The government would devise means to discourage victimization for participating in legitimate trade union activity.[125]

Workers responded to the formation of Congress ministries with joy and enthusiasm, hence the spurt in industrial disputes which followed is difficult to explain. Perhaps they imagined that the popular governments would take their side and intervene in settling the disputes to their advantage. In 1937, there were 379 disputes causing a loss of 8.982 million man days and in 1938 these figures shot up to 399 disputes with 9.198 million lost man days respectively.[126] In 1939, though the number of disputes was slightly higher, at 406, the cumulative loss suffered was much less, the man days lost were only 4.992 million. The outbreak of war in September and the resignation of Congress governments produced a dampening effect on labour. The popular governments took a hard line on lightning strikes. These were not condoned and the manner in which the government used the police to break up demonstrations showed that in practical terms nothing had changed. 'Section 144 was frequently used and within only a few months' time, the Congress Ministries revealed themselves more and more as functioning against the working class and trade Union Movement.'[127]

The communists in the AITUC defended recourse to direct action as a vitally important right of workers which must continue to be exercised in furtherance of the cause dear to them. Karnik says, 'In some places the communists deliberately organized strikes and other activities, not for securing workers' demands, but for discrediting Congress ministries. Some clashes with the police were deliberately brought about. The use of lathis and arms was inevitable under these circumstances.'[128] Labour unrest was largely caused by economic difficulties, the wage cuts which were not restored and the job losses which could not be regained. Workers also wanted unions to be recognized by the employers and accepted as legitimate bodies which gave voice to workers and the question was whether it was the government's duty in this regard which had been promised but not taken up seriously.

The employers' behaviour was no less in question as it showed strong resistance on the issue of union recognition. They had their own frame of reference and cooperating with the government had a low priority when it clashed with their interests. In Kanpur, the textile strike which began in 1937 never quietened down due to employers' intransigence demonstrated by not implementing the award made by the Congress Enquiry Committee, though the workers had accepted it. It led to a general strike in 1938.[129]

The most notable development of the 1937–9 period was the enactment of the Bombay Industrial Disputes Act, 1938. This was the first time the Gandhian philosophy on industrial relations, as practised at Ahmedabad, was given a legislative form. It provided for notice of change to be served to the other party and for 'settlement through negotiation and conciliation and, in the last resort, arbitration. An elaborate machinery was provided by the Act for conciliation and arbitration. The award of the arbitrator was made binding upon both parties. The Act also provided for recognition of unions so that notice could be given and negotiations could be carried on.' In the absence of a union, the government appointed labour officers who may intervene and ascertain the wishes of workers.[130] However, during the consideration of the Bill, the Communists mounted a strong protest; the main grounds being the provision that strikes would be illegal during the period conciliation was in progress and four months were provided for this. The communists believed, moreover, that under the Act, a favour would be done by recognizing the company unions, while the militant unions would bear the brunt of official discrimination.

The AITUC denounced the Bill as, 'uncalled for, reactionary, retrograde, and prejudicial and harmful to the interests of workers.' It was seen to repudiate the Congress election manifesto and ignoring the recommendations of the Royal Commission on Labour.[131] On 7 November 1938, at its call, over one hundred thousand workers conducted a one-day protest strike and demonstration. It produced police violence and firing in which several workers were killed and many others injured. In an official enquiry the blame for violence was put on the communists. Though somewhat unpopular at the stage of enactment, the machinery created under the Act was freely used by labour in subsequent years and later, in an amended form, it became the mainstay of the government's labour policy.

Trade unions grew in number and membership. Leaders were free to organize new unions and workers flocked to them to conduct their strikes or to negotiate with the employers. Whether they also became organizationally more mature and stable is less certain. In the jute industry they remained in their infancy, though in 1937 about two lakh workers had struck work. 'The groundswell of labour protest in the jute industry during the two general strikes of 1929 and 1937 was accompanied by the same phenomenon: quick flare up followed by speedy withdrawal.'[132] Once the strike was over, workers went their way and hardly remembered their unions. In 1943, in a 250,000 strong labour force, the 16 unions which existed had only 3,000 members.[133] Workers were strong on militancy but weak in organization and very low on accepting the union as their collective voice which needed loyal support and nurturance over several years.

The onset of war, accompanied by tough government regulations, brought about a radical change in the economic and political environment. The long-term problems of rationalization, over capacity or other structural troubles were put on the backburner and labour unrest which had turned so rancorous in the immediate past became more manageable. In the Congress ruled provinces it was not uncommon for workers to engage in spontaneous action, dragging the labour minister, or the premier, into particular disputes and insisting on a decision which might involve not just economic questions pertaining to wages, bonus or retrenchment but also local political issues churned up by competing labour leaders. This would no longer happen. The immediate effect was the deferment of proposed strikes and a breathing spell granted to the affected industry.

A fairly typical situation of unrest now transformed by war is described by Murhpy on the Coimbatore Textile Mills (extracts only):[134]

> As the trade crisis worsened, industrial unrest increased. On 19 July 1939 the Southern India Mill owners' Association announced that fifteen mills would curtail production by 50 percent from August by dismissing the night shift workers. Initially, both the Mill Workers and the Textile Workers' Unions opposed the reduction, maintaining that since the mills had not passed on the benefits to their workers during the prosperous years the workers should not be expected to suffer during the bad years ... The negotiations over the proposed reduction and dismissals revealed the close relationship between the Congress government and Textile Workers' Union which it supported against the Mill Workers' Union. Giri (the labour minister) persuaded the mills to delay the dismissals until he had time to consult the two unions involved ... In response to the rank and file's repeated requests for militant action, Ramamurty (leader of Mill Workers' Union) agreed that unless the mill-owners were prepared to lift some of the burden of the depression from the workers there should be a general strike in the Coimbatore district from 11 September. But he repeated his appeal for the workers to take no action until then...
>
> The proposed strike and the possible conflict between the two unions was averted with the outbreak of war in September 1939 which very quickly restored prosperity to the Indian textile industry. Within a brief period the mills had resumed full production and, anxious for the workers' cooperation to maintain high productivity, the mill owners made sweeping concessions. Increases in wages and the lifting of the threats of dismissals ended the labour unrest and the need for a general strike ...

The war lifted the pall of depression over the industry. While industrial unrest subsided and managements changed their focus from cutting losses and staging strategies of survival to the more exciting task of raising production and earning higher profits, while the government decided to act with greater firmness to maintain stability and order. Restraints were imposed on civil liberties and many political activists were put under detention. The official history of the AITUC records: 'The government launched a ruthless attack against the trade union and peasant leaders in India, arrested and detained without trial hundreds of them under the Defence of India Act.' The government seemed to be particularly keen to keep under detention people engaged in communist activities.[135] For the communists, it was an imperialist war and, for this reason, they were anti-British and this position happened to coincide with that of the nationalists.

In the AITUC, a sharp cleavage of opinions emerged between the followers of M.N. Roy and the nationalists; the former were ideologically committed to opposing fascism and lent full support to the authorities in the mobilization for war and the raising industrial production in aid of the war effort; hence, strikes and agitations were to be explicitly avoided, but not the others who were less convinced. In March 1940, the matter came to a head and the General Council passed a resolution of which the operative part disowned Roy's position; it said, 'participation in war which is not likely to result in the freedom of the people of India will not benefit India, much less will it benefit the working classes of India'.[136] This resolution was readopted at the XVIII Session at Bombay in September 1940. The differences between M.N. Roy's followers and the others reached the point of no return. Ironically, it was at this very session that the merger of the two all India trade union centres was also formalized. The unity achieved after many years of sincere effort was again on the rocks. The Roy group almost immediately broke off and resigned from the General Council and then proceeded to set up a rival centre called the Indian Federation of Labour.

However, for the Indian labour movement, the war produced yet another irony, in June 1941. Germany invaded the Soviet Union, the communists here received a letter from the British Communist Party to change course and support the war. Once again a deep division emerged in the ranks of the AITUC. It took the CPI six months to realize that a total transformation of the character of war had taken place and they had to reorient themselves to support the war. Results swiftly followed, the ban was lifted, the CPI became legal and its leaders released to work on the same side as the government. At the XIX session, the AITUC found it impossible to adopt any resolution on the war due to the constitutional bind that political resolutions would be adopted only if they received a three-fourth majority, and this was not achieved. M.N. Roy had already raised the slogan of 'Peoples' War', and now the communists adopted it.

The Roy group not only supported the war, it also demanded that coalition governments be formed in the provinces and they should extend unconditional cooperation to the British in the common cause of combating fascism. Roy criticized Congress' rejection of the Viceroy's offer to expand the Executive Council. This forthright act of dissidence cost M.N. Roy dearly; his membership in the Congress was first suspended; later, instead of expulsion, he was allowed to resign. Thus ended his well directed factional political work in the Congress to veer it to the left and take a more progressive stand on deeper ideological issues. Thereafter, in 1940 the Royists decided to form the Radical Democratic Peoples' Party. The Indian Federation of Labour starting in 1941 became the political affiliate of the new party under the common leadership of M.N. Roy.[137]

Quite often, political leaders were incarcerated and that produced comparative quiet. In Bombay, the Industrial Disputes Act was in force and it kept work stoppages at a low level. Though the war supporters asked labour to desist from strikes, they were not always successful in this. The main cause was inflation and the steady, un-arrested climb in the cost of living index. The Bombay textile workers staged a dearness allowance strike on 5 March 1940. Within six months of the start of the war, prices had shot up and this strike lasted for 40 days. Similar strikes took place in other industrial centres affecting jute, textiles, iron and steel, municipal workers, coalminers and oil workers. The government was without a policy on the question of dearness allowance, given the priority of the war expenditure on all other claims on the budget and it was most unwilling to do anything tangible to grant relief and reduce hardship. Taking a cue from the government, the employers too resisted the demand for dearness pay and the number of disputes rose from 322 in 1940 to 359 in 1941 though the man days lost declined. The first two years of the war did not strain workers unduly. Moreover, Rule 81-A was promulgated under which strikes and lockouts were prohibited, instead, an adjudication machinery was put in place to settle disputes.

III. 1942–5

War and India, Cripps Mission, Quit India Movement, Stalemate

The Congress failed to secure a declaration on Britain's war aims for India. Churchill was leading Britain and the only worthwhile goal for Britain was to continue to rule and let Indians compose their differences and come up with a constitutional scheme that would be acceptable to the Muslims, the depressed classes and the princes. A dominion status at the end of the war was a distinct possibility, but Indians would have to cooperate fully in the conduct of the war and may receive it as a duly earned reward. There was the added condition that Britain would retain some residual responsibilities in the governance of India over an interim period, which may be phased out gradually. However, in the winter of 1941–2, Britain and its allies were courting military disasters in a seemingly unending chain. In February 1942, Singapore fell to Japan and soon thereafter the British conceded defeat in Burma and withdrew their troops from that country. War was at India's doorsteps and the most threatening military fact was that the Bay of Bengal was totally under Japanese control while the entire coastline of India was undefended and exposed. Unaided, on its own resources, an adequate defence was beyond India's capabilities, more so because most of the Indian army was in full deployment elsewhere, mainly in North Africa. So the only option was to resist a possible Japanese advance into India by mobilizing people on a higher cause of national defence. The Viceroy understood the peril to which India was exposed and took the first step toward forging a common objective.

Majumdar writes,

> 'Just before the Japanese had entered the war, the Government of India had released, on 3 December 1941, the satyagrahi prisoners together with Azad and Nehru—probably the first fruits of the expansion of the Governor-General's Executive Council. Shortly after the Japanese entry into the war (7 December, 1941) the Viceroy made a public appeal for a united national front. But it fell on deaf ears. Events soon showed that the Japanese danger had not in any way favourably changed the attitude of the political parties toward British rule in India.'[138]

The Allies were anxious to rally India against Japan and, towards this end, Chiang Kai-shek and his wife visited India in February 1942, met Indian leaders and wrote to the British authorities to concede the demands of the Congress,

> one of which was the recognition of India's sovereign status and the formation of the Indian national government. The War Cabinet, however, frowned on such an intervention howsoever well-intentioned. Churchill wrote a polite letter to Chiang Kai-Shek expressing the hope that His Excellency would be so kind as not to press the matter contrary to the wishes of the Viceroy or the King-Emperor. At the same time he formed a group of ministers to study the course of Indian affairs from day to day and advise the War Cabinet accordingly.[139]

President Roosevelt, too, got involved since he knew that the defence of India would have to be a United States responsibility and sounded the British government on the possibilities of reaching a settlement with Indian leaders. To him Churchill cabled a political message on India.

> We are earnestly considering whether a declaration of Dominion Status after the war, carrying with it, if desired, the right to secede, should be made at this juncture. We must not on any account break with the Moslems, who represent a hundred million people, and the main army elements on which we must rely for the immediate fighting. We have also to

> consider our duty towards thirty to forty million untouchables, and our treaties with the Princes states of India, perhaps eighty millions. Naturally we do not want to throw India into chaos on the eve of invasion.[140]

Churchill misled Roosevelt on the composition of the army. In March 1942, it was disclosed by Linlithgow to the Secretary of State for India, Amery, that Muslims comprised 35 per cent of the army while the non-Muslims, including the Sikhs and the Gurkhas, made up 65 per cent. Churchill was still persuaded by US efforts to do something meaningful in India, so that Indians would fight to defend their country. Americans were also not pleased at Churchill's announcement that the applicability of the Atlantic Charter was limited to European countries which the Germans had overrun, not to the colonies of European powers in Asia and not to India. A decision was taken—perhaps because Attlee thought that a cabinet discussion on the declaration to be made on India was needed. The President was duly informed; while at the same time the Viceroy issued the gravest possible warnings at the risks the British government took in regard to the minorities, particularly the Muslims. Thereupon, Sir Stafford Cripps who had recently joined the cabinet was sent to India to discuss the scheme of the declarations before making it public.[141]

At this juncture, the three key people in authority, Churchill, Amery and Linlithgow were opposed to any political progress and the former two decided on such a cut and dried a proposal that it had to be either accepted or rejected, ignoring Attlee's suggestion that the person being sent should have wide powers to negotiate a settlement in India. Cripps was given strict terms of reference within which he should negotiate with Indian leaders, 'for the purpose of obtaining their immediate support for some scheme by which they can partake in an advisory or consultative manner in the counsels of their country.' Positions in the Executive Council could be offered, but without embarrassing the defence and good governance of the country. He was asked to bear in mind the supreme importance of the military situation.[142]

The strategic thinking in the US establishment was that defending India might not be possible without its substantial military involvement and, if this be the case, the nationalist opposition to British rule must be won over because, as in Russia and China, it would have to be a people's resistance to invasion requiring sustained political cooperation and backing from the masses and not just the military defence. This would be the only way to keep American casualties to the minimum and assure success in the war; moreover, there was the rather serious implicit threat of the Congress, still in opposition, opening the door of negotiation with the Japanese in the hope that they would redeem their pledge of restoring independence to India. The pressure the US exerted was never so strong as to cause misgivings in Churchill's mind, but sufficiently well intended to induce a positive response.[143] Churchill's own position, backed by Amery and Linlithgow, was strong as a rock that British rule over India could not possibly cease, particularly because the strong Muslim minority, the princes and British commercial interests expressed their solidarity with them; also because the important province of Punjab which provided the single largest contingent in the army was strongly on their side; and, in any case, they just could not hand over power to the Hindu majority and plunge India into interminable chaos and civil violence between religious communities, races and caste groups.

The proposals Cripps brought with him had so many obvious drawbacks that their acceptance without further consideration and substantial revisions was well nigh impossible. Gandhi summed them up somewhat uncharitably as a 'post-dated cheque on a crashing bank'. The position the Congress Working Committee took was that the proposals were, 'fettered and circumscribed and certain provisions have been introduced which gravely imperil the development of a free and united nation'.[144] The reference was to the option given to provinces and states to opt out of India if they so wished. Not only was the demand for Pakistan conceded in principle, one or more native states could also, on the basis of lapsed paramountcy, assert their independence and leave India totally Balkanized.

However, the crux of the matter rested on two immediate questions. One was the defence and the position of the British Commander-in-Chief in the new arrangement and, the second, whether the new government would be in charge of a cabinet, or would it function as an expanded Executive Council of the Viceroy in which, as hitherto, the veto right would continue to vest in him. As it transpired, despite numerous attempts made by the US representative Col. Louis Johnson, no solution could be found, since the promise of a cabinet form of government comprising popular leaders, first made by Cripps, possibly without authorization by Amery and Churchill and rejected by them, was at the last stage disowned by him too. And on the question of the veto, it was impossible for Linlithgow to agree and yet continue to discharge the onerous responsibilities cast on him without it. In his view, the abandonment of the veto in the midst of a perilous war was not only fraught with incalculable risks involving the defence and unity of India, it was also in total contravention of the 1935 Act.

The only way the proposals could fit in the 1935 Act was to reconstitute the Executive Council and let it function as freely as it might, subject to the Viceroy's veto, exercisable wholly at his personal discretion, which included the power to override, if necessary, the unanimous opinion of all its members. This position was unacceptable to the Congress leaders who were earnest in their negotiations and willing to lead the government and steer India towards a stronger defence and resistance to the Japanese invasion. Gandhi was quite opposed to the entire exercise from the start and had left for Sevagram without any involvement in the negotiations; so, no one was surprised when the Cripps' Mission eventually collapsed and he returned to report his failure, blaming the Congress for it. The failure of Cripps' Mission was well orchestrated and Linlithgow along with Amery and Churchill felt relief that he returned empty handed, as indeed they may have hoped he would never succeed.[145] Jinnah and the other leaders were barely brought into the negotiations though the Viceroy made it clear that their consent too would be required.[146] The Viceroy seemed to have received threatening messages from Jinnah, Firoz Khan Noon, who was a member of the Executive Council and the governor of Punjab, on the dire consequences of transferring power to the Congress and leaving the Muslims to their fate.

The failure of the Cripps Mission demonstrated beyond doubt that, in respect of the nationalist position, there was nothing more the British would do; there could be no longer any hope of progress on the formation of an all-party national government while the war was on, so it was for the Congress to consider what options it had, to break the political stalemate. Gandhi gave up on the British and the Congress again returned to him for leadership and guidance.

Meanwhile, the American army and air force started preparing for a long defensive fight against the Japanese who, it was feared, might start the invasion through the mouth of the Ganga and swiftly capture Bengal. British military planners considered the possibility of the strategy of substantial withdrawal, only to fight back with the help of American arms to recapture India and restore British rule. What would Congress do? Earlier, in December 1941, on the issue of non-violence, the Congress decided to leave Gandhi alone while it was following the path of political expediency. Nehru accepted the sheer unavoidability of preparing for an armed defence of India. However, in March–April 1942, the talk was of the military following the scorched-earth policy and the government acting in that direction.[147]

Gandhi by now made up his mind and said clearly that the British should withdraw from India, leaving India to God or to chaos; he also raised objections to the posting of foreign troops in India. He entertained serious doubts that once the British withdrew, Japan would still invade India, because it was at war with the British Empire, not India as such. He also considered the possibility of opening negotiations with Japan. In a draft of a resolution which the CWC did not accept, Gandhi wrote, 'Britain is incapable of defending India. Japan's quarrel is not with India. If India were freed, her first step would probably be to negotiate with Japan.'[148]

Indians should defend the country against Japanese aggression in the manner of non-violent non-cooperation. Being unarmed, this is what they could do. Alternatively, India would take such measures as were possible and this included organizing military forces. Nehru accepted the alternative. However, the unequivocal preaching of the Gandhian doctrines found only partial support among Congress leaders, with Nehru, Maulana Azad and several others disagreeing. On the question of a Japanese invasion and the use of military means to defend the country, there was an impasse in the Congress. This was gradually overcome as Gandhi prevailed but with the compromise that the Congress would be agreeable to the stationing of Allied Forces in India to resist the Japanese army and help China; however, it was impatient to achieve the national purpose. Gandhi wrote to Roosevelt that the Allies may keep their troops in India at their expense to resist Japanese aggression and to defend China, but India should be a free country to signal and accept the arrangement. In the event, the British did not agree to withdraw from India and this led to the July 1942 resolution which declared the Congress' intention to start a non-violent struggle to achieve its objective under Mahatma Gandhi's leadership.

The Congress once again returned to Gandhi and sought his guidance on the manner of conducting the next struggle. Gandhi convinced the Working Committee members that it would be a national disgrace for the Congress to remain inert while British misrule and high-handedness became ever more blatant. Yet inexplicably, he was of the optimistic view that the authorities would still not take any drastic action against the Congress to curb the agitation owing to the ominous proximity of the Japanese; indeed, they would be impelled to seek a settlement with the Congress as soon as the movement was launched. Azad did not agree and warned that Gandhi and the other leaders would be arrested and the people so paralysed as to be unable to offer any resistance to the Japanese.[149] He proved right but, when the issue was under discussion, he and Nehru failed to persuade the CWC and Gandhi prevailed, though on the assumption of British behaviour which probably rested on the memory of the Gandhi–Irwin Pact. Gandhi was determined to offer resistance to the British while resting on the improbable assumption that it would lead to a settlement along with a genuine transfer of power. Clearly he ignored the inexorable logic of the war and the imminent threat to India from the Japanese who were already close to an attack.

The rapid development of political events and their polarization between the short period, March to July 1942, proved beyond doubt that the Cripps Mission was a disaster. In early May, Gandhi took the important decision in his own mind that the Congress must lead a big satyagraha movement. It rested less on the political juxtaposition of forces and more on the moral premise that the British by their conduct had forfeited any moral ground for support in India. He said:

> I used to say that my moral support was entirely with Britain. I am sorry to have to confess today that my mind refuses to give any moral support to Great Britain, because the British behaviour towards India has filled me with great pain. I was not quite prepared for Mr. Amery's performance or the Cripps Mission. These revelations in my estimation have made Britain morally wrong. Therefore, though I do not wish any humiliation and defeat for Britain, my mind refuses to give her moral support.[150]

By the time the AICC met on 7 August to consider the Quit India resolution, it had already been discussed by several people. There were Congress leaders like C. Rajagopalachari who were opposed to it and had taken a public stand against any such move. Rajaji was of course a disciplined Congress man and he resigned from the Legislative Assembly as well as the primary membership of the Congress, while others came around. Gandhi had written in an article 'I can but do or die'. Thus the decks were cleared for the launch of a fresh movement. Meanwhile, the government made full preparations during this period to forestall the agitation by carrying out pre-emptive mass arrests of the prominent leaders, while excluding the supporters of the war efforts, particularly the Royists and the Communists. Accordingly, in the early hours of 9 August, all the prominent leaders of Congress were arrested. This Gandhi never expected and imagined that he would still meet the Viceroy and tell him about his plans before launching the movement as he had done earlier and, in this, he had totally misjudged the British mood. The Viceroy had been preparing since August 1940 to deliver a direct blow to the Congress if there was a declaration of war by it and to crush the organization as a whole. However, for two years Gandhi had not walked into the trap and had prepared the ground for yet another mass struggle following a prolonged period of truce.[151] The repression that followed showed that Gandhi was under a totally wrong impression about the manner in which the government would react. Indeed, the warnings were already given and Nehru had pointedly said that at the end of the movement the Congress might be totally crushed. Yet, having prepared the country to expect a big satyagraha movement, neither he nor anyone could backtrack. As Gandhi had sensed it, the people at large were seething with unrest and the government was becoming increasingly unpopular. Expectedly, as it turned out, the movement broke all bounds. The doctrine of non-violence was not always adhered to and considerable activity led by the lesser leaders, as underground agitators, caused sabotage, disruption, destruction of public property, attacks on government offices, police stations and so on. Before the end of the year, however, the government was in full control and its harsh repressive measures had clearly triumphed.[152]

The Quit India movement having being crushed, there was nothing much left of the parallel centre of power led by the Congress. The British power in India was now supreme and politically ascendant—even more than it was under the viceroyship of Lord Willingdon. However, the real gainers were the spokesmen of political Islam, who, while affirming their loyalty to the British and assiduously challenging the power of nationalism, downgrading it as representing the Hindu opinion, were able at the same time to establish a claim of parity with the Hindus, which the British conceded. Past events show a remarkable continuity in the British-Muslim relationship. It can be readily traced to the Minto-Morley Reforms which, on an extraordinarily systemic nonchalance, granted the Muslims, more or less on a platter the right to a separate electorate. Later, the Muslim League raised their 14 demands with the nationalist leaders, which were granted by the British government in the 1935 Act. The Muslim League was viewed as the political arm of the compact minority of 80 million Muslims and as a strong bulwark of the imperial government. The British desired to retain their loyalty and support. Particularly in view of the strong presence of the Punjab and the NWFP Muslim soldiers in the army, the British considered it politically expedient to grant more concessions to the Muslims if it would further weaken the voice of Indian nationalism, or enable them to accord it a still lower ranking as a party of the Hindu community.

Jinnah mastered the art of intransigence in politics and all he needed to do to win favour with the British was to oppose Gandhi and the Congress, advise the Muslims not to take part in nationalist movements, while asserting the Muslim claim to power. At first, this took the form of adequate safeguards for Muslims and later, he raised it to parity so that the Hindus, howsoever represented, would never have a majority in governance at the Centre and further on thereafter, to a major share in power exceeding 50 per cent of the seats of power.

In the post-Quit-India political scenario, the Viceroy found two strong backers, one, the well-organized, strong presence of the Muslims, led most remarkably and single-mindedly by Jinnah and the second, the relatively weak, secular voice of ideologically committed Communists and Royists. The Muslim leaders helped the Viceroy in the overall governance of the country, while the latter were on his side if only for the duration of the war and importantly contributed towards preserving industrial peace in aid of the war. The Communist Party and the Radical Democratic Party of M.N. Roy also made significant contributions in ensuring that, barring mainly Ahmedabad and Jamshedpur, most of the industrial centres in the country remained aloof during the Quit India Movement.

Yet, there were no political prizes for them. Now it was Jinnah as the unquestioned leader of Muslims who had the strongest political voice in India and it was avidly heard to be reassured in various ways. Much earlier, the Viceroy, while speaking on the importance of the Congress coming over to work the Federation said, well before the war broke out, that India's unity depended on it and, if the Congress didn't join and stayed away, Jinnah would break the unity of India.[153] Given these forebodings it might have been impractical to do something later that would counter-weigh the negative politics of unceasing intransigence by the Muslim League, probably because no other political force of any reckoning existed at the time which the British might have propped up. And they themselves could not possibly undergo the metamorphosis of becoming sincere supporters of Indian nationalism and agreeing to negate their Raj in India, though this is what Gandhi wanted to see happen and endeavoured to accomplish through satyagraha. Linlithgow believed in the British Empire and was committed to do everything that would sustain it. He found it wonderful to find the Muslim League on his side against the Congress.

The Quit India movement was the last Gandhi launched, but the way it was conducted, the leadership slipped into the hands of the small band of socialists and revolutionaries who had no faith in Gandhian non-violence. It became a singularly non-Gandhian opposition to the British rule. The Congress had made no preparations for it, so whatever programme of action was in evidence was planned as expedient by socialist leaders like Jayaprakash Narayan and elements of the underground revolutionary movement who believed that violence alone would work against the British.

Gandhi could not take responsibility for the many violent acts which in turn brought forth the full force of savagery that the government was capable of unleashing. In 1943, perhaps to expatiate for the hopeless incompetence and utter mismanagement of the 1942 movement and the sufferings caused to the people who had taken part in it, he decided on a self-purification fast. He had misjudged and miscalculated and may have realized his personal responsibility for the exhortations he had made, on 'do or die', asking each individual to engage in action even without any leadership or guidance. The self-purification fast was to last for 21 days from 9 February to 2 March 1943. The government offered to release him, which Gandhi refused, but declined to set him free. There was great consternation in the country because it was feared that Gandhi may not survive the fast in prison. Three members of the Viceroy's Executive Council resigned in protest against government's obduracy, while Gandhi moved close to death, but he miraculously survived. He was released in March 1943 on health grounds.

In 1944 he announced that there was a change in his thinking, he decided to give up, 'Quit India' and not hinder the war effort; also that he had no intention of offering civil disobedience again. He would be satisfied with a national government in full control of civil administration and wanted the British to make a declaration of full independence for India. This was rejected by the Secretary of State. So the only way forward was to find a common cause with Jinnah.

However, his parleys with Jinnah were entirely fruitless. Jinnah's political status rose as one at par with Gandhi while the latter got nowhere.[154] There was not much left of Gandhi's role in the struggle for independence or the unity of India.

In June 1945, Amery made a statement in the House of Commons,

> that whereas since March 1942 there had been no further progress towards the solution of India's Constitutional problem, and whereas, the working out of India's new Constitutional system is a task which can only be carried through by the Indian peoples themselves; and while His majesty's Government are at all times most anxious to do their utmost to assist the Indians in the working out of a new Constitutional settlement, it would be a contradiction in terms to speak of the imposition by this country of self-governing institutions upon an unwilling India. Such a thing is not possible, nor could we accept the responsibility for enforcing such institutions at the very time when we were, by its purpose, withdrawing from all controls of British Indian affairs.

The concrete proposal was that the Viceroy's Executive Council should be reconstituted and appointments to it may be, 'in proportions which would give a balanced representation for the main communities, including equal proportions of Muslims and Caste Hindus'. This statement assured complete victory to the Muslim League which as the sole representative of Muslims would have total equality with the Congress as the party of caste Hindus. The Scheduled Classes, Sikhs and European groups would have separate representations through their recognized bodies and forums. Amery added that, 'none of the changes suggested will in any way prejudice and prejudge the essential form of the future permanent Constitution or Constitutions for India'.[155]

The Amery proposals led to the Shimla Conference.[156] Earlier, Lord Wavell had watched the Gandhi–Jinnah talks ending on a note of complete futility. The Shimla Conference might provide a breather from the failed talks and possibly lead to agreement on the composition of an interim government under his leadership. Soon thereafter, direct rule of governors in Section 93 provinces would end. Fresh elections would be called and that would clear the air. However, the one notable weakness of the Amery' statement, or the purpose of the Shimla Conference, was that the question of India's independence was nowhere mentioned and expressions were used instead which indicated that the habit of dodging it was still at work.

> The conference, however, foundered on the issue of the League's claim to be the sole representative of Muslims with the right to nominate Muslims to the Executive Council. To this neither Lord Wavell nor the Congress would agree. Lord Wavell felt it was the Viceroy's prerogative to select able persons for the Council and the Congress felt as a national party it could suggest a panel of names comprising Muslims, Hindus, Parsis, Christians and others.

In addition, Jinnah demanded a special safeguard that the Viceroy's veto would be exercised in favour of Muslims in a case where a decision of the Council was found objectionable by Muslim members. This too the Viceroy could not accept. The failure of the Shimla Conference provided Jinnah the ostensible grounds to explain it as due to the non-compatible political vision of a united India by the Congress with that of the Muslim League of partition, leading to the creation of Pakistan. Indeed, the League would take part in the Interim government if His Majesty's government would make an announcement accepting the Muslim demand for self-determination and also agree to giving Muslims equality in the Council with all other communities. His fear was that the Congress might use the power it would wield in the Council to strangle Pakistan.[157]

The political stalemate resulting from the failure of Amery's initiative was still unbroken when, in the summer of 1945, in the British general elections, the Labour Party secured a providential victory resulting in the ousting of the India-hating Tories and the formation of a Labour Party government led by Clement Attlee. The new Prime Minister speedily took the initiative in September 1945 to declare the government's intention to transfer power for full self-governance in India and to convene a constituent assembly for the purpose. The elections in India, that followed showed that Attlee had made a major break with the Tory policies. It was no more divide and rule; now it would be divide and quit. He was determined to withdraw British rule from India and willing to go beyond the formula Cripps had brought with him in 1942, but the details and the procedure for withdrawal needed to be worked out.

Financing the War, Inflation, Famine, Ineffective Controls

In 1941, the population of British India registered a sharp, somewhat abnormal growth of 40 million people over the 1931 population of 256 millions. In the 1921–31 decade the totals had risen by only 22 million. By comparison there was no spurt in the population totals of the Indian states. Between 1921 and 1931 it increased by 10 million and in the decade 1931–41 by only 11 million.[158] The growth in the population of British India was partly natural and in part contrived and deliberately inflated at the enumeration stage; hence it was artificial. The Muslim League had asked for this and it was heard in most of north India. It required adding to the number of women in the family who must remain in purdah and out of view. A competing game was played by the much less popular and effective Hindu Mahasabha.

Accordingly, it was suspected that most of the inflationary additions were in the Muslim populations in the different provinces, but mainly in Punjab, Bengal and Assam. A procedural change in enumeration made it easier to falsify family totals. Instead of the composite household schedules, the census count was taken on individual slips. The advantage claimed for this was that it would facilitate a small sample of two per cent to be drawn from the census total for further investigations and P.C. Mahalanobis is credited with the idea. As a young ICS officer in charge of census work, Asok Mitra saw and grasped the damage the new method had inflicted.[159] The 1941 census formed the basis of partitioning provinces and drawing borders.

Agricultural statistics suffered from the opposite defect of under-estimation. In Bengal, the area under rice was found to be underestimated to the extent of 3.5 million acres, 'The total production of a crop was obtained as the product of the acreage under the crop and the average yield per acre. The general practice followed was to express the average yield in terms of the "standard" or "normal" yield by means of a condition factor.' Normal yield was the average on average soil in a year of average rain, et cetera. The subjective estimates thus derived resulted in an unknown degree of error.[160] However, later studies showed that the extent of under estimation of yields was probably much less and could form the basis for estimating national income from year to year.

For the principal food crops, rice and wheat, the acreage under cultivation remained nearly the same in the three years, 1939–40 to 1942–3. In rice it was (in 000 acres) 31,613 in 1939–40 which declined to 31,108 in 1940–1, rose slightly to 31,344 in 1941–2 and further to 31,846 in 1942-–3. Thereafter it increased significantly by more than 3,000 in the next three years. However, wheat acreage did not rise at all, fluctuating from year to year within narrow bounds. As far as production is concerned, 1939–40 was a better year and rice output was estimated at (in 000 tonnes) 27,562 which fell to 24,025 in 1940–1, rose marginally to 27,092 in 1991–2 and declined to 26,580 in 1942–3. Compared to 1939–40, in the year of great peril, that is 1943, the rice output was lower by one million tonnes. In the next year it was much better at 32,904, indeed above the levels recorded in the previous two decades.

However, for the people whose main staple in diet was rice there was a disturbing trend of declining level of availability and sufficiency in the country as a whole. As a result, rice prices rose, from (the weighted average in rupees per tonnes) 114.5 in 1939–40 to 132.6 in 1940–1, 150.0 in 1941–2 and 289.6 in 1942–3. The climb continued thereafter to reach

300.9 in 1943–4 and 314.8 in 1944–5. Rice must have become less and less affordable to the many who had no option but to buy it in the open market. The subsistence farmer, who never had much marketable surplus in the first place, might have considered it more prudent to conserve the crop he grew for his family's consumption.

Wheat prices also rose; so there is some question whether people who depended wholly on the market had any choice at all. Rice could not be afforded by the poorer classes and wheat and flour were only a shade less unaffordable.[161] Rice imports from Burma used to raise its availability till they stopped completely in 1942 when it came under Japan's occupation. The stoppage of rice imports made Indian consumers totally dependent on domestic production and those who depended on the market, on the marketed supplies.

Domestic trade in rice was subject to the policies of provincial governments. In May 1942, the Viceroy promulgated the Foodgrains Control Order, but in the absence of a requisite machinery it could not be put into effect. Attempts at price fixing had the opposite effect of establishing a black market in foodgrains. 'The Governor of Madras adopted sterner measures; he prohibited the export of rice beyond provincial boundaries in June 1942 and then made rice trade a state monopoly in September 1942.' As a result, the price of rice rose much less in Madras than in Bengal.[162] In fact, the entire eastern India was and had been deficit in food production and, especially during the war, it produced a systemic, persistent shortage owing to low overall availability of rice. Apparently there was very little inter-regional trade in rice, since the traders would have just sufficient stores to meet the local demand of urban consumers within the district or adjoining districts. At the same time, in 1942, the government's military policy in the deltaic region of Bengal became exceedingly hurtful, actually destructive of local capabilities in trade and transportation.

Expecting a Japanese invasion at the mouth of the Ganga, the government decided on a scorched earth policy, or denial of any facility to the invader, as the only defence that was available to India. Asok Mitra says:

> The Denial policy in its turn had two prongs. First the destruction and/or the forcible removal by the constabulary of the bulk of privately stored rice, not only in merchants' warehouses but also in private households as well (where paddy is stored in marais) in coastal rice growing districts of Midnapur, 24-Parganas, Khulna, Bakarganj and Noakhali. Anyone who resisted was denied even the cash compensation for the rice removed or destroyed.

This was not sufficient.

> The other prong of the Denial policy was the destruction of rice-carrying barges and boats and the indigenous goods transport vehicles like bullock carts in southern 24-Parganas and Midnapur. This kind of denial not only destroyed with little or no compensation in most cases—thousands of crores worth of investment on the waterways and dirt roads. It also wiped out the means of transportation of vital grain supplies from the surplus districts of Bengal to the deficit or marginal districts.[163]

There was also a third prong: the forcible evacuation of people. Thousands of poor and ignorant people at very short notice were evacuated and they suffered from food shortage, lack of medical help and elementary amenities. Meanwhile, in the absence of imports, the price of rise first rose, then skyrocketed. Asok Mitra says that the stoppage of imports and the sharp rise in price

> made mincemeat of purchasing power, market forces, intra-family distribution, entitlement and what have you. Had rice and paddy been available at even 40 per cent of the level of normal years, these phrases might have had some meaning. In that event the enterprise, the public spirit and the abundance of good sense of the common people—that you helped others to be able to help yourself—together with their ideas of supplementing cereals by fruits, spinach, watercress and other locally raised vegetables would have saved my subdivision. The sense of equity, efficiency and honesty with which dry relief

> was dispensed and community gruel kitchens were run by the local relief committees emboldens me to say so.[164]

The Bengal famine was an extremely tragic direct effect of the war economy and military doctrines. To a large extent it was man-made, worsened by the sadistic and diabolical attitudes of the provincial administration, released by the repressive policies of the government on crushing the Quit India movement. The military, on the other hand, quite obviously had no credible intelligence on Japan's war aims as far as India was concerned and its short-term military objectives. For Japan, the annexation of Burma had achieved the credible military purpose of cutting off supplies from India to China, while the total control over the Bay of Bengal gave the Japanese military security from any counterattack by sea from a base in India.

However, the British military mind conjectured and imagined in ignorance that the Japanese invasion would come via the deltaic region of Bengal and the only defence was to deny the invader any facilities or human support in the politically alienated Bengal. This policy then utterly destroyed whatever material resources the communities possessed for self-defence against a famine. Had it been a slowly advancing naturally caused food famine, people would have responded differently, though even then they would have suffered much and some loss of life would have occurred. In the Bengal famine of 1943 the government at least partly caused food scarcity and contributed to its disastrous consequence by the Denial policy.

Moreover, the district of Midnapur was devastated by a killer cyclone on 16 October 1942, while the Denial policy was being implemented. The news was withheld for military reasons. Midnapur had also taken active part in the Quit India movement. The cyclone killed over 3,000 people in the first 15 minutes of its impact. The Japanese estimated the death toll during the night at over one hundred thousand and they may have been right.

The cyclone killed more men than women. Men had come out to salvage what was left in their homes and many of them never returned. Children were orphaned and women became destitute. Relief was denied for the administratively plausible though immoral reason that people there had tried to overthrow the alien government and were to be suppressed and deserved no help from the government. However, at the time, there was little rice anywhere. Women with babies in arms started moving out and trekked to Calcutta 'They had been compelled, in consequence of the district magistrate of Midnapur's orders forbidding relief or dole, to trudge perilously on to Calcutta in search of gruel.'[165] Many died of exhaustion in Calcutta. This was because their men had died earlier in the cyclone and most of them came from very poor homes with low energy levels in their bodies.

Governments in Calcutta, Delhi and London never quite believed that Bengal was in the throes of a great famine and thought that the real problem was hoarding of rice not its absence. This version was readily believed, but Asok Mitra, as the SDM of his subdivision, found little support for this theory. A.K. Sen shows the data to establish the point that the index of per capita availability of food grains in Bengal declined from 130 in 1942 to 109 in 1943. Without further corrections, the data would point to hunger for many but not a killer famine.[166] Apparently, the Bengal government had no information on the stock position from month-to-month or year-to-year and perhaps even at the all-India level, the government of India knew no better. However, the facts that are not in question are that the military demand for food grains and all other foods was a matter of the highest priority and the government acquired a part of the marketed outputs for this purpose.

Moreover, Calcutta and other cities and towns had to be supplied with rice, especially for the working class in the factories and war-related workshops, who needed to be fed. This too was a responsibility that was accepted by the government. These demands were met mainly by buying and storing foodgrains in excess of current consumption and allowing for waste on various counts. Food entitlement of the poor and the very poor came last on priorities. There was no rice for them in the market and they died in the thousands, adding up to about 3-3.5 million in all.[167]

The government never declared 'famine' in Bengal, perhaps because it was not prepared to be deflected from war-related preparations to famine-related duties. The famine code of 1883 would then have had to be put into effect, which would have involved the government in organizing a works programme to provide employment to the destitutes and arrange for distribution of food or foodgrains, sugar, salt, kerosene oil and other bare necessities to enable them to survive. The government did not have the food stocks and it faced considerable difficulties in arranging for imports. Most of the rice-producing countries in South East Asia were under Japanese occupation and the sea routes were totally under its control.

This traditional source of supply was undoubtedly cut off, though wheat could still be imported, provided London would allocate shipping for the purpose. The British government had other priorities and could not find convincing reasons to make reallocation of shipping and release money or arrange for credit to pay for the imports. On its part, the Government of India was either too lethargic to organize a public distribution system and divert whatever foodgrains it was able to procure into it to protect lives and sustain consumption in the poorer sections of population, or, given the information it had on rice production and food shortage, it did not consider it necessary to make it a matter of urgent concern to take any drastic step. Food shortage was admitted in Bengal and in the rest of the country, and provincial governments were doing whatever was within their means to conserve their rice outputs for local consumption. However, Bengal did not produce enough rice and could not have contributed any significant quantity of it towards the government's procurement drive. Consequently the government, even if it had correctly learnt the facts and understood its gravity, would not have found it possible to procure sufficient rice at short notice and distribute it to the needy. Instead, the government had to depend on wheat and use its powers to obtain it in the wheat producing provinces, principally Punjab.[168] Later, wheat was supplied to Bengal but the normal trading profit was still allowed as an incentive, so by the time shipment and storage costs were added it was sold at unconscionable high prices to the consumers.

In January 1943, the Government of India decided to buy foodgrains from surplus provinces and sell them in the food deficit areas.

> By August 1943 one million tonnes of grain had been procured in that way. Trusting its new ability of handling the problem in this way, the Central government abolished price controls and sanctioned the free trade in rice in Eastern India. However, the limited stocks stored by the government did not suffice to discourage hoarders. Bengal rice traders invaded neighbouring provinces and drove up prices everywhere Alarmed by this development, the Central government abandoned its experiment in August 1943 and imposed price controls once more; this, of course, could only encourage the speculations of hoarders. The Government of Bengal was neither willing nor able to adopt energetic measures as the Governor of Madras had done.[169]

Quite the contrary, the popular government used its powers to introduce a communal element in the food supply and distribution system.[170] The idea was to intimidate Hindu traders and improve their conduct. The Bengal government just carried on. Possibly, it was baffled by the large number of deaths but little was distributed. The provincial government got into the act of providing relief only after a new governor was in position and Lord Wavell replaced Linlithgow as the Viceroy of India. The governor who presided over the Quit India movement, the killer cyclone and the famine has been painted in dark colours and probably had a demonic trait in his personality.

Throughout the war, the money supply grew, at first at a steady pace and then from 1943, it became very brisk. In 1939, the currency in circulation was (in million Rs.) 2251.9 which increased to 9370.3 in 1943 and further to 11086.8 in 1944, 13057.7 in 1945 and 13346.2 in 1946. Growth in deposits kept up with the pace and increased from 1585.3 in 1939 to 5403.9 in 1943, 6796.2 in 1944, 7469.9 in 1945 and 8043.7 in 1946. This was an unprecedented growth in money supply with the public.[171] The principal source of growth in the monetary stock was deficit financing which was incurred partly by the Government of India's own expenditure on defence and partly on behalf of the British government which was paid in the form of blocked sterling securities. The latter formed the basis as securities for increased defence spending by the government.

The Government of India spent Rs. 17,400 million on behalf of the British government between 1938–9 and 1945–6. It grew from a manageable sum of Rs. 40 million in 1939–40 to Rs. 530.0 million in 1940–1 and then very rapidly to Rs. 3,254.8 million in 1942–3, Rs. 3,778.7 million in 1943–4 and Rs. 4,108.4 million in 1944–5, then declined to Rs. 3745.4 million in 1945–6. And, though the war was over, India still had to spend on behalf of the British government another Rs. 516.2 million (revised).[172]

The fivefold increase in money supply built up inflationary pressures which showed up in market prices. Up to June 1943, prices rose more or less in an uncontrolled manner, but thereafter the various measures the government took to control and ration essential goods stabilized the prices to some extent. The government also sold some gold and silver to mop up excess money supply from the public. However, as production was principally diverted to meet military needs civilian consumption fell and the city poor who were dependent on the market were particularly hard hit. They had no access to the black market which developed as shortages became endemic and controls replaced market mechanism.

> The war saw the beginning of economic planning. From 1943 onwards a series of economic controls were instituted, to control capital issues, to prevent speculation and hoarding, to enforce saving and to control the production and distribution of cloth. A Department of Planning was set up in 1944 whose work was made use of by independent India's first Planning Commission. But the war's greatest legacy to the future was the sterling balances.[173]

On 31 March 1939, India's sterling debt was almost Rs. 4,700 million. This was wiped off and India emerged a creditor nation. The Reserve Bank's accumulated foreign assets totalled more than Rs. 17,000 million, though these were mostly illiquid and could not be freely drawn on by India to pay for imports.

Within six months of the commencement of the war the government had to put on the policy agenda entirely different sets of questions related to war finance, inflation, hoarding and speculation in scarce goods and, above all, the problem of food insecurity. The government proceeded to make the transition from depression to problems of economic management during the war, but without any intellectual apparatus to guide it on the difficult questions which inevitably came up.

Between 1939 and 1945, the Indian army increased from less than 200,000 to about 2 million and much of the needed equipment and supplies for the armed forces were procured by diverting real resources from civil consumption to war. It was a huge build-up. Additionally, nearly $300 million worth of material was transported for war use to the actual war theatres. India never became a war theatre except for a short period when the Japanese army literally knocked at the north-eastern border and several cities were bombed. At this stage, the Andaman and Nicobar Islands were under Japanese occupation and the Bay of Bengal was in the Japanese navy's control, with no possibility of resistance being offered from Indian shores.

On 21 February 1942, a month before Cripps' arrival in

New Delhi, General Molesworth, Deputy Chief of General Staff in India, had publicly admitted to the practically hopeless situation of India's defence, particularly of the long coastline which lay completely exposed.[171] The problem of arranging for India's defence, though intrinsically intractable, due to the absence of an air force and navy in force strength, was made worse by the opposition of the Congress to the war under imperial dispensation. However, no party or organization opposed voluntary enlistment for serving in the armed forces and there was no problem of manpower shortage for recruitment to the army or to man the greatly expanded production of war-related goods and material which could be conceivably produced in India.

However, India was very short in the supply of trained technical personnel and the government had to arrange for training in skills essential for the production of light weapons and military stores. Though the Allies depended on India for military supplies, the Government of India or the British government did not consider it in their interest to create the industrial infrastructure to produce weapon systems such as tanks or field guns in India, perhaps for political reasons.

The deprivation suffered by the civilian population may be gauged by the scale of diversion of industrial production. According to Tomlinson, it was estimated that all mill production of woollen textiles, all factory production of leather and footwear, all organized production of timber, nearly three-quarters of the steel and cement production, over two-fifths of paper production, about one-sixth of cotton textile production and the entire 'normal' quota of 600 million yards of cotton yarn were directed away from the civilian economy to serve military requirements.[175] As a result, prices rose and scarcities became general, to be suffered most by people least able to do so.

However, the worst impact was on foods and essential commodities. With 1939 = 100, the price of rice was at 218 in December 1942, 951 in December 1943 and following price controls and rationing it declined to 333 in December 1944.

In early 1945, 42 million urban consumers were on the rationing system. This was an extraordinary turn around for an unprepared government. Rice became terribly scarce and together with the sky-rocketing prices, it contributed greatly to the enormous number of deaths in the great Bengal famine of this year. Wheat prices also rose rapidly but at a steadier pace; the index in 1942 stood at 232, a year later at 330 and in December 1944 at 381. By comparison, prices of cotton manufacturers, for reasons given above, rose very fast to reach 414 in December 1942 and 501 a year later, but declined to 285 in 1944.[176] With the surrender of Japan, war ended for India. This was followed by peacetime inflation and the crisis conditions caused by foodgrains shortages. State intervention became a permanent feature of India's economic management.[177]

Labour and War, Tripartitism, Inflation, Ambivalent Unions

Inflation was not a serious threat for labour till the end of 1941. It became serious in 1942 when it started cutting into the standard of living of workers. Labour demanded dearness allowance as a protection against further erosion of real wages. The government's response was to stall the demand and, instead, there was a call for a conference of Labour ministers in 1940 and again in 1941, to coordinate provincial labour policies with the centre and also to meet the representatives of capital and labour in January 1941 to establish a broad-based consensus in support of increased production for the war.

The subjects discussed by the labour ministers were undoubtedly of immediate interest to labour. These were: sickness insurance, recognition of trade unions and holidays with pay. Other related matters, such as industrial housing and hours of night shift were also under consideration.[178] However, on dearness allowance, the government acted as if it was not a matter to be considered seriously or it displayed studied indifference.

However, in Bombay, the government took an early lead

in 1940 by raising the question with the Bombay Mill Owners' Association. It inquired of the mill owners if they were prepared to give their workers a war bonus if they made increased profits owing to war conditions. This was in line with the experience of the First World War and the memory of the consequences of delayed action in granting the war bonus that triggered a spate of spontaneous strikes. The government also thought of profit sharing as a possibility. In fact in November 1941, ten mills in Bombay had to consider a notice served by the operatives which asked for: a bonus, an increase in dearness allowance and an increase in basic pay. In December 1941 the mills announced a war bonus of two annas in a rupee or 12.5 per cent of the wage earned in 1941, payable in February 1941. At Sholapur, the mills decided to follow suit.

In August 1941, the unions pointed out that the index number of articles of food had risen to 145 and it was of great concern to the workers. In June 1942, the Committee of the Association convened an urgent general meeting to decide the question of a sliding scale of dearness allowance and the matter was accordingly resolved. A formula was announced recommending a dearness allowance for 26 days of work in a month on the expectation that the official working class index number would probably range between 144 and 163. Workers were informed in June 1942, though in July it became apparent that the index number would cross 163. Consequently in July 1942, the Association again resolved to revise the dearness allowance formula for the index number to rise further, but stay in the range of 164 to 183. At the end of December, it was felt that the index would be 188. In another urgent meeting it was resolved yet again to extend the dearness allowance formula for the index number ranging between 184 and 203. Every time this was done the Bombay government issued press notes approving the Association's actions.[179]

Workers demanded most of all a raise in money wages that would prevent a further fall in their already very low standards of living and, on occasions, using the strike action, they succeeded. In 1940, the jute mill workers also secured a ten per cent raise in wages. They, too, resisted a forced deduction from wages as their voluntary contribution to the war fund.[180] However, the communists-led AITUC and the IFL asked workers to refrain from strikes and stick to their posts. Thereafter, the government took the historic policy initiative to call the first Indian Labour Conference and it met on 7 August 1942 under the chairmanship of Dr. B.R. Ambedkar, who was inducted into the Viceroy's expanded Executive Council early in that year.

This conference had permanency as a part of its plan. Under the agenda item at the plenary conference, 'Labour Welfare and Labour Morale in War-Time', all the delegates referred to the pressing problem of food supply.

> It was considered essential that adequate supply of foodgrains and other essential commodities at reasonable prices should be ensured to the workers. One of the principal difficulties in this respect was the question of transport and the Central Government was asked particularly to remove or lessen the difficulties in this respect by granting, if necessary, a very high 'priority' for the transport of foodstuffs.[181]

Meeting thirteen months later in September 1943, the Tripartite Labour Conference, as it was now called, discussed and arrived at some conclusions on 'involuntary unemployment due to shortage of coal, raw materials, etc.' and elicited the view from the government that the relief was necessary, but of a purely temporary nature and it should be payable for a period of about one month. A lengthy discussion took place on 'the Principles for Fixing Dearness Allowance', and the consensus was that it was undoubtedly desirable to have general uniform principles but no decision was taken on the specifics; differences in opinions were noted. As far as the government employees were concerned, the policy of the Central Government was to grant as much dearness allowance as seemed possible in the form of essential articles at concessional rates. An important conclusion reached at this conference was to introduce standing orders in industrial concerns employing more than 250 or more people as soon as possible and to give them statutory force. Later, a law on the subject was enacted in 1946.

The AITUC decided to observe 9 August 1942 as the All India Dearness Allowance Demand Day. Unknown to it, or by a sheer coincidence, the Quit India resolution was adopted by the AICC on the previous day, so the movement happened to commence on this date. In Bombay, the issue had already aroused workers and, on 2 August at a largely attended meeting of workers, a resolution moved by N.M. Joshi was adopted, asking the government to announce a dearness allowance for its employees and to ask the employers to do the same.

As it turned out, the entirely worthwhile initiative of the Bombay Mill Owners' Association in resolving the matter with the support of the provincial government was not repeated anywhere else in the country. On the contrary, at Kanpur there was violence and, as the unions saw it, 'Nazi savagery was let loose by the authorities.'[182] Progress was piecemeal; the railwaymen won their demand and a meagre dearness allowance was granted in June 1941 itself, which meant a wage increase of 5 to 7.5 per cent. In November, the rates were revised. Gradually as the railway workers pressed their demand for higher dearness allowance and sufficient supply of food grains at controlled prices industrial relations heated up. In 1943, the railwaymen asked for adjudication of their demands, but this was turned down by the Railways Board. Instead, the authorities declared that they would vigorously pursue the policy of enlarging the scope of railway grain shops both in quantities and in the range of articles supplied and that a reduction in the price of the necessities of life would be made.[183]

Among the railway unions, conflicting positions were taken by the communists and the nationalists. The former took the position that,

> the railway workers manning the vast transport system, feeding the people and the front, are guarding the most vital artery. Transport has to be kept running for the defence of the country, for the army and the people. At the same time, the wooden bureaucracy would not be moved to see that these 'transport soldiers' of the rear are properly fed and kept in 'fighting trim.

The workers had their duty towards defence and should maintain the railways system in an efficient condition. The moderate leader, Jamnadas Mehta, President of the All India Railwaymen's Federation, told the workers in plain language, 'either go on for a strike or accept what the Board has given and keep quiet'.[184] In the event the strike ballot was not taken though the dispute continued to simmer.

Throughout the war, strikes were called, though their durations were kept short. The government referred the disputes to compulsory conciliation and on its failure thereafter, at its discretion, to adjudication. However, on the most important questions of dearness allowance and adequate foodgrain supply at controlled prices, satisfactory replies failed to emerge, mainly because there were severe constraints. The government could not allow a more generous policy on wage increases for fear of starting a vicious price-wage spiral, nor take the responsibility for supplying adequate foodgrains because it did not have the stocks to distribute. An ad hoc policy was being serviced by ad hoc policy instruments. Not withstanding these constraints, the government was still able to take basic decisions to advance the welfare of workers by appropriate enactments.

The highest priority was to maintain peace and order in the interest of increased production. In March 1942, a general order was issued applicable to all undertakings under the Defence of India Rules, 81A, requiring a notice of 14 days to be served of any intended strike. Earlier, this condition applied only to the public utilities, but now its sweep covered other undertakings as well. Moreover, once a dispute was referred to a Court of Inquiry or a Board of Conciliation, any strike during the pendency of the dispute would be illegal. In 1942, the government proposed certain amendments to the Trade Unions Act, 1926, requiring employers to recognize the registered trade unions and to empower them with the right to negotiate with the employers on matters affecting the common interests of its members. The power of withdrawing recognition was vested in the government, not the employers.

Earlier, the government had written to the Employers' Federation of India to recommend to its member organizations to adopt a liberal policy towards the unions, even if they had reservations on their leaders. The employers opposed both moves with the argument,

> that unless there was a radical change in leadership, recognition of the type which the Government proposed to bestow on unions would not only fail to confer any benefit on labour, but was likely to be a positive danger to the industry and its war efforts. The real need, therefore, was good leadership by men who came into the movement purely as trade unionists, pledged to rectify the economic grievances of men and not to mix them up with politics.[185]

Actually, there was a case for tightening up government control over unions.

In August 1942, the government issued another order banning lock-outs without serving the 14 days notice. Now the same regulation applied to both workers and employers. Under the modified rule, both strikes and lockouts would be illegal unless a 14-days notice was given or till two months had elapsed after the conclusion of conciliation or adjudication proceedings. These measures curbed workers' freedom, but the most genuine workers' grievance which the government was unable to meet pertained to dearness allowance and insufficient supply of grains at controlled prices. Workers in the railways devised the method of stay-in strike and resumed work after the authorities gave assurances that they would do their part on obtaining the needed food supply.

In coal mining, the government reversed the policy of not permitting women to work underground because despite an increase in the number of collieries, the level of employment in the mines had declined, resulting in a fall in coal production, which in turn resulted in the stoppage of production in many factories and the lay-off of workers. According to the government, there was a critical shortage of coal cutters due to higher wages in the many workshops and factories which were set up to engage in war-related production and had attracted the coalminers. The solution was to allow both men and women to work together in the mines, so that while men would do coal cutting, the women could work as loaders together earning more as husband and wife and it would also lower absenteeism.[186]

In addition, the government decided to recruit more male labour and this was to be supplemented, if possible, by preventing the employment of mining labour in neighbouring works. The government's decision on permitting women to work underground was protested by the AITUC in August 1943, while still welcoming the decision to establish a statutory Miners' Welfare Fund. The AITUC blamed the capitalists' greed for profit for the crisis in coal production and demanded the taking over of mines by the government. N.M. Joshi also raised these issues in the Assembly.

Led by Dr. Ambedkar, the government introduced a major war innovation in the labour policy, to convene on the ILO pattern tripartite meetings comprising the Central and Provincial Governments together with the employers and trade unions to discuss common problems affecting labour and requiring policy responses from the government. Under the 1935 Act, the government aimed at securing uniformity in labour legislation and the consideration of matters of all India importance at these meetings. Under the Act, labour found place both in the list of subjects reserved for provinces as well as on the list of concurrent subjects. This necessitated coordination and concurrence between the centre and the provinces on the proposed labour legislation. The government was equally keen on securing as wide an area of agreement as possible between the employers and the unions before enacting any new legislation or amending the existing laws. In the tripartite meetings labour was represented by the AITUC and the newly organized, M.N. Roy's, Indian Federation of Labour. Likewise, employers too were represented by two organizations.

The first Plenary Tripartite Conference met on 7 August 1942 to deal with procedural matters, its constitution, to deliberate on the issues listed on the agenda and what the participants were expected to do. This was followed by the first session of the Plenary Conference which met on 6 and 7 September 1943.

> There were eight items on the agenda, all of which were of immediate interest to the unions. These were, provision of relief for involuntary unemployment due to the shortage of coal, raw materials, etc.; social security and minimum wage regulation; principles underlying the determination of the cost of living bonus; provision for approved and recognized regulation of working conditions on a contractual basis in larger factories; rules of procedure for the Plenary Conference of the Tripartite Labour Organization; establishment of Tripartite Labour Organization in the provinces; representation of labour in the legislatures and other bodies; and model rules for provident funds.[187]

Dr. Ambedkar observed that the deliberations in the Standing Labour Committee and the Plenary Conference were of value to the government:

> these discussions had been extremely useful, and in all matters in respect of which unanimous conclusions had been reached the Government had not been slow in giving effect to them, as was shown by the enactment of the War Injuries (Compensation Insurance) Act, and the National Service (Technical Personnel) Amendment Ordinance, and in the administration of the Industrial Statistics Act and the establishment of an employment service.[188]

The second session of the Plenary Conference had an equally impressive agenda. It was also attended by the representatives of several princely states. An issue of pressing nature was the future of workers who were employed in war production and the related question, of how employment would be organized during the transition period from war to peace. On the status of tripartite deliberations, Dr. Ambedkar made it clear that both the Plenary Conference and the Standing Labour Committee functioned in an advisory capacity, not legislative. Moreover, the government would not surrender its right to determine the questions which would be discussed in these bodies, afresh. What was possible was that various interests could suggest items for the government's consideration before the agenda was decided.

The Standing Labour Committee also discussed several weighty matters and Dr. Ambedkar attended its meetings as well. In the fourth session of the Standing Committee in September 1944, he announced the government's decision to introduce the fair wage clause in contracts entered into by the Central Public Works Department and also to appoint a Labour Investigation Committee to investigate wages, earnings and other conditions of labour. The government kept the participants occupied with concrete proposals and used the discussions to firm up its ideas on the more controversial questions.

The Indian Trade Unions (Amendment) Bill, 1943 was circulated in the Standing Labour Committee and discussed, but soon it was apparent that there was no unanimity on compulsory recognition of unions. On state insurance covering sickness and injury, a broad consensus emerged based on the report prepared by Prof. B.P. Adarkar. The employers wanted to ensure that it would be a contributory scheme to which the government, the employers and the workers would make their contributions and, if there was a deficit, the government would cover it. This plea was not accepted since the government was not sure that it would be right for it to grant a subvention for a small number of people who would be covered by the state insurance scheme.

The Second World War had ended when the next Tripartite met in November 1945. It was now named as the Indian Labour Conference. The discussions and conclusions were on several subjects. These were in respect of lowering the hours of work from 54 to 48 per week and the amendment to the Factories Act for the purpose; the involuntary unemployment resulting from the working of controls in respect of which no statutory remedy could be anticipated; the attitudes of employment exchanges during strikes and lockouts; the industrial canteens which should be provided under a proposed legislation; the proposed amendments to the Workmen's Compensation Act, 1923 and the Trade Union Act, 1926. The conference in fact considered a draft bill on the former and one on the latter. It also discussed a draft on the Industrial Employment (standing orders) Bill and the delegates made several suggestions, which were noted.

In August 1942, a political upheaval that had been building up as a latent force with the commencement of the war suddenly found expression as the Quit India Movement all over the country. The government responded with great force using every instrument of suppression it had, to put it down and restore its authority. The vengeance employed by the government produced revulsion and anger even among war loyalists. The AITUC adopted a resolution saying,

> The general council of the AITUC condemns the action of government and authorities in resorting to indiscriminate firing upon unarmed people, in using excessive force through the police and the military, in putting unjustifiable and uncalled for restrictions on the liberty of speech, press, movement and association and in adopting humiliating punishments like flogging and imposing of collective fines on whole communities and virtually placing the country under military rule.[189]

This was followed by the observance of 25 September 1942 as the Anti-Repression Day. The trade unions' ranks were severely depleted during the Quit India movement. Nine members of the working committee and 30 of the General Council of the AITUC were imprisoned. For the first time ever, the General Council appealed to the trade unions and labour movements in the US. to bring pressure on their government to urge the British government to adopt a policy of conciliation towards the people of India, to put an immediate end to repression and to concede the national demand for transfer of power.[190] This message was duly cabled to leading personalities of labour movements in the UK and US.

Despite political setbacks, the trade unions and their membership increased rapidly during the war years in a climate which was highly conducive to unionization. On one hand, the level of employment rose steadily and, on the other, the decline in standard of living also proceeded unchecked. Additionally, with the fall of Burma, the availability of rice in India declined and the government found it difficult to maintain supplies of food grains to meet the demand of ration card holders. Moreover, the numerous wage cuts enforced by the employers during the years of depression had not been fully recovered by 1939 and, during the war, real wages stayed below the 1929 level.

Accordingly, though 1939 was in no way a normal year, for purposes of comparison, the rise in wartime earnings and the decline in real wages were calculated by treating it as the base year.[191] If it could be realistically asserted that, broadly considered, the wage level in 1929–30 was at the subsistence level, during the war years it declined to levels which were often below subsistence, though increased participation rates in working families did help the labour force in the daily struggle of survival. Another negative development of the wartime economy was rapid growth of population in large cities, the marked worsening of congestion in working class localities and a noticeable decline in the level of urban amenities.

The wartime purpose of convening the tripartite body

was an obvious one, to overcome the government's political isolation and also to involve both employers and workers along with the government agencies to find ways and means of enhancing wartime industrial production. The government felt the need to support labour at the apex level, to increase hours of work in the factories, permit employment of children in factories, allow women to work underground in mines and to take other measures to overcome shortage of labour wherever encountered. Labour's cooperation was urgently sought, because in several industries strikes were called on the issues of dearness allowance and war bonus. From the perspective of the labour movement, the invitation to take part in the tripartite forums represented a clear increment in its political standing and it reinforced the status already accorded to it in the 1935 Act. In the eyes of the ordinary workers, this meant that the trade unions which they were being urged to join, indeed had legitimacy and might not be attacked by the employers without inviting the ire of the authorities. Joining unions and taking part in its agitations might be safe and the workers need not fear victimization.

This summary of the work of the tripartite system of consultations shows it functioning as a sensitive advisory body to the government in a sphere of very great importance for the conduct of the war economy. The economic policies which the government developed were not the result of careful thought and preparation, but more of inescapable necessity, and these were urgently implemented through ad hoc controls for which no precedents existed. Matters of great importance, such as distribution of food grains at fair prices, were deferred till 1942 when the Japanese war reached India's doorsteps. Now army movements and defence stores which needed to be shipped and the consumption requirements of a very large military establishment were given priority, mostly at the cost of civilian consumption, and this included industrial workers.

Unrest followed which fuelled the Quit India revolt that developed spontaneously and without any guidance from the Congress High Command. The remedies lay in augmenting and perfecting the needed large body of administrative controls to meet the minimum essential requirements of the population, on one hand, and to secure political cooperation of as many parties and elements in the society as were forthcoming, on the other. This proved most elusive throughout the war, the popular element being totally absent in the political administration of the country at the centre. Moreover in 1942–3, as monetary expansion increased well beyond the capacity of the economy to absorb the increased supply of money, serious problems of economic management emerged and these were complicated by an unsatisfactory situation on the food front.

The plain facts are that the government had no clear idea of the stocks of food stuffs in the country, nor how to meet the requirement of the civilian population in addition to that of military consumption. Furthermore the government did not know how to administratively coordinate the policies of surplus and deficit provinces and discourage profiteering both on government and private accounts. The backdrop of inflation which began in 1942 and gained strength in 1943 was caused by the large expenditure incurred by the government to buy great quantities of materials required for the war which was met by deficit financing. This was admitted by the government later.

Perhaps the term inflation was not known to the rulers of the country and the inevitable connection between money supply and prices was not understood. The poor grasp of the inflationary phenomenon was made worse by the bureaucratic drive to suppress facts and delude the public by putting the blame on other mostly contributory factors. The government issued several orders through ordinances in May 1943 to bring the inflationary process under control, deal with the cloth famine which occurred during 1942–3 and the paper famine which developed in the following year, and so on without end.

The answer lay in tight controls and rationing measures

but when belatedly introduced their effectiveness remained generally lower than anticipated or acknowledged by the authorities, due to inefficient administrative procedures and poor coordination between the centre and the provinces. A major problem was the inadequacy of the transport system, particularly lack of engines and spare parts for the railways which were imported before the war, but could not be obtained due to disruption in shipping and breakdown in trade relations between India and the UK. Similarly, motor vehicles could no longer be imported for civilian use and shortages were made worse by requisitioning existing vehicles for war purposes. The position in regard to coastal shipping was much worse again, as the existing vessels were requisitioned by the government for military use. Moreover, the Japanese had sunk most of the tonnage in the Bay of Bengal during their naval operations.

All this and the many details, which were published as the war came to a close, show complete lack of advance planning and administrative preparation to cope with wartime shortages and the unavoidable breakdown in established trading arrangements, as for instance, the shortage of coal leading to closure of factories. War finance required a proper understanding of the ideas of inflationary gap and coordinated deployment of demand dampening fiscal and monetary policies in addition to price controls and rationing, to protect the minimum nutritional needs of the population.

The colonial government, which during this period included a majority of Indian members in the executive council, was found to be singularly inept at meeting the daunting tasks that confronted them. The denouement of tripartite forums under the guidance of B.R. Ambedkar may be the sole exception to this characterization and, at the end of the war, these were still usable to cope with the very grave problems that emerged.

ENDNOTES

1. Gandhi was warned in London by Sir Samuel Hoare, the Secretary of State, 'that if the Congress tried to force the pace by 'direct action' the Government would crush it with all the force at its command'. B.R. Nanda, *Mahatma Gandhi, A Biography*, London, George Allen and Ruskin, 1958, Ch. 36, 'End of the Truce', esp. p. 331.
2. Ibid. Ch. 37, 'Total War'; also Bipan Chandra's, *India's Struggle for Independence 1857-1947*, (op. cit.), pp. 287–8.
3. B.R. Nanda, *Mahatma Gandhi* (loc. cit.), p. 345.
4. Judith M. Brown, *Gandhi and Civil Disobedience The Mahatma in Indian Politics*, 1928–34, (op. cit.), Cambridge University Press, 1977, p. 323; also pp. 321–3.
5. R. C. Majumdar, *History of the Freedom Movement in India, Vol. III*, (op. cit.), pp. 477–8.
6. Tara Chand, *History of the Freedom Movement in India*, Vol. IV, Government of India, Publications Division, Ministry of Information and Broadcasting, p. 187. Raj Mohan Gandhi writes under the subtitle, 'Fast, Release and Reflection', 'in India the new arrests did not greatly lift morale. Not that Gandhi or anybody else thought they would. The disobedience struggle seemed to be on its last legs, and Congress supporters dispirited and in disarray.' *Mohandas, A True Story of a Man, His People and an Empire*, New Delhi, Penguin/Viking, 2006, p. 384.
7. B.R. Nanda, *Mahatma Gandhi* (loc. cit.), p. 365.
8. R.C. Majumdar, *History of the Freedom Movement in India*, Vol. III (op. cit.), p. 483.
9. Ibid., pp. 406–9; Quote on p. 406.
10. Bisheshwar Prasad, *Bondage and Freedom. A History of Modern India*, Vol. II (*1707-1947*), New Delhi, Rajesh Publications, 1979, Ch. 12, 'Provincial Autonomy', esp. pp. 428–34.
11. Tara Chand, Vol. IV (op. cit.), pp. 216–17; also John Glendevon, *The Viceroy at Bay*, London, Collins, 1971, Ch. 2, p. 25.
12. Tara Chand, Vol. IV, p. 216.
13. Ibid., p. 217.
14. Bisheshwar Prasad (loc. cit.); the detailed discussion of the Governor's powers and responsibilities is in pp. 436–9; and A.B. Keith, *A Constitutional History of India, 1600-1935*, London, Methuen & Co. Ltd., 1936, pp. 348–50.

15. Sir Reginald Coupland, *The Constitutional Problem in India*, Oxford University Press, 1945, p. 134.
16. Ibid., pp. 135–6.
17. Ibid., p. 147.
18. John Glendevon (loc. cit.), pp. 71–2.
19. Sir Reginald Coupland, *The Constitutional Problem in India (Part II)* (loc. cit), The reference is to a speech delivered by Sir Cowasji Jehangir, President National Liberal Federation at its meeting in December, 1936, p. 7.
20. J.P. Eddy and F.H. Lawton. *India's New Constitution. A Survey of the Government of India Act, 1935*, London, McMillan & Co. Ltd. 1935, pp. 94–5 and 219–27.
21. A.B. Keith (loc. cit.), pp. 376–8; quote on p. 378.
22. Vera Anstey, *The Economic Development of India*, London, Longman, Green & Co., Fourth Edition, 1952, p. 493 Table A on p. 492.
23. Ibid., Footnote on p. 493.
24. Ibid., Table B on p. 494.
25. S. Sivasubramanian, *Annual Estimates of National Income of India, 1900–1 to 1946–7*. New Delhi, Oxford University Press, 2000, Tables 3.6 and 3.7.
26. Ibid., Appendix Table 3(a).
27. Ibid., Table 6.1.
28. Clive J. Dewey (Ed.), *Arrested Development in India: the Historical Dimension*, New Delhi, Manohar Publications, 1988, p. 7, also Neil Charlesworth's article, 'The Impact of the Interwar Depression on Agriculture in the Bombay Presidency. A Case for Further Arrested Development', in the book (op. cit.) esp. Table 1.
29. S. Sivasubramanian *Annual Estimates of National Income* (loc. cit), pp. 383–5.
30. For the Bombay Presidency, Charlesworth writes:

    As prices started to fall and then slumped dramatically in the space of a few years, it does seem unlikely that employers could have forced down wages as rapidly and consistently as the general decline in prices demanded. Real wages for labour, as in the industrial west, therefore rose, in the short term anyway. This was regarded as economically harmful since, with the rise in real wages costs, 'agriculture cannot hope to be as remunerative as it has been for the past twenty years.' Similarly, the balance of the relationship between the landlord and tenant might have shifted significantly against the landlord. The key influence here was the relative scarcity of cash rents in the Bombay Presidency, (loc. cit.), p. 288.

31. Ibid., Table 3.
32. Ibid., p. 296.
33. 'Agrarian Change in Pre-Independence Punjab', *Essays in the Commercialization of Indian Agriculture* (op. cit.), pp. 59–61.
34. Christopher John Baker, *The Indian Rural Economy 1880–1955, The Tamil Nadu Countryside*, Delhi, Oxford University Press, 1984, Ch. 4, 'The Markets', Quote on p. 232 and p. 253.
35. Ibid., pp. 262–5, Quote on p. 262.
36. Ibid., p.297, also pp. 296–303.
37. B.R. Tomlinson, *The Political Economy of the Raj 1914–1947, The Economics of Decolonization in India*, The Macmillan Press Ltd. 1979, p. 43.
38. Dietmar Rothermund, *India in The Great Depression, 1929–1939*, New Delhi, Manohar, 1992 (op. cit.), p. 39. Reference is to Schuster's speech on 28 February 1930 defending the policy on contraction of currency.
39. Amiya Kumar Bagchi, *Private Investment in India, 1900–1939*, Cambridge University Press, 1972, Table 3.3 and pp. 85–7, also B.R. Tomlinson, *The Economy of Modern India, 1860-1970*, Cambridge University Press, 1993, p. 69.
40. B.R. Tomlinson, *The Political Economy of the Raj* (loc. cit.), p. 45, also pp. 45–56.
41. Ibid., p. 36.
42. Dietmar Rothermund, *India in the Great Depression* (loc. cit.), pp. 54–4, also B.R. Tomlinson, *The Economy of Modern India, 1860-1970* (loc. cit.), pp. 69–70.
43. Ibid., p. 67.
44. A.K. Bagchi, Footnote on p. 89.
45. Ibid., p. 216.
46. Aditya Mukherjee, *Imperialism, Nationalism and the Making of the Indian Capitalist Class* (op. cit.), p. 105.
47. Dietmar Rothermund, *India in the Great Depression* (loc. cit.), p. 50. Rothermund discusses Norman's role in Indian economic affairs and the part played by Schuster in pp. 21–57.
48. B.R. Tomlinson, *The Economy of Modern India* (loc. cit.), pp. 148–9.

49. B.R. Tomlinson, *The Political Economy of the Raj* (loc. cit.), p. 129, also Dietmar Rothermund, *India in the Great Depression* (loc. cit.), pp. 76–8.
50. Ibid., pp. 76–7. Rothermund says: 'It was an irony of fate that the Reserve Bank which was set up so as to safeguard British interests against the potential Indian Finance Minister emerged under Smith's guidance as a stronghold of Indian interests and proved to be particularly irksome to a conservative British Finance Member like Grigg.' p. 77.
51. *History of the Reserve Bank of India (1935-51)*, Bombay, Reserve Bank of India, 1970, p.162.
52. Raymond W. Goldsmith, *The Financial Development of India, 1800-1977*, Delhi, Oxford University Press, 1983. Goldsmith has briefly reviewed the GNP estimates made by Sivasubramanian, Madison and Heston and found considerable differences in their estimates. See, Table 2.1 which gives Annual Data on Income, Production, Prices and Bank Rate, 1913–46. He relies on Sivasubramanian's estimates as raised by 10 per cent to shift from net to gross national product, pp. 66–70.
53. In Ahmedabad, the most extraordinary fact was the availability of Gandhi as the leader-cum-moral force which brought together his followers and admirers both among workers and mill owners to work the trade union around positive lines, sticking as much as may be humanly possible to peaceful arguments and quiet agitation. See M.V. Kamath and V.B. Kher, *The Story of Militant But Non-Violent Trade Unionism, A Biographical and Historical Study*, Ahmedabad, Navajivan Mudranalaya, 1995. In January 1932, even as Gandhi faced arrest almost immediately on his return from the Round Table Conference he sent this message to Ahmedabad and labour, 'Vindicate the honour of your country, give up liquour, wear khadi, remain united, obey Anasuyabehn and Shankarlalbhai, educate your children, work honestly while guarding your rights, do not hate millowners, contribute your mite to the *yajna of swaraj*', Ibid., p. 281.
54. Rajnarayan Chandavarkar, *Imperial Power and Popular Politics: Class Resistance and the State in India, c.1850-1950*. Cambridge, Cambridge University Press, 1998, p. 115; also by the same

author, *The Origins of Industrial Capitalism in India, Business Strategies and the Working Classes in Bombay, 1900–1940,* Cambridge University Press, 1994, Chapter 9, 'Epilogue: Workers' Politics, Class, Caste and Nation'.

55. M.V. Kamath and V.B. Kher (loc. cit.), p. 327.
56. ICHR, *Labour Movement in India 1931-1937*, Vol. 14, (Indian Council of Historical Research, New Delhi), Bombay, Popular Prakashan, 1988, pp. 717–24. Quote in V.B. Karnik, *Strikes in India*, Bombay, Manaktalas, 1967, p. 251.
57. Ibid., pp. 260–1.
58. Rajnarayan Chandavarkar, *The Origins of Industrial Capitalism*, pp. 364–5 and footnote on p. 364.
59. V.B. Karnik, *N.M. Joshi, Servant of India*, Bombay, United Asia Publications, June 1972, pp. 95–6; also the government's preparedness to deal with the threats posed by the communists, in ICHR, *Labour Movement in India*, Vol. 14, pp. 582–5.
60. Moni Ghosh, *Our Struggle. A Short History of Trade Union Movement in TISCO Industry at Jamshedpur*, Calcutta, Firma K.L. Mukhopadhyay, 1973. It may be due to the frequent presence of national leaders that Jamshedpur workers participated in Gandhi's movements, especially the civil disobedience in 1930. See G. Ramanujam, *Indian Labour Movement*, New Delhi, Sterling Publishers Pvt. Ltd., 1986, pp. 35–40.
61. The evidence to this effect was placed before the Whitley Commission and again before the Labour Investigation Committee, 1946. See, Mahesh Kumar Mast, *Trade Union Movement in Indian Railways*, Meerut, Meenakshi Prakashan, 1969, pp. 5–7, and the chapter, 'The Movement: Genesis and Growth'.
62. Ibid., p. 8, also Chapter three, 'Main Features of the Movement'.
63. The Act is reproduced in ICHR, *Labour Movement in India*, Vol. 16, pp. 738–46, also pp. 747–51 and pp. 754–9.
64. Ibid., p. 750.
65. Eamon Murpjy, *Unions in Conflict. A Comparative Study of Fourth South Indian Textile Centres, 1918-1939*; Australian National University Monographs on South Asia No. 5, New Delhi, Manohar Publications, 1981, pp. 105–11.

66. All the 13 points were answered by N.M. Joshi who also suggested major deletions and reformations to make the unity worth having again. Prem Sagar Gupta, *A Short History of All Indian Trade Union Congress (1920–1947)*, AITUC Publications, September 1980 (op. cit.), pp. 198–207 especially 'Comment', pp. 201–6.
67. Ibid., pp. 210–11.
68. Ibid., p. 258.
69. Ibid., p. 270–1. The unity lasted till 1940 when the CSP decided to expel the communists.
70. Ibid., p. 274; for an account of communist infiltration in the Congress, See G. Ramanujam (loc. cit.), pp. 37–9.
71. K.M. Munshi, *Indian Constitutional Documents*, Vol. 1, *Pilgrimage to Freedom (1902-1958)*, Bombay, Bharatiya Vidya Bhavan, 1967, pp. 41–2.
72. Bipan Chandra (op. cit.), p. 312; also pp. 312–16. Nehru voted against the resolution for entry into the Councils together with two socialist members who had been included in the CWC by him as the President.
73. A brief narration of events is given in A.K. Majumdar, *Advent of Independence*, Bharatiya Vidya Bhavan, Bombay, 1963, pp. 133–4. According to Moore, 'while Muslim parties were able to consolidate their control over the Punjab, Bengal and Sind, the Congress was able to secure control of the Muslim minority provinces and to deny the Muslim population any say in their government. A sense of exclusion and even persecution drove the Muslims into hostility against the Act for the scope it afforded to Hindu Raj'. R.J. Moore. *End Games of Empire, Studies of Britain's Indian Problem*, Delhi, Oxford University Press, 1988, p. 16.
74. A.K. Majumdar, 'Historical Introduction', *Indian Constitutional Documents, Munshi Papers*, Vol. II, Bharatiya Vidya Bhavan, Bombay, 1967, p. XXIV.
75. K.M. Munshi, *Indian Constitutional Documents*, Vol. 1. (loc. cit.), p. 44. Also Chapter V, 'Constitutional Relations with the Governor', pp. 48–54.
76. Rajendra Prasad who was then the President of the Indian National Congress gives a detailed account of the developments that followed the Muslim League resolution of March 1938. See his, *India Divided*, Third Edition, Hind

Kitabs Ltd., Bombay, 1947 (first published in January 1946), pp. 146–53.

77. John Glendevon (loc. cit), Soon after the war broke out, on 4 September 1939, the Viceroy invited leaders to see him. The author records:

    Jinnah asked the Viceroy to strengthen his hand. He wanted something positive to take back to his followers preferably a complete reshaping of the constitution. Linlithgow asked him if he wanted him to turn the Congress Ministries out. 'Yes! Turn them out at once. Nothing else will bring them to their senses' ... Jinnah was asked, 'How was India to obtain self-government if not by democracy?' Jinnah replied that the escape from this impasse lay in partition which was not an answer to the question.

78. R.J. Moore, *The Crisis of Indian Unity*, Oxford, Clarendon Press, 1974, p. 30. Quotation from Azim Husain, *Fazli-Husain: A Political Biography*, Bombay, 1946, p. 310 (cited by Moore); Chapter 6 especially the section 'The Play for Sectoral Support'.
79. R.J. Moore, *End Games of Empire* (loc. cit.), p. 110.
80. Sir Reginald Coupland, *India A Restatement*, Oxford University Press, London, 1945, pp. 183—4.
81. Ibid, Chapter VIII, 'The Muslim Reaction'.
82. Sir George Schuster and Guy Wint, *India and Democracy*, Macmillan and Co. Ltd., London, 1941, p. 343. The book is in two parts. Wint is the author of Part I and Schuster of Part II. Earlier, the latter was the finance Secretary in the Government of India for five and a half years. On the constitutional questions he wrote, 'My own belief is that the constitutional problems cannot be completely or finally solved in advance. I believe that the essential thing is to get down to the practical work, and that, in the handling of the actual tasks, solutions for what look like intractable problems will be found, while new problems hitherto unforeseen may reveal themselves.' pp. 385–6.
83. Tara Chand, Vol. IV, (loc. cit.), p. 241. He writes, 'As usually happens in party politics, the party in opposition accused the party in power of all kinds of genuine and imaginary misdemeanours, delinquencies and wickedness. In view of the communal composition of the legislature, accusations

become draped in communal colours, which made the distinctions sharper, and the gulf between the communities wider.'

84. See S.M. Burke and Salim Al Din Quraishi, *The British Raj in India. An Historical Review*, Karachi, Oxford University Press, 1995, pp. 74–89. 'Sir Syed's political philosophy started the trend which ultimately convinced the Muslims that they and the Hindus constituted two irreconcilable nations.' (p. 81). Elsewhere the authors write,

    The Hindu intelligentsia derived its theory of nationalism from the British example and from English literature. It craved representative institutions as practised in England and the British colonies. To the Muslims, the parliamentary system in Indian conditions meant their permanent subjection to the Hindus. It was bad enough for them to be ruled by the British; to be ruled by their erstwhile subjects, the Hindus, was unthinkable. Not surprisingly, the Muslims largely held aloof from the Indian National Congress, which adopted British democracy as the model for India. (p. 92)

85. Sir Reginald Coupland, *The Constitutional Problem in India* (loc. cit.) Chapter, XVII, 'The Muslim Reaction', esp. pp. 190–8.
86. H.N. Brailsford, *Subject India*, Bombay, Vora and Co. Publishers Ltd., First Published in India, March 1946, p. 97. Shortly after its publication in England the export of this book to India was prohibited. 'The ban has now been lifted and it is possible to produce an Indian edition.' (Preface to the Indian Edition). About Congress he wrote,

    Its strength is unevenly distributed. Its hold on Bengal is relatively weak, and in the Punjab its influence is negligible, while in Hindu India it is a Great Power. It is nonetheless, a grave mistake to call it a Hindu party, as Mr. Churchill has done. Its purpose is not to advance Hindu confessional interest, though in fact the great majority of its membership, as of the Indian population, are Hindus ... The idea for which it stands is Indian Nationalism.(p. 32)

87. *The British Raj in India* (loc. cit.), pp. 348–51. The other, entirely different perspective, is provided by Bipan Chandra's well argued defence of Indian nationalism in the aftermath of poor election results, as a critique of Jinnah's sweep of communal politics.

    Jinnah had now to decide what to do: to stick to his semi-nationalist, liberal communal politics which seemed to have exhausted its potentialities or to abandon communal politics. Both would mean going into the wilderness. The third alternative was to take to mass politics which in view of the semi-feudal and semi-loyalist social base of the League and his own socially, economically, and politically conservative views could only be based on the cries of Islam in danger and the danger of a Hindu Raj. Jinnah decided in 1937–38 to opt for this last option. And once he took this decision he went all the way towards extreme communalism putting all the force and brilliance of his personality behind the new politics based on themes of hate and fear. From now on, the entire political campaign among Muslims of this tallest of communal leaders would be geared to appeal to his co-religionist's fear and insecurity and to drive home the theme that the Congress wanted not independence from British imperialism but a Hindu Raj in cooperation with the British and domination over Muslims and even their extermination as also destruction of Islam in India.

Bipan Chandra (loc. cit.), p. 435

88. Ibid., p. 324.
89. For a vivid description of Congress rule given by a Pakistani historian who reiterates the arguments by the Muslim League, see, *A History of the Freedom Movement Vol. IV, 1936-47,* Part I and II, Renaissance Publishing House, Delhi (first published, 1970), Reprinted in India, 1984. (Pakistan Historical Society Publication, No. 56). 'The Congress in Office 1937-39', by Jamil-ud-Din Ahmad, pp. 26–32.
90. John Glendevon (loc. cit.), p. 115.
91. Sir Reginald Coupland, *The Constitutional Problem in India* (loc. cit.), Chapter IV, p. 26.
92. Ibid, pp. 137–8.
93. Ibid, pp. 139.
94. Ibid, p. 55 also, Tara Chand, Vol. IV (loc. cit.), pp. 251–4.
95. Tara Chand, Ibid, p. 278.
96. R.J. Moore, *Churchill, Cripps and India, 1939-1945,* Clarendon Press, Oxford, 1979, p. 7.
97. R.P. Masani, *Britain in India,* Oxford University Press, 1960, p. 166. Also A.K. Majumdar (loc. cit.), is of the opinion that Congress should not have resigned in a fit of petulance. p. 161.
98. Ram Gopal, *How India Struggled for Freedom,* Bombay, The

Book Centre Pvt. Ltd., 1967, p. 416. A.C. Guha describes the preparations that were being made well before the outbreak of the war, having taken it for granted that a war with Germany was inevitable. Accordingly, they alerted the Government of India to make necessary preparations. *India's Struggle for Quarter of a Century* (op. cit.), p. 400.

99. See the testimony of P. Moon in *Divide and Quit*, London, 1961. pp. 24–5, Quoted more fully in A.K. Majumdar, *Advent of Independence* (loc. cit.), p. 150. Also Gandhi's view on unconditional cooperation which he knew would not find support in the CWC. p.151.
100. *Christopher John Baker*(op. cit.), p. 304.
101. Bipan Chandra (loc. cit.), pp. 329–30.
102. Sir Reginald Coupland, *The Constitutional Problem in India*, Oxford University Press, 1945, p.139; also Bipan Chandra, Ibid., p. 330 and for a critical review, Dietmar Rothermund, *India in the Great Depression* (loc. cit.), Chapter, 'Remedial Action: The National Congress in a Provincial Blind', pp. 233–60.
103. S. Sivasubramanian, *Annual Estimates of National Income* (op. cit.), Table 3.23 p. 148.
104. Vera Anstey (op. cit), p. 576.
105. S. Sivasubramanian *Annual Estimates of National Income* (loc. cit.), Tables 6.9 and 6.10.
106. A.K. Bagchi, pp. 244–53; Quote on p. 250.
107. Ibid., pp. 284–5 including the quotation.
108. Morris D. Morris, 'The Growth of Large-Scale Industry' in *The Cambridge Economic History, 'C-1757-C.1970*, Dharma Kumar (Ed.), Cambridge University Press, 1983, p. 615.
109. A.K. Bagchi, Table 12.3, p. 372.
110. Dietmar Rothermund, *India in the Great Depression* (loc. cit.), p. 176.
111. Vera Anstey (op. cit.), p. 511, also pp. 517–18.
112. A.K. Bagchi, p. 381.
113. Ibid., pp. 375–7.
114. Ibid., p. 381.
115. Vera Anstey (op. cit.), p. 518.
116. S. Sivasubramanian, *The National Income of India in the Twentieth Century*, New Delhi, Oxford University Press, 2000, Tables 3.6 and 3.7.

117. B.R. Tomlinson, *The Economy of Modern India, 1860-1970* (op. cit.), p. 135.
118. *The Cambridge Economic History* (op. cit.), 'Railways', p. 750.
119. V.B. Karnik, *N.M. Joshi, Servant of India* (op. cit.), pp. 210–15.
120. Ibid, p. 98.
121. G.K. Sharma, *Labour Movement in India*, Jullundur, University Publishers, 1963, p. 46.
122. Prem Sagar Gupta, *A Short History of the All-India Trade Union Congress (1920–1947)* (op. cit.), pp. 284–5.
123. Ibid., p. 285.
124. Ibid., pp. 300–1, 305–7, 311–12 and 329–31.
125. V.B. Karnik, *Strikes in India* (op. cit.), pp. 278–9 (extract from the Bombay Labour Gazette, August 1937, p. 923).
126. Ibid., pp. 279–80.
127. Prem Sagar Gupta, (op. cit.), pp. 293–4, quote on p. 294.
128. V.B. Karnik, *Indian Trade Unions*, Bombay Manaktalas, 1966, p. 111.
129. G.K. Sharma (loc. cit.), pp. 99–100, also V.B. Karnik, *Strikes in India* (op. cit.), pp. 286–8.
130. V.B. Karnik, *Indian Trade Unions* (op. cit.), pp. 112–13.
131. Prem Sagar Gupta, (op. cit.), pp. 318–20.
132. Dipesh Chakrabarty, *Rethinking Working-Class History: Bengal 1890–1940*, (op. cit.), pp. 125–39, quote on p. 125.
133. Ibid., p. 127.
134. Eaman Murphy, *Union in Conflict, A Comparative Study of Four South Indian Textile Centres 1928-1939*, Delhi, Manohar, 1981, pp. 212–15.
135. Prem Sagar Gupta, (op. cit.), p. 326.
136. Ibid., p. 327.
137. John Patrick Haithox, *Communism and Nationalism in India. M.N. Roy and Comintern Policy 1920-1939*, Princeton University Press, 1971, pp. 296–7.
138. R. C. Majumdar, *History of the Freedom Movement*, Vol. III, (op. cit.), p. 613.
139. *Britain in India* (op. cit.), p. 180.
140. Ibid., pp. 180–1. (This is an extract from Churchill's *The Second World War*, Vol. IV, pp. 185–6).
141. Tara Chand, Vol. IV (loc. cit), (op. cit.), pp. 335–41.
142. Ibid., p. 341. Earlier in January 1942 Linlithgow had written to Amery that, 'We should stand firm and make no further

move because further transfer of power might mean pressure on us for withdrawal of Indian troops and Indian supply'. See *The British Raj in India*, 'The Cripps Mission', p. 362. A complete background of the Cripps Mission including the discussions in the War Cabinet are provided and discussed by D.N. Panigrahi in his notable work, *India's Partition. The Story of Imperialism in Retreat*, London, Routledge, an imprint of Taylor and Francis, 2004, Ch. 5, 'The Cripps Offer, 1942'.

143. For a detailed account of US involvement in Cripps' India Mission and reaction following its inevitable failure, see M.S. Venkataramani and B.K. Shrivastava, *Quit India, The American Response to the 1942 Struggle*, New Delhi, Vikas Publishing House Pvt. Ltd., 1979, Chapter Three, 'Britain 'proves' its sincerity'; also Panigrahi (loc. cit.), pp. 207–33.

144. A.C. Guha (loc. cit. , p. 491; Tara Chand provides a detailed review of Cripps' proposals and the discussions that followed, *History of the Freedom Movement*, Vol. IV(loc. cit.), pp. 335–61.

145. Roosevelt had tried to prevent the breakdown in talks but failed. Majumdar says:

> One of the most intimate associates of Churchill justly remarked: The President might have known that India was one subject on which he would never move a yard. Perhaps an inch would be more like it. Harry Hopkins, who carried on the negotiations with Churchill on behalf of Roosevelt, also felt that India was one area where the minds of Roosevelt and Churchill would never meet.

History of the Freedom Movement in India, Vol. III, (op. cit.), p. 631.

146. According to Bipan Chandra,

> An important reason for the failure of the negotiations was the incapacity of Cripps to bargain and negotiate. He had been told not to go beyond the Draft Declaration. Moreover, Churchill, the Secretary of State, Amery, the Viceroy, Linlithgow, and the Commander-in-Chief, Wavell, did not want Cripps to succeed and constantly opposed and sabotaged his efforts to accommodate Indian opinion, Bipan Chandra (op. cit.), pp. 455.

Guha. (ibid). cites Mauland Azad's letter to Cripps in which he says, 'You told me then (at the initial stage) that there would be a National Government which would function as a Cabinet and the position of the Viceroy would be analogous to that of the King of England vis-à-vis the cabinet', p. 494. Linlithgow had opposed the scheme earlier as amateurish and dangerous and if it were to fail there would be chaos'. John Glendevon (loc. cit.), pp. 218–26.

147. According to Guha:

> many residential houses were demolished to convert a number of villages into a war depot or airfield or soldiers' camps. Similar things took place in many districts in Bengal. Village after village was turned into deserts or military centres. Then there was the Scorched Earth Policy or the Denial Policy – leading to the destruction of all vehicles of conveyance such as boats, carts, cycles and sources of drinking water, etc. ((loc. cit.), p. 502).

148. R.C. Majumdar, *History of the Freedom Movement in India,* Vol. III, Calcutta, Firma K.L. Mukhopadhyay, 1963, p. 634.
149. Ibid., for extensive extracts from the Quit India resolution and discussion based on it, see pp. 639–64.
150. *A Centenary History of the Indian National Congress (1885-1985),* Volume III, jointly published by the All India Congress Committee and Vikas Publishing House Pvt. Ltd., 1985, p. 523. See Section 6: 'Preparations for a Struggle', pp. 522–1.
151. Bipan Chandra (loc. cit.), pp. 460–1. For the opposite view point holding Gandhi and Congress responsible for errors and follies and numerous instances of misjudgments and wrong tactics, see, B.B. Misra, *The Indian Political Parties. An Historical Analysis of Political Behaviour Upto 1947,* Delhi, Oxford University Press, 1976; esp. pp. 330–95.
152. Detailed descriptions of agitations and underground activities are narrated by several historians. Guha, being a former revolutionary turned Gandhian and an activist though under arrest during this period, provides the most vivid accounts in his *India's Struggle Quarter of a Century, Vol. II* (loc. cit.), pp. 532–83. According to Congress sources cited by the author, 'not less than 15000 (persons) were killed by police and military firings, aerial bombings and from lathi charges and other assaults'. Guha thinks that there may be some exaggeration in these figures. p. 562. Another, more detailed version occurs in Majumdar, *History of the Freedom Movement in India,* Vol. III (loc. cit.), pp. 646–78. Yet another historian, while taking the nationalist position, sums up the situation in these words: 'The rejection of Cripps offer was an error, and the 'August Movement' a failure. The British Raj in its

remaining years exacted a cruel price for these lapses'. A.K. Majumdar, *Advent of Independence* (loc. cit.), p. 187. Bipan Chandra, of course, forcefully disagrees with this perception. Moreover, contrary to the general impression about the role of communists, he says that the elemental quality of the Quit India Movement was demonstrated:

> by the fact that hundreds of communists at the local and village levels participated in the movement despite the official position taken by the Communist Party. Though they sympathized with the strong anti-fascist sentiments of their leaders, yet they felt the irresistible pull of the movement and, for at least a few days or weeks, joined it along with the rest of the Indian people. Bipan Chandra (loc. cit.), p. 468.

Much detailed information based on secret documents is provided in the lively book, *Quit India Movement, British Secret Documents* (Ed. Dr P.N. Chopra), New Delhi, Interprint, 1986. The volume carries a foreword by Zail Singh, President, Republic of India. The period covered is 1942 and 1943; also Tara Chand, Vol. IV (op. cit.), pp. 377–88.

153. In an interview K.M. Munshi had with Lord Linlithgow in May 1939 the subject was the federation and the latter said:

> I am not keen on it for myself. If the federation was not to come now, it will never come. And if it does not come, I honestly think India's unity will be in danger. You know the forces at work. There is the Pakistan Movement; it is absurd, but it is not quite dead. And Sir Sikander is preparing some federal scheme of his own. The Muslims do not want the federatioin. But unless Hindus and Muslims sit on one Cabinet and learn to look at India as a whole, the communities will continue to fall apart.
>
> To this Munshi said, 'Mr. Jinnah also does not want the Federation.' Linlithgow's response was, 'Muslims don't want any Federation – this or any other.' Again on the Muslims' attitudes, Linlithgow's opinion was as clear as this: 'They are bound to dominate the country any way. It is a compact minority of 8 crores. But it will prove much more difficult to Indian unity if the Federation does not come into existence.

K.M. Munshi, *Indian Constitutional Documents,* Vol. I (loc. cit.), p. 389. Also see John Glendevon (loc. cit.), p. 177 and pp. 184–5.

154. R.C. Majumdar, *History of the Freedom Movement in India,* Vol. III (op. cit.), pp. 670–8 and 692–6.

155. K.M. Munshi, *Indian Constitutional Documents, Munshi Papers* Vol. II, Bombay Bharatiya Vidya Bhawan, February 1967, pp. 11–15.
156. Based on Wavell's journal and quoted by D.N. Panigrahi (loc. cit.), 'From Simla Conference to Partition.' pp. 261–5.
157. Ibid., pp. 265–6.
158. National Income of India (op. cit.), Table 1.2.
159. The census of 1941 was damaged by the play of communal considerations.

    > Ever since the resolution on Pakistan was adopted by the Muslim League, the latter had been sedulously pushing the idea of geographical partition. Geographical areas like Kushtia formed transitional lands from one majority community to another but here the difference between the numerical strength of the two major communities in the 1931 count had been marginal, that is, within the range of error or doubt. These areas naturally became objects of the most serious attention in the campaign for inflating the population of a particular community.

    Asok Mitra, *Towards Independence 1940-1947. Memoirs of an Indian Civil Servant*, Bombay Popular Prakashan, 1991, pp. 24–6; quote on p. 25.
160. S. Sivasubramanian *The National Income of India in the Twentieth Century*, pp. 51–6, quote on p. 53.
161. Ibid., Tables 3(b) and 3(e).
162. Dietmar Rothermund, *An Economic History of India* (op. cit.), pp. 123–6; quote on p. 123.
163. Asok Mitra, *Towards Independence* (loc. cit.), pp. 104–13; quote on p. 105.
164. Ibid., p. 106.
165. Ibid., p. 118.
166. A.K. Sen, *Poverty and Famine. An Essay on Entitlement and Deprivation*, Delhi, Oxford University Press, 1981, Chs. 4, 5 and 6, Table 6.2, p. 61.
167. Ibid., Appendix D, 'Famine Mortality : A Case Study'.
168. Ibid., pp. 75–83. Sen rejects the food availability decline (FAD) theory on the ground that official data showed that food shortage was manageable, though to break the famine a large stock of foodgrains was essential. According to him the government, 'was, in fact, fairly right in its estimation of overall food availability, but disastrously wrong on the theory

of famines.' p. 80. The picture drawn by Asok Mitra is very different. In the famine afflicted districts there was *no food* and the Bengal government didn't seem to care for providing relief.

169. Dietmar Rothermund, *An Economic History of India* (op. cit.), pp. 123–5.
170. Tara Chand, Vol. IV, p. 409. The Muslim League ministry brought in Muslim traders in the lucrative business of food distribution. The government supplied the capital and met losses suffered by traders in the early stages.
171. *The Cambridge Economic History*, Table 9.13, p. 767.
172. Ibid., Table 12.11, p. 943.
173. Ibid., p. 944.
174. B. Shiva Rao gives the text of his broadcast and frank admissions by him at a Press Conference of the likely developments in the Bay of Bengal. Later still in March 1942, in an address to the Rotary Club of Delhi, he said 'Everybody in India is asking: what are we going to do to keep the Japanese out? From the point of view of the army in this enormous battle front we shall hold vital places, what it is necessary to hold in order to make India safe, but we cannot hold everyone...' *The Framing of India's Constitution: A Study*, 'Historical Background', The Indian Institute of Public Administration, New Delhi, 1968, pp. 35–6. According to the author, these statements have received singularly little attention. In India anxieties had manifestly deepened; these statements made a profound impression on Gandhi.
175. B.R. Tomlinson, *The Political Economy of the Raj* (loc. cit.), p. 96.
176. Ibid., Table 3.3 on p. 94.
177. D. Rothermund (loc. cit.), pp. 125–9.
178. ICHR, *Labour Movement in India 1941-1947*, Documents, Vol. 23 (Eds. M.N.V. Nair and Praful Bidwai), pp. 25-26. The discussion that follows is based on this volume.
179. Ibid., pp. 45–9
180. Sukomal Sen gives a catalogue of strikes during the war years on various demands such as, dearness allowance, war allowance, bonus, supply of foodgrains at fair prices in his book, *Working Class of India. History of Emergence and Movement, 1870-1970*; esp. Ch. 17. 'Eventful Course of Working Class Struggles During World War, 1939-45', Calcutta, K.P. Bagchi & Co., 1977

181. *Tripartite Conclusions, 1942-1967*, Ministry of Labour, Government of India, 1968. p. 6.
182. ICHR, *Labour Movement in India*, Vol. 23, pp. 45–9.
183. Ibid., p. 58.
184. Ibid., p. 65
185. Ibid.
186. ICHR, *Labour Movement in India 1941-47*, Vol. 24, pp. 387–9.
187. Ibid., Vol. 23, pp. 231–6.
188. Ibid., Vol. 24, pp. 451–2.
189. Prem Sagar Gupta, (op. cit.), p. 378, also pp. 377–88.
190. Ibid, p. 379.
191. See *Indian Working Class Movement* (op. cit.); in this book the index number of money earnings for factory workers earning less than Rs. 200 per month (1939=100) is placed in relation to the All India Consumers Price Index (1939=100) and a table of real earnings. In 1945 money earnings stood at 201.5, the CPI at 269 and real wages at 75.1 respectively, also Table 24 and 25.

Chapter 4

TRANSFER OF POWER, NEW DEMOCRATIC INDIA, DEVELOPMENT, 1946–57

The end of the Second World War changed the political scene in ways no political leader in the country anticipated. Britain emerged victorious but as a weaker power. World politics had two great powers, the USA and the Soviet Union and the newly organized United Nations with its power structure. These dwarfed the role of Britain, though its empire was still intact. The all-important question which needed to be answered was whether Britain could still retain its Indian empire or admit the inevitability of transfer of power to the Indians. The Labour government answered the question by admitting the latter. It then proceeded to find a mechanism and suitable ways to do so while preserving the vitally important economic, political and military links between the two countries or the successor states in the Indian subcontinent. The paradox which soon enveloped this quest was that while Britain had implicitly conceded the Muslim claim to Pakistan, the government still wanted to accommodate it in a formula of Indian unity. This proved impossible and the only strategy that actually worked was 'divide and quit'. The new government was confronted with an enormous load of problems, under the threat of a famine, which was averted.

I. 1946–9

Communal War, Partition, New Constitution, Integrated India

In a move to break the deadlock which followed the collapse of the Shimla Conference, the new government in Britain announced its decision to go beyond the 1942 proposals, transcend the 1935 Act and endeavour to secure an agreement with the Congress and the Muslim League in devising a constitutional arrangement which would enable them to accept transfer of power leading to dominion status at par with the Westminster Statute. It would be for India to decide whether to stay as an equal member in the British Commonwealth or leave it. There would be elections in India. Both the Congress and the Muslim League decided to contest them, first for the Central Assembly and later for the provincial legislatures.

Meanwhile, the military trial of some INA officers in the Red Fort in Delhi opened on the main charge that, 'they had waged war against the King', together with other charges and the Congress decided to defend them. The trial created great patriotic fervour and the INA officers became the heroes of India. Subhas Chandra Bose, who had escaped from India in 1940 and organized the INA with the help of the Japanese, was hailed for his patriotism and the Congress leaders stumped the country in applauding Bose, the INA and its officers on trial. This built up a powerful nationalist sentiment among the people and they rallied to the Congress' call.

The Congress, riding on this patriotic wave, swept the elections to the Central Assembly, which, however, showed that while the Congress truly represented the non-Muslim electorate, securing over 91 per cent of the votes, the Muslim League was the sole representative of the Muslims, winning 86 per cent of their votes. This buried the question of whether any other party could represent the Muslims in the Viceroy's Council. The results of the elections for the provincial assemblies were less dramatic and the non-Muslim League politicians were elected in sufficient numbers in the Muslim majority provinces of Punjab and Bengal to form coalition governments with the backing of the Congress.

Beginning in early 1946, the Muslim League leaders, including Jinnah, were heard employing violent language in demanding Pakistan or else the population of India would be put to the sword. This was known to Lord Wavell as well as to others, but it was ignored. The Cabinet Mission, under the leadership of Lord Pethick-Lawrence, the new Secretary of State for India with Sir Stafford Cripps, President of the Board of Trade and A.V. Alexander, First Lord of the Admiralty, as members, had arrived on 25 March 1946. The mission was preceded by a visit by a Parliamentary Delegation in January. The arrival of the Cabinet Mission soon after and their meetings with important political leaders had toned up the political climate and may have contributed to the outbreak of intemperate language.

The Parliamentary Delegation had formed the opinion that the League would not join any constitution-making body, nor would it take part in any interim government. It appeared from the behaviour of the top Congress leaders, who were basking in their great popularity while the focus of public agitation was the INA trials (which some Congress leaders were prominently leading) that they scarcely understood the sharp swing in the political mood and perceptions of the Muslim League.

The failure of the Shimla Conference had apparently convinced the League leaders that the British government would concede the demand for Pakistan only in the face of a resounding demonstration of the inexorable logic of the two-nation theory; if it meant obstructing the Congress demand for independence this too must be unavoidably done. The logical consequence of this reasoning was that the British should not hasten their departure, they must first settle the question of partition of India, then leave.

This required a move away from high level negotiations to mass politics, invoking the fury and rage of the Muslim masses around the slogan, 'Islam in Danger', to make a frightening impact on the Hindus. It was not the Congress that needed bullying, nor was it a matter of creating the proper impression on the new Labour Party government in the UK, which, contrary to past experience, was keen on hastening the pace towards self-government for India as a whole. It were the Hindus who must be made to register the power and thrust of Muslim opinion and see it as a menace. The League was keen that all other options implied in the 1942 proposals of the Cripps Mission should be abandoned, for instance, that the whole of Punjab or Bengal might have a voice on whether they would each want to have a Constitution-making body to themselves. Lord Pethick-Lawrence's statement on 4 December 1945, that 'India should attain her full and rightful position as an independent partner state in the British Commonwealth and the desire of Parliament to do everything within our power to promote speedy attainment of the objective', probably spurred the League to think in terms of militant methods to attain their cherished goal.[1]

The irony of the situation was that Wavell had perceived an altogether different threat, of a fresh 'Quit India' type of movement being launched by the Congress to coerce the British Government to arrive at a settlement with the nationalists. In fact, the Congress was actually cooperating with him, even while championing the cause of the INA soldiers with the aim of securing their release and little else. However, the Viceroy's perceptions were coloured by past events and he still saw the Congress as the party of revolt. The British in India never perceived the League as a threat to peace and now, since it was beginning to happen, they decided to acquiesce and see what happened, or just feign to ignore the threat to governance which the League's spokesmen clearly implied. They acted thus, as indeed they were psychologically totally unprepared to see their trusted political ally in a new rebellious, violent mood.

The INA agitation took a violent turn in several places,

particularly Calcutta, which was often led by students. This continued till January 1946, when the C-in-C announced the remission of the sentence of life imprisonment and the three INA officers were released to be welcomed as heroes by the people. The student-led demonstrations in Calcutta were backed by large-scale strikes and shut downs. These were quelled by the police, which opened fire several times killing not less than 30 persons. The combined agitation of the students and workers indicated an upsurge resting on deeper anger and resentment against the government. The confrontation was followed by more demonstrations and police firing in February. An INA Officer, Abdul Rashid, was convicted and sent to jail and this inflamed public resentment further. Guha recounts:

> Military vehicles (not less than a dozen) were set on fire by the mob; tram cars, tram depots, military jeeps carrying loudspeakers, post offices, etc. were set on fire. On the night of 17 February 1946, the Governor announced that he had asked the military to help in restoring law and order. There were some attacks on Americans and they were asked by the Government not to go out of the barracks. The city was declared out of bounds for the Americans.'[2]

Disturbances continued for six days and so did casualties in police firing. The Muslims and communists also took part in the demonstrations. Their participation was evidence of the spontaneous nature of the upheaval; it was not led by any political party, though several Muslim League leaders were swept into it.

Another demonstration, if one was needed—of deepening anger and spreading unrest in the country—came in a wholly unexpected form in the naval mutiny, which broke out on 19 February 1946, delivering a great shock to the authorities. The immediate cause was the appalling scale of discrimination practised between the Indian Other Ranks (IOR) and the British Other Ranks in matters of salary, food, accommodation, medical and travelling facilities and even in the matter of training and on the actual fighting front. Use of abusive and filthy language against the IOR was common and this could be no longer tolerated. Though all these facts were known to the higher officers, nothing was done. In addition, there was the impending threat of demobilization with no future occupation to look forward to.

In fact, the trouble began much earlier, on 1 December 1945 which was to be celebrated as Navy Day. It was observed that objectionable political slogans were scrawled all over the ship and, on a small scale, it happened again on 2 February. The naval mutiny took a serious turn when the city people in Bombay and Calcutta joined hands in the demonstrations and caused much damage. 'Meetings and processions to express sympathy, as also strikes and hartals were quickly overshadowed by the barricades that came up, the pitched battles fought from housetops and by-lanes, the attacks on Europeans, and the burning of police stations, post offices, shops, tram depots, railway stations, banks, grain shops and even the YMCA centre.' The communists gave a call for a general strike which brought out a large body of workers to the streets and the city of Bombay was brought to a halt. The Royal Indian Navy mutiny spread to other naval centres where military establishments were affected. According to Bipan Chandra, 78 ships and 20 shore establishments felt the impact of the mutiny. The mutiny was eventually crushed and the ratings surrendered following appeals made by Sardar Patel, Nehru and Jinnah. A temporary communal unity was observed among the ratings, though while the Muslim ratings went to the League office to seek advice, the rest went to the Congress and Socialist party offices. Jinnah's advice to surrender was addressed to the Muslim ratings and they acted as advised.[3] Heavy casualties were reported as the police and British troops repeatedly opened fire, often indiscriminately, leaving many civilians among the dead and the wounded.

Elsewhere in the country, the disturbances and the mood of violence so noticeable among the demonstrators showed, that the quelling of the 1942 revolt had caused deep wounds.

In the speeches and slogans at Congress rallies, it was a common theme that the officers who had gone far beyond the line of duty to batter the nationalists should be in turn punished. These demands were particularly sharp in UP where the Governor did confess on 19 February 1946, 'that officials in UP in 1942 used on occasion methods which I cannot condone and which dragged out in the cold light of 1946 nobody could defend'.[4] These demands raised considerable anxiety among the British and two related questions were asked. Firstly, if the Congress started another movement to force their hands what could be done? The answer was that at this stage it would be possible, given the forces at the command of the government, to suppress it completely. The second question was: What would they do next? There was no answer. The military chiefs in the changed scenario were less sure about the loyalty of Indian troops to take part in crushing another nationalist uprising.

The Viceroy thought it would be difficult to hold on to India and administer it properly in view of the general shortage of British civil servants, more so because several were due to retire, or had expressed a wish to be relieved and retire. The Viceroy had correctly sensed the uneasy feeling among a section of British officers that they no longer knew why they were here, what they were doing here and, whether facing so much antagonism, even amongst the educated and affluent sections of the population, was at all necessary? The new government in the UK took note of these immediately relevant aspects of the political and administrative dimensions of the Indian problem and proceeded to expedite the process towards a settlement without, however, uttering the word 'independence'. They still hoped that the Indian leaders would go through the inevitable ordeal of arriving at a trilateral settlement, with the British, the Congress and the Muslim League, in a spirit of compromise and, in the end, agree to retain the historic ties with the British Commonwealth.

Members of the Parliamentary Delegation who were in

India for one month wrote separate notes on their impressions and the political perspective the government could realistically have about the course of negotiations in search of a settlement. The idea of Pakistan received wider concurrence, not because it was intrinsically sound, but that it would have to be conceded to avoid widespread bloodshed and to preserve British interests. The British government in all probability had already concluded that Pakistan would have to be conceded to the Muslims in some form.

The contributions of the Parliamentary Delegation encouraged the Attlee government to take the next step and send the Cabinet Mission to India with a renewal of the 1942 proposals. However, it had an important proviso that it was open to negotiations and modifications; further, that there should be a treaty between Britain and India covering financial, commercial and military aspects. Nevertheless, even as the Cabinet Mission was charged with the responsibility of securing on agreed settlement by exploring all possible alternatives and, while it was authorized to come to an agreement with the Congress and the League, they should not allow the minorities to produce such stalemates as would cause the breakdown of a settlement, nor could a minority have a veto over the progress sought by the majority. As Attlee explained in parliament, without disclosing the Mission's terms of reference, 'within the terms laid down by the cabinet, these Ministers must be able to act; but on major matters of policy that will refer back for cabinet decision. If they are going to negotiate they must have the power to negotiate.'[5] One problem was the position of Lord Wavell, so he was made a formal member of the Mission.

The big unresolved question was the nature of compromise that would be acceptable to Jinnah.

> The question before Jinnah was how to change the map of India. It occurred to him that having been in power for over 700 years over a good part of India, the Muslims should gain that authority at least over a part of India. He said that the Muslims would not demand their share of power in the Government of

> India but they would demand a share of land in the subcontinent of India. That was a revolutionary thought which aimed at suzerainty, no matter how limited it was, and at what cost. He desired to be the architect of a state, no matter how truncated or how moth-eaten it might be'.[6]

This position had evolved over the past five years and it was given steady encouragement by the Viceroys and senior British civil servants. Slowly though painfully, Gandhi, in his personal capacity, and the Congress (mainly Nehru and Sardar Patel) acquiesced in the idea. Yet, the possibility of keeping India united lingered and the Cabinet Mission strove to devise an acceptable formula for the purposes.

The next stage of development was visualized as an orderly pace of progress, but no one anticipated the tempest that actually followed. The political tempo that was unleashed by the elections and arrival of the Cabinet Mission, the preceding events of the INA trials, the mutiny of the naval ratings, the public demonstration of disaffection by the armed forces and the police, produced an unprecedented polarization of power at the two wholly incompatible political centres, namely the Congress and the Muslim League. It could produce only chaos, disorder and civil violence. Yet, all the key decisions still remained with the British. Gandhi's long-term objective and the Congress leaders' immediate goal was to secure formal acceptance of their claim of representing the most broad-based nationalism that could ever exist in India's vast diversities, hence to be the successor power to the British Raj and to arrange it by the legitimate constitutional device of a transfer of power. To obtain this overriding objective the Congress leaders slowly, with unavoidable reluctance, conceded the claim of the Muslim League to a share of Indian territory for the Muslims in the earmarked districts of the provinces in which they had a clear majority, to become the Muslim dominion called Pakistan. The League's position had been clearly spelled out in the April 1946 convention of Muslim legislators wherein a resolution was adopted which declared,

> that the Muslim Nation will never submit to any constitution for a United India and will never participate in any single constitution making machinery set up for the purpose and that any formula devised by the British Government for transferring power from the British to the Peoples of India, which does not conform to the following just and equitable principles, calculated to maintain internal peace and tranquillity in the country will not contribute to the solution of the Indian problem.

Then followed the scheme of partition and separate constitution-making bodies for the two successor states.[7]

In the context of the well established position of the Muslim League, Cabinet Mission made efforts to keep India united but, with a centre so weak by design, that if it did not work, and the British left, the successor state would not probably survive and a civil war would inevitably follow. The strongest hints that this might indeed happen became clear with the Congress taking the stand that whereas it would take the lead in forming an interim government, the formation of the Constituent Assembly should proceed apace and it must have full freedom in deciding the form of the Constitution for independent India. This implied that there was no finality to the Cabinet Mission's proposals, though it had been accepted by the Congress. The Constituent Assembly could re-work or alter the plan in new ways. Thereupon, the League withdrew its acceptance of the Cabinet Mission's plan and took the strategic decision to take the final plunge, to force the issue and wreck everything that was being put in place to preserve, in howsoever fragile a manner, the desired political unity of India.

Meanwhile, the new Secretary of State advised Wavell to give precedence to nationalism over communalism and invite Nehru to form the Interim Government. This spurred the League to acquire, as it were, a pistol in its hands and demonstrate its use by the call for Direct Action by the Muslims to fight for Pakistan.[8] The Cabinet Mission's plan gave the Muslims the critically important option to decide after ten years to continue to stay with the Union or to secede, and this formed the basis for its acceptance of the proposals. Now, since that pathway was no longer open, the League decided to observe 16 August 1946 as Direct Action Day, making it clear that the Muslims were not going to be restricted to non-violence.

The Muslim League Premier of Bengal, Suhrawardy, declared that if the Congress was put in power, Bengal would announce defiance; there would be a declaration of independence by Bengal or the formation of a parallel government and that the Centre would be denied revenue, et cetera.[9] Following an intensely communal propaganda and preparation, the gruesome direct action was focussed on Calcutta, which witnessed for about four days horrible scenes of unstoppable rioting, wanton killings and enormous losses of property.[10] The political focus of rioting was meant to be the city of Calcutta; for, elsewhere in Bengal, the observance of direct action was generally uneventful. The political issue which apparently tormented the League's leadership was whether, in the event of the partition of Bengal between the Muslim majority and the Hindu majority areas, Calcutta would be included in Pakistan or allowed to remain in India. Perhaps some pressure could be built up to have a plebiscite in Calcutta, in which case the Scheduled Caste Hindus might be impressed on to vote with the Muslims and win the case for Pakistan. This possibility had no doubt become increasingly unlikely since the government had already decided that in view of the fact that the Muslims comprised no more than 25 per cent of Calcutta's population it would in any case remain in India. Jinnah, at one stage, found it quite galling at having to be content with an eastern Pakistan, with the partitioned Bengal which excluded Calcutta, and described it as mere 'husk'.

The Calcutta killings and its aftermath of more riots elsewhere totally altered the political perspectives of the Congress and the Labour Government. Rioting had spread, from Calcutta to Noakhali in East Bengal, then to Bihar and from there to Punjab. In Sind, it was feared that if riots started and spread to rural areas the small Hindu minority would be exterminated. To the government, it now became unavoidable that the partition of India would have to form part of the withdrawal plan of the British, with the grant of dominion status to the two successor states.

The Attlee government was also convinced that this very complex and demanding task could not be discharged by Wavell. He was now found wanting in political sagacity and finesse in coping with the crisis that had taken a terrible law and order turn and was getting out of hand. There was little indication that Wavell had as yet truly grasped the full significance of the Attlee government's resolve to unwaveringly move towards just one objective, to transfer power to the Indians. Wavell had actually developed a strange and totally militarist plan of gradual withdrawal, first from the Hindu majority provinces and then stabilize the British power in the Muslim majority areas, mainly in north-western India, till a peaceful handover could be worked out.[11] Not only were there no takers for such ideas, the Labour government found them irksome. Clearly, Lord Wavell had come to the end of his resources. He now looked for a solution and wrote to the King: 'I failed, after many hours of conference, to get any definite policy from your Majesty's Government.' The government had already decided on a new policy; moreover, 'in the Prime Minister's words, new policies called for a new man'.[12] His replacement, Lord Mountbatten, was much younger, more dynamic and willing to move forward with new ideas, greater diplomatic initiative and at a faster pace. The Labour government also wanted to quash a theory Jinnah had formulated, perhaps with the connivance of the English Mullahs around the Viceroy, that the British should just lay aside all such ideas as the Cabinet Mission was exploring and continue to rule India for the next 15–20 years with the support of the Muslims.[13]

Mountbatten had already succeeded in securing from the Prime Minister a firm date for quitting India, namely June

1948. His diplomatic skill then lay in achieving two quite remarkable results. One was to persuade the Congress and the League to close the chapter on the Cabinet Mission's proposals and all that had preceded them. Second, he evolved the idea of a clear choice to the Congress and League leaders that they both could have strong Centres and fashion their respective constitutions to fit with their political ideas on democracy and governance, and administer their respective countries accordingly. However, Pakistan would be formed only of the Muslim majority districts in the provinces of Bengal and Assam in the East and Punjab in the West.

The third result, on which the success of the main scheme depended crucially, was to determine the future of the princely states in a manner that was supportive of the idea of strong dominion-status countries as the successors to British India. British paramountcy would totally lapse on the date the two countries would be free, and the only course open to them, collectively or individually, was to accede to one or the other dominion on the basis of geographical contiguity or any other equally relevant consideration.

However, all this required that the corresponding level of authority needed for accomplishing the job should be entrusted to him, and he was duly empowered. According to Tara Chand: 'Thus armed, he did not merely negotiate and persuade as his predecessors the War Cabinet emissary Cripps and the Cabinet Mission had done but he negotiated, persuaded, decided and imposed his decisions.'[14] In fact, Attlee's historic statement of 20 February was based on the revised draft prepared by Lord Mountbatten: 'Lord Mountbatten not only approved the public terms of his appointment and the confidential directive he received but very largely drafted them. He almost literally "wrote his own ticket".'[15]

Mountbatten's critically important move towards the achievement of the British objectives was to change the tactics of withdrawal by antedating it. From orderly retreat it was altered to the doctrine of riddance; 'they realized what they were doing was not so much handing India her freedom but washing their hands off her; and once the mood of disillusion was upon them, they would listen to no voices which counselled calm reflection and deliberation.'[16] Scrapping his earlier plan because of strong objections raised by Nehru, Mountbatten asked V.P. Menon, his Reforms Commissioner, to prepare a fresh scheme which he did in hot haste. Mountbatten then showed it to Nehru and obtained his agreement in writing. Jinnah accepted it verbally.

The idea of dominion status formed the firm feature of the new draft plan and the possibility of the balkanization of India was eclipsed. The Indian Independence Bill, 1947 fixed the new date of transfer of power as 15 August 1947. By this time, the exasperating experience of the Interim Government, working with the League's ministers, determined to obstruct its normal functioning which resulted in the demand for their resignation, had convinced everyone that a common Indian Centre would never work; it was better to accept the partition as the lesser evil. However, its announcement on 3 June greatly disturbed the people in the provinces which would be partitioned.

Raging riots followed and great killings in Punjab occurred on both sides. The civil services and the armed forces now divided between the two states failed to quell the riots. Consequently, horrible scenes of bestiality and plunder were witnessed; perhaps 100,000 young women were abducted, looting and rape were inflicted on the fleeing people, and about ten million people on each side had to migrate and somehow cross the border to a feeling of safety.[17] They faced extermination by death or exile. This was the price paid for the tactics of granting independence in great haste, without any preparation or advance warning on the scale of tragedy that might be enacted. It is obvious that the principal actors at the time had lost control over the grim chain causation of riots, arson and killings and the uprooting of communities which accompanied the partition of India, but it is in this tragic way that the British chapter in India closed.

The Constituent Assembly, based on the theory of adult franchise with indirect elections, was created by the Cabinet Mission as a political decision outside the framework of the Government of India Act, 1935. Based on the 1941 census for British India, it was decided that members to the assembly would be elected in the ratio of roughly one for one million by the provincial assemblies acting as electoral bodies. The number of representatives allotted to each province was proportional to its population, this being the nearest substitute to adult suffrage. Subsequently, the number of seats to the main communities in each province was allocated in proportion to the population. At this stage, the principle of separate electorates was introduced and members of the three communities viz. general, Muslim and Sikh would vote separately to elect their representatives. This made a total of 292 for British India. Four seats were added for the Chief Commissioner's Provinces and British Baluchistan. The maximum for Indian states was given as not exceeding 93, though the method of selection was not specified. So an appropriate procedure through consultations with the rulers would have to be devised.

By the end of July 1946, elections to the Constituent Assembly in respect of 296 seats were completed. However, it could not be convened partly because the main proposals of the Cabinet Mission were embroiled in a far reaching political controversy. This led the League to reject them and decide to struggle for Pakistan by recourse to direct action. Also, for similar reasons, the formation of an Interim Government was postponed. In the rapidly changing scenario it was not clear to any one whether the Muslim League would join the Constituent Assembly, and if it didn't, could the Constituent Assembly still proceed with its work and frame a constitution? The Congress meanwhile had decided to join the Interim Government on the understanding that the 1919 Act notwithstanding, the cabinet would function as a responsible government without the Viceroy exercising his discretion or veto power. It also decided to get the Constituent

Assembly functioning, as it would mark the fulfilment of a demand it had made for over a decade.

In the matter of convening the Assembly and the procedure to be followed in the conduct of its business, several controversies arose. Nehru, having formed the government on 2 September 1946, insisted on having his say on the important principle that the Constituent Assembly must assert its political autonomy and should not function as a creature of the British cabinet. Eventually, rather reluctantly, the Viceroy issued invitations to convene the Assembly. Jinnah described it as, 'one more blunder of a very grave and serious character' and advised the League representatives not to participate in its work. The assembly met on 9 December without the League's members or any representatives from the princely states. The Viceroy also wanted to appoint the provisional Chairman but did not insist on it and agreed to the procedure of the oldest member being elected as the Chairman. Dr Sachidananda Sinha being the oldest parliamentarian in India was elected as temporary Chairman and delivered a fine address.[18]

Two days later, Rajendra Prasad was elected as the President of the Assembly. In his reply to the felicitations Prasad made the important observation:

> This Constituent Assembly has come into being with a number of limitations, many of which we will have to bear in mind as we proceed. But, it must also be borne in mind that the Assembly is a sovereign body and is fully competent to conduct its proceedings in the manner it chooses to follow. No outside power can meddle with its proceedings. I also believe that it is competent to break the limitations attached to it at its birth. It should be our effort to get free of these limitations and frame a constitution which will assure all men and women of this country, no matter of what religion, province or shade of opinion that their rights are fully respected.[19]

Two days later, on 13 December, a resolution on the aims and objects was moved by Nehru which declared the Assembly's 'firm and solemn resolve to proclaim India as an

Independent Sovereign Republic and to draw up for her future governance a constitution'.[20] Dr M.R. Jayakar, moving an amendment, said that the resolution lays down the fundamentals of the constitution, such as, a Republic; a Union; present boundaries; the status of provincial authorities; residuary powers; minority rights; fundamental rights, most of which did not fit in with the Cabinet Mission's statement of 16 May. Therefore, further consideration of the resolution should be postponed. The amendment was withdrawn and it was decided that the resolution would be taken up again on 20 January when the Assembly would meet after the adjournment.

The resolution was subsequently adopted on 22 January, all members standing. Two hundred and ten members attended—155 Hindus, thirty Scheduled Caste representatives, five Sikhs, six Indian Christians, five representatives of backward tribes, three Anglo–Indians, three Parsis and four Muslims. The Muslim League's representatives were absent. According to the League, the Assembly was a 'rump' and the resolution was 'illegal, ultra vires and not competent of the Constituent Assembly to adopt'. It should be dissolved forthwith.[21]

The Assembly met again on 27 April for five days and on 14 July 1947 when the Indian Independence Bill was already being considered by Parliament. This time, the League's representatives of the forthcoming Indian Dominion also took their seats. The representatives of the princely states, excepting Jammu and Kashmir and Hyderabad, attended as full members. At the same time, members of the divided provinces of Bengal and Punjab legislatures ceased to be members and the Indian parts of the two legislatures had to re-elect their representatives. The Indian Independence Act, 1947 was passed on 15 July by the House of Commons and the following day by the House of Lords. It received Royal Assent on 18 July. It fixed 15 August as the day when full transfer of power would be effected in the two dominions and British paramountcy over the princely states would lapse. The Constituent Assembly then met on 14 August, as reborn, fully sovereign—all fetters having fallen – able to frame a constitution for independent India afresh, as if the Cabinet Mission's proposals never existed.

The Interim Government was reconstituted as the constitutional Government of free India with Nehru appointed as Prime Minister. Lord Mountbatten continued as India's Governor General, as provided in the Indian Independence Act, but without any discretionary power as the head of the state. The Central Legislative Assembly and the Council of State ceased to exist on 14 August. Hereafter, the Constituent Assembly would have a dual function: constituent as well as legislative. The sanction of the Governor General before a bill could be moved in the legislature was no longer required and the legality of any legislative measure being repugnant to the Imperial law ceased to have any meaning or force. At the same time, till the new constitution came into existence, the Government of India Act, 1935 was amended and adapted to serve independent India. This was facilitated by the India (Provisional Constitution) Order 1947.

The Constituent Assembly worked tirelessly on framing the new constitution. Perhaps, about 75 per cent of the Indian Constitution is formed of the provisions of the 1935 Act, but it also incorporates important features from other countries. The chapter on Fundamental Rights is inspired by the US Constitution; the one on Directive Principles is taken from that of Eire. The federal form is borrowed from the Canadian Constitution, while the principle of responsible government is from the British system. The Assembly was greatly helped in its work by the expertise of the Constitutional Adviser, Sir B.N. Rau who prepared the draft Constitution for the consideration of the Drafting Committee. The latter worked on it further, and expanded it considerably. This was diligently read and amended by alert members in the Assembly, and as a result the size of the proposed Constitution grew. Thus, what was originally planned as comprising 243 Articles and 13 Schedules, became in the end a Constitution of 395 Articles and 8 Schedules. It was formally adopted on 26 November 1949 when it was signed by the President of the Assembly.[22]

On the princely states, the problem the Assembly faced was a simple one. They should sign the instrument of accession or, prior to this, send representatives in an agreed manner to take part in its proceedings. The Resolution on Aims and Objects had described the Union of India as comprising the territories of British India 'and such other parts of India as are outside British India and the States as well as such other territories as are willing to be constituted into the Independent Sovereign India', and it would be a Republic. This could create difficulties with the rulers who wished to preserve their titles and privileges, yet wanted to accede to India. Nehru said: 'I do not wish, and I imagine this Constituent Assembly will not like, to impose anything on the States against their will. If the people of a particular State desire to have a certain form of administration, even though it might be monarchical, it is open to them to have it.' However, there must be complete freedom and a responsible government in the states that wish to retain the monarchy in some form.[23]

For the British, the problems were already resolved by the Cabinet Mission, so that, 'paramountcy can neither be retained by the British Crown nor transferred to the new Government'. The relationship between the rulers and the British Crown would cease. This meant that the states would become wholly independent and they would have to negotiate their way into the Union.[24] Accordingly, several princes toyed with the idea of gaining sovereignty in some form, while the larger states even dreamt of becoming independent in every respect. Some of them thought that if the Muslim League joined the Assembly, the states with 93 representatives would hold the balance of power. However, this possibility soon faded. Could there be a confederation of states called 'Rajasthan'? The idea failed to take off. Instead, a number of rulers welcomed a closer association with the new Indian dominion because they believed that was what their subjects wanted and because they believed that, with the Congress, a unified India would be strong and prosperous.[25]

Mountbatten, though tied up with the principal task of securing the agreement of the Congress and the League to the idea of partition, missed no opportunity to send the signal that the British would do nothing to promote the balkanization of India and confer dominion status on any larger state which desired it. Finally, the Indian Independence Bill provided on the subject in S-7 (D) as reproduced below:

> The suzerainty of His Majesty over the Indian States lapses, and with it, all treaties and agreements in force at the date of the passing of this Act between His Majesty and the rulers of Indian States, all functions exercisable by His Majesty at that date with respect to Indian States or the rulers thereof, and all powers, rights, authority or jurisdiction exercisable by His Majesty at that date in or in relation to Indian States by treaty, grant, usage, sufferance or otherwise.[26]

This helped matters but, for Mountbatten and V.P. Menon, what worked most was the urgency accorded to the goal of securing a basket as full of apples as possible for Sardar Patel before 15 August, so that the remaining problem would be so scaled down as to be politically manageable. The states acceded only in respect of three subjects, namely defence, foreign affairs and communications, retaining their sovereignty over the entire internal administration as hitherto. The pace at which work was done deserves to be noted.

According to Hodson, the drafting of standstill agreements covering all non-acceded matters and a standard Instrument of Accession was completed between 26 and 31 July. The latter took three forms; for 140 states the accession would be for three subjects only and without any financial liability. The terms were borrowed from the 1935 Act.

> For about seventy states in Kathiawar, Central India and the Simla Hills which had never exercised full powers, the standard Instrument of Accession was such as to restrict their future power to those they already possessed. Finally, for over 300 estates and talukas in Kathiawar and Gujarat, which were not in any proper sense 'states' though ranking as such and being no part of British India, an Instrument was devised on the lines of the common accession form but reserving all residuary powers and jurisdiction to the Central Government.[27]

According to the signed documents the ruler was at liberty to accept or reject the new Constitution or enter into negotiations on matters pertaining to it. Barring the three states of Jammu and Kashmir, Hyderabad and Junagadh, all the states signed the documents before 15 August. The legal basis for executing the Instrument of Accession was the Government of India Act, 1935 which had been amended to provide for Accession as well as supplementary instruments of accession, at later dates.[28]

In respect of the three states which had not acceded, deeper political problems cropped up. Junagadh had actually acceded to Pakistan which was annulled later. It was followed by a referendum in February 1948 which went in favour of India. However, Pakistan never acknowledged it and continued to treat Junagadh as Pakistan's territory. In Hyderabad, police action had to be taken to put an end to the absurd situation created by the scheming Nizam and the terrible threat of communal disaster which the Muslim private armed force of the Razakars had posed and which was determined to preserve a Muslim state in the south as a political ally of Pakistan. This was also Jinnah's design. The government under the guidance of Mountbatten gave as much time as the Nizam had sought, but it was used primarily to obstruct any settlement that was consistent with the policy of accession. It was duly followed by a standstill agreement but that was of no avail. So, in September 1948, troops moved in and in about one week the Nizam's intransigence was overcome.

In Jammu and Kashmir the problem lay in the Maharaja's indecision, allowing himself to be misguided by false notions of independence all of which were shattered by the invasion of Muslim tribesmen of the Frontier, which was later backed by Pakistani troops. India was asked for military help and this was promptly provided after the Maharaja signed the papers. In all three cases, Pakistan emerged as the principal adversary, more or less continuing the communal civil war in different forms to weaken and hurt India's interests. These examples pointed to the horrendous consequences which would have been upon India if most of the rulers had not seen reason and delayed the accession beyond 15 August.[29]

Accession done and the standstill agreements signed, the first problem was to determine, how the states would be represented in the reborn Constituent Assembly. It was no longer fettered by any previous legislation, in the sense that all the extant Acts could be amended by the same Assembly exercising its legislative function. The second problem was to decide in whose name would they speak: the rulers, as the autocratic sovereigns of their states, or the people. In B. Shiva Rao's words:

> To start with, the position was that these states would accede to the Union of India through suitable Instruments; and their internal constitutions were not to be part of the business of the Constituent Assembly. All this changed with remarkable rapidity and the position as it finally emerged was that the States would occupy the same position as the other units of the new Union of India; and the new Constitution would also provide for their internal constitutions. The fundamental rights provided in the Constitution would also extend to them; so would adult franchise. And the same type of democratic institutions as were being set up in the Provinces of India would also be set up in the Indian States. The Constitution had, therefore, to be enlarged to provide for these radical developments.[30]

When the Constitution was almost ready for adoption, Sardar Vallabhbhai Patel told the Assembly that, unlike the 1935 Act, the new Constitution was 'not an alliance between democracies and dynasties, but a real union of the Indian people, built on the basic concept of the sovereignty of the people'.[31]

Even while the Assembly was still discussing the draft provisions, important political developments were taking place. The stage was prepared by amending the 1935 Act to insert a new Section 290-A, which transferred the authority to the Governor-General, 'to direct that the state or group of states should be administered in all respects as if it was Chief Commissioner's Province, or formed part of a Governor's or a Chief Commissioner's Province'. By another Section 290-B, the Governor General was empowered to treat for administrative purposes any area of an acceding state as if they formed part of the absorbing provinces.[32]

Thereafter, merger and integration progressed without let or hindrance. It began on 1 January 1948 and continued through 1949 and 1950. By the end of 1949, the number of such Unions of States was only six. In due course, financial matters were settled in accordance with the principle that the financial relations between the states and the Centre would be conducted along the same lines as between the provinces and the Centre with adequate provisions made for the period of transition. Thereupon, agreements between the Government of India and the states were signed and executed.[33] It may be noted that constitution making bodies did function in three states. Ultimately, only Jammu and Kashmir produced a distinct constitution to conduct the internal administration of the state. All the remaining states followed the procedure of issuing proclamations adopting the Constitution of India as applicable to them.[34]

By the end of 1949, independent India had accomplished the most difficult and complicated task of integrating the princely states with the rest of the country. National leaders pointed out that though partitioned, India was never as united as it had become. They had also successfully completed the arduous task of writing a constitution based an universal adult franchise and parliamentary democracy together with a charter of fundamental rights and directive principles to protect citizens' freedoms and provide guidance to the state in the discharge of its duties respectively.

India chose to be a republic; it shed the dominion status, yet found an eminently reasonable formula to retain membership in the British Commonwealth of Nations and acknowledge the Crown as its head. As each milestone was crossed, India was applauded and the government's popularity soared in spite of being in the midst of much distress, gathering economic crisis and food shortages. The people breathed easy as the worst of the communal nightmare was over and the refugees looked to the government and public support as plans for rehabilitation were unfolded and implemented.

Mahatma Gandhi's assassination by a lone assassin on 30 January 1948 was a devastating shock to the government and the people alike. Though communal riots had ended with the forced transfer of population from West and East Punjab respectively, people were angry and a section of Hindu society was unreconciled to the idea that the partition of the country was unavoidable and had become inevitable. More anger piled up as the sordid, beastly tales of barbaric conduct, mainly in north-west Pakistan, reached people. The undercurrent of a violent mood could be detected in the country. Moreover, India was at war with Pakistan on the Kashmir territory, though Gandhi talked about peace and brotherhood as if the deep cleavage caused by communal wars and the partition was merely a passing phase.

Gandhi stood very tall in the eyes of the people and was adored as a Mahatma; he spoke the truth and what he said must be accepted as true. Yet, his actions were inscrutable. He had opposed partition, and people in the far flung areas of West Punjab believed him and had imagined that in view of Gandhi's firm stand no harm would come to them. However in the face of tide of times, the Congress leaders' great craving for office, coupled with the charisma and drive of Mountbatten and the utter futility of the Interim Government, the demonstrated power and savagery of the two nation theory impacted everyone and Gandhi had given in and accepted the vivisection of India as the price for freedom. Otherwise the British would balkanize the country and leave, not later than June 1948. The choice was between partition with dominion status or something unimaginably worse. Gandhi accepted the former and asked the Congressmen and his followers to do the same. In fact, only after it was known that the super leader Gandhi had accepted partition, did the league leader, Liaquat Ali Khan, second to Jinnah, believe that Pakistan would soon be a reality. Thereafter, Gandhi speedily left Delhi and withdrew from the political scene.

Gandhi knew that the historic task of ending British rule was accomplished and what remained for him to do was to uphold the moral voice of truth and non-violence and serve humanity, especially the weak and downtrodden in India as much as he could do. Already by 1946, he knew there was little that he could do to influence the course of events. The Cabinet Mission's talks had collapsed and Wavell had endeavoured to install an Interim Government and convene the Constituent Assembly, facing the baffling prospect of accepting Congress' cooperation and rejection and mass action-based revolt from the trusted ally, the Muslim League. Politics in India was gathering pace on a momentum of its own, pushing leaders to the sidelines.

A saintly political leader like Gandhi felt that he was no longer in control, was actually out of step and perhaps no longer needed in a leadership role, while the suffering people of Calcutta and East Bengal needed him more. He heard his inner voice directing him to go to them and this is what he did. Truly, balm in hand, he was a Mahatma with the people who were terribly distraught and desperately in need of moral support. During the partition, Gandhi's presence greatly helped maintain peace, general tranquillity, even harmony among the Hindus and the Muslims. Riots in the east were speedily curbed by the police and the armed forces.

He was summoned to Delhi on a peace mission, though, while in Delhi there were several things he did. Among his most notable accomplishments should be included the setting up of a national government, following Independence, with several non-Congress ministers. Gandhi knew that Nehru and Sardar Patel did not get along well and often treaded on each other's toes, or so the two had felt and complained to him. In fact, in January, Sardar Patel was ready with his resignation because Nehru had threatened that, if Sardar Patel stayed in office, he would resign. Gandhi would not allow either of them to quit office and leave the government in disarray. He mediated and both the leaders heard him say in clear words, 'No'. And they agreed to divide their responsibilities in a more rational manner.

Nehru was undoubtedly the Prime Minister, but he could not interfere in Sardar Patel's sphere of work. The latter was doing a job for the country and he alone had the ability, stamina and drive to see it through to the end. Nehru was not cut out for such an arduous task. Gandhi's mantle fell on Nehru, but Patel was equally indispensable. Gandhi went on a fast for about 17 days before his end came, mainly to end Hindu–Muslim enmity by this act of penance. However, an additional goal he wanted to accomplish was to exert moral influence on the feuding leaders to compose their differences and place the interests of the country and its people above their hurt egos and pride. How inscrutable was Gandhi was shown by the fact that though Nehru met him an hour before the announcement on the previous evening that he would go on a fast, but without fathoming his masters' mind.[35]

Economy in Crisis, Food Scarcity, Resettlement of Refugees

Comparing the impact of the Second World War on the Indian economy with the First, Rothermund finds that there were both common and uncommon elements. As during 1914–18, in the period 1939–45,

> prices rose, industrial equipment was utilized to full capacity, capitalists made enormous profits and the gap between the rich and the poor widened. This time, however, there was no spurt of economic growth. The First World War had followed a period of worldwide economic expansion, in which India had shared to a modest extent. Industrial capacities installed before the war, were then fully utilized, including India's novel steel plant. The Second World War, however, followed a prolonged depression from which India had suffered more than the industrial nations of the West. In this period, hardly any new equipment had been installed and the renewal of outdated machinery had been postponed. The utilization of installed capacity soon reached its limits and thus prices increased as wartime demand grew. Moreover, Great Britain claimed a much greater share of Indian production in the course of this war than in the previous one.[36]

The requirements of the allies were almost as large as those of the Government of India. Acute shortages developed and there was no way excess liquidity in the economic system could be absorbed against the limited supplies of goods and services.

The wartime inflation continued on the termination of war partly because the changeover from wartime shortages and controls to peacetime normal conditions took time, but also for the reason that the cheap money policy was continued in the apprehension that soon there would be a glut and a depression might follow. Consequently, the kind of inflation India had, as deficit induced and fuelled by excess money, continued during 1946 and 1947. The Reserve Bank of India's (RBI) official view was that the economic policy could not be shaped properly partly due to politically unsettled conditions and partly by confused thinking.

> In India, mainly because of political uncertainties relating to the transfer of power, the course of the economy was far from smooth. On the whole, economic problems received less than due attention, and growth during the post-war years was insignificant; indeed, industrial production, an important segment, received a setback. There was even some confusion

> in authoritative quarters in the analysis of the economic situation and in policy prescriptions. In the beginning, although there was concern regarding the prolongation of inflationary pressures, the view prevailed for a while that a depression was likely soon after the war as a result of the abrupt contraction of public expenditure; it is worth noting that a similar view was widely held in the developed countries abroad.[37]

The only attempt to check excess liquidity was by way of demonetization of high denomination notes early in 1946. However, in view of continued budgetary deficits and increased private spending, stimulated by withdrawal of controls, inflation proceeded apace and prices rose faster. The *RBI History* has this to say:

> There was also a gradual retreat from the abnormal cheap money conditions of the immediate post-war period. Also, in the beginning, there was much confusion and indecision in regard to physical controls. This resulted in too rapid a swing in the direction of decontrol; but when this resulted in a sudden and serious rise in prices, there was a return, albeit reluctant, to controls, the desire to do away with restrictions ultimately being affirmed at the same time.[38]

On its part, the Bank was consistently opposed to cheap money policy. It counselled caution in the matter of dismantling of controls. In 1945–6, it resisted the suggestion from the government to lower the bank rate. Gradually, by 1949–50, the monetary situation was brought to normalcy, mainly due to absorption of excess money in the form of higher prices but also aided by the contractionist effect of the balance of payments deficits and finally the devaluation of the rupee by 30.5 per cent, which followed the devaluation of sterling in September 1949.

In retrospect, it is evident that over the decade, 1939–40 to 1949–50, the Indian economy showed no significant growth in overall terms. The diversification of industrial output achieved under the war stimulus was mostly counter-balanced by the deterioration in capital stock and the inability to acquire capital goods for replacement and expansion of capacity. Long-term data suggest that the period, 1940–4, was worse than that of any comparable period in the half-century. At 1938–9 prices, per capita output in the primary sector was Rs. 29, the lowest recorded. During 1935–9, it was already low at Rs. 30, while by comparison, during 1915–19, indeed throughout the 15-year period ending in 1924, a relatively high level of output at Rs. 34 was observed. Thereafter, a slow and steady declining trend set in, which could not be reversed till several decades of development, following Independence.

By comparison, both secondary and tertiary sectors performed better, though surprisingly, their levels of per capita output were well below the primary sector. In the secondary sector the past was bleaker and the series show a slow climb from a very low level of Rs. 7 during 1900–9 to Rs. 10 in the period 1930–44, followed by some improvement in 1945–9 and a setback to Rs. 10 in the next decade. The tertiary sector shows steady growth, practically without any break, up to 1929, a decline in the following decade and resumption of a rising trend thereafter. The economic series create the unmistakable impression that the population of India which started growing from 1921 onwards, practically taking no notice of the great depression and the war inflation, had a depressing effect on the standard of living of people as depicted by the per capita figures. The long period of economic stagnation, especially of non-advance in agricultural productivity, worsened the effect of demographic growth. The change in the base year to 1948–9 raises the output levels by the price level factor and placed it above 1938–39, but the pattern of per capita series does not change. Nirmal Kumar Chandra, who constructed the series, also produced a set at 1960–1 prices, but it looks somewhat artificial owing to changes that had occurred in the economic structure. Yet, if comparisons can still be made, it would appear that in 1945–9 the per capita output in the primary sector was the lowest at Rs. 136, compared to Rs. 165 in the decade 1910–19.[39]

The sterling balances that had accumulated in London could not be freely used, in part because the British economy, saddled in debt and repayment obligations to the US, was struggling to get back on its feet, and also due to the chronic shortage of dollars as the chief hard currency in the sterling area, sterling not being freely convertible. Moreover, the immediate problem in India was to somehow augment the availability of a wide range of consumer goods to restrain prices by imports as well as by increased production. Decontrols were expected to contribute substantially towards this objective; but the policies failed because the pent up demand asserted itself before industry could re-gear to raise production. This provided a great psychological boost to the speculators who intervened in the market, hoarding goods in short supply and earning huge profits. The shift in income distribution which the war economy and post-war inflation brought about resulted in accruals of large cash balances that waited for a favourable opportunity for release. The decontrol measures which were affected in the first year after the termination of the war came as a golden opportunity to traders and speculators. India needed to import, but was unable to do so more freely either against current export earning or the sterling balances till the industrial capacity in the West revived and got reoriented to meet market-related demand for goods. Consequently, though the Indian market was ready to absorb a wide range of capital goods, intermediate goods and raw materials to refurnish the industry and consumer goods to soak up excess demand in the economy and, ironically, also had the money, yet it just could not do much about it. India had to wait for its turn and this didn't happen till about 1950–1.

The British aim in the short-run was that India should earn dollars by restricting imports and contribute to the Empire Dollar Pool and the government had to restrict imports from the US and several other countries, principally Canada and Australia. The British Raj had doubtless ceased, but the constraints of the British economy effectively impinged on India's as well. So close was India's dependence on the UK, not only in broad trading relations but also in the networks of trading and manufacturing houses, reinforced by acquired habits of connectedness, that not much effort was made to develop alternative channels of supply and credit.

On sterling balances, there was much comment and criticism. A large part of the criticism in India along nationalist lines was triggered by the scarcely unfounded fears that a powerful section of British opinion was in favour of devising some method for scaling them down. This was on the flimsy grounds that the balances represented the scale of the war effort made by the Allies. The Indian contribution had been insufficient towards this and the gap between the proper share and the actual ought to be quantitatively estimated and the debt the British owed India should be reduced by this amount. This was buttressed by the still flimsier argument that the stores purchased by the Allies were at inflated prices and now a corrective factor should be applied to achieve the desired end. In the same class of misapplied facts and misconstrued reasoning, was the tricky argument that the gold sales of Rs. 500 million made by the Allies in India should be set off against India's contribution to the Dollar Pool. The British conservative opinion harped on the doctrine that however distressing conditions may be in India, it should nevertheless still stretch its resources as earlier and help bail out Britain's war-battered economy. After all, a draw on sterling balances would be a draft on real resources and a consequent claim on the British economy.

The RBI carried out detailed studies on the subject. The study made by J.V. Joshi, the bank's Economic Adviser, has been particularly referred to in the official history, so the salient points made by him may be recapitulated.[40] First, the total sterling balance of about £1,515 million which had accrued by the end of March 1945 was made of two parts. 'The credits received from the Secretary of State accounted for £969 million, the rest being the result of regular commercial transactions between the two countries.' On the issue of inflated prices, Joshi pointed out that an independent investigation had been carried out and published and it was 'satisfied that fair prices had on the whole, been secured for war stores and food bought by the UK in India'. In the event of Britain defaulting on her obligations, 'the sterling balances amounting to something over £1,000 million could be realized completely,' he said, 'by offsetting an amount of about £250 million against a lump sum payment to the British Government to cover the Indian Government's liability for the pension and provident monies of the British personnel and by the legal acquisition of British private investments in India estimated at £900–1,000 million.' This would have caused a sharp break in the relationship between the two countries. It could also damage Britain's image as a debtor country and so it was avoided. Moreover, India would have gained nothing if Britain had actually defaulted.

Eventually, a solution was arrived at in the form of temporary agreements, for six months at a time, to release a small amount of the balance to make payment in hard currencies. By 1948, the balances had already declined partly due to heavy imports of food and partly by capital transfers made by British residents in India who sold their businesses and repatriated the capital. The long-term settlement provided for: (i) release of £80 million over a period of three years, of which £15 million could be spent in dollars and other hard currencies over one year; (ii) purchase of annuities from the British government for the payment of pensions at a cost of £168 million; (iv) leaving a balance of £800 million to be settled subsequently.[41]

Industry needed to replace war-weary machines. In the case of the cotton textile industry, the need was strongly felt and in some ways the mills were better placed at the end of the war than before it. Actually, before the war quite a few mills did not have the money to renovate or buy new machines, so they continued to use antiquated machinery. Their fortunes changed for the better during the war and even shaky mills did well. In 1944, the industry sought out producers in the US and UK which could supply textile machinery but drew a blank. It became clear that the mills would have to wait for a return to normalcy before they could import new equipment. By 1948, prices soared and the mills learnt to their disappointment that the new textile machines were excessively priced. To the Tariff Board in 1948 which enquired into the economics of the industry, the Bombay Mill Owners Association reported that the prices of machinery were at four times the immediate pre-war levels and at about ten times those of 1932. The mills did not have the money needed for the purpose. Moreover, the delivery period stretched over several years. In fact machinery prices had shot up only partly due to cost inflation. There was also a heavy demand for textile machines from several countries which were keen on setting up the textile industry in the post-war period.

Nonetheless, the mills which had the reserves went in for modernization and by 1950, in the industry as a whole, Rs. 66 crores were invested in fixed capital and Rs. 137 crores in working capital, a total of Rs. 203 crores. Yet in the Bombay mills in 1950, around 90 per cent of the machinery was more than 25 years old. They were poorly maintained because the mills had difficulty acquiring spare parts. Such mills were in a rundown state. The industry had acquired a dualistic character. It had a modernized segment which could export its products on competitive terms and a stagnant one which lacked the means to do so but continued to function because of excess demand for cloth in the country and an overall insufficiency of production.

Even as the cotton textile industry coped with chronic problems of technological obsolescence and sub-standard mills, the policy environment worsened. In May 1946, the Post-war Planning Committee (Textiles) reported that it would be necessary to ensure increased supplies of yarn to the handloom weavers and other consumers and for this it would be necessary to leave at least 25 per cent of new spindles installed to be left uncovered by looms. Provinces may reserve a larger spindlage for this purpose. This was followed up in Madras where T. Prakasam, the new premier of the Congress government, announced in October 1946 that the government would be launching a khadi programme and to ensure its success it was decided not to allow any new cotton textile mill to be set up in the province, nor would the existing mills be allowed to expand capacity. The central government was to be asked to cancel any allotment of spindles and looms in the province under the post-war plans of development. Soon, the interests of handloom weavers found a political voice and to safeguard their livelihood the mills' needs had to be sacrificed.

Exchange controls devised during the war were placed on a permanent footing partly on the realization that foreign exchange scarcity was likely to be of a long-term nature and also as part of the government's determination to acquire greater control over the economy. The Foreign Exchange Control Act, 1947 was passed to check the import of non-essential goods and as complementary to the agreements with the UK on the release of sterling balances. Moreover, as a member of the International Monetary Fund (IMF), India was committed to maintain stability in the external value of the rupee. This was followed by quantitative licensing of imports which allowed for free imports of food, capital goods and certain essential raw materials and consumer goods, but also for the prohibition on import of luxury goods.

Controls of this nature had a bearing on foreign capital already invested in India, especially the scope for repatriation of capital and dividends and the policy towards further investment in Indian ventures. In April 1949, the government announced that remittance of profits would be freely permitted; if any foreign company was acquired by the government, remittance of proceeds would be allowed and reasonable facilities for the purpose provided; that there would continue to be considerable scope for further British investments in India.

In September 1949, since the overvalued sterling was already devalued, India had to follow suit and the rupee was devalued. India's trade, both exports and imports, was largely with sterling area countries and, due to persistent inflation, the domestic price level was already high, so devaluation was the only method available to preserve its competitive position. Moreover, neither smaller nor larger measure of devaluation would have served any purpose; the best course was to maintain parity in the sterling area countries while correcting for overvaluation against the dollar. By this act, India repeated what it had done when Britain went off the gold standard. The new Government of India opted to reaffirm dependence on the UK and the habit of preserving the connectedness of the Indian economy with the British was reasserted. Simultaneous devaluation of the Indian rupee with the sterling was not strictly required at that juncture, and a more self-confident government might have considered the option of waiting till the value of sterling balances rose in rupee terms. India would have gained by this.

In 1947–8, food shortages crippled government options. The government had strengthened the rationing system as the only way the urban population could be provided with essential supplies of food grains and sugar, among others. A shadow of famine stared at people. The harvests in 1945–6 and the following year were poor and aggravated the already climbing price level. The situation was made worse by the horrors of communal riots and forced migrations of people in north India. At Independence, India faced three sets of awesome problems: inflation, food scarcity and dislocation in production, transport and distribution systems, the last mainly due to the partition. To these were added the growing body of refugees from West and East Pakistan. Their numbers gradually added up to about nine million. A little more than half came in great waves of forced marches in horrible conditions from the West and needed immediate attention on a large scale. This resulted in considerable increase in budgetary deficits in successive years.

Tarlok Singh writes:

> During the four years that followed (1947–51), while there was a large element of trial and error in the public policies which were followed, in addition to resettling refugees, rehabilitation of rail transport and maintaining industrial peace, there were three constant preoccupations, to increase agricultural production, to expand industrial production and to control inflationary pressures.'[42]

Taken together the period, 1947–51 was marked by economic emergency and great stress on the government machinery. Under pressure of public opinion, the government at first relaxed food and cloth controls but, between November 1947 and July 1948, the WPI (1939=100) rose at an alarming rate, from 302 to 390, and the prices of cereals and textiles were much higher, so controls were enforced again. In 1949–50, with an improved harvest, the prices started to stabilize. The Prime Minister took a trip to the US in late 1949 to forge bilateral ties and to explain India's pressing need for wheat and other food grains, and the response was helpful. The food situation improved with the arrival of two million tonnes of wheat under a loan from the US. The partition made India's dependence on food imports a regular feature of economic management; this being the result of 82 per cent of the original population having to be supported by 69 per cent of rice production and 66 per cent of wheat production in the post-Independence period. The release of sterling balances aided in the fight against hunger and inflation and to tide over economic emergency.

Food was a major problem with the government ever since the Japanese occupation cut off Burma and the import of rice could not be arranged. In 1942, the government set up a department of food in the larger organization of agriculture. Its responsibilities were to import food grains and procure them within India to maintain a central reserve of supplies. In this year, the government decided to launch 'the grow more food campaign' as the only alternative to a bleak international situation. At the time of independence, the government lent renewed energy into the campaign since India faced shortages in both wheat and rice. The idea was to attain food self-sufficiency at an early date; the target date was set at March 1952. In 1949, India experienced great difficulty in importing cotton and raw jute from Pakistan. Pakistan had not devalued its currency simultaneously with the sterling, so the Indian rupee stood devalued against the Pakistani rupee and this caused much disruption in the established trade between the two countries. Consequently, the government found it necessary to add programmes of growing more cotton and jute to that of food in 1950.

During the war, food procurement was conducted under the Defence of India Rules. In 1945, the government gave orders under the rules, which a year later became the Essential Supplies (Temporary Powers) Act, 1946. At Independence, fairly tight control measures were in place and the government managed the problem of supplying food grains to deficit rural areas as well through a non-statutory or informal public distribution system. At Independence, the Centre took the responsibility of importing food grains on a state monopoly basis and allocating the supplies to the food deficit areas. The provinces maintained the rationing system or controlled distribution to their people, also made arrangements for local procurements. The system was reinforced by supplementary controls imposed on prices at wholesale and retail levels and food movement between districts. Six systems of procurement were in place. These were: intensive procurement, levy-cum-monopoly, levy only, monopoly purchase, levy on traders and open market purchases. Different provinces adopted the particular procurement system as suited their conditions.[43]

Sweeping Agrarian and Labour Agitations, More Laws

Part A: Agitations and Splits

The mass upheaval of this period, in addition to the political turmoil, also had a class character affecting peasantry, workers and white-collar employees. The anti-landlord agitations at the local level occurred during the 1930s and alleviation of peasants' economic conditions received priority in the legislative measures enacted by provincial governments. In 1945–6, the anti-feudal and anti-imperialism agitations became fused and were often led by the communists and left-wing Congress leaders at the district level. In an election rally, a prominent Congress leader in Bihar announced that within five days of coming to power the Congress would abolish the zamindari system. The announcement was devoid of realism. However, there could be no doubt that the agrarian crisis in the country was becoming acute. There were instances of forcible occupation of landlords' lands, and its reverse, the forcible harvesting of the standing crops in 1946, resulting in violent agrarian riots.[44] The Congress government in Bihar dealt with the situation by enacting the Bihar Maintenance of Public Order Act, 1947 which had stiff provisions to arrest the kisan leaders who were found to be leading the unrest. The progress of zamindari abolition with compensation took more time as it met with roadblocks of opposition and diversionary tactics in the Congress camp.

In UP, agrarian riots between the peasants and the zamindars became a common occurrence in 1946–7 and continued thereafter for several years. The Kisan Sabhas, though functioning since the mid-1930s, became active with the release of Congress workers from prison and a sharp shift in the political orientation of the Communist Party from a 'Peoples' War' and support to the colonial government, to one of active opposition and agitation and greater involvement in the agrarian conflicts on behalf of peasants and sharecroppers.

The presence of an outside leadership element connected to a political party emerged as a factor of crucial importance in mobilizing a particular village or group of villages against the identified zamindars around issues of concrete importance to the peasants. Open conflicts occurred with impurity, such as this one: 'A party of zamindars attacked the residents of village Hamirpur in district Sultanpur, destroying the crops and looting the houses. A few months after one person was killed and five others received injuries when a party of men headed by a zamindar attacked the peasants of village Kaima in the same district.'[45] Authors have cited similar instances of violent conflicts to show the intensity of agrarian disputes in UP, mostly over possession of land. The Congress election manifesto included the promise of abolition of intermediary rights, which formed the basis of the system of rent-collection-revenue-payment operated by the zamindars. In order to pacify the agitating peasants, the UP Assembly decided in August 1947 to abolish the zamindari system on payment of compensation, though the law to this effect was enacted four year later in 1951.

The two agrarian events that produced lasting political repercussions and have been described in considerable detail, are the Tebhaga movement in undivided Bengal in 1946 and the Telangana revolt of the tenants in the former princely state of Hyderabad, which too broke out in 1946 and continued for five years. The former did not survive the more powerful trauma of communal riots and the shift in affiliation of Muslim peasants towards the Muslim League, which smothered it. The Suhrawardy government, though apparently willing to enact a bill to meet the demands of the peasants to limit the share of landlords to one-third of the produce, with several provisions for various contingencies, instead chose to deal with the Kisan Sabha-led movement as a law and order problem and let loose police repression. This resulted in direct confrontations between the militant peasants, who insisted on forcibly securing their share of two-thirds of the harvested crops, and the armed police, followed by firing in several instances and arrests and externment orders being served on the leaders. The Bargardars Bill was allowed to lapse, though in a new form it was later enacted by the Congress government. The directing elements in the Tebhaga agitation were the communist cadre comprising mostly the recently indoctrinated middle class Hindu urban youths who had learnt Marxism while in jail and joined the Communist Party. In the face of police repression the Provincial Kisan Council admitted its failure to work out the 'forms of struggle'. So, to strengthen the volunteers, the Council decided to set up, 'Councils of Action', in villages to train volunteers. The hard question the local leaders faced but could not resolve was that, 'if the government succeeded in crushing the movement, there would be great demoralization among the peasants. The immediate question therefore was if and how to resist police repression. There was no directive on this question and the movement was allowed to drift.'[46] The Tebhaga agitation relied on cohesion among the peasants and the aborigine tribes settled in the area, but it was greatly weakened by the withdrawal of the Muslims' support, who increasingly turned to the Muslim League for guidance and gave up the struggle.

The Telangana revolt began as an agitation and culminated in an insurrection, made possible by the fact that several agrarian classes had effectively united under the leadership of the Communist Party towards a well-defined cause. In the first stage, the political cause was to agitate against the autocratic, feudal and oppressive regime of the Nizam of Hyderabad, which was relying ever more on the militant Islamic volunteer force of the Razakars to intimidate the poor peasants in the predominantly Hindu region of the state. The Razakars were supposed to aid the police, but in practice, they functioned on their own towards the realization of the goal of carving out an independent Muslim kingdom in the south. This rested on their confidence and organized strength to suppress the voice of the Hindu majority population of the state, which supported its merger with the Indian Union. The latter also sought greater scope for free expression of views and demanded an end to the minority terrorism of the Razakars.[47]

By conducting organizational work among the masses over a number of years, through the Kisan Sabha and other popular organizations, the Communist Party gained in membership and a large body of supporters, who helped in mobilizing wider sections of society, and they attended its rallies and meetings. The party mobilized people on the issues of forced labour, illegal exactions, evictions of small farmers on flimsy grounds as well as the Razakars' terrorism. Gradually, it took the form of organized resistance to the Nizam's rule. P. Sundarayya has recorded the events: 'The rule of the exploiters was coming to an end. Thousands of acres of land were confiscated and distributed and people's committees were being established. The Razakar armies were let loose on the people. People under the leadership of the Andhra Mahasabha and Communist Party began heroically resisting the Nizam's regime.'[48] It was an armed struggle with the Communist Party forming the backbone and receiving extensive support from a wide strata of the population, though mostly from the poorest peasants and landless labourers. The leading elements confiscated lands belonging to the landlords awaiting its redistribution, while the peasants benefited immediately either by not paying rent at all or much less than the demand; rural indebtedness was also either scaled down or cancelled entirely. 'The guerrilla squads moved like fish in water'.[49]

The second stage began when the Indian army moved in as a 'police action' in September 1948 and secured the surrender of the Nizam's forces in less than a week. Thereafter, the army units first rounded up and neutralized the Razakars, and this job done, started to work against the communists. The second stage was marked by large-scale withdrawal of public support for the guerrillas and their isolation from the politically articulate public opinion, which had strongly supported the 'police action' and wished to see an end to the insurrection. Considerable confusion then prevailed among the communist leaders, on what to do next, with one section clearly seeing no future for it. It was finally withdrawn in 1951, but only after the communists had suffered heavy losses.

The class conflict character of the exploding industrial

unrest as witnessed during 1945–7, was not unprecedented, since similar turmoil had occurred as recently as 1937–9, though its intensity was without a parallel. With the end of the war, a terrible situation confronted the workers. First, the war inflation showed no sign of abatement and the steady erosion of wages that had been going on during the last six years continued, while the employers showed no willingness to grant higher wages on mere pleadings and submission of demands by workers. Second, the pre-war threat of large-scale unemployment reappeared with the demobilization of troops and closure of war-related industries, occasioned by the total withdrawal of government orders without any alternative plan being put into operation for conversion of these industries to peacetime civilian uses. Third, the scarcity of essential goods had inexplicably become greater rather than less, and there was no way of knowing how long this painful condition would continue. Finally, the shortages of food grains and supplies of foodstuff generally, particularly in the cities, had become alarming.[50]

Workers took to strike action in a major way. In 1945, there were 820 industrial disputes involving 747,530 workers causing a loss of over 4 million man days. In 1946, the number of strikes rose to the unprecedented level of 1,629 involving close to 2 million workers and resulting in the huge loss of over 12.7 million man days. Most of the conflicts occurred in the cotton, silk and woollen mills, followed by engineering. Bombay led in the strike wave. In 1947, the situation worsened further. According to, G.K. Sharma,

> as soon as the Congress Party took over from the British Government, a fresh wave of strikes swept over the country. In September 1947, there was a general strike in 58 cotton mills in Bombay involving over one lakh of workers. Another important strike of cotton textile workers which took place in the Buckingham and Carnatic Mills, Madras lasted for over three months and involved a loss of over 12 lakh man-days. It was estimated that in 1947 the cotton mill industry alone accounted for 600 disputes involving about a lakh workers and resulting in time loss of about 71 lakh man-days.[51]

The Bombay government quickly created a Ministry of Labour and appointed an enquiry committee to report on industrial conditions. The committee found workers to be in an 'increasingly aggressive frame of mind' and among the employers a mindset of 'hostility, obstinate resistance, inflexible and unsympathetic attitude to the workers' most legitimate activities and grievances'. The popular governments mainly appealed to workers not to make the already grave scarcity of food, cloth and other necessities worse by going on strikes.[52]

The intense unrest was fuelled by economic causes but its spread and intensity is better explained by the renewal of political activity in the country and formation of Congress governments in most provinces. As in 1937–9, much was expected of them, and people were desperate in seeking redress for conditions that were not getting better. The strike wave was far reaching and included postal workers, railway employees, teachers in UP, municipal services, banks, printing presses, hotels, petty shops and the non-gazetted and clerical staff of the government. Solidarity strikes also took place for the first time in support of postal employees, though they had stayed away from the trade union movement. But ignoring this aspect, the AITUC gave a call for strike in support of their demands and it received a substantial response from the communist and socialist-led unions. In the same class may be placed the strike ballot conducted by the All India Railwaymen's Federation for a general strike in the entire railway system in support of their economic demands; and it received total endorsement. However, just a few days before the strike was to commence the government announced a package of concessions which included cash wages of 90 million rupees, and the strike call was withdrawn. The government announced the setting up of a Pay Commission with almost immediate effect for all government employees, and this helped in cooling tempers.

The communists had been expelled from Congress and a split in the union movement was unavoidable. Actually

AITUC's dominance had turned the labour movement hostile to the Congress governments. As the Congress leaders viewed it, they had been inexplicably hostile in 1937–9 too. Now the Gandhian trade unionists looking into the future saw little prospect of the communists allowing them to function within the AITUC and steer the labour movement away from conflict to a fair understanding of the many perils the country faced and towards moderation in pressing their demands. This was paradoxical because during 1946–7, the official line of the communist leadership, under P.C. Joshi, was one of moderation towards the Congress and specially its leftwing leader, Nehru. Apparently, this position still allowed for the class struggle of the workers to continue, so the rank and file of the Communist Party followed the traditional course of intensification of class struggle, to prepare the working class for revolutionary action against the state and the capitalist system. For the Congress, the parting of ways was now fast approaching.

In November 1946, the Congress labour front, the Hindustan Mazdur Sevak Sangh (HMSS), asked their labour leaders to affiliate with the AITUC. Though, without the TLA of Ahmedabad, which declined to do so, there was little prospect of the Congress-led unions acquiring a dominant voice in the AITUC. This policy was soon reversed and in May 1947, the HMSS convened a conference of Congressmen in Delhi for the purpose of floating a new national centre of trade unions. The leading voices at the conference were those of Gulzarilal Nanda, Sardar Patel and the Congress President, J.B. Kripalani. The fundamental difference between them and the AITUC was whether the trade union was an organ of class struggle and committed to bring about nationalization of industries as an essential step towards socialism, or could it work for class harmony and promote workers' interests through peaceful and constitutional methods, including the state-provided legal machinery for conciliation, adjudication and arbitration. From this ideological stance may be derived the union policy on strikes.

For the HMSS, it was important that the weapon of strike should be kept in abeyance till all the constitutional methods were exhausted. In his letter of invitation Nanda said,

> The stand taken by the Trade Union Congress in reference to the principle and procedure of arbitration in the settlement of industrial disputes has been strongly disapproved by many prominent trade unionists. It is felt that it will militate against the best and most vital interests of the country and jeopardize its peaceful progress on democratic lines if at this stage a central organization of labour is not formed in harmony with the ideas and resolutions of the Indian National Congress.[53]

At the conference, which was attended by over 200 labour leaders, it was decided to form the Indian National Trade Union Congress (INTUC). It grew rapidly and in a year or so became the most representative organization of Indian Labour.[54]

The political line Sardar Patel established in his presidential address was to confront the communists in not just the AITUC but elsewhere as well. He denounced the communists as a party having few scruples as regards the means to be adopted as long as they were helpful in discrediting the Congress and defeating its programme. Moreover, their opposition to the government was blind and they had,

> thrown all regard for national welfare to the winds. We are passing through one of the worst crisis that faces a nation at any time. With the prospect of independence and freedom, several new problems are arising and the old ones are gathering intensity. Forces of national disintegration, the princes and the industrialists are all suddenly awakened to the new situation and are getting busy hatching their own plans to gain domination and privileges. Added to this, is the economic crisis. Even under normal circumstances we would have taken a good few years to recover from the effects of the last war. Food, clothing and other essential articles are in short supply. The railways are badly worn out and are in urgent need of repairs and renewals. The Government are doing their utmost to effect

> the recovery as speedily as possible. At a time like this when every ounce of energy should be utilized in building up the national economy and raising the standard of living of the masses, we are indulging in an orgy of destruction. As though this by itself were not enough, earlier political parties and trade union leaders seem to be bent on weakening the supply position still further, by stopping or cutting down production, by encouraging strikes and go-slow tactics. The irresponsibility and recklessness of these people pass all understanding. Strikes are launched on all conceivable pretexts and in utter disregard of the workmen's own interest and well being ... The strike mongers, there are reasons to believe, are now turning their attention to railways and coal mines. Perhaps it would be well for them to bear in mind that their success in these new fields would be nothing less than a calamity for the whole nation.[55]

In the INTUC the Congress forged a powerful political arm to wean workers from the communist and socialist trade unionists towards a system of industrial relations that was broadly supportive of the government's industrial and labour policies. The Congress could not possibly allow the political doctrines of class war and violent revolution to seep into people's consciousness, or let them consider the prevailing crisis conditions as the endemic feature of a decadent system that was in any case doomed, rather than as a passing phase which could be overcome. The first step towards complete success was independence and further progress would depend on the degree of trust and cooperation between the national government and the leading organs of the masses. the INTUC was meant to play a vital role in this regard.

The communists on their part found their influence ebbing. This was only partly due to direct competition offered by the Congress and socialist leaders in labour, peasant and student organizations,

> but in addition, among the educated opinion leaders in urban centres particularly, support for the communists weakened due to their open advocacy of Pakistan, coupled with their latest demand that the British should transfer power to all the nationalities of India towards a loose confederation to be

> negotiated by their representatives in a constituent assembly. This position was totally hostile to Gandhi's opposition to vivisection of the country. It was also opposed to the Congress high command's willingness to accept the scheme of Pakistan on the basis of double partition along strictly communal lines. The CPI's political ideas had drifted so far from that of the Congress, coincidentally during the preceding six-seven years, that on the eve of independence the leading communist elements could not at all grasp the significance of history's great moment that was now within sight, indeed approaching at an accelerating pace. Hence for them the occasion of independence was a sham, a surrender of the Indian bourgeoisie represented by the Congress to the British imperialists, further that Nehru, Sardar Patel and all the rest were the lackeys of the British having compromised on India's true national interests for the sake of the mere formality of transfer of power.[56]

This political line was approved at the second congress of the CPI in March 1948 and arrogantly led by the new General Secretary, B.T. Ranadive. 'The new line generated tremendous enthusiasm among the communists, and in the months following the congress, the CPI went on an adventurist spree, it launched a series of strikes and tried to convert them into a general strike. Ranadive expected an "imminent revolution".'[57] He expected a textbook type of revolution led by the proletariat which in turn would ignite the peasantry culminating in the intertwining of two stages of revolution, as had happened in Yugoslavia under Tito's leadership, and finally to the dictatorship of the proletariat headed by the CPI.

Several strikes did take place in the wide strata of the trade unions' stronghold, where the influence of communist leaders was particularly strong, and in Bombay and Calcutta violence followed the strikes. Sardar Patel had already anticipated it and the government was ready with its response. In West Bengal the CPI was declared illegal, a number of communist leaders were arrested, the office of the AITUC was sealed, and many escaped by going underground. The Bombay government followed suit and arrested some of the top communist and AITUC leaders. Severe methods of repression were initiated by other provincial governments, which included taking recourse to the Public Safety Acts. The communists, however, continued to issue calls for strikes. 'A few of these strikes materialized but most of them fizzled out. The communists had to pay a very high price for their adventurism. The AITUC lay prostrate, and could hold its 24th Session (1954), only after an expiry of five years. Its membership also dwindled from nearly 700,000 in 1948 to 100,000 in 1951.'[58]

Soon after the CPI's Calcutta congress, the AITUC found that its ranks were deserted. The communists were determined to use trade unions as their mass organizations and had no place for moderate leaders like N.M. Joshi who held the post of General Secretary. First, the socialists left, then N.M. Joshi too resigned, and by the middle of 1948 the communists were in total control of the weakened organization. In 1949, other left parties, which had refused to toe the CPI line, set up a parallel organization called the United Trade Union Congress under the leadership of Mrinal Kanti Bose, a veteran trade unionist and a former president of the AITUC. The socialists left the AITUC in disgust; they had been already edged out of the Congress by the new rule Sardar Patel made that no Congressman could remain a member of another party, such as the Congress Socialist Party, and must choose one or the other. They formed another competing trade union centre, called the Hind Mazdoor Panchayat. Later, the Indian Federation of Labour which by now had become practically defunct merged with it to from the Hind Mazdoor Sabha (HMS) in December 1948.[59]

In a short period of two years four parallel trade union affiliating organizations came into existence to give their political voice to labour. All the four centres were connected to the political parties that had brought them into existence; they provided the affiliating unions the needed resources in leadership, cadre support and backing at the all-India level. Of the four, the INTUC was born from the Congress' womb and was led by Congressmen, the AITUC was captured by the communists and functioned as the CPI's mass organization, the HMS was openly tied to the Socialist Party and led by its leaders, while the UTUC was entirely independent of any single party, but it was also the smallest of the four.

Part B: Workers, Unions and Parties

There is no observable direct relationship between the growth of class consciousness in the industrial workers and development of unions in three decades for them to accept unions and demonstrate solidarity in a steady manner, because it alternated with withdrawal from the unions and reverting into passivity. Most of them learnt to identify unions with their leaders and the particular stream of political awareness with the politics of union leadership. For workers, class consciousness in the ideological sense was the undifferentiated aspect of the idioms and slogans with which leaders ordinarily expressed their commitment to the cause for which a union or a centre of unions stood. In practice, there remained a profound disconnection between the query, 'Why workers join unions?' and the ideology of their leaders. This flowed largely from the enormous disparity between the workers and the leaders in education, culture and the capacity to forge linkages. Accordingly, a deep one-sided dependence came into existence, or an implicit trust of the former in the latter became the common characteristic of organized workers. The dependence behaviour may be interpreted to mean that the leaders were not just there to lead, but were also accepted in the dependency role. The mutual acceptance of this role relationship functioned as a binding code, being the result of numerous struggles workers waged in defence of their rights during which the leaders' skills, tenacity of purpose and endurance were put to test and they earned the workers' trust. Sustained work by leaders produced acceptance, it begat trust, and on these qualities a bonding relationship was formed between the two. Given trust, workers may follow their leaders even when the guiding hand was that of a political party whose character, ideology and leadership might be largely unknown to them. It was of course for the party leaders to judge whether the objective conditions in society, particularly the duration and extent of economic hardship workers had suffered, were of such maturity that a call to general strike could be made. Yet, workers alone would then decide whether to respond to it wholly, partially, or not at all. It is the response behaviour that may determine the degree of trust leaders still retained, or whether it was so eroded that the workers would be willing to replace them with others having a different set of ideological beliefs and political affiliations.

There may be one important reason why, despite widespread disillusionment among workers on the manner in which their struggles were conducted, leaders were still not replaced. It was the non-availability of acceptable replacements. Leadership was and is still a scarce resource, its supply was provided mostly from the ranks of middle class political activists, with very few developing from the midst of working class neighbourhoods or factory workers. At any point of time, the stock of union leaders was given and could not be augmented. If there was only one union and its leaders had demonstrably failed to produce the promised outcomes, workers normally would have just one choice, stick to the union and criticize the key leader asserting greater control over him, or withdraw from the union and sulk. However, in a large number of cases, the choice has not been so bleak because of the possibility that several unions may be competing over the same organizing territory, thereby providing more choice to workers. In a deeper sense the choice paradigm may be expressed as between strikes and labour courts, or as between leaders strongly committed to class struggle and others well-versed in labour laws and connected to the government through the party in power.

These choices corresponded to two diametrically opposite political cultures of industrial relations that were far removed from the bread and butter issues which mostly occupy workers' minds and actuate behaviour at the plant level. In practice, all trade union leaders, regardless of party affiliations, spend most of their time and energy on day-to-day matters pertaining to individual grievances, disciplinary issues, settlement of industrial disputes, negotiating a new agreement, presenting workers' cases before courts and tribunals, or pleading for understanding and support before senior government officials and ministers. This great bundle of activities is altogether time consuming, often very tiring, and in return there may be little or very little in the form of tangible gains for the leaders and their family members.

In the past, one-way sacrifices were made by young leaders in the making, indeed this was what their mentors expected and the only return was acknowledgement, affection and deeper solace provided to the young activists by their party leaders that they were truly rendering service to a greater cause. For the communists, the political cause provided the purpose for engaging in trade union work, this being necessary to build class consciousness in the large mass of mostly illiterate and ignorant workers, broadly tied down to narrow ethnic, religious or caste-based primary loyalties. Union activity would upgrade the level of consciousness by infusing doctrines of class cohesion, class struggle and identification of the immediate employer as just one element comprising the larger block of the entire capitalist system, whose basic impulse for expansion lay in profit motive, exploitation and capital accumulation.

The intellectual basis for a life of sacrifice has been the entirely secular, Western doctrines or dogmas of Marxism, later interpreted as Leninism, Stalinism and Maoism, with considerable variations in basic themes as well as points of emphasis. This is how a number of young scholars, college graduates and degree holders returning from the UK, joined the CPI and dedicated themselves to the allotted tasks in trade unions, kisan sabhas, students' organizations or other mass organizations—something which P.C. Joshi during his long tenure of 13 years as the General Secretary of the CPI, nearly half of it when the party was illegal, steadfastly aimed at and accomplished to a remarkable degree. Under his leadership, the criteria for membership were liberalized and the size of the CPI leapt in scale, and possibly turned more petty-bourgeois and less working-class or peasant-oriented in character. The change in membership lowered the class character and revolutionary orientation of many sections of the party and its front organizations. However, the basic motivation, indeed the defining purpose of anyone becoming a communist, was the power-centred political orientation of the party to seize power and hold the reins of government to accomplish the desired objectives. This led the CPI to gamble for power.

In 1948, the party deviated from an objective understanding of the underlying social reality, based on a correct grasp of socioeconomic facts, and made mistakes in interpreting them politically. It engaged in massive gambles for power, first leading the insurrection in Telangana, to be routed and devastated by the Indian army—during its post police action phase—followed by recantation and withdrawal. Secondly, the unbelievably delusionary call for revolution following the Second congress in 1948. This too was suppressed and the party suffered deep pains and bruises.

The CPI was then forced to review its political ideas. It had to recast its thinking around the entirely new phenomena of the new Constitution being actually practised and delivering electorally produced political results. It took the CPI four years to admit the fact that India was actually free, that independence was real and not a sham, that Nehru was not a lackey of British imperialism, and that nationalism was functioning as a progressive and positive force, achieving genuine, tangible progress.[60] As the CPI leadership with new faces recast itself ideologically, abandoned shibboleth and worn out conflict-centred politics, it had virtually to rediscover itself. After Sardar Patel's death, Nehru showed more consideration and understanding and allowed the CPI to re-emerge into legality and function normally in the political life of the country.

During Gandhi's lifetime, Gandhism in practice meant a life devoted to constructive work and steadfast dedication to non-violence, nationalism and the mobilization of the masses around the platform and programmes of the Congress. Gandhian trade unionism was focussed on non-violence, peaceful methods of persuasion, agitation, satyagraha if necessary, and strikes only as a last resort.[61] This philosophy opened the doors wide to seeking reconciliation of labour's interests vis-à-vis the employers through the legally determined course of conciliation and adjudication by courts or arbitration as agreed to by the parties. The government, while taking the responsibility for promoting peaceful settlements of industrial disputes through a legally constituted machinery, simultaneously took away certain basic rights of the workers or whittled them down significantly in the interests of public order. These were the right to strike to determine the scope of collective bargaining, to decide what trade unions could or could not do, or how their executive committees may be composed, et cetera. The Indian system of legalistic industrial relations has drained class consciousness and class struggle of their fury and bound the trade unions in various legalistic ways. This was acceptable to the Gandhians, though every aspect of legalism may be considered on its merits and a stand taken accordingly.

As far as competition in influencing the working class was concerned, the four centres of trade unions operated differentially in different industries and regions. For the INTUC considerable organizing had to be done in 1947 when it was formed. Those who came to it were primarily active in the textile centres of the country, though in the last decade several other industries had also come up, and the same group of leaders often stretched their time and energy to provide guidance to the new unions. The AITUC leaders were already well placed in the older unions, in the established textile mills, collieries and engineering units, but had to compete against both Congressmen and socialists. On ideological grounds, the strongest competition came from the ex-AITUC trade unionists who now worked under the INTUC banner and platform. In 1948, they competed with considerably greater success since the AITUC was low on popularity and no longer independent of party affiliations. Its policies were now determined by the CPI decision to use the communist-led unions for political purposes. In 1948, political strikes were called not to press for workers' demands but to raise their collective voice in support of a revolutionary cause. Even when the strikes did not fizzle out rapidly, or produced only a partial response, the net effect on ordinary workers was one of demoralization and disillusionment. The militant leaders swiftly disappeared from the scene on being arrested or going underground, and the situation ripened fairly rapidly for the INTUC leadership to enter the psychologically vacated space with promises to deliver swifter results at less cost through the recently created legal apparatus under the Industrial Disputes Act. The latter could also advantageously urge the provincial labour ministers to use their influence to expedite references of disputes to adjudication and opening conciliation procedings in other cases.

Cynically, it may be said that the advantage of partiality the INTUC trade unions enjoyed was due to shared political ties with the ministers and it had only a remote connection with Gandhism. Nevertheless, there could be no denying the fact that peaceful, constitutional methods of dispute settlement formed the core of their political philosophy and this was fully consistent with the operative philosophy of the Industrial Disputes Act. However, the experience of practical trade unionism brought out the inherent drawbacks of excessive dependence on government patronage. The persistent tension between the Gandhians and the communists in this field resulted in polarized industrial relations, which left out the other two centres, namely the HMS and the UTUC, from principal reckoning. These centres gradually became marginalized and confined to particular industries and areas. These were largely the industries where their leaders were already well established and left undisturbed on the strength of the effective leadership in the existing unions, as well as the good image and reputation of their leaders. Accordingly, the unions affiliated to HMS and the UTUC have continued to survive despite six decades of fairly intense inter-union rivalry.[62]

Part C: The Labour Policy

The labour policy which took shape during this period was the combined result of colonial thinking and the nationalist outlook which found reflection in the Karachi Resolution in 1931. The experience of Congress governments in law making and coping with industrial unrest during, 1937–9, and the advanced thinking of the National Planning Committee on the subject also contributed to shaping ideas. The colonial government had meanwhile already drifted considerably from the doctrines of laissez-faire and free collective bargaining towards a broadly defined framework of a paternalist labour policy which assigned fairly large responsibilities on the government to upgrade working conditions and promote industrial peace. The Royal Commission on Labour had asked for legislation to provide for amenities, safety and welfare in factories and for workers employed in mines, plantations, docks and the merchant navy, as far as it was possible, and within the means of industry to bear the cost, as well as in conformity with ILO standards and recommendations. The part of the public responsibility towards industrial peace did not produce a forthright response till the outbreak of the Second World War. The war experience showed that the institutional mechanism created under the Rule 81-A of the Defence of India Rules worked reasonably well. While there were shortcomings and much criticism from labour spokesmen on the actual working of the administrative aspects of the system, these were not such that they could not be overcome through a statute, which would assign duties and responsibility in a carefully worked out charter along with provisions for appeal to higher courts. Moreover, the working of the tripartite consultative bodies were found to be generally satisfactory by all the three parties, and labour in particular found the forums of the tripartite labour conference and standing labour committee useful to directly address their problems to the government as well as employers' representatives. The government, too, could address its concerns to other participants and invite their comments and suggestions on legislative proposals without getting bogged down in wider political arguments and controversies.

A major advance on the body of protective legislation was made by the colonial government in the form of the Industrial Employment (Standing Orders) Act, 1946. For the first time, this enactment introduced the rule of law in all industrial establishments employing 100 or more workers. According to V.V. Giri, the absence of standing orders clearly defining the rights and obligations of the employer and the worker, in respect of recruitment, discharge, disciplinary action, holidays and leave, was one of the most frequent causes of friction between managements and workers in industrial undertakings. The discussions on the subject at the Tripartite Labour Conferences revealed a consensus of opinion in favour of a separate central enactment making it obligatory for employers in large industrial undertakings to frame and enforce, with prior approval of the government, the standing orders defining precisely the conditions of employment under them.[63]

The colonial government also took fairly large steps towards promoting labour welfare by legally establishing, the Mica Mines Labour Welfare Fund Act, 1946 and the Coal Mines Labour Welfare Fund Act, 1947. These were financed by the levy of a cess on the concerned industries. The Factories Act was also amended in 1948, now providing for 48 hours a week in perennial factories and 50 hours a week in seasonal factories. The Mines Maternity Benefits Act was amended to provide women working underground a 10-week leave of absence before and six weeks after delivery. During these 16 weeks, maternity benefit was to be paid at the rate of Rs. 6 per week.[64] These nitty-gritty matters had not received much attention from the AITUC, though it raised a general demand for a comprehensive review of The Factories Act, to bring it in line with the analogous British legislation and to revise The Mines Act suitably. They also wanted legislation to protect workers employed in shops and commercial establishments, road transport services, the docks, plantations and municipalities, and to abolish contract labour, et cetera.

Some of these demands were voiced in the tripartite forums, and the government not just listened but paid heed and in several spheres started working on the bills. A number of them were presented to the Legislative Assembly during 1947 before Independence. Several others were taken up by the national government after the transfer of power. The fact that there was a plethora of labour legislation during, 1946–52, is largely due to the sustained homework that was already put in by the concerned officials. Moreover, in the tripartite forums all the interested parties had expressed opinions on them and generated the needed consensus. Member In Charge of Labour, B.R. Ambedkar, said in these forums that the government would implement as many suggestions for labour reform on which there was a broad consensus, as could be feasibly undertaken by the government. This commitment was demonstrated in the formation of legislative proposals.

On industrial relations proper, the government felt the need for an effective legislation to control labour unrest, though the respective positions of government and trade union leaders were far apart. The central government extended the DIR—Rule 81-A by another six months after the end of the war to retain effective control on industrial disputes. This gave officials the time to prepare a bill which would incorporate the essential features of the wartime rules in respect of compulsory conciliation and adjudication. The bill which was circulated for comments restricted the workers' right to strike so as to practically annul it. The General Council of the AITUC objected to the proposal to deprive workers of their right to withhold labour and argued more convincingly 'that the necessity to give notice of a strike can only be a condition of a civil contract and consequently its breach can only be treated as a civil wrong and not as a criminal offence as the bill seeks to do'. According to the General Council, the right to strike could be restricted if the industry concerned was publicly owned and managed and the state took the responsibility for speedy investigation and redressal of grievances of workers and was able to guarantee a living wage and decent working conditions.[65] While voluntary arbitration preceded by conciliation by the government machinery would be welcome to workers, not compulsory arbitration in any form, 'either in public utility services, or in other occupations, making awards binding on them and making strikes illegal during the period of proceedings of either conciliation or arbitration and during the period in which the award of the arbitrator is enforced.'[66] The Bill was passed in 1947 excluding the penal provisions against which the labour leaders in the Central Assembly had raised a strong voice.

The Industrial Disputes Act, 1947 remains till date the cornerstone of the industrial relations policy of the government. The Act formed part of the government's Five Year Programme for Labour, though for the union leaders, in total it was found too unsatisfactory to merit any support. 'The AITUC is of the considered opinion that the Five Year Programme for Labour recently prepared by the Government of India, considered as a whole, is very unsatisfactory as it does not go far enough in many directions and it does not go fast enough in any direction.'[67] In the meantime, the provincial governments of Bombay, Madhya Pradesh, Berar and UP enacted respective dispute legislation to control the protest function of labour and secure industry from the destructive part played by strikes, particularly lightning strikes and associated lockouts.

The Five Year Labour Programme, 1947 and the Industrial Truce Resolution of 1947 representing the mutually agreed positions of representatives of labour, management and government together defined the goals of social policy. Other important announcements were the Industrial Policy Statement of 1948, in which the principle of associating representatives of labour in the consideration of problems of industrial production was accepted. In addition, the government passed the Limitation of Dividends Act, 1948, as the counterpart to the policy of wage control.[68] These were followed by reports on profit sharing and fair wages by the two committees appointed by the government, though hardly any practical steps were taken or could be undertaken to convert their broad far-reaching ideas to implementable forms through legislation.

Unlike the Committee on Profit-Sharing, which had several dissenting notes attached to the report, the Fair Wages Committee was able to produce a practically unanimous report. On fair wages, a device was found to refer this criterion to the tripartite wage boards, whenever constituted, which they would keep in view while considering the determination of wage structures at the industry level. This procedure found acceptance among the unions, hence the demand for fair wages speedily ceased to be voiced in their agitations for social justice. The question of profit-sharing could not be resolved due to the several contentious issues pertaining to such terms, as capital employed, treatment of depreciation and taxation in the determination of gross profits, fair return on capital and labour's share in the surplus profits, et cetera. Thereafter, the unresolved problems produced numerous disputes around the contentious issue of bonus, till it was resolved by the enactment of the Payment of Bonus Act, 1964.

An important law that was enacted in 1947, prior to Independence, was the amendment to the Indian Trade Unions Act, 1926, to provide for a machinery to certify the bargaining agent and its compulsory recognition for purposes of collective bargaining. It provided for the right to organize by outlawing certain unfair labour practices. This Act entered the statute book but required an administrative decision to notify it on a certain date. This was not done and the Act, never enforced, has been practically forgotten. One reason for non-notification was that the years 1947 and 1948 were very disturbed for industrial relations and the AITUC was almost totally under the control of communists.

It has been suggested that the West Bengal government pointed out to the central government that under this law the communist-led unions would secure unchallenged recognition in most industries. This would place a very awkward difficulty before the provincial government, if it decided to take a hard line against the communists. The perceived threat did materialize and actually took a very serious turn in 1948 following the exit of the moderate leaders from the AITUC. The harsh measures the government then took practically banned the unions from functioning.

In Kanpur, the communist-led KPS, which was recognized by the UP government, planned a general strike in the cotton mills in 1948. The government acted to pre-empt the threat by withdrawing recognition and arresting the leaders. For the union it produced a catastrophic effect, in the almost total withdrawal of the workers from membership. This might be due to the strong moral standing of political leaders in UP and the workers' rejection of the communists' call for a political general strike.[69] At the same time, there is no denying that if the 1947 amendment to the Trade Union Act had been enforced, it would have caused the most serious embarrassment to the government in taking action against the offending union leaders. What the government did would have been counter to the provision and spirit of the law. The other even more basic reason is that the underlying philosophy of the amending Act happened to be totally counter to that of the Industrial Disputes Act which was also enacted at about the same time.

The Interim Government which passed both laws seemed to be moving in exactly opposite directions, one inspired by the US law, towards collective bargaining, based on the right of the certified agent to engage in it as a legal right, and the other, based on the wartime regulations in the UK and India, towards adjudication and restricted right to strike. It appears that the deeper meanings of the two laws were not fully grasped by the officials who prepared them, nor by the labour minister in the Interim Government, who was enthused by the Five Year Programme on Labour, and piloted the two bills in the Central Assembly. In the light of later experience, the government realized the force of the logic that it had to choose one of the two competing labour philosophies, and it opted to retain that of the Industrial Disputes Act, to further strengthen the role of the state in industrial relations as a social arbiter.

The government also took a major step in regulating the supply of labour which was mostly in excess of requirements for stevedoring work in the docks by enacting The Dock Workers (Regulation of Employment) Act, 1948. The Whitley Commission had recommended a policy of decasualization of labour to systematically match supply with demand and dispensing with the role of intermediaries. This Act provides for framing schemes of decasualization for the major ports by the Centre and in respect of minor ports by state governments. Other major advances were, the Minimum Wages Act, 1948 applicable to restricted employments as notified by the state governments, the Employees State Insurance Act, 1948 and the Coal Mines Provident Fund and Bonus Schemes Act, 1948. The question of fixing a minimum wage was examined by the Royal Commission on Labour and it recommended that the possibility should be examined for small industries in the unorganized sector. The ILO had also adopted a Convention on the subject in 1928. The 1948

Act authorizes the state governments to decide on the industries or employments in which minimum wages should be fixed.

On health insurance, the AITUC submitted a memorandum on the proposals prepared by Prof. B.P. Adarkar which was broadly in line with the scheme already launched in the UK. The government implemented the Adarkar proposals on due consideration of questions of coverage, costs and benefits, and the organization that would have to be set up to manage the scheme. This was entrusted to the organization to be created under the Employees State Insurance Act, 1948. Thus, by 1952, the government had implemented not just the programme proposed in 1947 but more. Through tripartite deliberations, it completely reversed the earlier colonial policy of laissez-faire. It adopted the opposite doctrine of purposive intervention to maintain industrial peace, indeed, to promote industrial harmony by assuming the role of a paternalist state concerned simultaneously with good industrial relations and the welfare of the workers within limits permitted by the economy and the resources of the state.

II. 1950–3

The Nehru Era (First Phase): First General Elections, Congress Splits, Government Advances

On 26 January 1950, the Constituent Assembly formally adopted the Constitution of India and in this respect its work ended. It reverted to the role of a legislative assembly. The government was led by two very senior, popular and powerful leaders, Jawaharlal Nehru and Sardar Vallabhbhai Patel. Though Nehru by conviction veered towards the left, Sardar Patel was more conservative in outlook and worked on the strength of the organizational support of the Congress. The economic portfolios in the government were held by non-Congress, pro-business politicians who had minimal support among the masses and functioned with the backing of Nehru and Sardar Patel. The interpersonal differences between the two leaders were rooted in their political orientations which started unravelling as they drew on their ideological moorings to find answers to the numerous policy issues.

Among the socialists, the group led by Jayaprakash Narayan could no longer combine Marxism with Gandhism with the realization that violence could not be accepted or justified for the attainment of their cherished goals. India was now free. The people would soon face a totally democratic election and elect their governments at the Centre and the states. The socialists, too, would have to find a mandate for themselves in the new milieu. Similar questions were raised within the Congress and there were differences of opinion not only on the directions of national policy but also on the relationships within the party, particularly its president and the government. Sardar Patel, whose voice was dominant in the CWC, took the stand that the government was answerable to the Congress Parliamentary Party, not to the Congress President. He prevailed, though during 1937–9 this was not the case and the Congress High Command insisted on its supremacy. However, then, none of the top leaders besides Rajaji who headed the Madras government had accepted any post in the government. They remained outside and maintained discipline in the legislative wings of the party.

Under the new Constitution the established British practice was accepted as proper and it was put into effect. Acharya J.B. Kripalani, the Congress President, was left out of the government and protested strongly. In 1950, the top job in the Congress came up for re-election. Sardar Patel's grip over the organization was firm and secure. He preferred Purushottam Das Tandon for the job. As lines were drawn, Kripalani, another contender, moved towards Nehru and a contest developed between him and Purushottam Das Tandon. On Sardar Patel's backing, Tandon won and this was interpreted as Nehru's defeat, though he had not openly supported Kripalani.

The year 1950 was a particularly disturbed year, owing to heightened communal tension in East Pakistan, which resulted in a mass exodus of Hindus and the question of war with Pakistan became real. The government was asked to take a firm stand on the issue, since Pakistan was either unwilling or unable to ensure the safety of the remaining Hindu population in their midst. Tandon's victory indicated a swing to the right and Nehru thought that his utility to the Congress and the government was exhausted. Yet Sardar Patel showed decency and affirmed his loyalty to Nehru. Acharya Kripalani decided to mobilize the dissidents, but within a few months their relations with the Congress leadership turned sour. The Kripalani-led dissidents took cover under Gandhian principles and criticized the government for deviating from Gandhian ideals. The possibility of their having to severe relations with Congress gained in strength, because the organization was ceasing to be an aggregation of nationalists of all hues, and under Sardar Patel's guidance it was being transformed into a disciplined political party.

At the deeper level, differences between the two titans in the government, Nehru and Patel, remained unresolved. Patel never thought that the Kashmir issue had been carefully handled by Nehru. And on Tibet, he had deep misgivings on China's political goals and aspirations. In October 1950, China invaded Tibet and converted the empty status of suzerainty into an exercise of sovereignty by the force of arms and virtual annexation. In November, Sardar Patel wrote to Nehru that communists were as good or as bad as imperialists. India should be alive to the new danger and should be strong on defence. Moreover, after the rebuff over Tibet, India should cease pleading for China's entry into the UN. He wanted Nehru to reconsider India's friendly ties with a host of countries including America, Britain and Burma. He even hinted at the question, whether the policy of non-alignment actually subserved India's interests and a shift towards the West might be the appropriate response to China's actions in Tibet.

Nehru said that China had acted foolishly, but India could hardly go to war on Tibet. In his view, India should not overdo the criticism of a neighbouring country. China was now united and emerging from the shadows of European domination. So India need not swerve from the course of friendship with a great country. Nehru did not believe that China would attack India since it was inconceivable that China would undertake a wild adventure across the Himalayas. Unfortunately, as later events demonstrated, Sardar Patel's judgement was nearer the hard truth on both issues, and Nehru in his lifetime had on more than one occasion to realize his mistakes. In domestic policies as well as in external affairs, Nehru was fully committed to left of centre policies, while it may be said for Sardar Patel that in national interests he systematically veered to the right, though not far right. However, two months before his death, Sardar Patel declared that Nehru was the leader, that Gandhi had appointed him as his successor and, as a Gandhian, he would follow Nehru's leadership.

Nehru had strong views but he understood the Congress equally well and knew the value of practical compromise. He knew that most of Gandhi's leading followers were not socialists, nor had leftist sympathies. All the leading stalwarts of the Congress, including Sardar Patel, Rajendra Prasad, Rajagopalachari (Rajaji), Acharya Kripalani, Maulana Azad had strong humanist sympathies, or were broadminded nationalists committed to truth, non-violence and the essential decencies of a civilized society. They respected private property, appreciated Indian enterprise gaining one milestone after another and believed in class collaboration as well as the importance of state-directed policies to achieve reconciliation of conflicting interests. The Constitution carried their stamp and they looked forward to working to realize the nation's aspirations through it.

Apparently Nehru too was satisfied with the basic features of the Constitution, though he did not rule out the possibility of amending it to maintain its serviceability. The Constitution should remain a live document, not a frozen one, and he perhaps understood better than many of his contemporaries that all the talk of zamindari abolition and agrarian reforms would fail to produce any progress if the provisions on property rights and compensation remained unchanged. Then a greater danger of upsurge of discontented masses might develop which would overwhelm the nascent democracy and force a complete rewrite of the Constitution.

On 26 January 1950 India became a republic and the office of Governor-General ceased to exist. Rajaji was the last Governor-General, though it was a titular post and he had used his office to offer advice and find compromises and solutions to the several questions which arose in the drafting of the Constitution. Nehru wanted Rajaji to be the successor from one office to another in a smooth transition and elected as President of India. He failed because the party, adroitly led by Sardar Patel, wanted to elect Rajendra Prasad, who had presided over the Constituent Assembly from inception, to the post. Nehru clearly lacked support. Moreover, the Congress would not accept a veteran leader like Prasad to be sidetracked or ignored. He had stayed with Gandhi since the Champaran agitation and was widely respected. However, his social, religious and political outlook were far more traditional and not to Nehru's liking.

The differences between the two, holding the highest offices in the country, again came up on the question of inaugurating the newly restored Somnath Temple in Gujarat. It was rebuilt with the support of Sardar Patel and K.M. Munshi among others. The President was asked to inaugurate the temple and he agreed. Nehru wrote to him not to do so, because it would send a wrong signal within the country and abroad; in fact he had never approved of the idea in the first place. Prasad disregarded Nehru's advice and did as he was asked to do. His speech on the occasion was a plea for reconciliation and moderation of religious beliefs and stressed Gandhian ideals. Nehru did not raise the matter again.

In December 1950, Sardar Patel died and this created a major vacuum in the Congress. As far as the government was concerned, Nehru stepped in quickly to take full leadership into his hands and then gradually asserted his commanding presence in the party organization as well. In May 1951, with an eye on the forthcoming general elections, Acharya Kripalani and his colleagues decided to leave the Congress and announced the formation of the Kisan Mazdoor Praja Party.[70] In the following months, the Congress too went through a major regrouping exercise. Nehru resigned from the working committee. This led Tandon to offer his resignation as the President of the party, and to pave the way for Nehru to get elected to this post, whereupon he could reconstitute the working committee as he wished. This is exactly what happened and Nehru became the sole leader of the party. Though the leading members often disagreed with his socialist ideas, yet they were eager that he should lead them in the forthcoming elections for the state assemblies and parliament. He was authorized to write the election manifesto and the resolution to be placed at the AICC. Nehru now had an upper hand and he combined the dual role of leading the government as well as the party to achieve complete political ascendancy in the country. The international position for the country and for himself, which he had been able to develop, was already rated as a notable achievement and it was expected to work to the advantage of the ruling party at the hustings.

The Nehru era had begun. The unique characteristic of Nehru's leadership was his dominance in formulating policies and giving expression to the nation's ideals while leaving much autonomy to the Congress organization to carry on in such practical ways as suited the leadership at the state and lower levels. The dualistic pattern that emerged was that the organizational leaders, seemingly accepted Nehru's policies and his direction in one or more spheres, but with little inclination to implement them with energy and conviction. The party accepted Nehru as its foremost leader and in turn Nehru accepted the party as it existed. He never tried to refashion the Congress.

The electoral system was a creation of the new

Constitution and the elections in December 1951/January 1952 were conducted according to the provisions of the Representation of the People Act, 1950. It rested on universal adult franchise and direct elections to both, the House of the People or the Lok Sabha, at the centre and the legislative assemblies or Vidhan Sabhas in the states. The House of the People had 489 seats, and of them 98 were reserved for candidates representing the Scheduled Castes and the Scheduled Tribes. The legislative assemblies had a total of 3,283 seats, 477 of which were reserved for the Scheduled Castes and 192 for the Scheduled Tribes.

Under this system the candidates securing the largest number of votes cast in the constituencies are declared elected, and the elected members constitute the house after every election. This system of elections usually produces a disproportionate representation with the high probability that a party that formed the majority in the house may have failed to win a majority of the votes cast. The system puts the smaller parties to severe disadvantage and forces them to periodically voice their opinions outside the elected bodies, where a willing audience may wait to cheer them, rather than inside the houses where they may not have any voice. The electoral system produces a kind of political dualism separating the insiders from the outsiders.

The 1952 elections were a major milestone in the country's political development. These were also an eye-opener to the newly formed parties which entered the fray with high optimism but found the results deeply disappointing. The popular votes for the House of the People at the centre totalled over 105.944 million, of which the Congress secured the highest at 45.0 per cent, the socialists 10.0 per cent, the KMPP 5.8 per cent and the CPI 3.3, though inclusive of its allies the total added up to 5.4 per cent. The communists were pleasantly surprised at the results, because till recently they were either in jail or worked underground, and their party organs had suffered greatly by government repression.

In the state assembly elections the communists won 62

seats compared to the over optimistic KMPP which secured only 35.[71] The unexpected performance of the communists and their front candidates created the impression that the country was getting polarized between them and the Congress and this unhealthy trend needed to be checked. There was not much factual basis for this apprehension since the combined votes of socialists and the Gandhians in the KMPP were more than twice that of the communists, though this was not reflected in the number of seats won. Moreover, the communists gained mostly in three states—Madras, Hyderabad and West Bengal—whereas the socialists emerged as an all-India party though thinly represented in most state assemblies. Nonetheless, the socialists advanced the political plank that the non-Congress opposition votes should be consolidated to present the electorate with a middle ground and to offset the influence of the communists. This realization was apparently equally shared by the KMPP leaders who visualized the unity of socialists and sarvodaya forces as highly desirable. As a result, at great speed the Socialist Party and the KMPP merged in just a few months after the elections and assumed the name of the Praja Socialist Party, enjoying a combined respectable voting strength of 16.7 per cent of the popular vote.

By the time the elections were held, India had effectively turned the corner. The traumas of partition and communal rioting had largely healed and the government was seen to be actively engaged in solving the remaining problems of refugee resettlement, as well as integrating the Muslim population in the more difficult task of resuming civic life in the broad framework of a secular polity. The adoption of the Constitution provided the government with the much needed legitimacy, and this was affirmed, indeed, as was the intention, by the 1951–2 elections, in accordance with its provisions. The newly inaugurated political system received the wide endorsement of the masses as demonstrated by the large number of candidates who entered the fray for seats in the assemblies and parliament under various party platforms, and the fact that nearly 60 per cent of the electorate had cast their votes. Taken together, with the lengthy process of the selection of candidates, the issuance of party manifestos and the actual campaigning to secure votes, the first general elections marked a great step forward towards the political mobilization of the masses and regrouping of society along discernible political lines.

Under the Constitution and its various institutions and symbols, a new India began to take shape. Hereafter, the past phase of nationalist struggle would steadily recede; indeed, the priorities were already so altered. Now there was no need to subordinate all the various issues of a sectional nature to the larger cause, which actually had already come to the fore under the provincial autonomy, developed under the 1919 Act and greatly invigorated under the 1935 Act. There was no need to even heed the powerful ever-present voice of Gandhi to abjure violence and cowardice and serve the country selflessly. All this would soon become memory, since on Gandhi's death there could not possibly be another leader of comparable political weight carrying his message forward. Gandhi's followers had already split into several camps. The leading elements were in power running the government, while some others who had seceded from the Congress were in the Opposition and the non-political group had withdrawn into implementing Gandhi's ideas through work on rural reconstruction, removal of untouchability, development of khadi and so on.

The biggest challenge to Indian nationalism came shortly after the elections. The question of redrawing the political map of India along linguistic lines was considered in the Constituent Assembly and was rejected, predictably because no one in the top echelons of Congress was in its favour. This was at complete variance from the earlier Congress position that the boundaries of provinces should be redrawn on linguistic principles and the map of the Congress organization reflected this principle. The Nehru Report which was adopted by the Congress also accepted the linguistic principle as the legitimate basis for redrawing political boundaries. In January 1948, Gandhi said that if new provinces were formed on the basis of language and if they were placed under the authority of Delhi there would be no harm. However, later, Nehru, Sardar Patel and Rajaji changed their position and opposed the demand because it would encourage fissiparious tendencies.

The elections provided the occasion to reorder Indian politics to accommodate provincial particularism, resting on the claim that it would strengthen the unity of India, not weaken it. Moreover, democracy would be more meaningful to people if the states' boundaries were recast to reflect India's diversity by separating population groups on the basis of language, because it would enable the business of the government at the state level to be conducted in the mother tongue of the people.

The communists had already made a large contribution towards politicizing the language sentiment in the Telangana agitation in the former State of Hyderabad. On 19 October 1952, Potti Sriramulu, a Congressman and a follower of Gandhi, started a fast-unto-death in Madras on this issue. Nehru received frantic telegrams but remained unmoved. Hartals were called, angry mobs stopped trains and the agitation spread. Sriramulu died 58 days into the fast and the Andhra area was plunged into chaos. Nehru decided to yield and in 1953 the government conceded the demand for a separate Andhra Pradesh. And the new state was formed out of Madras State. For the Telugu-speaking people 1 October 1953 was a day of major triumph when the new State of Andhra Pradesh was inaugurated.

The CPI emerged from the wilderness as a significant political factor in India, but was still not clear about the true nature of change that had taken place in the last five years. In early 1951, a delegation of four CPI leaders went to Moscow to seek guidance and met a formal commission comprising the top leaders of the Soviet Union, namely Stalin, Suslov, Molotov and Malenkov, who told the Indian communist leaders that the method of insurrection at this stage was not valid for India and they should not treat Nehru as the lackey of Anglo-American imperialism, in as much as the transfer of power was not fake. Moreover, the CPI should strengthen the forces working for world peace.[72] The party should organize a broad united front of four classes—the working class, the peasantry, the middle class and the national bourgeoisie, to struggle for the establishment of a genuinely democratic government, using the power of the state to transform the economy, freeing it from the stranglehold of British capitalism and monopolist big bourgeoisie. For some time to come, the communists should stick to a peaceful strategy and gain strength among the masses. The time for revolutionary action may come at a later stage, when the objective conditions had sufficiently developed, and the party could maintain its leadership role till success was achieved.

It was on the basis of the new tactical line that the CPI had contested the elections and found the exercise entirely worthwhile. This correction was badly needed, as the party, following the earlier Yugoslav doctrine, had adopted the path of insurrection and met with utter failure. Since then it was confronted with three distinct political paths for the future.[73] One was the classical path shown by the Soviet Union leading to dictatorship of the proletariat. The second was that of Mao Tse Tung, who led a coalition of pro-revolutionary classes and the peasant army to victory. The third, promoted by the right wing faction in the CPI, asked for support to the progressive elements in the government, particularly Nehru, to strengthen their hands vis-à-vis the conservative, right wing politicians in the Congress, to organize popular agitations, so that they may feel the pressure of the masses and move further to the left both in foreign policy and domestic economic and agrarian policies.

The New Tactical Line prepared by four Indian communists in consultation with the Soviet leaders was adopted by the CPI in 1951. They were told that in view of Indian peculiarities, the CPI would have to develop their distinct strategy to capture power and steer society towards socialism with due consideration of the objective conditions as they develop. There could be no doubt that the restraining hand was that of the Soviet leadership, which was at the time seriously engaged in reviewing their evaluation of Indian development. They had, in the meanwhile, decided that what the Soviet Union needed most was the strengthening of the peace movement throughout the world, India included, to ward off the threats to its security from the US-led imperialist forces.[74]

India's foreign policy emerged as a notable dimension of the broad vision of a newly freed people's quest for all-round development, self-reliance, support for the broad principles on which the United Nations was founded and freedom from power-centred entanglements. India chose to be independent in foreign relations in the same manner as it wanted to be free in domestic matters. This did not mean isolation, a withdrawal from world affairs, or neutrality as a creed. India's foremost need was to foster friendship with as many countries as would reciprocate and seek the support of the economically stronger countries in aiding India's national developmental efforts.

An independent foreign policy was inseparable from political independence. India's colonial experience showed that even on such an issue as the Second World War, India was committed to wage war on the Axis powers without being consulted or allowed a voice. India must remain free and determine what position to take on various international questions, solely on the basis of its independent judgement and in national interests. Nehru was the architect of this doctrine, and though questions were asked on what it might achieve, and doubts raised that it could fail on the way, it nonetheless carried the ruling party, most of the opposition and the articulate public opinion.

This foreign policy extended Gandhian doctrines to foreign affairs and reflected India's predisposition towards non-aggression, world peace and peaceful coexistence. India sought decolonization to proceed at a faster pace, to achieve freedom for the subject people in Africa and Asia, and an end to racialism and apartheid in South Africa. The policy was a mix of sentiments, realism and reason.

During 1947–53, the government rapidly learnt that there were four issues which dominated the foreign policy agenda. The first was its relations with Pakistan, the dispute over Jammu and Kashmir, the Security Council's resolutions and the attitudes of the US, UK and the Soviet Union on matters of concern to India. Relations with China and the issue of Tibet came next though the government systematically downplayed them. The third was the delay in withdrawal of European powers from their possessions in India. France moved slowly, Portugal not at all. Fourth was the essentiality of world peace, so that India might stay disentangled and concentrate on the development of the economy and society as its foremost concern.

India needed friendship, food grains and aid from the rich and powerful nations. If the government was to succeed in the exceedingly arduous task of bringing about a generally peaceful transformation of the colonial economy into a self-sustaining, development-oriented and democratic politico-economic system, which would be at peace with itself and the rest of the world, an indispensable prerequisite was the support of the developed countries over several years. The problem was how to get it across and secure its acceptance in a world torn by tension and divided into two hostile power blocs. India learnt the hard way, that whereas the economic aid message was accepted on mutually advantageous terms, which needed to be negotiated, on political issues harder attitudes defined the respective positions of powerful countries and they were unimpressed by India. For Nehru the first hard learning took place late in 1949 when he visited the US.

Nehru failed to create a favourable impression on the State Department and Dean Acheson was clearly disappointed. Nehru was asked questions on the Kashmir issue but instead of a political response, with an eye on American interests and what India and the United States could do together, Nehru showed a tendency towards rhetoric or a specimen of public speech and flashes of anger. India got the wheat aid it needed badly to ward off hunger and starvation, but not political understanding. This task was better accomplished by the US ambassador to India, in 1951–2, by Chester Bowles. He conveyed to the Americans and the State Department the immaturity and ridiculously simplified nature of the dictum that if Nehru was not with us, he was against us. At the Security Council, the US position, goaded and guided by British diplomats, hardened on the Kashmir question and Pakistan emerged as the favoured country. It was seen as pro-West and willing to act as a bulwark against communism. India's pro-China stand was found irksome, and in the judgement of strategic analysts not well founded on hard reasons, as for example, shown by China's contempt for the Indian position on Tibet.

Instead of trust, relations with the US were marked by mistrust. It became worse in 1953, when John Foster Dulles showed his dislike for Nehru. He offended Indian sensibilities on Portuguese possessions in India, saying that Portugal could keep Goa as long as it wished. He proceeded to sign a military pact with Pakistan with promises of economic and military aid in total disregard of India's protests. This was a major long-term setback suffered by India in foreign relations and it pushed Nehru to find other options to counterbalance the US–Pakistan pact, which could go against India.

At the UN Security Council, India's position on Kashmir failed to win support. In January 1949, there was a call for ceasefire which both India and Pakistan accepted. In February 1950, the Security Council asked both countries to withdraw their armies, which both countries stalled. However, by 1950 India regretted going to the UN first and prepared to formally divide the state on the basis of the status quo. No progress could be made since Pakistan now talked of the liberation of Kashmir as a cardinal belief of its people. The idea of a plebiscite failed to win support and no progress could be made because the Pakistani press linked the issue to the Islamic cry of jihad producing strong religious sentiments. Nehru felt that instead of a plebiscite there would be a civil upheaval not just in Kashmir, but elsewhere in India and Pakistan.

Meanwhile, Sheikh Abdullah started talking in terms of an independent Kashmir and could not understand why the UN ignored independence as a possible solution. With the government, he spoke in terms of greater autonomy for the state. He even suggested that Kashmir's accession to India was not final. An independent Kashmir would of course become a client state of America, or as he may have imagined, possibly turn into another Switzerland. In Jammu, the Praja Parishad agitated in support of full integration with India and relations between the two regions worsened. In 1953, Adlai Stevenson visited the Srinagar valley and met Sheikh Abdullah, and appeared to have extended more than moral support for his causes.[75] Matters swiftly came to a head and the government had to remove him from power and put him into detention.

Beginning of Planning, Stable Prices, Economic Growth

The industrial policy resolution of April 1948 assured the private sector that the existing enterprises would not be nationalized, though a number of key industries were reserved for government to own and operate them. The business community found the government to be supportive and the investment climate favourable. Sentiments improved as supply constraints were overcome, while profit margins remained high. The disquieting factor was that between 1947 and 1949 the price level had risen by around 14 per cent. To restrain prices and to augment the availability of goods in the market the government followed a liberal imports policy, though in one year, 1948–9, the sterling balances declined by Rs. 6 billion.

The government's highest priority no doubt was to do

whatever was possible towards the rapid rehabilitation of the refugees. At the same time, long-term economic problems demanded government's urgent attention. India must grow more food, and this required the enlargement of canal irrigation, increased supply of better seeds, fertilizers and other inputs. The government's foremost attention was drawn towards building several large multi-purpose river valley projects for harnessing river water, by constructing dams to produce hydro-electricity and lay out canals for irrigation purposes. America's Tennessee Valley Authority and the integrated project it managed was the inspiration and adopted as the model for similar projects in India. Nehru was enchanted by the idea and called them 'the temples of modern India'. The Bhakra–Nangal project was the most prestigious, though several others, like the dams on the Mahanadi, Rihand, Tungabhadra and Damodar were no less important.

The Bhakra–Nangal project compensated the refugees from West Punjab for the loss of the canal colonies. It would resettle the Sikh farmers on irrigated lands and bring them prosperity. In addition to irrigation, there would also be power and new industrial townships could be built to use it. The Bhakra dam was inaugurated by Nehru in the first week of July 1954. It was a remarkable achievement for which much credit is owed to its chief engineer, Harvey Slocum, who was earlier the construction superintendent of the Grand Coulee dam in America.

The government set up the Planning Commission in 1950 and in 1951 it issued a draft of the First Five Year Plan. Its focus was on agriculture, to raise food production, and enhance transport and communication. A novel feature of the First Plan was the concept of community development as complementary to agriculture with the larger responsibility for organizing rural societies around government-funded schemes suitably adjusted to local areas and community needs. The Community Development Programme was formally launched on 2 October 1952. The

First Plan, 1951–6, commenced in 1952 in the sense that the draft plan was revised and finalized only towards the end of the financial year. Most of the schemes included in it were already with the government. The scale of endeavour was quite modest and not expected to stretch the economy much. This was justified on the grounds that in the course of implementing it the government would acquire the confidence to consider bolder plans and the experience gained would improve the feasibility of the next plan.

India was a major exporter of cotton textiles at this stage. The assumption on which Indian exports rested was the continued supremacy of cotton. The textile machinery industry which was promoted and protected in the 1950s rested entirely on cotton as the basic raw material. However, the imported technology produced obsolete machines. There was little realization that new technological breakthroughs had taken place which led to the production of synthetic and blended fabrics. The textile industry in India, including the textile machinery industry, was unprepared to accept the new challenge and adapt to it. Instead both the government and the textile industrialists were keener to ensure that no segment of the industry was exposed to competition from abroad. In the domestic market, the availability of cloth at low prices was the priority, exports came next, and the fundamental malaise of technological obsolescence was left unattended. In 1952, the textile machinery industry was given protection and foreign exchange was released to import capital goods. India began to think in terms of self-sufficiency in the capital goods sector, but without sparing much thought on bringing in the new technologies that were reshaping the entire textile industry in the US and several other advanced industrial countries.

Government behaviour showed that it was a captive to nationalist aspirations and ideas of industrial development which were projected in opposition to colonial economic policies. There were other obstacles as well. The protected textile industry continued to depend on plain looms instead of automatic ones, even at the stage of machine manufacturing. Institutionalization of an already weak impulse of modernization was inexplicable, except as an extension of the urge for self-sufficiency and an escape from the hazards of freer competition from the more modern producers in other countries. The government, as it went into the planning mode, lost sight of the pressing argument that without modernization, Indian industries, clinging to obsolete and worn out equipment, would be condemned to mediocrity and sooner or later face elimination.

In the domestic context, the preferred mediocrity route steadily took the form of industrial sickness becoming a permanent burden on the economic system. It appears that the government, then grappling with the insurmountable problem of shoring up finances for the Plan, never could confront the question of modernization. Actually, insufficiency of finance, which the government endeavoured to control ever more tightly, rendered the talk of modernization akin to exploring an impossible proposition. The Indian textile industry which led in the exports in the early 1950s steadily lost ground as it predictably fell behind in modernization and gave up the quest for higher efficiency.

At the industry level, two major problems acquired urgency and in immediate need of the government's attention. One was economic stagnation and the other, unemployment. The labour force rendered redundant by technological progress could not be provided alternative employment and would soon swell the ranks of small cultivators or landless labour, while some might remain perpetually under-employed. Connected to this was the issue of saving village industries and the First Plan thought of a remedy. It was suggested that whenever a large-scale or modern industry threatened the existence of a village industry a remedy may be found in formulating a common production programme. On translating this idea into action, it would require: (a) reservation of spheres of production; (b) restrictions or non-expansion of the capacity of the competing large-scale industries; (c) imposition of a cess on production in the large-scale industry; and (d) arrangement for the supply of raw materials to the village industries. It also favoured the idea of coordination in research and training. Some of these ideas were already in the making or put into effect. In April 1950, the cotton mill industry was prohibited from producing certain varieties of cloth since their production was reserved for the handlooms. In December 1952 the mills were directed not to produce certain varieties of cloth in quantities exceeding 60 per cent of the production of the previous year. Later more restrictions followed.

Thus far, the development of industries was due to the business acumen of the private sector. The British led and Indians followed, except in Bombay, where Indian capital was able to organize independently to set up cotton textile mills but with strong dependency on British manufacturers, trading arrangements, managerial personnel and supervisory manpower. They used the legal instrument of the joint stock company in preference to partnership and individual proprietorship. This provided the combined advantage of extended partnership with limited liability and could be conveniently grafted on the joint family system. The supply of capital was always scarce and it had to be collected in small pools. All other inputs were utterly scarce and had to be imported, which made them quite costly. Only unskilled labour was plentiful and cheap, but its extensive, continued use in preference to more advanced capital-intensive technologies resulted in low productivity and considerable variability in quality. The private sector organized itself on the basis of the managing agency system which was dependable in part. However, it was an open question whether on its basis, the private industrialists would be able to take the country to the next higher stage of industrialization and development. Managing agencies had a tendency towards monopoly formation and restricting opportunities for new entrants, if not blocking entry altogether.

Under the managing agency system, the tendency was to expand the production base by expanding the technology already in use. This style had its advantages. The same management could enlarge capacities by recruiting and inducting fresh kinsmen, or by bringing in fresh managers on the expectation and promise of their total identification with the styles of the leading elements and securing acceptance as akin to family members into positions of authority in the management organization. Among other reasons, this kind of management style severely restricted the scope of development of the industrial groups under their control. Ordinarily the industrialists would take on only what they understood, provided it was not unduly complicated, and it could be profitably run within the limits of their resources, experience, existing skills and learning capabilities. Given these limitations, it was hardly possible to imagine that the established business families would show an interest and take the initiative to shift over to new industries that required greater amounts of fixed capital, perhaps even new designs of organizations, to manage them and to recruit and train fresh manpower. The reason is that quite apart from scarcity of capital and the undeveloped stage of the capital market, any such venture would necessitate excessive stretching of a given managing agency house, which in the course of making a success of new ventures might severely damage the cohesiveness of family-run businesses. Moreover, fear of failure or inability to recover their investment, or earn a satisfactory return on equity in the short run, plus an unwillingness to commit the time and energy for the purpose, might act as a deterrent.

Although the Bombay Plan was prepared by the leading industrialists and it could be supposed that in free India they were there to take the lead in promoting new industries, there was little evidence that they were actually prepared to do so. The government was expected to provide the leadership and to project detailed proposals of public-private partnership for setting up new undertakings and ensuring a secure market for them. Protection was a dire need. It was the same for finance and credit, power, raw materials, foreign exchange and several other things. In the first decade of independence, industry worked the technologies they already had and expanded output within their limits. They asked the government to provide all the other requirements, including leadership and controls for further development. The need to build a public sector along more modern lines was laid bare by the industrialists themselves, as was affirmed by an objective evaluation of the potentialities and limitations of the collective entity, called the private sector.

Free India's first population census was conducted in the first half of 1951. R.A. Gopalaswami, the new Census Commissioner, made several departures from earlier censuses on questionnaires, definitions and tabulations. For the first time, detailed demographic information was collected on each village. Asok Mitra, who conducted the Census in West Bengal, viewed it as a notable achievement. 'In every way the 1951 census marked the great divide between the pre-Independence era of the census as a tool for law and order (and, whenever necessary as an instrument of discrimination, divide and rule) and the post-Independence era of the census as a handmaiden of planning for cultural, economic and social development.'[76]

The Census revealed India's population at 361 million, showing a growth rate of 13.31 per cent over the previous decade. Average annual birth rate and death rate were estimated at 39.9 and 27.4 per thousand respectively. These were underestimates which implied that so was the population total. These facts were taken note of in the First Five Year Plan which devoted a section to the subject, 'Population Pressure: The Bearing on Development', and a plea was entered for a population policy as an essential part of planning. The pressure of the population was already so high that a reduction in its rate of growth was a major necessity. Accordingly, the government announced a policy on limiting the population by family planning in 1951.

Though a Family Planning Cell was created in April 1952, in the office of the Directorate General of Health Services, the first officer on special duty was appointed in 1956. The government lacked clear ideas on how to carry the family planning message to the masses and little progress was made. It was appended to the Health Ministry, which was politically one of the least important ministries in the government both at the Centre and the states. Moreover, the government was less sure on the values, norms and customs on childbearing among the masses and preferred the natural method of family planning, rather than the clinical approach. The latter was untried in India, and the government did not have the organizational infrastructure for the purpose. As a result, though the government accepted family planning as a goal, it could not meaningfully strive towards its practical realization for at least another decade. A major difficulty was political in nature. India's Minister of Health, Rajkumari Amrit Kaur, was opposed to all artificial means of conception control and preferred the 'rhythm method' or the 'safe period' method, which could only produce failure for all the effort made by way of research and propaganda.[77]

The policy of community development (CD) drew considerable attention and also received some acclaim. Albert Mayer, an American architect and planner had worked in Uttar Pradesh during 1948–52 and launched the Etawah pilot project aimed at improving the productivity of the land and the economic condition of the people. With the support of the Ford Foundation, the government promoted a number of similar programmes in several states. A typical community development project covered about 300 villages with a total population of 200,000 people. The purpose was to achieve a number of goals, such as, agricultural productivity, public health and sanitation, road building and education. There were also composite Development Blocks which promoted small industries alongside improved agricultural practices. A third parallel scheme aimed at imparting training to village level workers and social education organizers. Minimum achievable targets were set to provide safe drinking water, boring tube wells or building canals, tanks or same other method for improved irrigation, among a number of other goals. According to Mitra, 'the assumption, born of pilot work, led to estimates that in four years a CD programme following these general lines would bring about an increase in food production of roughly 50 per cent in each area. In addition there would be an increase in cash income per village of some 35 per cent.' Villagers would find work for 200 days instead of 120 to 135 days.[78] The goals were set on a realistic basis, yet less was achieved, and by 1954 the CD idea began to lose its shine. No new CD projects were inaugurated, and on completion, the existing projects were discontinued. Apparently, the altruism implied in community development could not survive the rise of agricultural classes and their assertion of leadership at the village level. The CD administration could not cope with their power and influence and it was decided to give up the effort.

> The scheme no doubt brought the caste-based as well as political factions to the forefront and in general provided the means of satisfying the age-old hunger for power by the rural elite. While this sharing of power cannot be equated with their participation in development programmes, the experience of the community development programme made it clear that it was difficult to secure peoples' participation in development without entrusting them with the responsibility for formulation and administration of the programmes. The prospects of development seemed better with such an integration than with continued conflict between the community development officials and the political elite.[79]

An additional reason was that the cost of CD projects was rising and the government looked for an alternative programme. The government was of course committed to rural development, but in future it would be done through the National Extension Service.

The community development programme highlighted the problem of implementation. The initial thrust of the programme was planned for areas which had enough water from irrigation, or assured rainfall, so that the project staff and specialists in crop production, plant protection, use of fertilizers, et cetera. might be able to produce measurable results in the form of higher yields and better farm management within a reasonably short period of time. The programme received financial and technical aid from America. Frankel points out:

> The community projects budgeted only one-third of the costs of land reclamation, drainage, irrigation and road building schemes, and relied on village contribution in labour and money for the remainder. Matching contributions were also required to qualify for government grants toward the construction of social amenities projects, including primary schools, community centres, and drinking wells. There was, therefore, an objective justification for creating and strengthening village institutions as grass root agencies for organizing the extensive popular participation necessary to carry out rural improvement schemes. At the centre of the community development programme was a plan to establish cooperative and panchayat institutions that aimed at reconstructing the whole village as the primary unit of economic and political action.[80]

However, unlike the original structure, in the final version of the plan, the coverage was increased to 120,000 villages covering nearly a fourth of the population in rural areas without the corresponding backing in money and expert manpower. The consequent dilution of resources inevitably followed.

The cessation of hostilities in Korea in 1952 produced a worldwide decline in general price levels. This happened in India too, and the government realized unanticipated gains due to a cyclical turn in world prices. A dis-inflationary trend developed in India, and the price level soon declined for the first time since the beginning of the war. The cost of living index (1939=100), reached its peak level at 390 in 1951 and declined in 1952. The public finances of the country moved ahead at a faster pace leaving behind the legacy of low levels of revenue that forced the government to balance the budget at a low proportion to the national income. This practice was already given up during the Second World War, but since then, the government went through several rounds of controls, followed by decontrols leading to surging prices, and the re-imposition of controls.

By the time the First Plan was underway, the political leadership was still in two minds on the question, though there was a broad consensus that the size of the Plan being altogether modest the government must rein in prices. By 1952, this goal was realized without the government making any contribution towards it. The planners faced a severe fiscal constraint as the share of tax revenue in national income was only about 5–7 per cent. It imposed economic and political discipline in deciding just how much the government could aim at by way of new taxes and what needed to be done to prioritize the use of existing capacity in industry. The planners believed that additional taxes would depress the level of savings and investment in the private sector, while any significant increase in deficit financing would further aggravate inflation. So the resources available for the First Five Year Plan were seen as the sum of: (i) normal expansion in revenue and capital receipts; (iii) withdrawal from sterling balances; and (iii) modest levels of foreign aid. In fact the disinflationary environment made the government bolder with deficit financing to meet the resource gap, particularly because the scale of foreign aid was expected to remain below the level provided in the Plan.[81]

The government found it encouraging that the acceptable level of deficit financing was far above what was earlier imagined as safe. Yet the compelling economic fact that the Indian economy was largely open was barely grasped. As happened during 1929–33, it was strongly swayed by cyclical swings in the world economy, and the government still lacked the capacity to even partially insulate it from adverse trade influences developing in the stronger market economies.

Another hard truth that needed to be confronted was that, indeed, as the country's tax ratio to national income was among the lowest in the world, so was the rate of savings. Both were a function of the very low proportion of national output being exported. Higher exports would have raised savings, because by definition, there was less domestic consumption by this amount. Moreover, exported commodities can be subject to customs duties and the income generated by exports can be brought into the income tax net. This meant that the inertia of low tax ratio and savings rate could be broken if the economy developed a significant export surplus. However, this important economic message was ignored because India's export surplus was very low and in normal conditions of economic growth it could rise only incrementally.

The Constitution and Labour, Respite from Conflicts

Labour welcomed the new Constitution. It reinforced the purpose which informed the government of free India to promote equity and economic freedom through a democratic political system. The Constitution guaranteed the fundamental rights of freedom of speech, press, assembly and organization. The political side of the labour movement always demanded these rights and now these were established as universal democratic rights for the people of India. The Constitution also had a section devoted to the Directive Principles of State Policy which addressed the concerns of labour more directly. These were in Articles 39, 41, 42 and 43 and suggested a long-term commitment to strive towards providing an adequate means of livelihood to all citizens, men and women equally, that both men and women should get equal pay for equal work, that within the limits of its economic capacity and development the state would make effective provision for right to work, to education and to public assistance in cases of unemployment, old age, sickness, disablement and in other cases of undeserved want; that provisions would be made to secure just and humane conditions of work, and also for maternity relief. Beyond these broadminded, humane commitments, the Constitution made a huge promise without any reference to the timetable or means available or the stage of economic development to do the following:

> The state shall endeavour to secure, by legislation or economic organization or in any other way, to all workers, agricultural, industrial or otherwise, work, a living wage, conditions of work ensuring a decent standard of life and full enjoyment of leisure and social and cultural opportunities and, in particular, the state shall endeavour to promote cottage industries on an individual or cooperative basis in rural areas.

Those who drafted the Constitution never meant the directive principles to be treated as promises, and these could not be enforced by appeal to higher courts, but were there to be pursued earnestly by successive governments, or to be viewed as political rights which citizens could claim and ask the government to provide. In the next two decades, both fundamental rights, especially the right to property, and the directive principles activated politics and it became incumbent on the higher courts to take positions on contentious issues. The chief planks of the Constitution, to secure for all citizens of India, social, economic and political justice, liberty of thought, expression, belief, faith and worship, and equality of status and opportunity, became livewire issues of political controversy and engagement.

A large part of the operative part of the Constitution rested on the 1935 Act. A common feature was the division of subjects into three lists: the Union, the States and the Concurrent. Since labour was a subject on which both the Centre and the states could claim jurisdiction, it was in the Concurrent list. This meant that both the Union and state legislatures could pass laws on labour, but if there was repugnancy in respect of any law between the central and the state laws, the former supersedes the latter, except in the case of a law for which the previous assent of the President was obtained. The Union List on labour is a comprehensive one, while the State List includes only relief of the disabled and unemployment. Given the lopsided distribution of subjects, there was never any risk of the Union ousting the legitimate jurisdiction of the states. However, the government soon realized that the enactment of a contentious law on labour was a lesser problem. The more complex and difficult questions of implementation had to be dealt with and resolved by the states. The difficulty was removed by defining in each legislation the term, 'appropriate government', to mean the state government, where the actual implementation could be done only by the state government. This requires prior consultations with state governments before the enactment of a proposed bill. It partially answered the difficult question of maintaining fair uniformity of standards throughout the country. Part of the remedy lay in the organization of the Indian Labour Conference and the Standing Labour Committee where among other matters the issue of ensuring uniform standards could be raised in the presence of central and state ministers or other officials.

While the adoption of the Constitution as the basic law, on which as a touchstone, all existing and future enactments could be tested, marked great progress for labour, there were two prominent exclusions which were deeply disappointing. The Constitution did not grant the right to collective bargaining and the right to strike. The right to form trade unions was also missing though, later, it was explained that this right was inherent in the fundamental right to organize, et cetera. under Article 19. The right to labour impliedly included the right to withhold labour, but did not include the right to strike. This matter was pressed in the courts though, since neither the Trade Unions Act nor the Industrial Disputes Act (both of which preceded the Constitution), included the right to strike and the government was opposed to it, the test failed, and labour could not claim it then or later. In fact, the labour movement was not united on the subjects of collective bargaining and the right to strike. The dominant Gandhian part led by the INTUC and the TLA of

Ahmedabad were opposed to the idea of pushing these demands to the extremes, the search for a compromise or a via media were better methods to look after the welfare of workers. A major compensatory advantage to the labour movement was the uniform extension of all labour laws to the 100 million people who lived in the erstwhile princely states which were now incorporated in the Union of India. Earlier, in this backward Indian India, barring a few states, trade unions could not be formed and labour was denied this right.

The Five Year Plan on labour announced before Independence was implemented to a substantial extent. One item on the agenda was the fixation of minimum wages in sweated industries and occupations including agriculture. This was a tall order and required considerable preliminary work, including investigations which were time consuming. Instead, the government enacted the Minimum Wages Act placing the responsibility for notifying minimum wages in the scheduled industries, occupations and agriculture on the provinces (states after 1950). The economic question which was not addressed, but could never be ignored, was whether the notified wages should follow market trends or lead them. It would have to be answered in the light of the experience and the extent of voluntary compliance, opposition or evasion the law received. The low-wage sweated sector was the least unionized in most urban areas, so the only hope for the successful extension of the coverage of the Act was that over time the habit of voluntary compliance would grow and the pressure of unemployment on the undeveloped labour markets, which exerted a downward pressure on wages, would diminish.

Another item was the rationalization of the dearness allowance rates. The government never took it up. It required the enactment of a comprehensive wage law which the government chose not to have. Yet another item was the promotion of fair wage agreements. The government attended to this subject by setting up a committee to examine the question of fair wages in relation to fair return on capital, the interests of consumers and the claims of the government. In 1947, at the Tripartite Industries Conference, it was agreed in a resolution that:

> The system of remuneration to capital as well as labour must be so devised that while in the interests of the consumers and the primary producers excessive profits should be prevented by suitable measures of taxation and otherwise, both will share the product of their common effort after making provision for payment of fair wages to labour, a fair return to capital employed in the industry, and reasonable reserves for the maintenance and expansion of the undertaking.[82]

The same committee, with the representatives of labour as members was asked to examine the problem of profit sharing along with the question of fair wages and make recommendations. The committee's work was a creditable performance. A fair wage was above the minimum wage but below the living wage. The minimum wage must be assured to workers regardless of paying capacity of the employing firm, but not the fair wages which could be determined keeping in view the capacity to pay and other relevant considerations. The government drafted a Fair Wages Bill in 1950 and circulated it for eliciting public opinion and comments. It never could go beyond this stage and was given up. Instead of law, the idea of wage boards for different industries was found more attractive and accepted. The task of fixing fair wages would be entrusted to the tripartite wage boards, whenever these were set up.

The Plantation Labour Act, in 1951 extended the reform of labour standards and working conditions to the plantation labour whose interests and concerns were raised on occasion, but usually heard in feeble voices which this poorly organized segment of the exploited working class could muster. The working of the Industrial Disputes Act showed that there was a need for hearing appeals. This led to the enactment of the Industrial Disputes (Appellate Tribunal) Act in 1950. The government appeared to be keen to re-enact the dispute legislation and put it on firmer foundations. In 1950, it drafted two bills, the Labour Relations Bill and the Trade Unions Bill. The government was willing to encourage collective bargaining and establish the legal basis of trade union rights, but was equally determined to retain a firm grip on industrial conflicts. According to Karnik, 'both contained useful as well as harmful provisions. There was a storm of protest against them. Influenced by it, the Government decided not to proceed with the Bills—and quietly dropped them.'[83]

V.V. Giri was the Labour Minister and he strongly canvassed against heavy dependence on the conciliation and adjudication machinery of the Industrial Disputes Act. This habit weakened unions because instead of organizing workers in a spirit of self-reliance and mutual accommodation with the employers, which is achieved through collective bargaining and practical ways of give and take, workers raised disputes in the hope of drawing government's attention, expected the union to work on the government machinery and secure favourable verdicts. These were persuasive arguments but he failed to carry conviction.

Following the 1952 elections, the new labour minister formally rejected collective bargaining as a philosophy of industrial relations on the ground that it carried with it the theory of sanctioning strikes and lockouts, without regard for inter-industry effects or the economic health of society. These coercive methods could be used only as a last resort, or preferably not even then. Instead, at the early stages of the dispute, recourse to conciliation should be undertaken and, on its failure, the government could decide on the merits of the dispute whether it should be referred for adjudication. At this stage, the disputing parties must wait for the courts/tribunals to announce their verdicts.

The government rejected the concept of sanctions or freedom to engage in industrial conflicts, as being antithetical to economic planning and the vision of orderly progress in a peaceful democratic political system. The communists were already in full battle cry against the government, determined to organize a revolutionary class war to topple capitalism and feudalism in India. They promoted strikes and street violence wherever they had influence in industry. Partly for this reason, the AITUC failed to take part in the tripartite deliberations and in the enactment of the several laws that had the good of the working class as their objective. Their wild actions strengthened the government's convictions not to let the grip over industrial relations weaken.

In 1948, the communists had decided to plunge the country into a violent upheaval which happened to be in close sequence to the communal riots and the partition-induced forced migration of population. The working class was also seething with unrest. The threat of famine loomed over the horizon and the government's resources were stretched to the limit. Yet, the government led by enlightened and farsighted leaders projected the newly freed state in liberating and moderating roles, in alleviating suffering and doing justice to the downtrodden. The labour policy formed part of the philosophy of moving forward to bring about incremental systemic changes in the organization of industries with the aid of a body of new laws. These would strengthen labour and usher in a more informed and humane relationships between the owners of capital and labour. Labour was obviously the weaker party and in any test of strength it was likely to come out worse and demoralized. The interests of society did not warrant such an outcome, it should be better to have neither victory nor defeat for either labour or capital. For their own good, as well as that of the society, it was important to keep the productive system functioning without disruption. This was the Gandhian method of non-confrontation and peaceful engagement in conflict resolution which was first put into law in Bombay in 1938.

This philosophy found wider acceptance not only in the government, at the Centre and the states, and the ruling Congress Party but also among labour leaders. the INTUC was committed to it; the HMS would not oppose it, while the leftist unions led by the CPI were strongly for class conflict-based industrial relations. Their philosophy of industrial relations was derived from the Marxist–Leninist ideology and in its practical aspects it formed part of the manner in which class relations were to be used to remake or wreck the very fragile democratic Constitution of free India. Between 1948 and 1951, the free institutions were powerfully assailed by the communists and produced several negative results. The law of preventive detention and the denial of due process in law were the two entirely adverse outcomes of this unproductive early contest. India needed to be defended against the communists' subversion of the rule of law.

The Bombay Industrial Relations (BIR) Act, 1946, based on the principles of reconciliation and compromise, created an elaborate machinery for the settlement of industrial disputes. One of the novel features of this Act was the system of representative and approved unions. Such unions could collect union dues and post notices. In a local area, they were the sole bargaining agents. The Act laid down a procedure to make any changes in the working conditions. Its purpose was to maintain industrial peace, especially in the conflict-prone cotton textile industry. However, in 1950, a major strike broke out in this industry on the question of fairness of union recognition under law, among other issues. The strike of 63 days' duration was led by the HMS against recognition granted to the Rashtriya Mill Mazdoor Sabha, affiliated to the INTUC. The economic issue was the bonus. The Industrial Court under the BIR Act awarded bonus to be paid at two months' basic wages in all mills except four. The award was not acceptable to the workers and the recognized union decided to make an appeal to the newly constituted Labour Appellate Tribunal (LAT). The mill owners also filed an appeal to reduce the bonus. Pending the appeals before the LAT the union and the Mill Owners Association signed an agreement for the payment of the first instalment of bonus. At this point, the Mill Mazdoor Sabha, affiliated to HMS, advised the workers to reject the agreement, refuse the instalment and demand three month's bonus, based on basic wages plus dearness allowance, and payable by all the mills, including the four left out by the Industrial Court.

This led to the call for battle on 14 August, if the demand was not conceded by then. The communists opposed the long strike which was contemplated, but still called a one-day strike on 14 August. Later they supported it. The strike was illegal under the Act; accordingly meetings and processions were prohibited by the police. Most of the strike leaders and members of the strike committee were arrested. There was a call for a general strike on 31 August, which was a big success. Police had to open fire and four people were killed. The strike took the turn of a general agitation and police opened fire on several occasions, killing more people. A total of 10 people were killed in police violence; around 1500 persons were put n jail. The strike went on for 55 days when LAT announced ts decision confirming the original award with some nodifications. On 16 October the strike was called off. It had failed and the workers were demoralized. The arrested leaders were prosecuted for calling an illegal strike and convicted by the court. Later, though they appealed, the convictions were upheld, first by the High Court and on further appeal, by the Supreme Court as well. The Mill Mazdoor Sabha leaders were dismissed by the mills and the Mill Owners' Association advised other mills not to hire them.[84]

The moral principle that emerged from the successfully called illegal strike was that, though recognized, the RMMS did not enjoy the confidence of the workers. Yet, under the law, it, alone, could represent workers and speak in their name. It was the legal status of the union which was effectively challenged and brought out the inequity of the legal procedure to determine the representative status of a union, even though it failed to enjoy the workers' support. The BIR Act survived intact. Recognition was first granted by the court on the basis of the verified membership of the unions. Later, the Mill Owners' Association accepted the recognized union for bargaining purposes.

It is apparent that among the textile workers the recognized union lacked credibility, but they would not demonstrate greater loyalty to the rival HMS by enrolling as its members. The law demonstrated that merely by going on a prolonged strike workers could not dislodge the legal status of the recognized union, more so since the dispute was already pending before the LAT. By going on an illegal strike, which was also unjustified, workers had shown contempt for LAT as well. In fact, the strikers and HMS had rejected the entire legal basis of dispute settlement. If the strike had been allowed to succeed, it would have uprooted the entire edifice of law on which the BIR Act and the LAT functioned. Nonetheless, the 1950 strike did demonstrate the sheer fragility of legal remedies for class related disputes.

The communist-led militancy in working class areas began to ease in 1951 and by the time election results were announced it was over. The Moscow guidance produced considerable debate within the CPI, mainly between the faction leaders who wanted to back Congress on its progressive policies and others who believed that the party had built a strong mass base in several parts of India and could wrest power by ousting Congress in the next election. The road to power did require a broad-based united front of classes and the exploited masses. It would not be possible to sustain that by supporting Nehru or toning down their attack against the Congress, which was steadily losing popularity and the support of the common people.

Class struggle could not be politically given up or scaled down. Indeed, it must remain the solid core of the party's ideology; yet, sectarian adventurism was wrong and should be given up. The CPI underwent a leadership change in mid-1951 and again just before the 1952 election. These were never explained, but there was a distinct change in the party's political orientation. Hereafter, as far as the communists were concerned, industrial relations would more likely be peaceful than turbulent.

The economy had started growing again. The sum of average daily employment in factories, mines, plantations, railways and posts and telegraph rose from (000) 5,010 in 1948 to 5,165 in 1949, 5,276 in 1950, 5,414 in 1951, 5,498 in 1952 and appeared to be stable at 5,475 in 1953. Thereafter, employment rose continuously every year in the following decade. Labour productivity in manufacturing rose alongside. With 1946 as the base year, it was 110.6 in 1950, 124.1 in 1951, 128.3 in 1952 and 138.9 in 1953 and, in the next 10 years, productivity rose together with total employment. 1950 was a year of low productivity compared to the previous two years. The index of money earnings (1939=100) declined to 334.2 in 1950 compared to 340.3 in 1949; thereafter it showed a gentle upward trend. In 1951, the index stood at 356.8, and in 1952 at 385.7, but declined in the next two years to 384.6 in 1953 and 381.2 in 1954. This was paradoxical since earnings per worker remained stable.[85]

The cost of living index (1939=100) showed alternating years of stable and rising prices. It remained stable at 371 in 1949 and 1950, rose to 387 in 1951, declined to 349 in 1952, rose again to 385 in 1953 and fell in the next two years. For the working classes, this was an unusual experience, a boon in the post-Independence period. Between 1949 and 1956, the cost of living index declined or showed zero change in four years and spurts in the other four years. Such a thing had not happened in many years! It began to be reflected in the index of industrial disputes or stoppages (1939=100). The highest level of 446.1 was recorded in 1947, but following the Industrial Truce Resolution which labour honoured, the index declined to 310.1 in 1948, 226.6 in 1949 and 200.5 in 1950, then rose to 263.8 in 1951 and fell to 237.2 in 1952, and again to 190.1 in 1953. Thereafter, industrial conflicts rose every year till 1957. By this time, the ITR was all but forgotten. Trade unions gained in membership and the labour movement grew from year to year while the average membership per union declined. Four competing trade union centres were engaged in forming new unions and enrolling memberships without bothering about their financial or organizational viabilities.[86]

III. 1954–7

Nehru Leads India, Linguistic Reorganization, Second Elections

The 1952 elections showed that the Congress received less than 50 per cent of total votes cast, while in three states, Travancore–Cochin, Madras and the newly created PEPSU (Patiala and East Punjab States' Union), it failed to get the majority in state assemblies. Moreover, factionalism was rife in the Congress organization and an unseemly tussle was observed for ministerships and attempts at ousting the chief minister. Nehru was the undisputed leader, not just of the Congress, but of the country, and support for him, which was a unique blend of loyalty, love and admiration, came from across the parties and all walks of life. By 1954, his reputation had travelled abroad and his unique foreign policy that steered India on the middle path of non-alignment received some grudging acceptance in the US and UK. In national politics, he felt the need for a vision for the future which would guide the formulation of Five Year Plans and policies and set the course of the socioeconomic development of the country for years to come.

The Congress moved to the left under Nehru's leadership by adopting the long-term goal of a socialistic pattern of society in 1954. In 1953, Nehru had tried to forge fresh ties with the PSP to strengthen the forces of democratic socialism, but found the stiff conditions presented by Jayaprakash Narayan unacceptable. The conditions were that the government would have to accept the demand for constitutional amendment on the fundamental right to property, to nationalization of banks, et cetera, and far-reaching agrarian reforms. By comparison, the idea of the socialistic pattern of society was a much diluted version of socialism; it was closer to *sarvodaya* and cooperation, rather than public ownership of the means of production, and compatible with the idea of a mixed economy with state regulations in the interests of the common good of the people.

Nehru thought that the new institutions, particularly cooperative farming, would go further in reducing the spectre of exploitation in rural India than a direct onslaught of property rights in land. The government would endeavour to improve the economic and social conditions of the masses in the Gandhian way. As an organization, the Congress went along with him, endorsing his ideas, but given its mixed class character and unwillingness to hurt its supporters in the privileged sections of society, this was nearly as far as was expedient to move to the left without becoming a leftist party. As a result, actual political behaviour of party functionaries, particularly at the state level, often did not match the leader's ideas. Moreover, it was observed usually more often in formal speeches and much less in actions. Gopal Krishna summed it up thus:

> The party, instead of being actively associated with the formulation and implementation of social reconstruction programmes, became a suppliant adjunct to the Government. Its only function being to endorse the policies of the Government when called upon to do so by the leader. In the states the machinery of the organization was used by rival factions to gain control over the Government, and then its power and patronage were utilized by the successful faction to control the party.[87]

Following the consolidation of the princely states and their integration into the Union of India, the country was truly one and never as united as now. The new challenge to the unity of India came from the insistent demand for reorganization of state boundaries on the basis of the language spoken and accepted as the mother tongue of the people. After the formation of the new state of Andhra Pradesh, this demand, especially in the Marathi speaking regions of the composite Bombay state, became unstoppable.

The government decided to yield to this demand and appointed the States Reorganization Commission to examine all the related problems connected with the demand for linguistic states. It reported in 1955 and, a year later, India's political map was partially redrawn to reflect the language principle though, for different reasons, both Bombay and Punjab were left bilingual.

Around this demand, a number of new multi-party political organizations had formed to carry on agitations along the lines of civil disobedience, strikes, stoppage of civic life, including demonstrations in defiance of law and propitiatory orders and wholly new forms of protest. There were several dimensions to the problem. The one that people asserted most was the obvious importance of their subnational identity coupled with a subtle demand that their distinct identity should not be submerged in the greater identity of Indian nationhood. Instead, it should be accorded a secure position within it, treating India as a great umbrella under which all the diverse people of this country may develop, enjoying their cultural autonomy and self respect without in any way impairing national unity.[88]

Linguistically defined ethnic societies sought the political right to promote their economic development and allocate scarce resources, including mineral wealth, forests and water towards maximizing the larger good of their people. It was asserted that the subnational sentiment was entirely compatible with the Indian Constitution, which gave wide powers to the states. It was also consistent with the idea of India as a functioning federation with strong unitary features. In any case, this problem in all essential respects was resolved by 1956, though the residual matters still took several more years of agitations, compromise and capitulation by the Centre to get it resolved.

By 1967, India was politically regrouped along ethnic demarcations of language, religion and tribe, as completely as was considered administratively feasible. The political map of India, by the end of 1967, was markedly different from the one that was inherited, post-Partition, in 1947. This was the second largest contribution made by democratic politics, though brought about by a combination of agitation and civil disobedience, even violent means towards coercing the government to act against its declared policies. The leaders and law makers who wrote the Constitution could never have anticipated the consequences of the politics of mobilizing ever-increasing sections of populace, through agitations, elections and political contests in various forms, which occurred over a period of about two decades since its adoption.

Nehru's foreign policy was a strong plank which gave rise to significant regrouping of political forces within the country. In 1954, Nehru formulated the five principles of peaceful coexistence and soon received support for them from the leaders of the Soviet Union and Communist China. India emerged as a dependable country in advancing the cause of world peace. The CPI leaders on their part developed major divisions among themselves on appraising India's position in a Cold War-torn world.[89] Ajay Ghosh went to Moscow in 1954 to seek guidance. On his return, he announced that while the CPI supported India's foreign policy, it would remain critical of Nehru's and the state governments' anti-people policies. Moreover, such was the impact of the 1952 election, and the progress the CPI made through parliamentary work, that it decided to transform itself from a cadre-based small party with a few thousand members to a party of the masses with a large body of members. Meanwhile, it was becoming clearer that India could not stay aloof in the Cold War. The US signed a military pact with Pakistan in 1954 and the latter began to be viewed as a dependable ally of the West. Earlier in February 1954, in support of Pakistan, the Western powers introduced a resolution in the Security Council for the induction of a temporary UN force into Kashmir to facilitate the holding of a plebiscite, but the effort failed as it was vetoed by the Soviet Union.

In the Security Council debates, the Soviet Union's stand

on the Kashmir issue showed that in its view the policy of the US and the UK was clearly of an imperialist character. It was indicative of the path of expansion, intervening in the internal affairs of Jammu and Kashmir under the UN flag, to introduce foreign troops there in order to turn this territory into their strategic base. India was asked to accept foreign troops in the Kashmir valley which had categorically turned down the suggestion.

The Soviet position moved closer to India and this undoubtedly helped lay the basis for greater cooperation in economic aid and trade and the strengthening of bilateral relations. The Indo-Soviet Trade Agreement of December 1953 valid for five years provided for payments in Indian rupees for imports from the USSR. The agreement covered 39 items including industrial plant and equipment, heavy electrical plant and equipment, machine tools and a vast array of machines which India sorely needed to replace worn out industrial assets. In return, India could export 20 items, mostly agricultural or primary products.

This was followed by the Indo-Soviet Steel Agreement signed in February 1955 to set up a steel plant at Bhilai. It was a major break in the trading pattern India had with the industrialized countries and marked the beginning of a new era. The terms provided for a credit of approximately Rs. 1,020 million, repayable at the very low interest rate of 2.5 per cent over a 12-year period. By comparison, the Western countries were charging interest at over 6 per cent. Additionally, India had the option to repay loans in rupees, which the Soviet Union would use to import goods from India. Later, the Soviet Union agreed to help in setting up the Institute of Technology at Bombay. It also gifted farm machinery for the government farm at Suratgarh.

The five principles of peaceful coexistence (1954), were broadly echoed by the Soviet Union and the two countries joined hands at the United Nations to work for the promotion of peace and the lowering of international tensions. The exchange of visits by Nehru to the USSR in 1955 and the return goodwill mission by Khrushchev and Bulganin, further strengthened the friendship between the two countries. Indian observations on the Hungarian crisis were taken by the Soviet leaders with forbearance and allowed to pass. It may be that the visit by Nehru was less substantive in political terms though, for him, even the symbolic aspect was important. On the other hand, the return visit of the Soviet leaders was meant to be of political significance. The two leaders extended support on Goa and took a pro-India position on Kashmir. Supporting the Kashmir Constituent Assembly's decision taken two years earlier, confirming the state's accession to India, Krushchev declared that the people of Kashmir had already decided to join the Indian Union, implying thereby that there was hardly any basis for taking a plebiscite on the question.

In 1954 and 1955, the Portuguese possessions in India became politically alive. The Socialist Party took the lead in forcing the issue by launching a satyagraha in Goa and other territories. In July 1954, the tiny enclave of Dadra was occupied by a group of socialist workers from Bombay. Encouraged, they entered another enclave, Nagar–Haveli, during the next month and secured it without a fight. On Independence Day, about 1,000 volunteers attempted to enter Daman, but were stopped by Indian police.

Following this episode, in 1955, a group of activists entered Goa shouting slogans and walked a couple of miles when they were attacked by the Portuguese police. Some were injured while others were arrested and they spent about 20 months in a Goan prison before being released. The Vatican was credited with the positive role it played in securing their release. One of the prisoners was Tridib Chowdhury, leader of the RSP and an MP. Nehru's government was not on speaking terms with the dictator, Salazar, who had pretentiously announced that Goa was a Portuguese community in India and it belonged to Portugal by injunction of history and force of law.[90] The government could do little to secure the release of more than 2,000 Indian prisoners in

Portuguese prisons, and may have sought the intervention of other powers, including the Vatican.

Nehru together with President Sukarno of Indonesia organized an Afro-Asian Conference in 1955 at the Indonesian city of Bandung in which 29 countries including India and China took part. At the conference, a political commitment was made to work together to end colonial rule everywhere, and for Nehru it was a great achievement. However, questions were posed whether the conference was non-aligned in character or was it anti-Western? The colonial powers of Europe were closely aligned with the US, and the latter, despite it dominance as a world power showed little interest in ending colonial rule. India was undoubtedly non-aligned on the issues of the Cold War and advanced the belief that only by accepting coexistence as a political principle could the ideal of world peace be achieved, but there was no question of remaining uninvolved on the issue of Portuguese enclaves in India. It was strongly anti-colonialism at the same time.

In Egypt, issues came to a head in July 1956. When Gamal Abdel Nasser nationalized the Suez Canal Company, jointly owned by Britain and France, which owned and managed the Suez Canal, Britain demanded action to reverse the decision and asked for international control over the canal. Nehru mediated but failed. In retaliation, Britain, with France and Israel as colluding parties, decided on a military invasion of Egypt. India condemned it as an act of aggression, while the US, whose prior concurrence had not been obtained, did not accept it as a proper act and exercised its weight to put an end to it. As a result of this pressure, the Anglo-French military alliance withdrew their forces and the Suez Canal stayed with Egypt.

The harder test came next. Soon after the Anglo-French invasion, came the dreadful news that Soviet tanks had entered Hungary and rolled into its capital, Budapest, to crush a popular government, following a nationalist revolt for an independent and representative government to rule their country. This was formed by replacing the earlier government led by the Soviet puppets government. Moscow's intervention put an end to the democratic government and restored communist rule, now backed by the Soviet armed might.[91] This too was an act of aggression. Soviet troops had entered Poland as well. Both were aggressive acts to preserve the hegemonic status of the Soviet Union, but India failed to call them as such and merely expressed its disapproval. Krishna Menon was directly criticized for this bias, while Nehru's reputation also suffered.

Hard political reasoning explained India's acknowledged dependence on the Soviet Union for support in the Security Council, where it was indispensable, and its very willing economic and technical aid towards India's economic development. Nehru never spoke on what weighed with India's actions, partly because his moral standing was in question, but more importantly, he was equally keen on maintaining cordial relations with the United States for the much needed economic ties. Moreover, the present crisis would soon be history. The West would concede the Soviet Union's dominance over the Eastern European countries and the logic of the Cold War prevailed. Amidst all this, India's foreign policy commitment to non-involvement and maintaining a fair distance from the two power blocs remained. Therefore, all that could be done under the circumstances was to engage in damage control. The Americans and British understood this and were willing to play along, but no one ever understood why Nehru permitted Krishna Menon to use his acid tongue so often, and mostly directed at the West.

In 1956, the foreign policy increasingly served the governments' deepening involvement in planned economic development. Two matters were of the foremost importance. India accepted its perpetual food deficit status and its need to import food grains to feed the people and keep the Plan afloat. The United States emerged as a major provider of food grains, happily for India, on a rupee loan and was willing to lend complementary aid in technical training and other ways. The first PL 480 agreement (Public Law or Food for Peace) was signed in August 1956. Following this, the food ministry signed another PL 480 agreement in September 1957 to import two million tonnes of wheat over a period of two years. This assured the continuity of the Second Plan.

The British were more belligerent and less suave. Following the Suez crisis, the British government showed their ire by expressing strong disapproval of the Second Plan's emphasis on industrialization and socialism, as well as India's acceptance of aid from the Soviet Union. It took the unusual step of asking all the Colombo Plan donor countries to jointly teach India a lesson and stop it in what it was endeavouring to do. This kind of belligerence was not expected and it cleaved the relations, principally with the UK and also all the older member countries of the British Commonwealth. Politically, India moved out of the Commonwealth connection and searched for firmer ties, more by way of dependence on the United States, though at the same time using the increasing closeness of relations with the Soviet Union as a counterweight to preserve an overall balanced international position. It can be said that the close informal ties with Britain which Nehru readily accepted in 1947–8 could no longer take the wear and tear of conflicting national pursuits and contradictions in conducting multinational relations, specially the strain of the Cold War, the Kashmir dispute, the West's close alliance with Pakistan, and these had to give way. In 1957, India effectively ceased to be under the British sphere of influence and moved out of it on an independent course. The Suez crisis and the disaster in Hungary proved to be the major markers in India's quest for a nationally centred independent foreign policy, though it had been taking shape since 1954.

The laws enacted to reform Hindu society deserve to be placed among Nehru's most notable achievements, mainly because the bills met with a large body of criticism and political opposition from the more conservative and tradition-driven spokesmen of Hindu society. The Hindu code was on the reform agenda of the British government and, in 1941, N. Ram was entrusted with the task of preparing a draft code. The British were convinced that the strong reformist movements among the Hindus in the last one century or more had prepared the society to have reforms codified in law. In 1946, a draft of the reform code was ready and, in 1948, under the leadership of B.R. Ambedkar, it was revived and revised by the select committee. It was called the Hindu Code Bill of which Nehru became a strong votary and champion.

The Code sought to raise the status of women in Hindu society and remove the caste-based disparities and discriminations. The Bill created the legal basis of equity for women—indeed as nothing comparable had been done so far—and for this reason alone it ran into a strong body of political opposition. President Rajendra Prasad was one of them, though he took the stand that the Assembly was elected on a restricted franchise and lacked the authority to enact such a bill; moreover, such a controversial legislation as the Bill should be passed following an open electoral contest. He prevailed, and the Bill was allowed to lapse to the great disappointment of Ambedkar, who was piloting it and expected greater and more consistent support from Nehru. As a mark of protest, he resigned from the government in October 1951 and founded an opposition party, called the Scheduled Castes Federation.

He failed to win a seat in the Lok Sabha in 1952 and later entered the Rajya Sabha. However, he no longer took an interest in the enactment of the several bills into which the earlier great tome, the consolidated Hindu Code Bill, was usefully split for ease of discussion and passage in parliament.

In the 1952 election, Nehru was opposed by an orthodox Hindu politician, Prabhu Datt Brahmachari, who was supported by several Hindu parties and organizations and won with a massive majority. The Congress, with a large majority in the Lok Sabha was returned to office with the expected mandate to proceed with the reform measures, and Prasad, now re-elected President of the republic, no longer pressed his views. Nehru argued, wrote to his challengers and persuaded others on the importance of the proposed Marriage and Divorce Bill, the Succession Bill and others dealing with adoption and guardianship. As a result, political protests were more subdued. though arguments against them were still advanced.

The strongest argument against the bills was that they were politically opportunistic moves, since, instead of legislating a common code, the Hindus were singled out for social reforms. Monogamy was undoubtedly the right principle to codify, but why should the law be applicable only to the Hindus, the Sikhs, the Jains and the Buddhists, and not the others, principally the Muslims? The reason cogently advanced was that whereas Hindu society had advanced sufficiently to accept and practise the more modern and liberal laws on the status of women, the Muslims evidently had not, and it would not be proper to enact a common code at that stage, though later at a more opportune moment it could be done. The Muslim MPs were grateful to the government for this religious sensitivity.

In the 1957 general elections, both the Congress and the communists improved on their previous performances. Owing to a split in the party, the PSP declined and it sharpened the three directional pulls already working on the party cadre, one of which was towards the Congress, which now advocated socialism and encouraged PSP members to return to the fold. The second was of Dr Ram Manohar Lohia with his agitational approach to mass politics. And the third was to stay with the party and strengthen it. However, overall the PSP declined politically and this condition remained un-arrested. In the 1957 elections, the Congress reached its peak position with one party dominance at the Centre. However, by this time, several competing parties had gained in strength in a number of states, most noticeably the CPI in Kerala, the Jan Sangh in UP where it made noticeable gains, while the CPI in West Bengal emerged in considerable strength.

The 1957 elections witnessed the participation of a large number of splinter parties and groups which caused splitting and diffusion of voting strengths. There were also instances of vote splitting. 'At many centres in the country much the same body of voters returned Congress candidates to the lower house of parliament at New Delhi but cast its votes in favour of candidates of other parties or in favour of independents to the state assemblies.'[92] This may have been indicative of voters' discernment in the choice of candidates, or more pertinently it was the politically expressed desire to be governed by another party at the state. After all, Nehru's government functioned mainly at the Centre. At the state level, the political spectacle was often dominated by unseemly faction-based rivalry among groups of local leaders.

The Congress noticed a decline in the people's loyalty and viewed it as a result of the widening gulf between the organization and the rural masses. More at the roots lay the numerous impediments placed on land reforms. The Congress legislators belonging to the landowning classes either slowed down or effectively diluted the contents of land reform legislation. While it was possible in various degrees to abolish the institution of intermediaries and instead create direct and simplified land tenure systems in various states, subsequent progress was tardy. This was the clearest sign that the Congress as an organization had deep differences with the programme the Centre proposed for more progress in land reforms and perhaps the character of planned economic development generally.

The heterogeneous class character of Congress pushed the government machinery in contradictory directions. These were more often reflected in the formation of factions which weakened the cohesiveness and drive of state governments still further. Those who strongly believed in peasant proprietorship of land had little sympathy with cooperative farming or the pooling of land under government auspices. Before the 1957 elections, the issues were mostly managed in a political sense, but left unresolved at the policy and implementation levels. On occasion, these took the form of clashes between the government and party organization on various questions; or the leadership of the chief minister faced challenges by a contending leading rival representing other class interests, or the politically active castes. Temporary solutions to such conflicts were usually worked out by the national leaders on an ad hoc basis, mostly by Nehru personally choosing one contestant over another. The conflict would then resurface on another occasion.

The CPI was steadily moving to the right and this facilitated their active participation in the second general election. The party did unexpectedly well in Kerala where it secured a bare working majority and formed the first ever communist government on the basis of a democratic election. The party followed the change in direction in the international communist movement closely. It took particular note of the disbandment of the Cominform in 1956, following the advocacy of peaceful coexistence of the competing sociopolitical systems of capitalism and socialism and the renewed emphasis of the Soviet leadership on preserving world peace. The CPI too found it expedient to put the doctrines of class war, violent social revolution and the use of state power to vanquish class enemies, on the outer shelves of its ideology. The communists, of course, would not give up violence, nor accept non-violence as a legitimate political creed in a democracy; instead the party decided that it was not really necessary any longer to assert that the roadmap of socialism had to be bloodied. This was reflected in the new party Constitution adopted in 1958 in which several threatening features were dropped. It could be interpreted as an indirect yet one more significant gain for democracy in India.[93]

The 1957 elections produced disarray among the socialists. Jayaprakash Narayan (JP) expressed disenchantment with party politics and moved towards the Vinoba Bhave-led Bhoodan (land donation) movement. He tried to unite the party. Dr Lohia had been expelled earlier and founded the socialist party which was committed to opposing the Congress. JP attempted to reunite the two but failed. In 1957, he gave up his membership of the PSP and devoted all his time to the Bhoodan movement as a peaceful method of land redistribution, and also in the quest for a party-less democracy. This was to be attained by mass education and awareness rather than political power. He was out of politics because he feared that the failure of parliamentary democracy would be a great disaster not only for India, but also for Asia. The present experiment should not fail and lead to one-party government. There was the ardent Gandhian, the saintly Vinoba Bhave, whose walking tour from village to village, unescorted by police, through the communist-led guerrilla campaign in the Telangana area of Andhra Pradesh, for land redistribution, showed the way to genuine progress. The Vinoba Bhave Mission sought the path of persuasion and conciliation, which India needed, not Marxism nor parliamentary democracy.

New political forces emerged in the 1957 elections. In Bombay, the state-based Samyukta Maharashtra Samiti (SMS) and the Mahagujarat Parishad, each fighting for a language-based division of the composite state, gained at the expense of Congress. The former had campaigned for a Marathi-speaking United Maharashtra and secured 5.5 million votes against 5.3 million cast in Congress' favour. The SMS managed to capture the municipal bodies in local elections in the cities of Bombay and Poona. The two groups demanded that the same principle of language-based demarcation of states should apply to Bombay as well, and there was a further demand by the SMS that the city of Bombay should form part of the Marathi-speaking state.

The communist government in Kerala led by E.M.S. Namboodripad introduced the controversial Education Bill in the assembly to correct known abuses in privately owned schools and colleges, including those run by the churches. It gave the state the power to take over schools that did not abide by the provisions in the Bill, on the status of teachers, managements' rights to hire and fire, salaries and working conditions. A strong opposition was mounted by the Christian organizations. They were deeply anti-communist, and this fact was reflected in the low vote polled by the CPI candidates in the constituencies where Christian voters were predominant. The churches were able to make common cause with the Nair Service Society which also ran schools and colleges. The Congress party now in opposition decided to take the opportunist route to join hands in opposing the Bill with those already doing it.

In Madras (later Tamil Nadu), K. Kamraj, leader of the backward castes, emerged as the foremost leader in 1954, replacing Rajaji as the Chief Minister. The latter was in retirement, but in 1956 he decided to enter public affairs once again on the plea that the Congress had become too complacent and the country needed an opposition party. He was also uncomfortable with the Congress moving left to build a socialist pattern of society. The Second Five Year Plan showed that the economic policies of the government would be influenced by socialist economics. His own thinking was strongly conservative and there was little common ground between him and Nehru. The answer was either a strong opposition functioning within the Congress, or, if this was not possible, to launch a party of the right outside it, to which likeminded people might gravitate.

In fact, the Congress Party still had several independent-minded people who put uncomfortable questions in parliament and expressed disagreement with the government. In September 1957, questions were asked on the propriety of the Life Insurance Corporation (LIC) making large investments in a private firm owned by Haridas Mundhra. Nehru's son-in-law, Feroz Gandhi, disclosed that the shares were bought at inflated prices well above their market worth and hinted at some sort of conspiracy which should be investigated. Conceding this point, the government appointed a retired judge to conduct the enquiry. Proceedings were open to the public and received considerable notice by the press. 'People flocked to the hearings, there to see the minister, his officials fumble under questioning or contradict one another. The final reports of the judge were damning, and exacted a price; both the minister and his secretary were forced to demit office.'[94]

Ten years after Independence, the Nehru government suffered a real political shake up. The Mundhra affair showed that, unknown to Nehru, but functioning under his strong umbrella, a fiscal impropriety of this kind was put through without any fear that it might be discovered and sully the reputation of the government. With the exit of T.T. Krishnamachari, Nehru lost an able finance minister. TTK was strongly committed to the Second Plan. He had the courage to take the blame for the taxation proposals needed for its finance and defend them in parliament on his convictions.

Economic Stabilization, Government Shifts Gears for Development

In the first seven years following Independence the government resolved several policy-related issues. One, that the economic model will be that of a mixed economy in which the private sector will have considerable freedom, but not the leading role in economic development. Moreover, as the Industries (Development and Regulation) Act, 1951 provided, no new industrial undertaking may be started or expansion of an existing unit taken up without a license from the government. So the development process will be a controlled one and regulated by laws.

Two, the public sector will play a larger role in industrial development. It may even overtake the private sector and become the leading agency for industrialization.

Three, by 1954, Nehru had visualized the long-term goal of economic planning and social development as the socialist pattern of society to be realized by blending the Gandhian sarvodaya principles with the egalitarian ideals of socialism through democratic and peaceful means. The Planning Commission created by him would produce Five Year Plans in smooth succession to organize the scarce resources of the country to build an economic structure of inter-dependent and mutually sustaining subsystems which would generate long-term growth and liberate the economy from the shackles of backwardness. Moreover, the vision of a socialist pattern of society would inform the formulation of Five Year Plans and act as a guide in devising policy instruments for their implementation.

Nehru looked for talent to man the Planning Commission and start the journey, and unsurprisingly found it among the capable ICS officers and a few economists who were already there and could be entrusted with the responsibility. He relied on people such as Sir V.T. Krishnamachari, ICS, Tarlok Singh, ICS and Gulzari Lal Nanda, a committed Gandhian trade unionist, and a few others, not more than ten in all. This group was joined by Professor P.C. Mahalanobis, a scientist and statistician of exceptional ability and dynamism. They were committed to working Nehru's vision into a Five Year Plan, so capable of being translated into reality.

In 1954, the ball was set rolling towards a bolder and more robust Second Five Year Plan. Nehru delivered the key speech on 9 November 1954 at the National Development Council. 'The picture I have in mind is definitely and absolutely a socialist pattern of society. I am not using the word in a dogmatic sense at all. I mean largely that the means of production should be socially owned and controlled for the benefit of society as a whole. There is plenty of room for private enterprise provided the main aim is kept clear.'[95] Mahalanobis invited a large number of distinguished economists from different countries and discussed his ideas with them. However, what emerged at the end of these discussions was a distinctive Mahalanobis product carrying an imprint of the Soviet Union's early models of industrialization.

In 1955, the Plan Frame for the Second Plan was circulated for wider discussion. In January 1955, at the Avadi session of the Indian National Congress, Nehru personally moved the resolution which committed the party to work to build a socialist pattern of society. However, the Plan Frame received heavy criticism and it took the government some time to finalize it. Industrialists welcomed the emphasis on heavy industries and accepted the agency of the public sector to put them in place, but not the restrictions placed on expansion of factory production in the private sector. The government was criticized for fostering the intrinsically inefficient small-scale industries and cottage industries in place of the modern factory system. The cost could be high and it may result in the collapse of the Second Plan. The Planning Commission's ideas on agrarian reforms, especially cooperative farming, met with strong resistance from the state governments and party organization. Beginning with 1955, the Five Year Plans and the Planning Commission faced unceasing criticisms and academic critiques during the next two decades. The country's politics produced new alignments of political parties around the many concrete issues which were encountered in the course of implementation, success and failure of the Five Year Plans.

The First Plan ended on 31 March 1956 as scheduled. The economy had grown at 3.7 per cent per annum, while agricultural production increased at 3.57 per cent per annum. Prices were stable and the government received encouraging signals from the IMF that a somewhat higher level of deficit financing and some rise in the price level might be healthy for the economy. The balance of payments showed accretion of foreign exchange reserves and the rupee could be viewed as a relatively strong currency in a weak sterling area.

By the end of 1950, the government could resettle the rural migrants who comprised the majority of 4.7 million refugees who needed help, on land in East Punjab, Rajasthan and UP. This was done on a quasi-permanent basis.

> It was another two years before Government could decide upon making the settlement permanent, taking into consideration the benefits that had accrued to the lands and to the occupying and cultivating tenants; and a further two years for it to decide on conferring proprietary rights on them, when it became clear that Pakistan's calculated evasion of a settlement with India of the evacuee property issue had petrified. The result of Government effort at finding gainful occupation for the urban displaced was slight.[96]

In respect of urban evacuees the claims to their properties were verified and the government decided on paying compensation to them, on the principle of providing small relief, since it had been unable to do more by way of training and employment. Over a few years, the maximum a claimant got was 20 per cent of the value of his property left in Pakistan. However, more than 95 per cent of the claims were below the highest level of Rs. 50,000 each. Venkatasubbiah says,

> By 1957, about a third of the total number of claimants (150,000 out of 450,000) had received compensation. In general it was a more prosperous Hindu community that came to India from West Pakistan after partition as against the Muslim community that left India for Pakistan. Notwithstanding what was done for it, and that was not much, large numbers of it in the north and east of the country were at times deeply frustrated, readily lending themselves as the spearhead of social discontent, and willingly exploited by political opponents of the Government.[97]

The fact that the discontent did not go out of control was mainly due to the large success achieved in settling most of the refugees on land and granting many of them proprietary rights over the evacuee properties they may have occupied, on finding them vacant.

The government appointed the Taxation Enquiry Commission to help it finance the next bolder plan and it reported in 1955 advising the government to both widen and deepen the tax structure placing relatively greater reliance on indirect taxes. However, the government wanted something more to bite, so in 1956 it invited the Cambridge economist Nicholas Kaldor to look into direct taxes and suggest additional handles of taxation if possible. This task he performed eminently well by recommending three additional taxes, namely a tax on wealth, a gift tax as a complementary measure and a personal expenditure tax and to simultaneously make income tax less progressive in order to reduce its disincentive effect. T.T. Krishnamachari (TTK), who succeeded C.D. Deshmukh as the Finance Minister, introduced all the three taxes at one go in the 1956–7 budget. In addition, the capital gains tax which had been withdrawn earlier was reintroduced; simultaneously, the income tax rates were made less progressive.

The Second Five Year Plan (1956–61) was a blend of three contradictory principles. First, that India must acquire basic and heavy industries in order to achieve self-sustaining growth in future, and for this purpose, substantial resources must be allocated on a priority basis.

Second, in order to achieve an output growth of 25 per cent over the plan period the scale of investment, taking the first criterion into account, must be of a given magnitude. The contradiction emerges in as much as investment made in the basic and capital goods sector would not generate output growth till they were fully prepared, and this may happen in later years. So, for the realization of the desired output growth, additional investment of a compensatory nature needed to be made in light industries and agriculture. This was not provided in the Plan.

Third, the Plan Frame even initially was under-funded; moreover, the Plan finances rested on unsure cost estimates and unrealistically optimistic gestation periods. The assumption made was that capital on the needed scale would be raised both from domestic sources and in the form of foreign aid and credits. It was further assumed that foreign aid would be offered at a sufficiently fast rate to keep up with the pace of investment, without causing delays or interruptions. To these may be added the critically important problem of food sufficiency, which did not form part of the investment frame of the Plan, so it lay in the larger area of political mobilization and public administration. Economists raised the question of inadequacy of wage goods entering the production stream at a sufficient pace to provide the equivalence to money wages as investment was stepped up, leading to the probability that an inflationary spiral would be set into motion. This was obviously the case, but the attendant risk had to be taken. The Plan was deeply import dependent, there was scarcely any reasonable basis for the expectation that the economy, despite a rising domestic demand for more inputs and consumer goods, would still be able to generate sufficient export surplus to pay for the needed imports of capital goods, raw materials and food; else the plan would stall midway.

For a developing economy, shaping its democratic polity on the basis of a detailed constitutional framework and with a socialist pattern of society as a long-term objective, the dependence on foreign aid from the developed capitalist countries must be deemed to have rested on political calculation rather than down-to-earth economics or investment accounting. Apparently, the Cold War world politics were factored into the Second Five Year Plan as an implicit assumption.

The relatively lower position of the private sector was posited in the Industrial Policy Resolution (IPR) adopted in April 1956, and it formed part of the Second Five Year Plan. The IPR announced that the state would progressively assume a predominant and direct responsibility for setting up new industrial undertakings and to develop transport facilities. The government would also engage in state trading on an increasing scale. Industries were classified into three groups and the share of the public sector was indicated in each. Seventeen industries were reserved for the public sector, although existing private sector undertakings would also expand; the private sector may be given the opportunity to participate in the joint sector. The entire industrial activity would be subject to government controls.

All this and more flowed directly from the government commitment to establish a socialist pattern of society. Tarlok Singh, who was a member of the Planning Commission later reviewed the problem of coping with diverse goals at the same time. He said,

> India's plans were drawn up within the framework of political democracy, economic development, and social change. Together, these pointed to three closely related objectives, the pursuit of welfare, the search for equality, and the desire for more even distribution of economic power. In practice, these objectives have been found most difficult to attain. The assumptions underlying them have not yet been fully analysed, nor have the means for achieving them been adequate. It would also be true to say that the objectives themselves have still to be formulated in a manner consistent with economic growth.[98]

India's political leadership found it necessary to follow diverse goals, mostly at the cost of economic growth, because this is what the articulate opinion makers wanted, and the government seeking a broad consensus for the planning process could not say with conviction that growth in disregard of distributive aspects would be accepted by the masses as legitimate. The Second Plan began with a budgeted outlay of Rs. 48,000 million which was raised a year later to Rs. 52,000 million. Of this sum, about 80 per cent was meant for capital investment; the biggest share at 29 per cent being earmarked for transport and communication. Next came the broad class of social services, housing and rehabilitation for which 20 per cent was allocated. Education and health formed part of social services. Irrigation and power received 19 per cent and an equal share was given to the category of industries and minerals. The lowest share of 12 per cent was set apart for agriculture and community development.

In absolute terms, the capital allocated for industries and mining showed a big jump of nearly 400 per cent, and this, relative to agriculture, became a target of considerable criticism, particularly as food production failed to rise and the resulting crisis made the outcome of the Plan quite uncertain.[99] The private sector was expected to invest Rs. 240,00 million. Thus, the planned ratio of the public and private sectors was 60:40. However, industrialists could draw comfort from the fact that three steel mills with a capacity of one million tonne of ingots each would be built and the resulting production of steel would greatly strengthen the engineering industries in future. Moreover, coal production would rise from 38 million tonnes to 60 million tonnes per annum, accompanied by an increase in cement production from 4.3 million tonnes to 13 million tonnes.

No one could object to such targets being set; the Bombay Plan prepared by the industrialists themselves visualized similar magnitudes of industrial expansion, and now that this was actually being done, it didn't matter much if it was the government that made the larger part of the investment. Moreover, the private sector had neither the capital nor the experience to create large management-based industrial organizations to undertake all the associated tasks simultaneously over a short period of time. Only the government could take the risks and do it.

At the very outset of the Second Plan, a major conflict developed on the question of the autonomy of the Reserve Bank of India. In January 1952, the RBI introduced the Bill Market Scheme to enable the scheduled banks greater access to the RBI for discounting the specially created bills to obtain advances. These were self-liquidating, with enhanced flexibility in credit creation, which the RBI desired. As an encouragement, the RBI charged interest at 0.5 per cent lower than the bank rates, and in addition, the stamp duty charged on the discounted bills was at a low rate of two annas for Rs. 1,000. The RBI would bear half the cost of the stamp duty. Commercial banks ordinarily borrowed against government securities at the bank rate. Now they could also borrow at a lower cost by discounting the bills. These were not the bills of exchange which arose in the course of normal trading transactions, but were created by banks by the permitted procedure of converting the bona fide trade bills into usance bills with a maturity of not more than 90 days (later 180 days), and carrying two signatures of which one was of a scheduled bank. The scheme was useful in augmenting credit during the busy seasons when credit stringency usually developed, and it gained in popularity. The key characteristic of the scheme was the provision of converting demand promissory notes into time notes and of accepting the creditworthiness of banks' borrowers on their certificates. The risk attended on these aspects was acceptable to the RBI.

In the 1956 budget, the Finance Minister, T.T. Krishnamachari, raised the stamp duty from two annas per Rs. 1,000 to Rs. 5 or 80 annas per Rs. 1000. This effectively raised the bank rate by 0.5 per cent though without any reference to the RBI. This was unprecedented and effectively took away the RBI's autonomy in fixing the bank rate. The Governor of the RBI, B. Rama Rau, protested and circulated a memorandum on the subject to his Central Board of Directors. Earlier, TTK told the Governor that the Bank was merely a section of the Finance Ministry and that he would have to accept the decision of the government, whether he liked it or not. The Prime Minister also objected and wrote to the Governor,

> Monetary Policy must necessarily depend upon the larger policies which a government pursues. It is in the ambit of those larger policies that the Reserve Bank can advise. It cannot challenge the main objectives and policies of government. There are apparently some sections of the business community who disapprove of our basic policies and who have in fact criticized them. They have every right to do so. But, it is surprising that the Reserve Bank should encourage this criticism and indirectly participate in it itself.[100]

The Governor could not acquiesce in a situation in which by taking fiscal measures the Finance Minister would run the monetary policy as well and thereby undermine the statutory autonomy of the Bank. He resigned. A leading member of the Board, Purshottamdas Thakurdas also resigned from the Board. He wrote: 'The happenings in the last couple of weeks are so extraordinary, one-sided and unprovoked that I feel it is not in the interest of the country that any non-official should avoidably keep up his connection with the Reserve Bank.'[101]

The tension between the government and the RBI eased somewhat but it did not abate due to fast emerging inflationary trends and the rapid decline in foreign exchange reserves. The government was determined to follow an expansionary course and this resulted in an unceasing recourse to deficit financing as well as credit creation. Within a year, crisis conditions surfaced. Wholesale prices rose by 8 per cent, while markets showed financial stringency. Money rates moved up and firms experienced difficulty in raising finance to meet the expenses necessitated by investment decisions. Clearly, investment demand was in excess of current savings, and what contributed to the conditions of stringency was that the government too was in the market raising loans for the Second Plan. Accordingly, the Finance Minister was in favour of an easier credit policy, while the RBI thought that the answer to stringency was in promoting savings with higher interest rates to attract more deposits.

The policy on open market operations augmented banks' reserves and greater permissiveness resulted in higher than normal credit-deposit ratios. This was found to be unsustainable and brakes were placed on the expansionary momentum. The bank rate was raised from 3.5 per cent to 4 per cent in May 1957. The government's consent was obtained in the several weeks of discussion the RBI had with it before the announcement was made. The government's loan programme followed. Selective credit controls were relied on more than before to prevent diversion of bank credit towards speculative trading. These fire fighting activities became the regular features of monetary and credit policy in the next decade, as the government generally chose an expansionary policy on money supply, leaving larger budgetary deficits to be financed by net money creation.

Within two years of the Second Five Year Plan, two disturbing trends developed. First, the sterling reserves were being drawn far more rapidly than provided for in the Plan. In 1957, imports had peaked and the government had to take strong counter-steps to lower the volume of non-essential imports. In the first two years of the Second Plan, the current account deficit rose to Rs. 8,210 million resulting and a loss of sterling balances by Rs. 4,790 million. Second, food prices started rising and in one year the rise of about five per cent was partly due to the decline in agricultural production by over 10 per cent, but also aggravated by the weakness in the procurement system. India had imported from the US, under PL 480, three million tonnes of wheat in 1957 and 1958. However, the greater deficit was in rice which could be made good only by further increase in domestic production. In addition, high budgetary deficits were pulling up prices since the overall supply of goods and services in the country including imports was insufficient to absorb the augmented money supply. Moreover, a sustained rise in prices in one year would lead to cost escalation and cost-push inflation in the next period. This was a spiral in the making, and corrective measures had to be taken.

As a first step, the financial targets of the plan were pruned and in physical terms the planned investment targets were lowered. The government focused hard on raising agricultural yields and food production without issuing price incentives to farmers, instead relying ever more strongly on cooperative farming and cooperative credit societies to do the job. This rested more on the imagined gains to yields on land which the pressure of the left wing of the Congress produced. The idea was to reduce inequality in land ownership and power structure in villages, which in turn would somehow raise land yields without the need for economic incentives. The Ministry of Food and Agriculture was not at all convinced that a greater push to cooperative farming and cooperative credit societies by itself would improve yields in the short period. The Ministry preferred to provide more agricultural inputs, better seeds, fertilizers and rely on improved crop planning to raise output, but all these would cost money and this was hardly possible given the Plan priorities and investment commitments.[102] As a consequence, the government courted failure on domestic production and had to import twice the amount of food grains than earlier believed necessary, and this necessarily lowered the foreign exchange allocations for the public sector.

By 1957–8, the Second Five Year Plan had to be grouped between the core and the non-core. The former included iron and steel, coal, power, the railways and ports. All other projects, including fertilizers, were placed on the deferred category. The Plan strategy of high focus on imports substitution coupled with a near absence of any understanding of export promotion through investments and incentives, led to the rapid descent of the Plan into a crisis mode. This led in turn to two side effects. On the domestic front, the government had to tighten its grip on procurement and distribution of wheat and rice and maintain price stability as much as seemed feasible. On the other hand, the policy of liberal licensing in favour of the private sector, which led to heavy imports in 1956 and 1957, possibly at a cost to the public sector, resulted in private sector targets getting over fulfilled while the public sector showed under-achievement. An early indication of this tendency was that the government agencies were able to spend on projects considerably less than the budgeted amounts.

A major problem which the planners failed to come to grips with, was that they could not extract additional surplus from the agricultural sector in the form of higher savings as desired by them, without first raising per capita production of agricultural crops and other outputs by making additional investments in the production and technological base of farming. Nor did they realize the economic implications of faster population growth, mostly in rural India, at a rate twice as high as envisaged in the Second Five Year Plan, particularly that it correspondingly lowered the potential surplus which could possibly be obtained through voluntary or forced savings. If the scale of aggregate investments systematically exceeded the flow of savings or market surpluses, allowing for measures for tightening private consumption, inflation would result. This message did come through in the first two years of the Second Plan, though the lesson learnt was that the government, having made the commitment to the core of the Plan, must push ahead anyhow with whatever means it could now mobilize. Meanwhile, a constitutional constraint which had to be kept in view was that even as the government augmented its fiscal resources, it had to allocate the larger part of additional revenues to the states under the scheme of revenue sharing as proposed by the Finance Commission.

In the 1957–8 budget, the government pressed hard on industry and private savings through the levies of direct taxes, and on private consumption through heavy indirect taxes, principally excise duties. This was the year of the great bout of taxation.[103] Indirect taxes raised prices through a cost-push mechanism, while the demand-pull factor raised prices more directly and people found the double burden excessive. The resentment of the wage and salary earning classes soon found outlets in agitations for dearness allowance and other forms of compensation.

In 1956–7, the WPI rose by 14 per cent and necessitated the imposition of selective credit controls mostly directed against food grains and other agricultural commodities. These rested on the dubious premise that the speculators were taking advantage of the expansionary forces in the economy and by hoarding goods in short supply hoped to make abnormal profits by raising prices. The problem which the selective controls aggravated was that the genuine needs for expanding credit to finance agricultural operations also suffered, and in the end the government downplayed rural credit even as it remained unrestrained in public spending by increased borrowing from the Reserve Bank.

> The proliferation of selective controls was largely, however, the result of government's preferences rather than Bank's. On the other hand while the Bank wanted the government to restrain public expenditure, it could not remain indifferent to

> the latter's concern about movement in the prices of key commodities like food grains and sugar, and of important agricultural raw materials or intermediate goods used by industry. The reintroduction of lending controls against sugar and food grains including paddy and rice in June 1957 was at the government's initiative, as were those on lending against sugar later the same month. In fact, government interest in selective controls extended to its highest levels, with Jawaharlal Nehru complaining to Iyengar about the Bank's allegedly flouting instructions to make large advances to millers and encouraging the hoarding of rice.[104]

H.V.R. Iyengar succeeded B.N. Rau as governor of the RBI and was more accommodative of the government's policies, though he did point out that in supporting the cooperative credit societies the bank was only following the long-range policy of promoting and strengthening their lending ability, including the larger societies which were formed by amalgamating several less viable ones. The moneylenders' grip over the agriculturists needed to be broken and the remedy was to build up an alternative credit providing institution of which the borrowers may become members and also use it to deposit their savings. It was possible, however, that the larger cooperative credit societies had come under the control of the same set of interests which were already deeply entrenched in rural society, often controlled the district level Congress organization, and also fuelled the speculative fever. It was a sheer irony that the short-term selective credit controls would be employed to defeat an entirely worthwhile long-term objective of the government, whose time span clearly extended far beyond the Second Five Year Plan.

On the food front, the situation was alarming. In 1956–7 imports of food grains of two million tonnes were made and in 1957–8 the government had to import another four million tonnes. Price controls and food rationing became an absolute necessity though that may not curb speculation. So the answer lay in devising some form of social control over wholesale trading in food grains. Given the shortages, prices could not be stabilized by any other devise.[105]

The problem of food shortage could be theoretically overcome by imports, but the government faced severe constraints. During 1955–7, the government was liberal in granting import licenses and the result was a large import of capital goods though largely by the private sector. There was considerable expansion in building and construction activities which was financed by banks, and there was a large commitment of banks' funds to private firms. Increase in foreign investment was also on private account. By comparison, the public sector was still getting organized and faced severe shortages of funds and most acutely the constraints emerging from the scarcity of foreign exchange. Defence expenditure was also growing. The US was providing extensive military aid to Pakistan and this necessitated a balanced increase in military spending by India as well, which now had a prior claim on the available foreign exchange earnings. As the government struggled to look for other options, some of the answers emerged politically from the logic of the Cold War and India's policy of non-alignment.

The United States soon emerged not only as a major provider of food grains on a rupee loan, but also as the aid giver in the field of technical training and other forms. Nothing was unconditional and there were indications that in order to facilitate the agreement, the Food Ministry played a helpful role in stalling the pressing demand for state trading in food grains. The pleas it took on the question of raising food production against the Planning Commission happened to be in substantial alignment with the policy line advanced by the United States to reorient the Plan priorities and against emphasis on heavy industries and socialism.

The criticisms of steel plants slowly lost their bite, because all three plants were built with foreign aid; of these the aid most forthcoming was from the Soviet Union which provided steady and consistent support for the Bhilai-based steel plant. German aid for the Rourkela plant and British aid for the

Durgapur plant followed. Meanwhile, India had become quite unpopular in Washington due in part to Indo-Soviet trade and aid agreements and the considerable warmth in their bilateral relations, but more by the one-sided criticism of Western policies, sometimes justified in themselves, but falling short on moral grounds as reflected in India's quiescence on the Soviet Union's brutal repression of the nationalist rebellion in Hungary. Yet in US policy circles, there was a growing realization that the only effective way to defeat communism was economic development and for this purpose US aid should be forthcoming. In addition, the PL 480 wheat loan against blocked rupee payment happened to be bilaterally beneficial; it lowered the mounting wheat stocks in the US, while strengthening food reserves in India.

An important consequence of foreign exchange shortage was the beginning of government's quest for foreign aid in any form which could be negotiated. In this search, the aid negotiating officials soon learnt a number of vital lessons. The British were treating the release of sterling balances as their aid to India, not in discharge of their wartime obligation. The probable line of reasoning was that their release resulted in a draft on the UK economy, so the quantum of sterling balances allowed to India must be within the capacity of what it could afford. If more was needed, strings would be attached to make foreign aid mutually beneficial.

Labour Shows Strains, Parties Accommodative, Policy Initiatives

Beginning with 1954, strikes increased in number resulting in heavier losses in man days. The lowest strike activity year was 1953 when 772 strikes took place. In the next year and thereafter in every year up to 1957, strikes increased in number from 840 (1954), 1,160 (1955), 1,203 (1956) to 1,999 (1957). Along with the number of workers involved, the man days lost also grew. Each strike depicted a breakdown in industrial relations and the failure of the industrial disputes settlement machinery to reach out to the dispute centres and engage in settlements. The number of workers involved is a rough measure of the reach of the strikes and their potential to mobilize workers in straight conflicts.

An equally rough estimate of damage done by strikes is provided by the data on man days lost. These losses aggregated to 3.382 million in 1953, 3.372 million in 1954, 5.697 million in 1955, 6.992 million in 1956 and 6.174 million in 1957. Most of the strikes occurred in the cotton textile industry and in the two most industrialized states, Bombay and West Bengal. However, the reach of the strikes was steadily increasing and covered more industries. For example, in 1956, while cotton textiles accounted for 203 strikes and lockouts, 195 strikes took place in iron and steel, 84 in mines, 50 in plantations, 34 in railways and 21 in jute. All the rest affected other industries. Fortunately, about two-thirds of the strikes were of a short duration, lasting for five days or less and kept the damage done by way of man days lost within limit.

Economic causes pertaining to wages, dearness allowance and bonus contributed importantly to the strikes, though an equally powerful cause was related to employment security which resulted in active opposition to the rationalization schemes which increased mechanization and produced job losses. These were resisted to the utmost and demonstrated the greatest solidarity among workers. An important non-economic cause related to the right of workers to representation and recognition of unions, which the employers often resisted, and this was of a kind for which there was no legal remedy.

Rationalization became a subject of public importance and received considerable attention by the government. In September 1954, the government formulated its attitude in the form of a resolution adopted by the Lok Sabha: 'The House is of the opinion that rationalization of the textile and jute industries, where it is necessary in the country's interests, must be encouraged, but the implementation of such schemes should be so regulated as to cause the least amount of displacement of labour in those industries providing reasonable facilities for the employment of such displaced labour.'[106]

Labour leaders urged caution on encouraging labour-saving machinery which increased unemployment and sacrificed man at the altar of machines. Yet, the cotton textile mills faced tough competition and in Kanpur the employers pointed out that if rationalization schemes were blocked, between five to nine thousand workers would be thrown out of employment as the mills were unable to compete due to higher wages in the city. In 1955, there was a protracted strike on the issue of rationalization and installation of new machinery in the Kanpur cotton textile mills, and it virtually crippled the industry. The issue of automatic looms and new machinery and the threat of unemployment so agitated labour that the trade union leaders chose to ignore the Industrial Truce Resolution and the agreement reached earlier to support 'rationalization without tears' and allowed themselves to be swept into conducting a three month long strike in Kanpur.

The same pattern of behaviour was repeated in 1956 in the Nagpur textile mills where the anti-rationalization strike lasted for five months.[107] More than wages, the threat of unemployment with no alternatives in sight pushed the factory labour to extreme action, of the kind that occurred during the 1920s and early 30s, when labour was barely organized and yet reacted with elemental energy to ward off a real threat. It was this welling up of popular anger that created unity among the rival trade union centres at Kanpur and Nagpur, though it did not survive the inevitable fizzling out of the general strike and, soon thereafter, the rivals started bickering again.

The government saw a new threat to industrial peace in the form of trade union rivalry, essentially between the bigger but committed to quieter Gandhian methods of decency in agitations and demands made on the employers, and the others believing in class straggle and militant trade unionism, which would so unsettle industrial relations in particular industries that the industrial relations machinery under the ID Act was unable to maintain industrial peace. Moreover, the Second Five Year Plan with its focus on basic industries might create additional stresses and strains in the economy and the government may have to ask people to tighten their belts and labour, in particular, to refrain from pressing wage demands. Clearly the former industrial relations policy that was developed with the pronounced inclination to meet as many of labour's demands as remained unfulfilled during the war period, and were justified and reasonable, could not be pushed indefinitely. New devices were badly needed to keep the bulk of the labour force on the side of the Five Year Plans and retain its support for industrialization.

The government's response to growing labour unrest and politicization of the labouring masses was two-fold. One, to appeal to the left wing socialist idealism of people to understand the long-term implications of government licensing and controls in terms of: (i) enforcing the planned pattern of investment and restricting the working of purely market-based economic impulses; (ii) counteracting unhealthy trends in the private sector towards monopoly and concentration of wealth; (iii) better regional balance in locating new industries; (iv) protecting and promoting small-scale industrialists, while also encouraging the formation of a new class of entrepreneurs; and (v) ensuring optimum scale of production by adopting advanced technology wherever feasible.

The development of public sector with direct support from the Soviet Union and several East European countries showed that the government's commitment to work towards a socialist pattern of society was serious and it already enjoyed considerable international backing. This message was powerfully projected towards the communists and it produced favourable results. Under Nehru's leadership India's foreign policy of non-alignment, though somewhat leaning towards the Soviet Union and the communist block of countries, subserved in remarkable ways the domestic policies of industrial development with industrial peace; it succeeded in winning the CPI-led AITUC to its side.

The Soviet Union made an assessment of world capitalism and the role of the US in the light of its survival needs. The Soviet leaders also came to the conclusion that peaceful transition to socialism was possible, and it was in this context that India's Five Year Plans, the emphasis on the public sector, and the responsibility accorded to the government to steer society towards a socialist pattern fell in place. In India, the CPI almost totally changed from the revolutionary path to constitutional means towards socialism at the Amritsar Congress in 1957. 'Moscow also was so much convinced of the effectiveness of the parliamentary method that it advised the Indian communists to avoid confrontation with the Nehru Government even when the latter had developed a serious contradiction with the communist led Kerala Government.'[108]

The CPI would now work for peace and democracy and lead popular movements to correct the negative tendencies in the government while strengthening the positive ones. The party strove to strike a united front with the PSP and 'this cooperation also extended to the field of industrial relations. This understanding rested on the principle of controlled agitations.'[109] According to Madhu Limaye, 'it was chiefly political considerations that led the CPI and PSP leaders to work for the withdrawal of the Central Government Employees strike notice in 1957. The lacklustre conduct of the strike in 1960 can also be understood only in the context of the attitude of the PSP and CPI to Jawaharlal Nehru.'[110]

The other thrust of labour policy was addressed to the Gandhian tradition. The code of discipline and related policy tools had a high moral tone and phrased in such highly principled terms that no decent person could ordinarily disagree. The code of discipline promoted the following principles, among others, to maintain proper discipline and cordial human relations so as to ensure maximum production in the wider national interests. The principles agreed on by the representatives of government, employers and workers were: (i) no strike or lockout without notice; (ii) no unilateral action should be taken in any industrial matter; (iii) no recourse to go-slow tactics; (iv) no damage should be deliberately caused to plant property; (v) no resort to acts of violence, intimidation, coercion or instigation; (vi) to use the existing machinery for the settlement of disputes; (vii) to seek rapid implementation of awards and agreements; and (viii) to avoid any action which disturbed cordial industrial relations.

In practical terms, the code implied that the managements would not increase workload except by mutual agreement or encourage unfair labour practices; that they would endeavour to draw a line between discharges justified by any wrongdoings by the workmen concerned and others, which must be preceded by warnings, reprimand or suspension; in other words, by treating termination from service as an extreme punishment. The unions similarly agreed not to permit demonstrations that might not remain peaceful or turn rowdy or any kind of unfair labour practices.

The 15th Indian Labour Conference in 1957 took an extraordinary decision on need-based minimum wages and proceeded to lay down the norms for its computation. The Minimum Wages Act, 1948 was already in place to fix minimum wage rates to prevent sweating and excessive exploitation of labour. However, the unions pressed for need-based minimum wages which must by definition be above the subsistence level wage rates that were notified under the Act. Accordingly, a formula was decided on, which defined a standard working class family to comprise three consumption units plus one earner; the minimum food requirement was to be calculated on the basis of 2700 calories for an average Indian adult engaged in moderate activity. To this may be added clothing needs for four at a total of 72 yards and a minimum rent for housing as charged by the government for low-income groups in subsidized housing schemes. Further, an addition of 20 per cent of the total minimum wage should suffice to provide for fuel, lighting and other miscellaneous items of expenditure. These norms were to be used as guidelines to fix minimum wages for industrial workers. The authorities concerned were charged with the responsibility of justifying the instances of non-adherence to these norms by citing relevant circumstances.

This was a significant moral victory for the trade unions, though they soon learnt that this particular recommendation bound no one, at any rate not the government. It disowned any commitment to the formula when the matter was formally raised by the Second Pay Commission appointed in 1957, that had received several representations from the central government employees' associations to implement the formula on the need-based minimum wages. The Pay Commission, nonetheless, did the calculations to determine just what sum the norms would add up to and the implications thereof.

The Pay Commission noted that the need-based wages formula made no allowance for the employers' ability to pay, which had to be done while fixing the minimum wages under the Act. The calculated need-based minimum yielded a figure of Rs. 125 compared to the upper limit of Rs. 52.50 with some exceptions for wages under the Minimum Wages Act. This was then compared with the per capita income at current prices of Rs. 291.50 or a total of Rs. 1166 per annum for a family of four members, or Rs. 97 per month. The need-based minimum wage was accordingly considered to be pitched so far above the per capita income as to be obviously beyond the capacity of the country to accept and implement. The Commission also worked out a lower norm of food intake of 2100 calories of vegetarian diet and reworked the expenditure for three consumption units at Rs. 52 per month. Adding to this the other items of expenditure the total amounted to Rs. 70.73 per month at the consumer price index of 115 (1949 =100).

The publication of the Pay Commission Report led to

several controversies on such matters as optimum diet, balanced diet and adequate diet, while the government sat tight and did nothing to implement any part of the need-based minimum wages. The trade unions continued to raise the issue as often and in as a many forums as possible for nearly a decade, and then it died a slow death.

The Second Plan contained several observations on the direction industrial wages should take; one, that real wages should rise slowly; second, that the wage level should correspond to workers' expectations as far as possible; third, the idea of fair wages should be implemented at the industry level by the wage boards and by the tribunals, while fixing wages through awards made by them. So far, these showed no discernible trend. Fourth, the concept of living wages should be kept in mind as a long-term objective, while its realization in the near future was clearly impracticable.

The planners made no effort to formulate a wage policy in the face of the enormous diversity of wage payment systems prevailing in the country and the very large, wholly unaccountable, wage differentials that existed in the same industry across regions. Moreover, the inadequate data base was a major handicap, so a wage census should be conducted. If wage uniformity and some order in the system of wage payments was to be aimed at, it had to be done industry by industry and at a pace that would be considered acceptable to the employers and also contain labour unrest. At the government level, this could be done by the pay commissions, though the Second Pay Commission would make recommendations for the central government employees only. At the industry level, the tripartite wage boards would be the appropriate agency, and at the region-cum-industry level the tribunals must continue to adjudicate wage-related disputes and give awards. This was the existing system and it was left untouched.

The appointment of the Second Pay Commission was the result of a last minute climb down by the government in the face of a threatened general strike by post and telegraph employees on the midnight of 8 August 1957. For several years past, in fact since 1954, on different pretexts and excuses, the government had stalled the demand for dearness allowance and several other matters. The railways too agitated and decided to take a strike ballot in August 1957, but later the idea of a strike was dropped. The ports and docks workers had actually conducted a token strike in November 1955. The government promised to consider their demands, though no action followed. Another strike was threatened in October 1956 but it was not called and the government was given more time to consider their demands. If the strike had materialized other employees of the central government would have followed suit. It was at this juncture that the government issued an ordinance, declaring the strike illegal; later it was allowed to lapse. Karnik says, 'the promulgation of the ordinance was another grave mistake. It showed that the government was neither willing to face a strike, nor was prepared to allow workers the alternative remedy of adjudication for the settlement of their dispute. This was in contravention of its declared policy that the remedy of adjudication was always open to workers.'[111]

The error in the workers' perception was that the policy meant for industrial and commercial workers for settling their industrial disputes could not possibly be applicable to the large body of government employees who were bound by entirely different sets of rules and protocols, and were regulated by the Constitution. Yet, disputes continued to arise. In the case of the ports and docks workers, the government put up a stiff resistance to their fairly reasonable demands, which were focused on the implementation of the Choudhari Report. In the event, a strike followed, violence occurred, and then the government decided to give in and settle the dispute in 1958. There was much unrest among a whole range of government employees who found the emergence of the inflationary trend and the government doing nothing about it, very disturbing. The Second Plan started its term with considerable labour unrest, but in the course of two years of rising prices the government could only think of ad hoc remedies.

Within the government, the formulation of a logically coherent policy required answers to two questions. One was the question of collective bargaining and the other pertained to the political dynamics of the labour movement. On the former, the resignation of V.V. Giri in 1954 as the Labour Minister virtually sealed the issue and collective bargaining lost out. Giri remained a strong defender of the policy of internal settlement. In October 1953, as a Minister of Labour presiding over the Indian Labour Conference he said,

> The spirit of self-confidence and self-reliance, engendered by healthy bargaining has given place to the habit of importunity and litigation. That is bad enough, but what is worse is the deplorable effect that this dependence on a third party has brought about in the outlook and attitudes of the parties towards each other. In a system of straight forward bargaining, there is no doubt a keen struggle during the period of negotiations, but except in a few cases that lead to strike or lockout, the parties conclude their bargaining in a spirit of 'give and take'—in an atmosphere of goodwill and understanding. Neither party entertains any sense of humiliation or feels the urge for retaliation and revenge. But that is not the case with compulsory arbitration.

Litigation produces 'transient truce, but not lasting peace'.[112] The position Giri took was not acceptable to the employing ministries, which were opposed to the very idea of the Labour Ministry deciding the policy on labour under their charge. They would not shed ministerial control, or admit trade unions as a legitimate party for bargaining on behalf of their employees. The latter did have the right of representation to be heard, but there could be no bargaining with the sovereign government. This was the hard line the government took as the employer.

On the side of labour too, there was no unity on the question. The INTUC was not at all committed to the philosophy of collective bargaining and totally unwilling to give up the crutches of support which the I.D. Act and its arm, the IRM, provided. In fact, reliance on the law was the main strength of the INTUC affiliated unions against their rivals, the AITUC and the HMS affiliated unions. There were also deeper issues on which the government thinking and policies clashed with those of the unions. On the issue of rationalization the big strike at Kanpur was in the nature of a labour revolt against the entire establishment. It left deep unhealed scars on trade unions and weakened the industry. There was just no solution to the problem of mechanization that was acceptable to labour and unavoidably it required the authority of the government to restore normalcy.

Similarly, on the issue of wage restraint which the Planning Commission advocated, and which the government desired that it should be accepted, though there did not exist the slightest chance that the trade union movement would willingly fall in line. The government used inflation to enforce it, or prevent real wages from rising, but lacked the will to accomplish the aim through the wage determination bodies, or by enacting a wage law which would empower it to directly fix wages. The government and labour were in a conflict relationship on issues which directly and immediately affected labour, which showed as strikes increased in number and imposed even heavier costs in man days and production lost.

The politics of labour was very divisive. From its inception, the INTUC was organized to oppose and restrict the influence of communist and socialist movements among workers. While the INTUC talked to the HMS to create amity, nothing came of it. There could only be rivalry and contest with the communist-led AITUC unions. The two held opposing viewpoints. Indeed there was nothing in common between the Gandhian doctrine of class harmony, of persuasion and use of moral force to produce a change of heart leading to class collaboration and mutual acceptance of each other's interests, while admitting differences in goals and perceptions as legitimate, and the ideology of class war which the communists propagated. The INTUC sought the support of state governments, where most industrial disputes occurred, and openly received it. The communists were in the opposite war camp and unfailingly denounced the Congress, the government and the INTUC.

In comparison, the socialists were going through an intense internal struggle on issues raised by Asoka Mehta's thesis on 'Compulsions of a Backward Economy'. The thesis led to seeking areas of agreement with the Congress and the government in the implementation of the Five Year Plans. In a developing economy like India, 'the chief problem is economic growth, and therefore, the major question for union is subordination of immediate wage gains and similar considerations to the development of the country'.[113] If this idea was accepted, it would result in the unions seeking a durable policy of constructive cooperation which would ultimately be beneficial to the working class. However, it required the acceptance of austerity in the short run. The internal struggle sharpened as positions hardened and led to a formal split in the PSP, with the dissenting leader, Dr Ram Manohar Lohia forming another Socialist Party in 1955.

These pulls and pressures produced doubts and ambivalence among the socialists and an inclination to prefer a soft and politically accommodative stance in labour policy. It produced results. Even the CPI-led AITUC took the position that the Second Five Year Plan deserved to be supported and the government should have a fighting chance to take it to successful completion.[114] The so-called tender mindedness of the government was less the influence of Gandhian ideas and more a product of political necessity in a democracy where opposition and cooperation occurred as transient features, while the government appeared ever eager to garner as much support for its national endeavour as it could get. On ideological grounds, virtually the entire labour movement was supportive of the idea of planned development led by the government.

Amidst so much tension, collective bargaining made

steady progress. It was mostly practised by the Indian subsidiaries or affiliates of multinational corporations which were already in the habit of practising collective bargaining in their home countries and had a body of concepts and tools to make it work. Mary Sur refers to the Dunlop Rubber Co. as the earliest organization (1947) to sign an agreement with the unions. The others were the Bata Shoe Co. (1948) and the best known, the Indian Aluminium Co. (1951). These were the forerunners in industry to accept and work with collective bargaining. These were followed by the Imperial Tobacco Co. (1952–4) and several others in 1955–6.[115] The TISCO crossed a milestone in its industrial relations policies in 1955 when it signed, for the first time, a collective bargaining agreement with the recognized union and has done so ever since. Other companies no doubt had these examples before them, but preferred the legal route of the ID Act instead, and settled their labour disputes through courts. The difference between the two sets of companies was as one of modernity and tradition. 'In the companies which showed willingness to meet and discuss in detail with their unions there is no doubt that management thinking was rather advanced. As yet modern conceptions of the role of management, particularly in industrial relations, were only slowly gaining acceptance in Indian industry.'[116]

ENDNOTES

1. A.K. Majumdar (Ed.), *Indian Constitutional Documents, Munshi Papers*, Vol. II, Bharatiya Vidya Bhavan, Bombay, 1967, For the text of the statement, see pp. 17–20, and also for the subsequent statement made on 19 February 1946, p. 21.
2. A.C. Guha, *India's Struggle Quarter of a Century 1921-1946*, Part II, Publications Division, Government of India, August 1982, pp. 718–22, quote on p. 720.

   The fact that the INA trials had ignited a mood of national rebellion could not have been missed by the British rulers. The spirit was sometimes disquietingly violent as is evidenced by posters posted in Delhi that for every INA man sentenced 20 English dogs would face the threat of death. The threat must have been palpable to promote the Viceroy to warn Nehru in November 1945, that any incitement to violence would not be tolerated by the government. In April 1946, Wavell warned Gandhi that there were still a great many thousand British soldiers in India who did not subscribe to his doctrine of non-violence and might be very violent if British lives or property suffered.

D.N. Panigrahi, *India's Partition The Story of Imperialism in Retreat*, London, Routledge, an imprint of Taylor and Francis, 2004, (loc. cit.), p. 272; also p. 270. On INA-related references see *India's Struggle for Independence* (loc. cit.), pp. 476, 477.

3. Ibid., pp. 479–83, quote on p. 480; also A.C. Guha, Part II, pp. 732–5.
4. Ibid., p. 475.
5. A.C. Guha (loc. cit.), pp. 744–5.
6. B. Sheik Ali, 'Political Parties and their Motives', in Amrik Singh (Ed.), *The Partition in Retrospect*, Anamika Publishers and Distributors (P.) Ltd., 2000, p. 367.
7. Khaliquzzaman, *Pathway to Pakistan*, Lahore, Orient Longmans, 1971, pp. 340–1.
8. V.P. Menon, *The Transfer of Power in India*, Orient Longman, Bombay, p. 288. Menon catalogued the events:

    the situation was causing the Government no little anxiety. Communal tension had already increased in the towns as a result of the Muslim League's call for 'direct action'; moreover, there was widespread labour unrest in the country. Lord Wavell felt that a representative Central Government was most urgently needed. The Secretary of State was keen that having progressed thus far the Government should not lose initiative and proceed with the formation of an Interim Government and could not allow Jinnah's non-cooperation to hold up its formation.

9. Ibid., p. 294.
10. A.C. Guha provides a detailed account of events during, the 'Great Calcutta Killings', as he calls them which included the partisanship of Suhrawardy's government, inaction of the police and passivity of the Governor. See A.C. Guha (op. cit.), pp. 771–93; also H.V. Hodson, *The Great Divide, Britain-India-Pakistan*, Karachi, Oxford University Press, pp. 166–8.
11. D.N. Panigrahi (op. cit.), pp. 281–3. 'The breakdown plan, which Lord Wavell had authored and for which he received

much odium from Indians, who described it as "Plan Balkan", was an article of faith for him. He kept repeating his ideas on the subject to the British government at home' (p. 283). For a favourable review of the Breakdown Plan, see H.M. Seervai, *Partition of India Legend and Reality*, Emmenem Publications, Bombay, 1987, pp. 87–91.

12. H.V. Hodson (loc. cit.), pp. 189–90.
13. Panigrahi records: 'Wyatt wrote that he met Jinnah on 24 May 1946. Jinnah suggested that the Cabinet Mission should put the statement on one side and the British should remain as the binding force in the Indian Centre for some 15 years and deal with defence and foreign affairs for Pakistan and Hindustan consulting the Prime Minister of each state.' V.P. Menon, *Transfer of Power* VII no. 373, p. 686 and D.N. Panigrahi (loc. cit.), pp. 313–14. On English Mullahs, B.R. Nanda says, at the time of the Cabinet Mission, 'there were, it seemed to Congress leaders, "English Mullahs" around the Viceroy who were not sorry to give a parting kick to the party who had been primarily responsible for challenging and liquidating the Raj and for wrecking promising British careers in the ICS and the Indian Army', *The Making of a Nation, India's Road to Independence*, New Delhi, HarperCollins Publishers India, 1998, p. 294. 'The British civil servants' negative position on Indian independence largely reflected the Churchillian view that however the negotiations might proceed no grounds should ever be allowed which would lead to total exit of British power from India. This was duly reflected in the debate in Parliament on Attlee's statement on February 20, 1947.'
14. R.C. Majumdar *History of the Freedom Movement in India*, Vol. IV (op. cit.), p. 504.
15. H.V. Hodson (loc. cit.). pp. 192–200; Quote on p. 199.
16. Leonard Mosley quoted by Tara Chand, ibid., pp. 507–8.
17. According to Mountbatten the population involved in the disturbances and forced migration was only three per cent of India's total. This factor raises the gross estimate to over 10 million and could make it the costliest surgery ever made in the remaking of the political map of a country. See, H.M. Seervai, *Partition of India* (loc. cit.), Ch. X, esp. 'Mountbatten's Responsibility for the Massacres and the Migrations in Punjab', p. 167.

18. K.M. Munshi, *Indian Constitutional Documents, Munshi Papers,* Vol. II, (op. cit.), pp. 79–86. Sinha compared the honour to the conferment of the Knighthood of the Garter by Queen Victoria on Lord Palmerston who, however, wrote to his friend, 'I have gratefully accepted Her Majesty's gracious offer as, thank God, there is no question of any damned merit about the honour conferred on me.'
19. Ibid., p. 107 and p. 109.
20. Ibid. The full text of Nehru's speech is reproduced on pp. 110–22. Churchill's comment on the work of the Constituent Assembly without the Muslim League's representatives was something like the absence of the bride in the church when the marriage was going to take place, referred to by Dr. Shyama Prasad Mookerjee in his speech following Dr. Jayakar's amendment, p. 129.
21. B. Shiva Rao, et al., *The Framing of India's Constitution: A Study,* The Indian Institute of Public Administration, New Delhi, 1968, (loc. cit.), p. 80. The Congress position was reflected in the legal opinion of K.M. Munshi that the Assembly represented the population as a whole; that it was not represented by delegates representing different communities, but an organ of a sovereign people; Ibid., p. 77.
22. An important factor that contributed in large measure to the smooth functioning of the Constituent Assembly and the completion of its labours in a satisfactory manner and spirit, was the broad view in which the Congress, with guidance from Gandhi, had selected nearly 30 non-Congressmen and securing their election on its ticket. They were legal minds or had considerable experience as administrators or represented other elements in national life. All minorities were represented on the Congress list of nominations. Experts like N. Gopalaswamy Ayyanger, Hriday Nath Kunzru, Alladi Krishnaswamy Ayyar, S. Radhakrishnan, H.C. Mookerjee were invited to make their contributions as members of the Assembly and this they did diligently. B. Shiva Rao (loc. cit.), pp. 96–8. For the record of the progress see ibid., Chapter, 'Progress of the Constitution Through the Assembly,' pp. 107–18.
23. K.M. Munshi, *Indian Constitutional Documents, Munshi Papers, Vol. II* (loc. cit.), pp. 110–20, quotes on p. 113 and p. 119.

24. Statement made by Sir Stafford Cripps at a press conference on 16 May 1946. Ibid., p. 35.
25. Ian Copland, *The Princes of India in the Endgame of Empire, 1917–1947*, Cambridge University Press, 1997, Ch. 7, entitled, 'Fin de-Siecle', esp. p. 239.
26. K.M. Munshi, *Indian Constitutional Documents, Munshi Papers*, Vol. II (loc. cit.), p. 232.
27. H.V. Hodson (loc. cit.), 1969, Ch. 19, 'The Accession of the States'.
28. For texts of Instruments of Accession see K.M. Munshi, *Indian Constitutional Documents, Munshi Papers* (loc. cit.), pp. 418–32.
29. The political history of states' accession with Mountbatten as the central figure is related in H.V. Hodson, *The Great Divide* (loc. cit.). There was considerable potential for trouble as was shown by the rulers of Bhopal, Indore, Travancore and Jodhpur besides the three states, which held out. The 'Junagadh Affair' is described in Chapter 24, 'Conflict in Kashmir' in Chapter 25 and 'The Recalcitrance of Hyderabad' in Chapter 26. The subsequent story of 'The Integration of the States' is told in Chapter 27. Also in Ian Copland, *The Princes of India* (loc. cit.), Copland says, 'No sooner had the ink dried on the princes' IOAs, than Patel and Menon began to plot their downfall. This project, which took about two years, involved, in more or less chronological order (although the processes overlapped), the amalgamation of the states into larger administrative units/or merger with the erstwhile provinces, their rapid democratization, and their total subordination to the federal centre,' (p. 262). The details are given on pp. 261–8.
30. B. Shiva Rao et al., *The Framing of India's Constitution* (loc. cit.), p. 117. The Chapter, 'The Indian States', pp. 511–57, covers the entire range of issues that arose in the course of drafting the Constitution and the political merger of the states with the Union of India.
31. Ibid., p. 130.
32. Ibid., pp. 532–3 and pp. 537–8.
33. Ibid., pp. 540–1.
34. Ibid., pp. 541–3.
35. H.V. Hodson (loc. cit.), pp. 424–5.
36. Dietmar Rothermund, *An Economic History of India From Pre-*

Colonial Times to 1986, London, Croom Helm, 1988, Chapter 9, p. 48.

37. *History of the Reserve Bank of India (1935-51)*, Bombay, Reserve Bank of India, 1970, p. 676.
38. Ibid., p. 677, also see, pp. 678–83. In 1946 when the government and the Bank had to take a position on the par value of the rupee towards the fixed exchange rates decided by the IMF, it was necessary to make a conjecture about the probable trends in price levels in India and the UK. The experts' opinion was veering round to the view 'that Indian prices, in all probability, would decline during the early post-war period and the index might be stabilized at about double the pre-war level, i.e. at 200. On the other hand, prices in the UK were likely to rise by about 5 to 10 per cent to 180–90.' Ibid., p. 604. The rupee was left undisturbed at 1s6d for the time being.
39. See Table 4 in 'Long-term Stagnation in Indian Economy, 1900–75' in *The Retarded Economies*, Delhi, Oxford University Press, 1988 p. 162 also C.K. Johri, *Industrialism and Employment Systems in India*, Delhi, Oxford University Press, 1992, Table 7.1, p. 226.
40. *The History of the Reserve Bank of India* (loc. cit.), pp. 613–14. For the diffused views of the Governor and others on the Dollar Pool, see pp. 615–18.
41. Ibid., pp. 628–9. For a critical review see, National Planning Committee publication, *Currency Banking and Public Finance*, Bombay, Vora & Co. Publishers Ltd. November 1948, pp. 167–71. On the stores, installations and equipment taken over by the government the criticism takes the line that no one knew the real value.

> Much of this is either unusable, obsolete or impossible to be removed bodily by Britain without incurring a disproportionate cost of transport. Rough estimates made of sample stores, etc. calculated the value of all those at over Rs. 500 crores. But even if these sample valuations should be accepted as giving a correct basis for calculating the total amount involved, the benefit received by India, from the standpoint of serviceability of an up-to-date character of the material, is scarcely commensurate with the amount fixed as the price, and deducted from the total sterling due to us. (p. 170).

42. Tarlok Singh, *India's Development Experience*, Delhi, Macmillan India, 1974, p. 13.
43. V.M. Dandekar, *the Indian Economy*, 1947–92, Agriculture, Vol. I, New Delhi, Sage Publications, 1994, Ch. 3, 'Food Administration'.
44. Radha Kanta Barik, 'Congress Politics and Peasant Unrest in Bihar, 1946–47' in *Myth and Reality*, ibid., pp. 398–405. The author gives instances of one landlord's head being chopped off, the ear and nose of another similarly dealt with. 'The violent nature of the class struggle in the countryside became clear around the month of October 1946.' p. 404. He further says that 'peasants' struggles in some areas were camouflaged as communal riots. (p. 405).
45. H.D. Malaviya, 'Agrarian Unrest After Independence' in *Rural Sociology in India* (Ed. A.R. Desai), Fourth Revised Edition, Bombay, Popular Prakasn, 1969, p. 385. This article forms part of the author's book, *Village Panchayats in India* (pp. 206–10). Also see in the same volume, the article by Dr P.C. Joshi, 'Land Reforms in India'. Joshi gives the following quotation from the UP Zamindari Abolition Committee Report,

    The age-long simmering discontent bursting into acts of open defiance and sometimes of violence in our province and other parts of India has reached a critical state. Whatever forbearance and self-restraint we find in the countryside among the tenants is due to the hope that those who are running the State will undo the wrong done to them. Once that hope has gone, the tenant will be driven to desperation. The discontent may develop into revolt and our social security may be threatened by the outbreak of violence. Our scheme of Zamindari abolition contemplates payments of equitable compensation. p. 448.

46. See the three articles by Sunil Sen extracted from his book, *Agrarian Struggle in Bengal, 1946–47*, entitled, 'Tebhaga Chai', 'The Bargardards Bill' and 'The Dilemma' reproduced in A.R. Desai (Ed.). *Peasant Struggles in India*, Bombay Oxford University Press, 1979. The Tebhaga struggle in the Jalpaiguri district of North Bengal is vividly described by Ranjit Das Gupta in 'Peasants, Workers and Freedom Struggle, Jalpaiguri, 1947–57' in *Myth and Reality* (loc. cit.), esp. pp. 435–49. Das Gupta says: 'That the Tebhaga struggle itself remained localized and did not spread to other parts of the Duars was another manifestation of the Communists'

limitations. The communist leadership was also found to be confused and ill equipped for the task of facing the state repression'. (p. 447).

47. D.N. Dhanagre wrote a D.Phil thesis on the subject, provides the background and narration of events in an article, 'Social Origins of the Peasant Insurrection in Telangana (1946–51)' reproduced from *Contributions to Indian Sociology* (No. 8, 1974), in A.R. Desai (Ed.) *Peasant Struggles in India* (loc. cit.), pp. 486–516.
48. P. Sundarayya, who actually led the movement, wrote a book, *Telangana People's Struggle and its Lessons* from which the article, 'The Communist Movement in Andhra: Terror Regime 1948–51' is taken in A.R. Desai (Ed.) *Peasant Struggles in India*, Ibid., p. 553. Also see three other articles by him in this book entitled, 'Telangana', 'Hyderabad State—Its Socio-Political Background' and 'Entry of Indian Army and Immediately After'.
49. C. Rajeshwar Rao, another communist leader of Telangana, wrote a book from which the article, 'The Post-war Situation and Beginning of Armed Struggle' is extracted, ibid. The title of the publication is *The Historic Telangana Struggle—Some Useful Lessons from the Rich Experience.* Dhanagre (loc. cit.), writes, 'Fighting with the Indian army over 2000 peasants and party workers were killed. By July 1950 the number of communists and active participants detained had reached 10000 (Pritt 1958: 319–20). This should suffice as an index of the degree of intensity of the insurrection.' p. 505. Sundarayya puts the losses at twice this figure of killed. The reference is to Pritt, P.N., 'Oppression in India', *The Labour Monthly*, 32(7), 1950.
50. In Bombay the cost of living index (1939=100), rose to 246 in 1946 and 265 in 1947, in Madras it rose to 239 in 1946 and 277 in 1947, in Kanpur the climb was much higher, to 328 in 1946 and 378 in 1947. These figures understate the pace of inflation and mainly show the behaviour of controlled prices. In the post-war years, as the grip of the government slackened, the black market flourished; there was also much corruption in the food rationing departments. Food rations were reduced in view of lower availability of food grains in the government stocks which forced the workers to buy in

the open market at higher prices. Speculation in essential commodities was rife.

51. G.K. Sharma, *Labour Movement in India*, Jullundur, University Publishers, 1963, p. 115.
52. Ibid., p. 113.
53. *Trade Unions and Politics in India* (op. cit.), p. 83. Also V.B. Karnik, *Strikes in India*, Bombay, Manaktalas, 1967, pp. 325–8. For the AITUC perspective, see Prem Sagar Gupta, *A Short History of the All-India Trade Union Congress (1920–1947)*, (op. cit.), pp. 479–88.
54. V.B. Karnik, *Indian Trade Unions A Survey*, Bombay, Manaktalas, 1966, pp. 150–3.
55. Quotation from G. Ramanujam's *Indian Labour Movement* (op. cit), p. 55–6.
56. There was a conflict of opinion between P.C. Joshi, the General Secretary of the CPI and other members of the Politburo. Joshi thought that independence was genuine and that the Indian bourgeoisie had a progressive character, so there should be a united front of all progressive forces against the imperialists and the reactionary forces. This position was gradually ousted and replaced by the opposite view that independence being fake, opposition should be mounted and the masses prepared for the revolution for which the existing political instability lent the needed psychological context. See T.R. Sharma, *Communism in India, The Politics of Fragmentation*, New Delhi, Sterling Publishers Pvt. Ltd., 1984, Ch. 2. 'Strategy I: Independence to Palghat Congress'. The role played by Cominform and Soviet spokesmen in causing confusion in India is broadly described by S.N. Talwar, in his PhD. thesis, *Under the Banyan Tree. The Communist Movement in India, 1920–1964*, New Delhi, Allied Publishers Pvt. Ltd., 1985, pp. 271–4.
57. Ibid., p. 274.
58. G.K. Sharma, *Labour Movement in India* (op. cit.), p. 124.
59. *The Indian Trade Union Movement* (op. cit.), pp. 199–203. The progress made by HMS over the decade 1949–59 is given in a table on p. 202, which in fact shows progressive decline both in the number of affiliated trade unions and total membership. The progress of UTUC is shown in a similar table on p. 204 and, in its case, the decline is less marked.
60. *Communism in India* (loc. cit.), Ch. 2 'Strategy I: Independence to Palghat Congress', esp. pp. 42–50. The author gives a

detailed account of the ideological issues raised by the three factions in the CPI. Also Talwar (loc. cit.), p. 279–85.

61. For a concise and faithful presentation of Gandhi's ideas, mostly in his own words, see R.N. Bose, *Gandhian Technique and Tradition in Industrial Relations,* Research Division, All India Institute of Social Welfare and Business Management, Calcutta. The foreword by the Chief Minister Dr B.C. Roy carries the date as June 1956.
62. For an excellent early review of the performance of the four trade union federations, see Charles A. Myers and Subbiah Kannappan, *Industrial Relations in India,* Bombay, Asia Publishing House, Second Revised and Enlarged Edition, 1970, pp. 149–57.
63. V.V. Giri, *Labour Problems in Indian Industry,* Second Edition, Bombay, Asia Publishing House, 1959, pp. 128–9.
64. Prem Sagar Gupta, *A Short History of the All-India Trade Union Congress* (op. cit.), pp. 463–4. The volume records, 'The AITUC also submitted memorandums regarding Adarkar report on Sickness Insurance; Amendment of the Payment of Wages Act; Implementation of Adjudicator's Awards, Maximum Rent That May Be Charged to Industrial Workers; Need for instituting Tripartite Committees for Coal, Textiles, Plantations and Other Industries.'
65. Ibid., p. 465; also pp. 464–7.
66. Ibid., p. 465.
67. Ibid., pp. 481–2, also pp. 483–4.
68. Myers and Kannappan (loc. cit.), p. 311. The Industrial Truce Resolution was adopted in December 1947. 'Government succeeded in arresting the deteriorating industrial relations situation. The worst was over in 1947. Time loss to industry in 1948 on account of work stoppages was less than half of what it was in 1947.' Also A.S. Mathur, *Labour Policy and Industrial Relations in India* (op. cit), p. 117 and G. Ramanujan, *Indian Labour Movement* (op. cit), pp. 62–3. The book gives the text of the resolution.
69. See S.M. Pandey, *As Labour Organizes: A Study of Unionism in the Kanpur Cotton Textile Industry,* New Delhi, Shri Ram Centre for Industrial Relations, 1970, pp. 94–5. The Indian Trade Unions (Amendment) Act is discussed in considerable detail by K.N. Subramanian in his *Labour Management Relations in*

India, Bombay, Asia Publishing House, 1967, pp. 141–8. Omitting the political aspects, the author gives three reasons for the non-enforcement of the Act. These are: (i) the new definition of the term 'industry' in the amendment Act could be extended to government servants as well including the police and armed forces; (ii) the new term 'unfair practices' might impair government rules on conduct, service and punishments, et cetera. This would be an extension of the first objection; (iii) the non-enforcement of the amendment Act appeared to offend the ILO Convention no. 98: Right to Organize and Collective Bargaining, 1949 and Convention No. 87. The government could not ratify this convention since it found it necessary to impose reasonable restrictions on registered unions in respect of the number of outsiders on executive committees or the conditions subject to which registration may be granted or cancelled. However, it is not at all self-evident whether subsequent amendments to remove these non-fatal drawbacks would not have served the purpose if the political circumstances were more favourable. According to Subramanian, 'it was, therefore, imperative that if India wanted to give effect to the ILO Convention, she overcome her internal difficulties which came in the way of a legislation similar to the Amendment Act of 1947'. p. 147. Needless to say this has not been possible till date.

70. Ramchandra Guha, *India After Gandhi. The History of The World's Largest Democracy*, London, Picador, Pan Mcmillan & Co. 2007. pp. 132–3.
71. Myron Weiner, *Party Politics in India. The Development of Multi-Party System*, New Jersey, Princeton University Press, 1957, Ch. 4.
72. 'Rajne Palm Dutt had advised that it was the peace movement, the struggle for peace, in the course of which the four class alliance, the National Democratic Front, could be forged, to depose Nehru's regime and propel the CPI to power in a coalition government.' See Victor M. Fic, *Peaceful Transition to Communism in India. Strategy of the Communist Party*, Bombay, Nachiketa Publications, 1969, pp. 39–52, Quote on p. 48.
73. Bhabani Sen Gupta, *Communism in Indian Politics*, New Delhi, Young Asia Publications, 1978, pp. 37–47. Indian communism

was visualized as 'an independent national force'. 'As an independent party, charting its own political path through its own accumulated experience, the CPI would hopefully develop into a strong national force. Independence of external control appeared to be an essential coefficient of operating within the Indian Parliamentary system as the main Party of Opposition to the bourgeois government.' p. 43.

74. Gene D. Overstreet and Marshall Windmiller, *Communism in India*, Berkeley, University of California Press, 1959, Ch. 13. 'The Return to Constitutional Communism'.
75. Ramachandra Guha, *India After Gandhi* (loc. cit.), pp. 244–56. 'It was rumoured that Sheikh Abdullah would declare independence on 21 August—The day of the great Id festival-following which he would seek the protection of the United Nations against 'Indian aggression'. Two weeks before that date Abdullah dismissed a member of his Cabinet. This gave the others in the pro-India faction an excuse to move against him.' p. 255.
76. Asok Mitra, *The New India. 1948–1955. Memoirs of an Indian Civil Servant*, Bombay, Popular Prakashan, 1991, pp. 69–70 quote on p. 70, also pp. 85–6.
77. See the article by J.R. Lele and Asha A. Bhende, 'Population Policy' in J.N. Mongia (Ed.), *India's Economic Policies 1947–77*, New Delhi, Allied Publishers Pvt. Ltd., 1980.
78. Asok Mitra, *The New India* (loc. cit.), pp. 93–7; quote on p. 96.
79. C.H. Hanumantha Rao, 'Agricultural Policy' in *India's Economic Policies* (loc. cit.), p. 121.
80. Francine R. Frankel, *India's Political Economy, 1947–2004, The Gradual Revolution*, Second Edition, Delhi, Oxford University Press, 2005, pp.102–3.
81. Against the expectation of Rs. 2,030 million in foreign aid, India received only Rs. 580 million. This raised the budgetary deficit from the planned sum of Rs. 2,900 million to about Rs. 4,840 million. To this may be added deficit financing by state governments at about Rs. 480 million, raising the total to Rs. 5,320 million. See H. Venkatasubbiah, *Indian Economy Since Independence*, Second Revised Edition, Bombay, Asia Publishing House, 1961, pp. 255–7.
82. V.B. Karnik, *Indian Trade Unions* (op. cit.), p. 156.
83. V.B. Karnik, *Strikes in India* (op. cit.), p. 335.

84. Ibid., pp. 341–4.
85. The data on employment cover 19 industries including personal services but excludes shops and establishments. The index of productivity is based on the index of employment in factories, mines and railways and the index of output in the above: it is output over employments.
86. *Labour-Management Relations in India* (loc. cit.), Ch. V. 'The Present State of Trade Unionism'. The chapter gives a large body of factual information with comments. Indian trade unions are compared with the British and American models and found deeply deficient on several counts.
87. Gopal Krishna's essay, 'One-Party Dominance—Development and Trends' in *Party System and Election Studies,* Centre for the Study of Developing Societies, Bombay, Allied Publishers, 1967, p. 29.
88. In 1956, there was an opposite political move to merge Bihar and West Bengal states and revive the colonial composite province in a truncated form. However, in West Bengal a strong agitation against it was mounted and it had to be dropped. The Congress tasted defeat on this issue in a by-election for a parliamentary seat in Calcutta and the West Bengal government decided to bow before the popular opinion.
89. For an insider's view on the differences on political questions within the party see, E.M.S. Namboodripad, *The Communist Party in Kerala. Six Decades of Struggle and Advance,* New Delhi, National Book Centre, A. K.G. Bhavan, December, 1994, esp. pp. 99–113.
90. Ramachandra Guha, *India After Gandhi. The History of the World's Largest Democracy* (op. cit.), pp. 177–8.
91. Ibid., pp. 165–6.
92. Ibid., The chapter, 'The Law and the Prophets', pp. 226–41.
93. Myron Weiner (Ed.), *State Politics in India,* New Jersey, Princeton University Press, 1968. Articles by Paul R. Brass on Uttar Pradesh and Marcup. F. Franda on West Bengal are of greater interest. The developments leading to the Amritsar Congress are ably discussed in Victor M. Fic in *Peaceful Transition to Communism in India. Strategy of the Communist Party* (loc. cit.), Ch. 9. 'The Amritsar Thesis.'
94. Ramachandra Guha, *India After Gandhi* (loc. cit.), pp. 299–300.

95. Quoted in Francine R. Frankel, *India's Political Economy* (op. cit.), p. 117.
96. H. Venkatasubbiah, *Indian Economy Since Independence* (loc. cit.), pp. 23–5; quote on p. 23; the repeated failure to settle accounts with Pakistan over immovable urban property has been put to the fact 'that the total value of such properties left behind by migrants in India was at least three times the total value of similar properties left behind in India by migrants to Pakistan and this made urban refugees feel more exasperated at each successive failure'. p. 25.
97. Ibid., p. 25.
98. Torlok Singh, *India's Development Experience* (loc. cit.), 'Welfare, Equality and Economic Power', p. 129.
99. H. Venkatasubbiah (loc. cit.), Chapter, 'Planning'.
100. G. Balachandran, *The Reserve Bank of India, 1951–1967*, Delhi, Oxford University Press, 1998. pp. 1151–64, quote on p. 1151.
101. Ibid., p. 1164.
102. Francine R. Frankel (loc. cit.), writes:

    The food ministry's solution to the food crisis, which it argued before the Planning Commission, was a reorientation of agricultural policy to restore the priority for the introduction of scientific practices over changes in organization as the foremost instrument of increasing agricultural productivity and surpluses. Among other policies, they pressed for greater investment outlays on agriculture for improved seeds, pesticides, and especially fertilizers; and remunerative prices for rice and wheat in order to provide an incentive for increased private investment in improved inputs. (p. 147).
103. The revenue raised by excise duties were a mere Rs. 851 million in 1951–2 which rose to Rs. 1,287 million in 1955–6 and sharply to Rs. 2,333 million in 1957–8. The contribution of excise duties to the growth in total revenue of the Centre in one year amounted to nearly 64 per cent.
104. G. Balachandran, *The Reserve Bank of India* (loc. cit.), p. 72.
105. The contradictory dimensions of various policy options and pressures operating on the government are discussed by Frankel (loc. cit.), pp. 143–7.
106. Quoted by R.C. Saxena in a textbook by him, *Labour Problems and Social Welfare*, Seventh Edition, Meerut, Jai Prakash Nath & Co., 1959, p. 438.
107. G.K. Sharma (loc. cit.), pp. 136–7 and S. M. Pandey (loc. cit.),

pp. 96–113. Pandey narrates the sequence of events that led to the strike.

108. S.N. Talwar (PhD Thesis), *Under the Banyan Tree. The Communist Movement in India, 1920–1964,* New Delhi, Allied Publishers Pvt. Ltd., 1985, pp. 309–12.
109. Madhu Limaye, *Socialist Communist Interaction in India,* Delhi, Ajanta Publications (India) Ltd., 1976, p. 107.
110. Ibid., p. 108.
111. V.B. Karnik, *Indian Trade Unions* (op. cit.), p. 197.
112. V.V. Giri's inaugural lecture at the Labour Economic Conference at the Lucknow University Campus in January 1958. Reproduced in T.S. Papola, P.P. Ghosh and Alakh N. Sharma (Eds.), *Labour, Employment and Industrial Relations in India,* Presidential Addresses at ISLE Annual Conferences. Delhi, B.R. Publishing Corporation, 1993, p. 21.
113. Harold Crouch, *Trade Unions and Politics in India,* Bombay, Manaktalas, 1966, Chs. VI, VII and VIII.
114. Ibid., pp. 212–17.
115. Mary Sur, *Collective Bargaining. A Comparative Study of Developments in India and Other Countries,* Bombay, Asia Publishing House, 1965, Ch. V, VI & VII.
116. Ibid., pp. 64–9; quote on p. 64.